MAXWELL MACMILLAN CHESS SERIES

Play Anti-Indian Systems

Maxwell Macmillan Chess Openings

Executive Editor: PAUL LAMFORD

Technical Editor: JIMMY ADAMS

Russian Series Editor: KEN NEAT

Some other books in this series:

ADORJAN, A. & HORVATH, T.
Sicilian: Sveshnikov Variation

BASMAN, M.
The New St. George
The Killer Grob

CAFFERTY, B. & HOOPER, D.
A Complete Defence to 1 e4

GLIGORIC, S.
The Nimzo-Indian Defence

KEENE, R.D.
The Evolution of Chess Opening Theory

KOVACS, L.M.
Sicilian: Poisoned Pawn Variation

MAROVIC, D.
Play the King's Indian Defence
Play the Queen's Gambit

NEISHTADT, I.
Play the Catalan
  Volume 1 – Open Variation
  Volume 2 – Closed Variation

POLUGAYEVSKY, L.
The Sicilian Labyrinth, Volumes 1 & 2

PRZEWOZNIK, J. & PEIN, M.
The Blumenfeld Gambit

RAVIKUMAR, V.
Play the Benko Gambit

SILMAN, J. & DONALDSON, J.
Accelerated Dragons

TSEITLIN, M.
Winning with the Schliemann

VARNUSZ, E.
Play the Caro-Kann
Play the Ruy Lopez

WATSON, J.L.
Play the French

A full catalogue is available from:
Maxwell Macmillan Chess, London Road, Wheatley, Oxford, OX9 1YR.

Play Anti-Indian Systems

by

Egon Varnusz

MAXWELL MACMILLAN CHESS

MAXWELL MACMILLAN INTERNATIONAL PUBLISHING GROUP

UK, Europe, Middle East, Africa

Maxwell Macmillan International Europe
Purnell Distribution Centre, Paulton, Bristol BS18 5LQ, UK
Tel: (0) 761 413301. Fax: (0) 761 419308. Telex: 44713

USA, Canada, Latin America, Japan

Macmillan Distribution Center, Front & Brown Streets, Riverside, New Jersey 08075, USA
Tel: (609) 461-6500. Fax: (609) 764-9122.

Australia and New Zealand

Maxwell Macmillan Publishing Pty Ltd, Lakes Business Park, 2a Lord Street, Botany, NSW 2019, Australia
Tel: (02) 316-9444. Fax: (02) 316-9485.

Pacific Rim (except Japan)

Maxwell Macmillan Publishing Singapore Pte Ltd,
72 Hillview Avenue, No 03-00 Tacam House, Singapore 2366
Tel: (65) 769-6000. Fax: (65) 769-3731.

First Edition 1991

Library of Congress Cataloging-in-Publication Data
applied for

British Library Cataloguing in Publication Data
Varnusz, E.
Play anti-Indian systems
I. Title
794.12

ISBN 1-85744-015-3

Cover by Pintail Design
Printed in Great Britain by BPCC Wheatons Ltd, Exeter

Contents

Preface

The reader of this book need not rush to his bookcase looking for sources on the Anti-Indian – the term has been coined by the author. Other books deal with it under different headings: the Queen's Pawn Opening, the Colle System or the Indian Systems.

The opening is very popular, played by ordinary club player and world champion alike, yet it is a touch neglected by theorists. Let us see what it is all about.

After 1 d4 ♘f6 Black intends to play an Indian variation. However, *White omits c4 at an early stage of the opening and replies 2 ♘f3.* This move meets general principles ('Develop your pieces!' Do not make too many pawn moves in the opening!) and often succeeds in practice since the variations are not only correct but may also take the opponent by surprise.

Needless to say, a scrutiny of White's dangerous weapon is also a must for devotees of the Black side of Indian Defences. The Contents list demonstrates the idea at a glance. The Anti-Indian is an opening which is easy to learn and provides White with simple methods to counter the Indian Defences. Furthermore, the reader is free to select from the material: he might play the main lines against the King's Indian but choose the Anti-Indian against the Benoni.

This small book presents the variations popular with masters, so the author had to omit a few lengthy lines. Let us draw the reader's attention to the illustrative games (116 in number), which provide an enjoyable survey of the typical middle- and endgames arising from the opening.

From the numerous sources consulted, the author wishes to express his indebtedness to Jimmy Adams' *Torre Attack*, Kondratiev and Stoliar's *Benoni Defence* and the volumes of *Tournament Chess*, *Informator* and *Encyclopaedia*.

Egon Varnusz
Budapest 1991

Part I:
Torre-Petrosian Attack
1 d4 ♘f6 2 ♘f3 e6 3 ♗g5

Introduction to Chapters 1-7

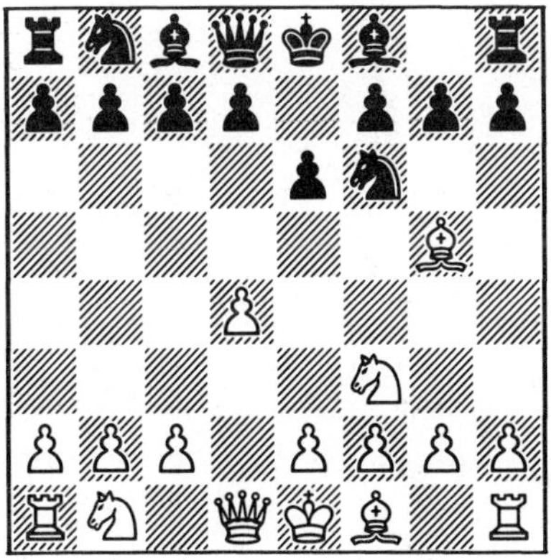

It was in 1925 that the young Mexican master, Carlos Torre, crushed the great Emanuel Lasker in an astonishing game at a tournament in Moscow. Torre's victory put him and his variation into the limelight and his further wins encouraged a number of top players to play the variation. After Torre's retirement however, the opening was hardly played in strong tournaments. The revival of the Torre line is to Petrosian's credit. When young, the Soviet grandmaster admitted he had difficulty in coping with the Queen's and Nimzo-Indian complex and was looking for a simple, easy-to-learn system. He found that the Torre Attack was an adequate antidote and the later World Champion kept it in his repertoire ever after. The names of Torre and Petrosian represent two extremes in chess, demonstrating that this opening suits the tactician and the positional player alike.

The basic idea is simple. White attempts to paralyse Black's forces by an early pin and threatens to occupy the centre immediately by e2-e4. Should Black counter this by ... d5 he can expect trouble from the weak e5 square. White's c3-d4-e4/e3 pawn structure is typical of the variation.

As shown by the Illustrative Games, this apparently modest White set-up quite often develops into a decisive attack in no time.

And another remark: White's tournament record in this line is better than one would expect after making an unbiased assessment of the opening analysis. The idea is correct and is not inferior to other main variations, whilst it often crosses the opponent's preparation. Needless to say, the system is to be scrutinised from Black's viewpoint as well.

The Torre-Petrosian Attack has been, and still is, championed by many outstanding players of the game: Marshall, Trifunović, Spassky, Vaganian, Timman, Yusupov, and, *nomen est omen*, the Filipino Eugenio Torre, to name but a few.

1 Torre-Petrosian Attack: Without an early ... c5

1	**d4**	**♘f6**
2	**♘f3**	**e6**
3	**♗g5**	

This chapter analyses the lines immediately deviating from the main variation 3 ... c5. Of these, 3 ... h6 is the most popular, providing the best chances for Black to equalise. Before turning to this and to the other main variation, 3 ... d5, here are some rare replies:

(a) 3 ... b6 4 e4 h6 transposes into 1.122

(b) 3 ... ♗e7 4 ♘bd2 h6 (4 ... b6?! 5 e4 ♗b7 6 ♗d3 c5 7 e5 ♘d5 8 ♗xe7 ♕xe7 9 ♘e4 0-0 10 0-0 ±) 5 ♗xf6 (5 ♗h4!?) 5 ... ♗xf6 6 e4 d6 7 ♗d3 ♘c6! 8 c3 e5 9 d5 ♘e7 10 ♘f1 c6 11 c4 g6 12 h4 (12 ♘e3 ♗g7 13 ♕c2 0-0 14 g4) 12 ... h5 13 ♘e3 ♗g7 14 ♘d2 ♗h6 ∓ Kristensen-Conquest, Hastings 1989/90. Playable is 4 ♘c3 d5 5 ♗xf6 ♗xf6 6 e4, a transposition to the French.

(c) 3 ... d6 or 3 ... c6 would give White a significant advantage in space. A warning lesson from the latter: 4 e4 ♕b6? 5 ♘bd2 ♕xb2 6 ♗d3 ♕b6 7 0-0 d5 8 ♕e2 dxe4 9 ♘xe4 ♘xe4 10 ♕xe4 ♘bd7 11 c4 h6? 12 ♕xe6+! fxe6 13 ♗g6+ and mate! Stringe-Gebhard, Germany 1924.

1.1

3	**...**	**h6**

Black wants to get rid of the pin. Clearly he will retain both his bishops in the main variation, but the manoeuvre gives away a tempo and allows White to grab the centre.

1.11

4	**♗h4?**	

1.111

4	**...**	**g5!**

Vigorous! Less incisive is 4 ... b6 5 e3 ♗b7 6 ♘bd2 (6 ♗d3 c5 7 0-0 ♗e7 8 c4 cxd4 9 ♘xd4 d6 10 ♘c3 ♘bd7 11 ♖e1 a6 12 ♗f1 ♖c8 13 ♖c1 g5 14 ♗g3 h5 15 f4 ♖g8 Larsen-Andersson, Buenos Aires 1980) 6 ... c5 (6 ... d6 7 c3 ♘bd7 8 ♗c4 ♗e7 9 0-0 0-0 10 ♕e2 c5 11 ♗a6 ♗xa6 12 ♕xa6 d5 13 ♖fd1

♖c8 14 ♕e2 ♖e8 = Ermolinsky-Romanishin, Simferopol 1988) 7 c3 ♗e7 (7 ... d6 8 ♗b5+ ♘bd7 9 dxc5 bxc5 10 ♘c4 ♕c7 11 0-0 ♗c6 = Aaron-Botvinnik, Leipzig 1960) 8 ♗d3 cxd4 (8 ... d6 9 0-0 0-0 10 ♖e1 cxd4 11 exd4 ♘bd7 12 a4 a6 13 b4 ♘d5 14 ♗xe7 ♕xe7 15 ♕b3 ± Larsen-Andersson, Biel 1976) 9 exd4 ♘c6 10 0-0 0-0 (10 ... ♘d5 11 ♗g3!) 11 ♖e1 ♖c8 12 a3 ±.

Black can also play the waiting move 4 ... d6, for example 5 ♘bd2 g5 6 ♗g3 ♘h5 7 e3 ♗g7 8 c3 ♘d7 9 ♗e2 ♘df6 10 0-0 ♕e7 11 e4 ♘xg3 12 hxg3 0-0 = Seirawan-Ehlvest, Skelleftea 1989. Black is a whole tempo up on lines discussed in Chapter 10, where Black plays ... h6 and ... g5 after he has already played g6. 4 ... c5 is also sufficient; see 1.112 below.

5 ♗g3 ♘e4

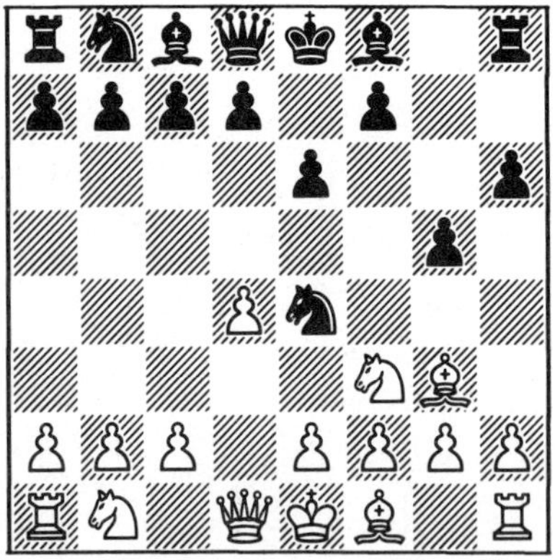

Despite a slightly spoilt pawn structure, Black has a comfortable development and the two bishops. No wonder 4 ♗h4 has disappeared from tournament practice.

6 ♘bd2

6 ♕d3 ♘xg3 7 hxg3 ♗g7 8 ♘c3 d6 9 0-0-0 ♘bd7 10 e3 a6 11 ♘d2 b5 12 f4 ♗b7 13 ♔b1 ♕e7 14 ♘b3 0-0-0 15 a4 c6 16 ♘a5 ♘b8 = Larsen-Byrne, Las Palmas 1976, or 6 ♘fd2 ♘xg3 7 hxg3 d5 8 e3 c5 9 dxc5?! ♗g7 10 c3 ♕c7 11 e4 0-0 12 ♗e2?! ♖d8 13 exd5 ♖xd5 14 0-0 ♘a6 15 ♗f3 ♖d8 ∞ Kan-Antoshin, USSR 1955.

6 ... ♘xg3
7 hxg3 ♗g7

7 ... b6?! 8 e3 ♗b7 9 ♗d3 ♗g7 10 c3 d6 11 ♕e2 a6. Black has got to keep his bishops as compensation for his weakened pawns. 11 ... ♘d7?! 12 ♗a6 ♕c8 13 ♗xb7 ♕xb7 14 0-0-0 d5 15 e4 ± Spassky-Gobet, match 1987.

8 c3 d6
9 e3

9 e4! is more to the point, e.g. 9 ... ♕e7 10 ♗d3 ♘c6 (10 ... ♘d7!?) 11 ♕b3! a6 12 0-0-0 b5 13 ♖he1 ± Tseitlin-Stempin, Polanica Zdroj 1989.

9 ... ♘c6

9 ... c5? 10 dxc5 dxc5 11 ♘e4! ±.

10 ♗d3 ♕e7

10 ... ♗d7 11 ♕c2 ♕e7 12 0-0-0

a5 13 e4 a4 14 a3 ♘a5 15 ♖de1 0-0-0 16 ♔b1 ♔b8 17 e5 d5 18 g4 ∞ Petrosian-Botvinnik, USSR Ch 1951.

11 ♕c2 f5!

Black has equalised, e.g. 12 e4 ♗d7 13 0-0-0 fxe4 14 ♘xe4 0-0-0 15 ♔b1 ♕f7! 16 ♕b3 ♔b8 17 ♖he1 ♖he8 Hort-Browne, London (BBC) 1979.

1.112

4 ... c5

Leading to the variations of Chapter 4, with the addition for Black of ... h6, favouring the defending side.

5 e3 b6

Apparent deviations are often no more than changes in the order of moves. Here is an overview.

(a) 5 ... cxd4 6 exd4 d5?! 7 ♘bd2 ♗e7 8 ♗d3 0-0 9 ♕e2 ♘c6 10 c3 a6 11 0-0 ♖e8 12 ♘e5 ♘xe5 13 dxe5 ♘d7 14 ♗xe7 ♖xe7 15 ♘f3 ± (±) Zilberman-Kholmov, USSR 1990.

(b) 5 ... ♗e7 6 ♘bd2 b6 7 c3 (7 ♗d3 ♗b7 8 0-0 cxd4 9 exd4 0-0 10 c3 d6 11 ♗xf6 ♗xf6 12 ♗e4 ♗xe4 13 ♘xe4 ♗e7 14 ♘fd2?! d5 = Z.Nikolić-Rivas, Bor 1986) 7 ... ♗b7 8 ♗xf6 (8 ♗d3 0-0 9 ♕e2 cxd4 10 exd4 d6 11 ♗xf6 ♗xf6 12 ♘e4 ♗e7 13 g4 ♖e8 14 g5 d5 ∞ Z.Nikolić-Horvath, Yugoslavia 1984) 8 ... ♗xf6 9 ♗d3 ♘c6 10 ♕e2 d5 11 dxc5 bxc5 12 e4 ∞ Hulak-King, Moscow 1990.

6 ♘bd2 ♗e7

(a) 6 ... ♗b7 7 c3 cxd4 8 exd4 ♗e7 9 ♗d3 d6 (for ... ♘c6 see Chapter 4) 10 ♗xf6 ♗xf6 11 ♘e4 ♗e7 12 0-0 ♘d7 13 ♖e1 0-0 14 ♗c2 ♘f6 15 ♕d3 g6 16 ♘g3 ♔g7 17 ♖xe6 ♗xf3 18 gxf3 ♖e8 ± Kovačević-Polugayevsky, Haifa 1989.

(b) 6 ... cxd4 7 exd4 ♗b7 8 ♗d3 ♗e7 9 0-0 0-0 10 ♕e2 d6 11 ♗xf6 ♗xf6 12 ♘e4 ♗e7 = M.Tseitlin-Averkin, USSR 1983.

7 c3 ♗b7
8 ♗d3 ♘c6
9 0-0 cxd4
10 ♗xf6!?

For 10 exd4 0-0 11 ♖e1 see 4 ... b6.

10 ... ♗xf6
11 exd4 0-0
12 ♘e4 ♗e7
13 ♘g3 d5?!

13 ... d6 (13 ... f5? 14 d5!) 14 ♖e1 ± (I.Sokolov).

14 ♕e2 ♗d6
15 ♖ae1 ♖c8
16 ♔h1

I.Sokolov-Kir.Georgiev, Haifa 1989; 16 ... ♖e8! ±.

1.12

4 ♗xf6 ♕xf6

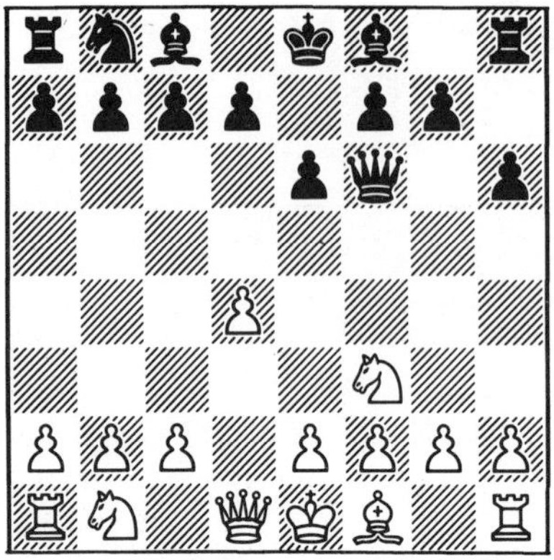

5 e4

The occupation of the centre is a natural consequence of White's play. 5 ♘bd2, however, is also worth considering: 5 ... c5 (5 ... d6 6 c3 ♘d7 7 a4!. A typical manoeuvre to gain space. 7 ... a5 would now loosen Black's pawn structure. 7 ... g5?! 8 g3 ♗g7 9 ♗g2 0-0 10 a5! ⩲; see Illustrative Game No 1. Or 7 g3!? g5 8 ♗g2 g4 9 ♘h4 h5 10 0-0 ♗e7 11 e4 ♕h6 12 f4 ♘f8 13 e5 d5 ∞ Salov-Pr.Nikolić, Belgrade 1987, or 7 g3!? g6 8 ♗g2 ♗g7 9 0-0 0-0 10 a4 a5 11 ♕b3 e5 12 e4 ♘b6 13 ♘c4 ♘xc4 14 ♕xc4 ♕e7 15 ♖ad1 ♗e6 16 d5 ♗c8 17 ♘d2 h5 ∞ Kosten-Adams, London 1990) 6 ♘e4 (6 c3?! cxd4 7 cxd4 g5 ∞; see Illustrative Game No 2) 6 ... ♕f5 (6 ... ♕d8?! 7 dxc5 ♗xc5 8 ♘xc5 ♕a5+ 9 ♕d2 ♕xc5 10 e4 ±) 7 ♘g3 ♕f6 8 e3 (8 e4!?) 8 ... cxd4 9 exd4 b6 10 ♗e2 (10 ♗d3 ♗b7 11 ♘e4 ♗xe4 12 ♗xe4 d5 =) 10 ... ♗b7 11 0-0 h5!? 12 ♘e5! ♕g5 Vaganian-Taimanov, USSR 1983; 13 ♗f3! ∞.

Similarly, White can delay with 5 ♘c3, e.g. 5 ... d5 6 e4 c6 7 ♗d3 ♘d7 8 ♕e2 (8 a3!?) 8 ... ♗b4 9 a3 ♗xc3+ 10 bxc3 0-0 11 0-0 c5 12 ♕e3 b6 ±/= Izeta-Sunye, Salamanca 1990.

1.121

5 ... d6

(a) 5 ... ♘c6?! 6 c3 d5 7 ♘bd2 ♗d7 8 ♗d3 0-0-0 9 e5 ♕e7 10 b4 g5 11 ♘b3 g4 12 ♘fd2 ♕g5 13 0-0 f6 14 b5 ♘xe5!? 15 dxe5 fxe5 16 c4 h5 17 ♕e2 e4 18 ♘xe4! ± Vaganian-Psakhis, USSR 1983.

(b) 5 ... d5?! 6 ♘bd2 c5 7 ♗b5+ ♗d7 8 ♕e2 cxd4 9 exd5 ♗b4 10 0-0 ± van den Bosch-Wijhaus, Holland 1941.

(c) 5 ... g6!? 6 ♘c3 ♗g7 7 ♕d2 a6 (7 ... d6 8 0-0-0 **♕e7!?** 9 e5 d5 10 h4 ♗d7 11 ♔b1 ♘c6 12 ♗e2 0-0-0 13 ♘a4 b6 14 a3 ♘b8 15 ♘c3 ♔b7 ∞ Klinger-Romanishin, Palma de Mallorca 1989; **8 ... ♘c6** 9 ♗b5! 0-0 10 e5 dxe5 11 ♗xc6 exd4! 12 ♘e4 ♕e7 ∞ Hodgson-Eingorn, Illustrative Game 5) 8 0-0-0 b5!? 9 e5 ♕e7 10 ♘e4 d5 11 exd6 (11 ♘c5!?) 11 ... cxd6 12 ♕b4 d5 13 ♘d6+ ♔d7! 14 ♘e5+ ♗xe5 15 dxe5 ♘c6 16 ♕f4 g5 ∞ Hodgson-Lputian, Hastings 1986/87.

1.1211

6 ♘bd2

(a) 6 e5 (aggressive!) 6 ... dxe5?! (6 ... ♕e7!) 7 dxe5 ♕e7 8 ♘c3 ♘c6 9 ♗d3 (9 ♗b5!) 9 ... g5! 10 ♕e2 ♗g7 11 ♗b5 ♗d7 12 ♗xc6 ♗xc6 13 0-0-0 ♕b4 14 ♘d4 ♗xg2 15 ♖g1 0-0-0 ∞ Shirazi-Christiansen, USA 1984.

(b) 6 c3 ♘d7 7 ♗d3 (7 ♘bd2 g5!? 8 ♘c4?! g4! ∓) b6 8 0-0 ♗b7 9 a4 a6 10 ♘bd2 ♕d8 11 ♘e1 c5 12 ♕g4 cxd4 13 cxd4 e5 14 f4 ± Dreyev-Kengis, Barnaul 1988.

6 ... ♘d7

(a) 6 ... g5 7 c3 ♘d7 8 ♘c4 ♗g7 9 ♗d3 ♕e7 10 ♕e2 b6 11 0-0-0 ♗b7 12 ♖he1 0-0-0 13 ♔b1 ♔b8 14 ♘a3 ♘f6 15 ♘d2 ♕d7 16 ♗a6 ± Yusupov-Gurgenidze, USSR 1982.

(b) 6 ... ♕e7 7 ♗d3 g6 8 0-0 e5 9 c3 ♗g7 10 ♘c4 0-0 11 ♘e3 ♘d7 12 ♖e1 ♘f6 13 a4 c6 14 dxe5 dxe5 15 a5 ♘g4 16 ♘c4 ♗e6 17 ♕e2 ♖ad8 = Dreyev-Romanishin, Lvov 1987.

7	**♗d3**	**g6**
8	**c3**	**♗g7**
9	**a4**	**♕e7**

After 9 ... a5?! 10 ♘c4 the threat is 11 e5.

10 a5

White has a slight advantage in space. 10 ... a6 11 0-0 0-0 12 ♖e1 e5 13 ♕c2 ♘f6 14 ♘c4 ♘h5 15 ♘e3 ♗e6 (15 ... ♘f4 16 ♗c4) 16 ♗c4! ♖ae8 17 ♗xe6 fxe6 18 dxe5 ♖xf3! 19 gxf3 ♗xe5 ∞ Psakhis-Makarichev, USSR 1983.

1.1212

6 ♘c3

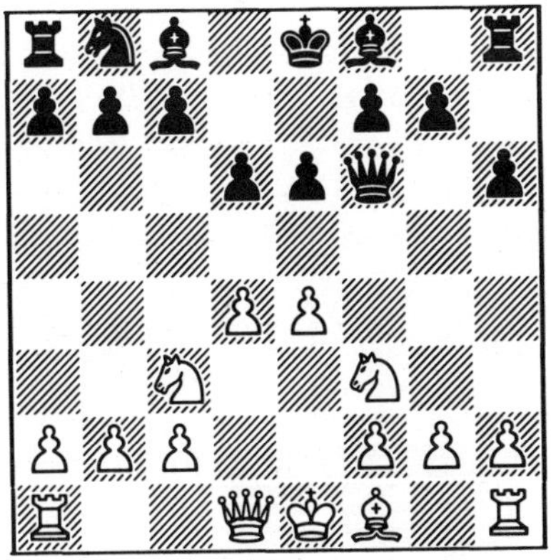

1.12121

6 ... c6

(a) 6 ... g5 7 e5! (7 ♗b5+ c6 8 e5 ♕d8 9 ♗d3 d5 10 0-0 c5 11 dxc5 ♗xc5 ∞ Gurgenidze-Parma, USSR-Yugoslavia match 1966) 7 ... ♕e7 8 h4 g4 9 ♘d2 h5 10 f4 gxf3 11 ♘xf3 ♘c6 12 ♗b5 ♗d7 13 ♕e2 dxe5?! 14 ♗xc6 ♗xc6 15 ♘xe5 (King-Summermatter, Lucerne 1989) 15 ... ♗d7! ±.

(b) 6 ... g6!? 7 ♕d2 (7 ♗b5+ ♘d7 8 e5 ♕e7 9 d5!? ∞ Shabalov-A.Ivanov, USSR 1987) 7 ... ♗g7 8 0-0-0 ♘c6 (8 ... ♕e7!? see 5 ... g6) 9 ♗b5 0-0 10 ♗xc6 (10 e5 see 5 ... g6) 10 ... bxc6 11 e5 ♕f5 12 ♖he1 c5 13 ♘e4 dxe5 14 dxe5 ♗b7 15 ♕e3 ♗xe5 16 ♘xe5 ♕xe5 17 ♘xc5 ♕xe3+ 18 fxe3 ♗xg2 19

♖d7 ∞ J. Piket-Nijboer, Wijk aan Zee 1990.

(c) 6 ... a6 7 e5 ♕d8 8 ♗d3 d5 9 ♘e2 c5 ∞ Terpugov-Botvinnik, Illustrative Game No 4.

7 ♕d2

7 e5 ♕d8 ∞ (7 ... dxe5?! 8 dxe5 ♕f4 9 g3 ♕b4 10 a3! ♕a5 11 b4 ♕c7 12 ♘e4 ± Petrosian-Taimanov, Illustrative Game No 3).

7 ... e5
8 0-0-0 ♗e7

8 ... ♘d7 transposes into 1.12122.

9 ♔b1 ♘d7
10 h4 exd4
11 ♘xd4 ♘e5
12 f4 ♘g4
13 h5

± Hodgson-Zsu.Polgar, Haifa 1989.

1.12122

6 ... ♘d7

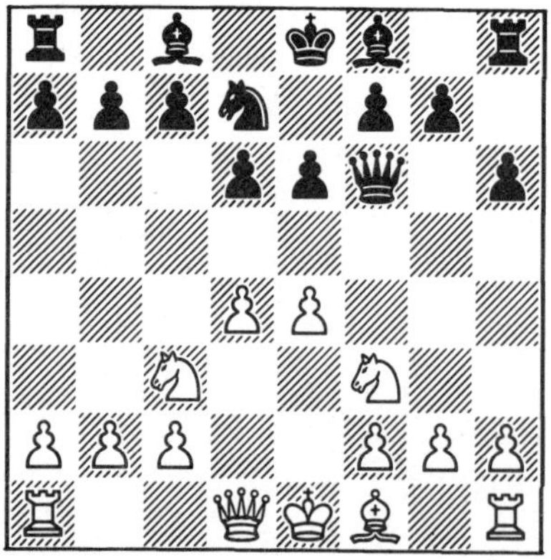

7 ♕d2

7 d5 exd5?! (7 ... e5) 8 ♘xd5 ♕d8 (Lerner-Makarichev USSR 1982) 9 ♕d4! ±.

7 ... c6

7 ... a6 8 0-0-0 ♕e7 (8 ... c5?! 9 e5!) 9 ♗d3 g6 10 ♖he1 ♗g7 11 h4 0-0 12 e5 d5 13 ♘e2 c5 ± Yusupov-Bischoff, Munich 1990.

8 0-0-0 e5

8 ... ♕d8 9 ♔b1 ♗e7 10 h4 e5 11 dxe5 dxe5 12 g4!? ♕c7 13 ♗e2?! ♘f8! 14 g5 h5 15 ♕d3 ♘g6 ∓ Blatny-Tolnai, Stara Zagora 1990.

9 dxe5!?

9 h4?! ♗e7 10 ♕e3 ♘f8! 11 ♗e2 ♘e6 12 ♗c4!? ♗d8! ∓ Hodgson-Rogers, Wijk aan Zee 1989.

9 ... ♘xe5

9 ... dxe5? 10 ♘b5 ♖b8 11 ♘xa7 ♘c5 12 ♘xc8 ♖xc8 13 b4 +− Klinger-King, Lucerne 1989.

10 ♘xe5 ♕xe5
11 f4 ♕a5
12 ♗c4 ♗e7
13 ♔b1 b5

White stands slightly better: 14 ♗b3 ♕b6 15 ♖hf1 0-0 16 e5 ± Plaskett-Ward, Hastings 1989/90.

1.1213

6 ♗d3 ♘c6

(a) 6 ... g6 7 0-0 ♗g7 8 e5 ♕e7 9 ♕e2 ♘d7 10 c4!? c5 11 ♘c3 cxd4!

12 exd6 ♕xd6 13 ♘b5 ♕b6 14 b4! 0-0 15 c5 ♕d8 16 ♖ad1 ∞ Sideif Zade-Ivanov, USSR 1985.

(b) 6 ... e5 7 c3 ♗e7 8 ♘bd2 0-0 9 0-0 ♘c6 10 dxe5 ♘xe5 11 ♘xe5 dxe5 12 ♕e2 a5 13 a4 ♗c5 = Spiridonov-Zaichik, Polanica Zdrój 1984.

(c) 6 ... ♘d7 7 0-0 (7 ♘bd2 e5 8 c3 g6 9 ♘c4 ♗g7 10 d5 0-0 11 ♘e3 h5 12 ♕e2 ♗h6 = Hoi-Browne, Reykjavík 1988) 7 ... g5 8 c3 ♗g7 9 ♘bd2 0-0 10 b4 e5 11 d5 h5?! 12 ♘c4 ♖e8 13 ♘fd2 g4 14 f3 ± Sandler-Plaskett, Hastings 1989/90.

7 c3 g5!?
8 ♘bd2

8 h3 (8 ♕b3 g4 9 ♘fd2 h5 ∞, 8 0-0 ♗d7 9 ♘bd2 0-0-0!?) 8 ... h5 9 h4 g4 10 ♘g5 ♗h6 ∞ (Browne).

8 ... g4
9 ♘g1 h5
10 ♕b3 ♗h6
11 ♘c4 e5

11 ... h4!? 12 ♘e2?! (12 ♖d1) 12 ... h3! ∓.

12 dxe5 ♘xe5
13 ♘xe5 dxe5
14 ♘e2 h4
15 ♖d1 c6
16 a4 ♗g5!

Black has the upper hand (I. Ivanov-Browne, US Ch 1989).

1.122

5 ... b6
6 ♗d3

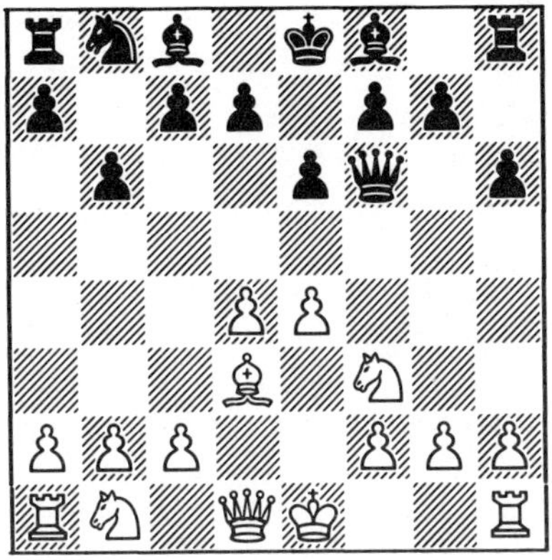

6 a3 (preparing 7 ♘c3) 6 ... ♗b7 7 ♘c3 d6 8 ♕d2 (8 ♗b5+ c6 9 ♗d3 ♘d7 10 0-0 ♕d8 11 ♕e2 ♗e7 12 e5 ± Petrosian-Portisch, Erevan 1965) 8 ... ♘d7 9 0-0-0 g5 10 ♘b5!? ♔d8 11 h4 g4 12 e5 ♕g7 13 ♘e1 a6 14 ♘c3 d5 15 f4! ± Korchnoi-Keres, Illustrative Game No 6.

6 ... ♗b7

6 ... ♗a6?! 7 ♗xa6 ♘xa6 8 0-0 ♗e7 9 ♕e2 ♘b8 10 ♘c3 0-0 11 ♖ad1 c6 12 e5 ♕g6 13 ♘e4 ± Ekström-Taimanov, 1983.

7 ♘bd2

The same position emerges after 2 ♘f3 b6 3 ♗g5 ♗b7 4 ♘bd2 e6 5 e4 h6 6 ♗xf6 ♕xf6 7 ♘bd2.

Black has more possibilities after 7 ♘c3?! ♗b4! (7 ... g5!? 8 ♕e2 ♘c6 9 e5 ♕g7 10 ♘e4!? g4!? 11 ♘f6+ ♔d8 12 ♘d2 ♘xd4 13 ♕e3 ♗c5 14 ♕g3 ♗e7 15 ♕f4 ∞

Murshed-Conquest, London 1989) 8 0-0 ♗xc3 9 bxc3 d6 (9 ... 0-0? 10 ♘d2! e5 11 f4! exf4 12 e5 ♕h4 13 ♘e4 d5 14 g3! ♕h3 15 ♘f6+! gxf6 16 ♖xf4 ± Cifuentes Parada-Ligterink, Wijk aan Zee 1988) 10 ♗b5+?! ♘d7 11 ♕d3 ♕e7 12 ♗a6?! ♗xa6 ∓ Larsen-Timman Tilburg 1980.

7 ... ♕d8

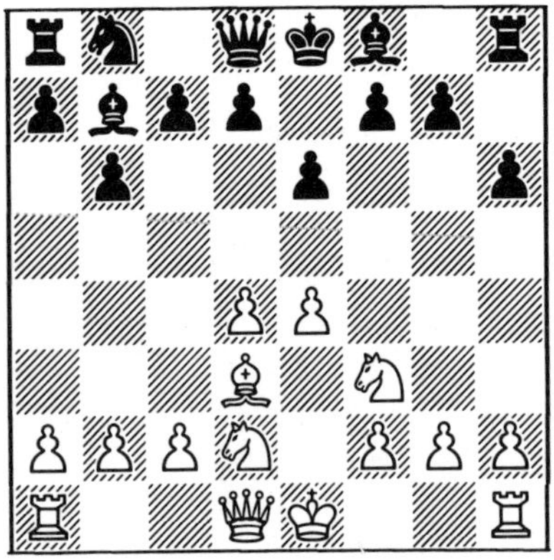

7 ... d6 8 ♕e2 a6 (8 ... ♕d8 9 h4 a6 10 0-0-0 ♘d7 11 g4 g6 12 c3 ♗g7 13 ♔b1 ♕e7 14 ♘f1 ± Kärner-Ornstein, Tallinn 1977) 9 0-0-0 ♘d7 10 e5 (10 ♔b1 e5 11 c3 ♗e7 12 ♘c4 0-0 13 ♗c2 ♖fe8 14 d5 ± Korchnoi-Karpov, Illustrative Game No 7) 10 ... ♕e7 11 h4 b5 12 ♔b1 d5 13 ♘b3 c5 14 dxc5 ♘xc5 15 ♘bd4 0-0-0 16 h5 ± Dorfman-Sokolov, USSR 1983.

8 ♕e2 ♗e7

8 ... d6 9 a4! a6 10 0-0 ♗e7 11 d5! exd5 12 exd5 ♗xd5 13 ♖fe1 c5? (13 ... ♔f8!) 14 ♘h4 ♖a7 Vaganian-Kengis, USSR 1982; 15 ♕g4! ±.

9 0-0-0

9 c3 d6 10 ♘c4 ♘d7 11 h4 a6 12 ♘e3 ♘f6 13 ♕c2 c5 = Wirthensohn-Keene, Dortmund 1978.

9 ... d6
10 h4 a6

10 ... ♘d7 11 g4 ♘f6 12 g5 ♘h5 ∞; 11 ♗a6!? (Lerner).

11 ♘c4

11 g4 ♘d7 12 g5? hxg5 13 hxg5 ♖xh1 14 ♖xh1 ♗xg5 ∓ (Lerner).

11 ... ♘d7
12 ♘e3 ♘f6
13 e5 ♘d5
14 ♘xd5 ♗xd5
15 ♗e4 ±

Lerner-Yudasin, USSR 1983, Illustrative Game No 8.

1.2

3 ... d5

Black has a stronghold in the centre but has problems in activating his light-squared bishop. The move is not very popular since now or later on White can switch to the Queen's Gambit, which may not be to the liking of Black, who initiated an Indian line.

In the following variations Black

delays ... c5.

4 ♘bd2 ♗e7

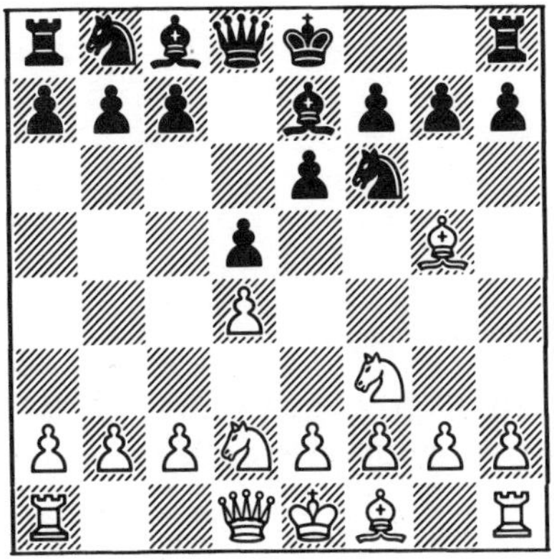

5 e3

5 c3 b6 6 e3 ♗b7 7 ♗b5+ c6 8 ♗d3 ♘bd7 9 0-0 0-0 (9 ... ♕c7!?) 10 a4 c5 (10 ... a6!?) 11 a5 c4 12 ♗c2 b5 13 a6! ♗c6 14 ♘e5 ♘xe5 15 dxe5 ♘d7 16 ♗xe7 ♕xe7 17 f4 ± (17 ... f5? 18 ♘f3 ♘c5 19 ♘d4 ♗d7 20 g4! ± Hort-Pia Cramling, Dortmund 1986).

5 ... ♘bd7!

Black has to look out for the e5 square. 5 ... 0-0 6 ♗d3 b6? 7 ♘e5! ± Timman-Geller, Illustrative Game No 9.

6 ♗d3

6 c3 came into consideration to counter 6 ... b6 by 7 ♗b5!.

6 ... 0-0
7 c3 b6
8 b4

More active is 8 e4!?.

8 ... ♗b7
9 ♕b1 h6
10 ♗h4 ♘h5
11 ♗g3 ♕c8
12 ♗e5 ♘hf6
13 0-0 c5

Chances are balanced. Petrosian-Andersson, Amsterdam 1973.

ILLUSTRATIVE GAMES

1 d4 ♘f6 2 ♘f3 e6 3 ♗g5

1) **Vaganian-Plaskett**
Hastings 1982/83

3 ... h6 4 ♗xf6 ♕xf6 5 ♘bd2 d6 6 c3 ♘d7 7 a4! g5?! Merely by weakening his own pawn structure, Black cannot hinder White's development. **8 g3! ♗g7** 8 ... g4 9 ♘h4 ± **9 ♗g2 0-0 10 a5! ♖b8 11 0-0 e5** Losing control of f5 – yet is there a suitable plan for Black? **12 e3 ♕e7** The waiting ... ♖e8 and ... ♘f8 would be more advisable. **13 e4 exd4** 13 ... f5 14 exf5 ♖xf5 15 ♖e1 ±. **14 ♘xd4! ♘e5 15 ♖e1!** Preparing the following manoeuvre of the knight. **15 ... ♖e8 16 ♘f1 ♘c6 17 ♘c2!** Following Tarrasch's principles, White does not ease his opponent's task by exchanging pieces. **17 ... ♕e5 18 ♘fe3 ♕c5** 18 ... ♘xa5 19 ♘d5 ♘b3 20 ♖a3 c6 21 ♖xb3 ±±. **19 ♘d5 ♘e7 20**

b4 ♕c6 21 ♘d4 21 e5 ♕d7!. **21 ... ♕d7 22 ♕d2 ♘xd5** 22 ... c5 23 ♘f5 ±. **23 exd5 ♖xe1+** More stubborn was 23 ... ♖e5. **24 ♖xe1 ♕d8.**

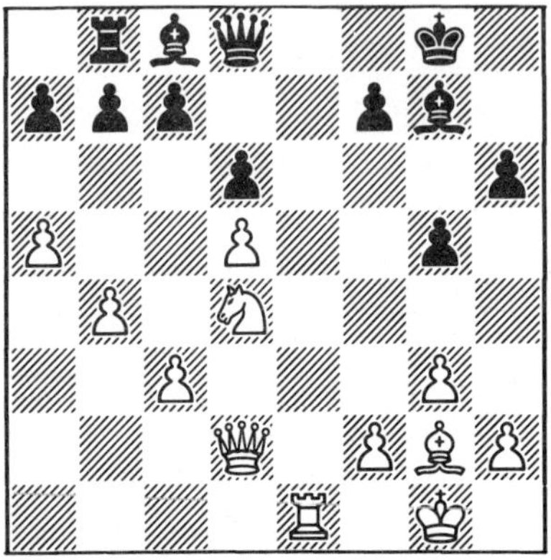

25 a6! The culmination of White's strategy! The c6 square is a hole, the need to protect which makes Black swap his only active piece, and consequently, decisively undermine his king's position. **25 ... ♗xd4 26 ♕xd4 b6 27 h4! ♗d7 28 ♗f3 gxh4** 28 ... ♕f8 29 hxg5 hxg5 30 ♕f6 ♕g7 31 ♕xg7+ ♔xg7 32 ♖e7 ♖d8 33 ♗h5 +-. **29 gxh4 ♕f8 30 ♔h2 ♖e8 31 ♖g1+ ♔h7 32 ♕f6 ♖e5 33 ♗d1! ♗f5 34 ♗h5 ♗d3 35 ♗xf7 ♖e8 36 ♖g3 ♗b1 37 ♖f3 ♖d8 38 ♗g6+ ♗xg6 39 ♕xf8 ♖xf8 40 ♖xf8 1-0** (Notes partly drawn upon Vaganian's)

2) **Lechtinsky-Velimirović**
Banja Luka 1985

3 ... h6 4 ♗xf6 ♕xf6 5 ♘bd2 c5 6 c3?! cxd4 7 cxd4 ♘c6 8 e3 g5!? 8 ... d5, 8 ... ♕g6!?. **9 a3** 9 h3 h5 10 g3 ∞; 9 ♗d3!? **9 ... g4 10 ♘g1 h5 11 g3!?** 11 ♘e2 h4 12 ♘c3 g3 13 ♕f3 gxf2+ 14 ♔xf2 ♕g6 ∓. **11 ... d5** 11 ... b6. **12 ♗g2** 12 h3 e5 13 dxe5 ♕xe5 ∓. **12 ... ♗d7 13 ♘e2 h4! 14 ♘f4 ♕g7 15 ♘b3** 15 ♕b3 ♗d6 16 0-0-0? ♘a5 17 ♕d3 ♗a4 ∓. **15 ... ♗d6 16 ♖c1 b6 17 ♖c3 ♘e7 18 ♕d2 ♖c8 19 ♖xc8+ ♗xc8 20 ♗f1** 20 ♔d1 ♗d7 21 ♔c1 ♗a4 22 ♕d3 ♔d7 ∓. **20 ... hxg3 21 fxg3 ♗xf4 22 exf4 ♘f5 23 ♗b5+** 23 ♔f2 ♘d6 24 ♗d3 ♗a6 ∓. **23 ... ♗d7 24 ♗xd7+ ♔xd7 25 ♕b4?!** 25 ♔f2 ♘xg3; 25 0-0 ♕h7 ∓. **25 ... ♘xg3 26 ♘c5+ ♔e8 27 ♖g1 ♕g6 28 ♕a4+ ♔f8 29 ♖xg3 bxc5 30 dxc5 ♖xh2 0-1** (Velimirović)

3) **Petrosian-Taimanov**
Moscow 1960

3 ... h6 4 ♗xf6 ♕xf6 5 e4 d6 6 ♘c3 c6?! 7 e5 dxe5?! 8 dxe5 ♕f4 9 g3 ♕b4 10 a3 ♕a5 11 b4 ♕c7 12 ♘e4! a5 13 ♖b1 axb4 14 axb4 ♘d7 15 ♘d6+ ♗xd6 16 exd6 White has obtained a significant space advantage in the opening. The d6 pawn keeps the opponent's forces cramped. **16 ... ♕b6 17 ♗g2 0-0 18 0-0 ♖d8 19 ♕d2 c5 20 ♖fd1 ♖a2?** Seemingly active, this move is inferior to ... cxb4 with some counterplay. After the text Black will get chances only by sacrificing a pawn.

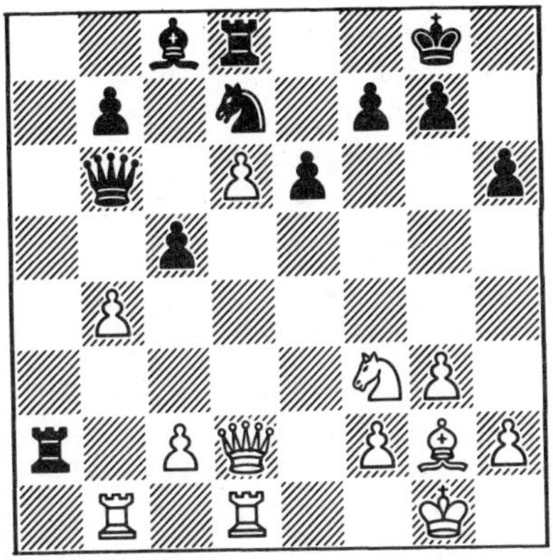

21 b5! c4!? 22 ♕c3 ♕c5 23 ♘d2 ♘b6 24 ♘e4 ♘a4 24 ... ♕*any* is met by 25 ♕d4!. **25 ♕a5 ♕b6 26 ♕b4 e5 27 ♖a1?! ♕d4! 28 ♖ab1 ♕b6 29 ♕xc4 ♗e6 30 ♕c7! ♖c8** 30 ... ♕xc7? 31 dxc7 ♖xd1+ 32 ♖xd1 ♖xc2 33 ♖d8+ ♔h7 34 ♘f6+!. **31 ♕e7 ♘c5 32 ♘xc5 ♕xc5 33 ♗e4 b6 34 ♖d2 ♖a4 35 ♗c6 ♗h3 36 ♖e1 ♔h7 37 ♕xf7 ♕b4 38 ♕d5 ♕c3 39 ♕d3+ ♕xd3 40 ♖xd3 ♖d8 41 d7 ♔g6 42 f3 ♔f6 43 g4 1-0**

4) **Hodgson-Eingorn**
Reykjavik 1989

3 ... h6 4 ♗xf6 ♕xf6 5 e4 By transposition; the game actually started 1 d4 ♘f6 2 ♗g5 e6 3 e4 h6 4 ♗xf6 ♕xf6 5 ♘f3. **5 ... g6 6 ♘c3 ♗g7 7 ♕d2 d6 8 0-0-0 ♘c6** 8 ... a6!?; 8 ... ♗d7!?. The text allows an annoying pin. **9 ♗b5!** 9 d5?! exd5 10 exd5 ♘e7 ∓ **9 ... 0-0 10 e5**

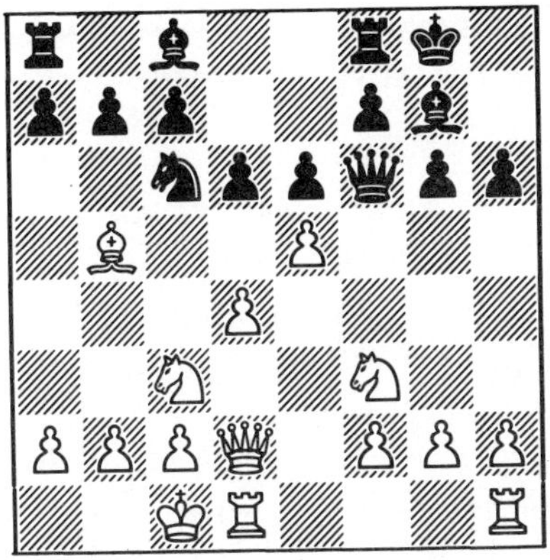

White appears to be gaining substantially in the centre, e.g. 10 ... ♕e7?! 11 ♗xc6! ±. Black has a bold reply. **10 ... dxe5 11 ♗xc6 exd4! 12 ♘e4 ♕e7 13 ♗a4 c5 14 ♖he1 ♖b8** Intending ... b5. It is clear that Black has potentially a massive pawn roller. Indeed, White is soon obliged to return the extra piece in order to break the pawn centre. **15 ♕f4! e5 16 ♘ed2 exf4 17 ♖xe7 b5 18 ♗b3 c4 19 ♘xc4 bxc4 20 ♗xc4 ♖b7! 21 ♖de1 ♗f6 22 ♖7e4** 22 ♖xb7 holds the balance. Now Black can open up the position for his bishop pair. **22 ... d3! 23 c3** Uncomfortable, but letting Black capture on b2 is even worse. **23 ... ♗f5 24 ♖e8** 24 ♖xf4? ♗g5! 25 ♘xg5 d2+ 26 ♔xd2 ♖xb2+ ∓ **24 ... g5 25 h3 h5 26 ♗b3?!** 26 ♖xf8+ ♔xf8 27 ♖d1 g4 28 hxg4 hxg4 29 ♘d4! ♗xd4 30 cxd4 = (Hodgson) **26 ... g4 27 hxg4 hxg4 28 ♘d4 ♗g6**

29 ♘c6 ♖xe8 30 ♖xe8+ ½-½ Although Black still has winning chances after 30 ... ♔g7.

(Notes based on Eingorn's)

5) **Terpugov-Botvinnik**
Moscow 1951

3 ... h6 4 ♗xf6 ♕xf6 5 e4 d6 6 ♘c3 a6 7 e5 ♕d8 8 ♗d3 d5 9 ♘e2 c5 This is already the French Defence. **10 c3 ♘c6 11 0-0 ♗d7 12 ♕d2 ♕b6 13 ♖ad1** After 13 dxc5! ♗xc5 14 b4 the initiative falls into White's hands. **13 ... cxd4 14 cxd4?** White should hold d4 with a knight. **14 ... ♗e7 15 ♘f4?** This stereotyped move costs White a pawn. **15 ... g5! 16 ♘e2 g4! 17 ♘e1 ♘xd4 18 ♗xa6 ♘c6 19 ♗c4?** A blunder, yet 19 ♗d3 was just as hopeless. **19 ... ♗g5 0-1**

6) **Korchnoi-Keres**
USSR Championship 1965

3 ... h6 4 ♗xf6 ♕xf6 5 e4 b6 6 a3 ♗b7 7 ♘c3 d6 8 ♕d2 ♘d7 9 0-0-0 g5!? 10 ♘b5!? ♔d8 10 ... ♕d8? 11 ♕c3 c6 12 d5! **11 h4 g4 12 e5 ♕g7 13 ♘e1 a6 14 ♘c3 d5 15 f4!** The threat is 16 f5! exf5 17 ♘d3 then ♘f4 and ♗d3. **15 ... f5!?** Black does not wait idly for White's attack to be unleashed. It turns out that the opening of the position is dangerous for both sides since Black will have counterplay in the centre and along the long diagonal. **16 exf6 ♕xf6 17 h5?** White attempts to surround the g4 pawn but he underestimates his opponent's chances. 17 ♘e2! c5 18 c3 or 18 c4!? ±. **17 ... c5!** Reacting to emergency? Black opens a file to his own king, but in a few moves it turns out that White's king is more vulnerable. 18 ♘e2 would be too late now owing to 18 ... cxd4 19 ♘xd4 ♘c5 and ... ♗g7. **18 dxc5 bxc5 19 g3 ♗c6** 19 ... d4? 20 ♗g2 **20 ♖h4 ♖g8 21 ♘d3 ♖b8 22 ♘f2 c4 23 ♘xg4** 23 ♖xg4 ♖xg4 24 ♘xg4 ♕g7! 25 ♗e2 ♗c5∓. **23 ... ♕e7! 24 ♖e1?** Better is 24 ♕e3! although the text continuation is still dangerous after the queen move.

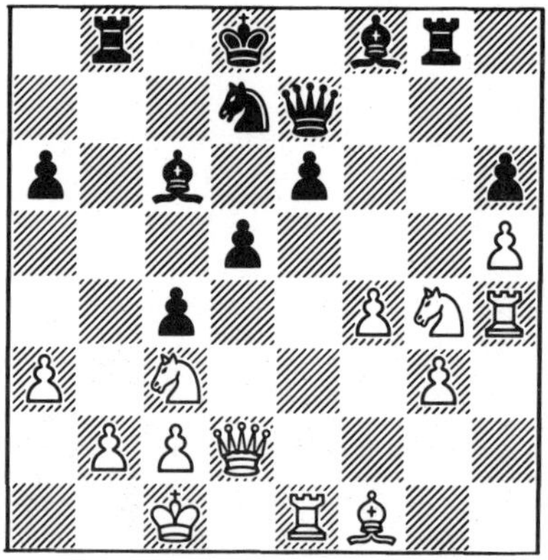

24 ... ♖xb2!! An attractive 'destroying' sacrifice. Its beauty is considerably increased by the small number of attacking pieces involved. **25 ♔xb2 ♕xa3+ 26 ♔b1**

♗g7 27 ♘e5 ♔c7! 28 ♘b5+ The last resort. **28 ... axb5 29 c3 ♗xe5 30 fxe5 ♖xg3 31 ♖h3 ♖g5 32 ♖he3 ♘c5 33 ♖f3 ♗e8 34 ♕a2 ♕xa2+ 35 ♔xa2 ♖xh5 36 ♔a3 ♘e4 37 ♖f8 ♗d7 38 ♔b4 ♖xe5!** Allowing the penetration of the opponent's rooks, but Black has a combination up his sleeve. **39 ♖a1 ♖f5 40 ♖h8 ♖f2!** The final point! 41 ♖a7+ is met by 41 ... ♔b6!! 42 ♖xd7 ♖b2+ 43 ♔a3 ♖b3+ 44 ♔a2 ♘xc3+ 45 ♔a1 ♖b1+ mate! **0-1**

7) **Korchnoi-Karpov**
Hastings 1971/72

3 ... h6 4 ♗xf6 ♕xf6 5 e4 b6 6 ♗d3 ♗b7 7 ♘bd2 d6 8 ♕e2 a6 9 0-0-0 ♘d7 10 ♔b1 e5 11 c3 ♗e7 12 ♘c4 0-0 13 ♗c2 ♖fe8 13 ... exd4 14 cxd4 ♖fe8 ⩲. **14 d5 c5?!** 14 ... c6! 15 ♘e3 b5 opens the queen-side. **15 ♘e3 ♗f8 16 g4! ♕d8 17 g5! h5** 17 ... hxg5 18 ♖dg1 ±.

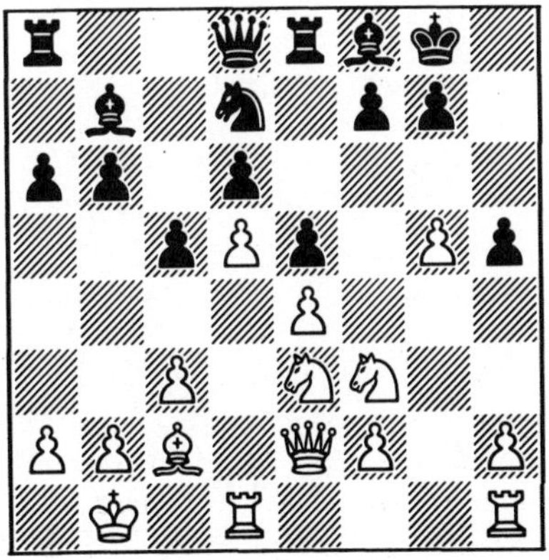

18 g6! fxg6 19 ♖hg1 ♕f6 20 ♘g5 ♗e7 21 ♘e6 ♘f8! 21 ... ♖ac8? 22 ♖g2 ♘f8 23 ♖df1. **22 ♘c7 ♕f7 23 ♖df1?** 23 a4!, then ♗d3, shows more urgency. **23 ... b5 24 ♘xa8 ♗xa8?!** 24 ... ♖xa8!. **25 c4 ♖b8 26 ♗d3 ♕e8 27 ♖c1 ♗f6 28 ♖g2! ♖b6?** 28 ... b4!. **29 ♖cg1!** 30 ♖xg6! is the threat. **29 ... ♖b8 30 ♕f1 b4** 30 ... ♗b7 31 cxb5 ♗c8 32 bxa6 ♗h3 33 ♕e2 ±. **31 ♗e2!** Black is unable to parry the breakthrough. **31 ... h4 32 ♖xg6 ♕xg6 33 ♖xg6 ♘xg6 34 ♗g4 ♘f4 35 ♕d1 b3 36 axb3 ♗b7 37 ♘g2!** An exemplary attack on the king. 37 ... ♘xg2 38 ♗e6+ leads to mate. **37 ... ♗c8 38 ♗xc8 ♖xc8 39 ♕g4 ♖e8 40 ♘xf4 exf4 41 ♕xf4 ♗e5 42 ♕xh4 ♖f8 43 b4 ♗d4 44 bxc5 1-0**

8) **Lerner-Yudasin**
USSR 1983

3 ... h6 4 ♗xf6 ♕xf6 5 e4 b6 6 ♗d3 ♗b7 7 ♘bd2 ♕d8 8 ♕e2 ♗e7 9 0-0-0 d6 10 h4 a6 11 ♘c4 ♘d7 12 ♘e3 ♘f6 13 e5 ♘d5 13 ... ♘e4? 14 d5! exd5 15 ♘xd5 ♗xd5 16 ♗xe4 ±. **14 ♘xd5 ♗xd5 15 ♗e4 c6** 15 ... ♗xe4 16 ♕xe4 d5 17 ♕g4 0-0 18 ♖h3 ±. **16 ♔b1 b5 17 g4!** White wants to pin down the entire kingside, so Black is forced to make a weakening move. **17 ... h5!? 18 gxh5 ♖xh5 19 ♖dg1! ♗f8** 19 ... g6? 20 ♖xg6!. **20 ♘g5** 20 exd6 ♕xd6 21 ♘e5 ♖xe5! 22 dxe5 ♕xe5 ±. **20 ... ♖h6 21**

♗xd5 cxd5 22 ♕f3 ♖a7 23 ♖g4! ♖d7! 24 ♖f4 ♕c7 25 ♖e1 dxe5 26 dxe5 ♗c5 White's first attack has not got through. Still, he has the advantage in space and can easily regroup his pieces in the blocked position.

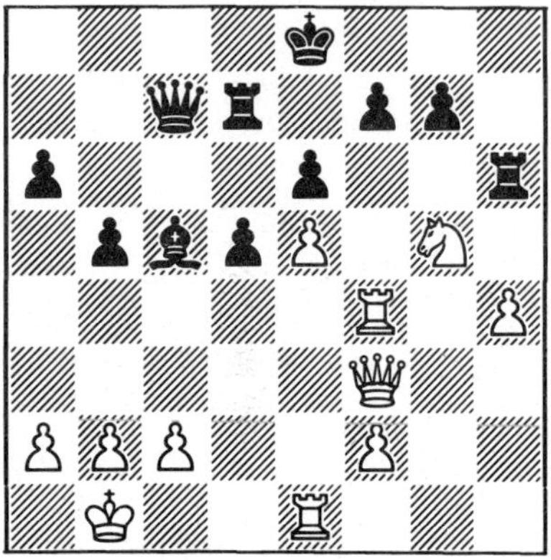

27 a3 a5?! Creating a weakness! **28 ♖d1 b4 29 a4 ♗a7 30 ♕e2 ♖e7** 30 ... f5? 31 exf6 ♕xf4 32 ♕xe6+ ♔d8 33 fxg7 ♖xe6 34 ♘xe6+. **31 ♖g4** 31 ♖d3 f6! 32 exf6 gxf6 33 ♘xe6 ♕xf4 34 ♘xf4 ♖xe2 35 ♘xe2 ♖xh4 36 ♖xd5 ♖e4! 37 ♘g3 ♖e1+ 38 ♔a2 ♗f2 ∞. **31 ... ♕c6 32 ♘f3 f5!? 33 exf6 gxf6 34 ♖g8+ ♔d7 35 ♖dg1 ♕c4** 35 ... ♕xa4? 36 ♕a6 +−; 35 ... e5!? 36 ♖1g7 ♗c5 ∞. **36 ♕d2 ♖h5 37 ♖8g4! ♕c5 38 ♖f4! ♔c7 39 ♘d4 ♔b7 40 ♘b3 ♕c7?** 40 ... ♕b6 41 ♖xf6 ♖xh4 42 ♖e1 ±. **41 ♖xf6 ♖xh4 42 ♖xe6!** Radically forcing the issue. 42 ... ♖xe6 43 ♕xd5+ ♖c6 44 ♘xa5+ ♔b6 45 ♕b5+ mate! **42 ... ♖d7 43 ♕d3 1-0** (Notes drawn from Lerner's analysis)

9) **Timman-Geller**
Linares 1983

3 ... d5 4 ♘bd2 ♗e7 5 e3 0-0?! 5 ... ♘bd7. **6 ♗d3 b6?! 7 ♘e5 ♗b7 8 ♗xf6!** 8 f4 ♘e4! **8 ... ♗xf6 9 f4! ♗xe5! 10 fxe5 ♕h4+ 11 g3 ♕h6 12 ♕e2 ♘c6** 12 ... f6 13 ♘f3 ♘d7 ±. **13 0-0** The light-squared bishop will disappear from the board, as if 13 c3 f6!. **13 ... ♘b4 14 ♖f4! ♘xd3 15 ♕xd3 a5!** Geller makes every effort to bring his bad bishop into play. His kingside however, is weak, his queen is idling on the edge of the board and the c7 pawn needs protecting. **16 ♘f3 ♗a6 17 ♕c3 ♗e2 18 ♕c6 ♕h5 19 ♔g2 ♖ae8 20 ♖e1 ♗a6** 20 ... ♗xf3+ 21 ♖xf3 ♖e7 ±. **21 g4 ♕g6 22 ♔h1** 22 ♔f2 f6. **22 ... ♖e7 23 g5!?**

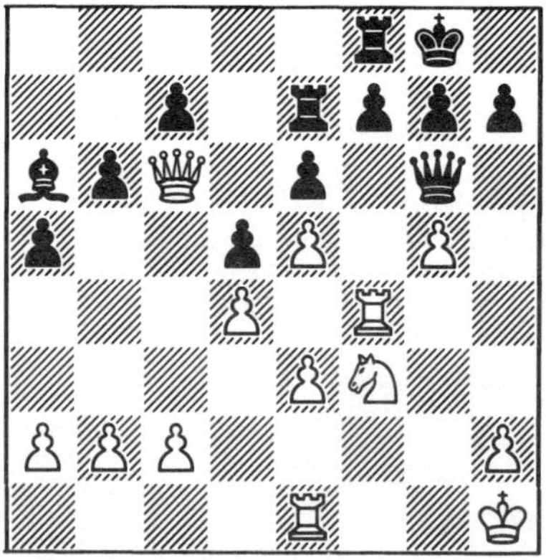

Aiming to checkmate the queen rather than the king. **23 ... ♕h5 24 ♔g2 ♖b8 25 ♔f2 ♕g6 26 ♖f6!? ♕e4 27 ♖f4 ♕g6 28 ♖c1 ♖c8?** 28 ... ♔h8 ±. **29 ♖f6! ♕e4**

(diagram)

30 g6!! Depriving the queen of the g6 square. Whichever pawn recaptures the reply is 31 ♖f4!. 30 ... gxf6 is met by 31 exf6 ♖ee8 32 gxf7+ ♔xf7 33 ♘g5+. **30 ... ♖f8 31 ♖f4! fxg6** 31 ... ♕xg6 32 ♖g1 ♕h5 33 ♖h4 ♕f5 34 ♖g5 ±±. **32 ♖xe4 dxe4 33 ♕xe4 c5** 33 ... ♗c4 34 ♕g4 h5 35 ♕xg6 ♖7f7 36 ♕xf7+! ♔xf7 37 ♔g3 ±±. **34 c4 1-0**

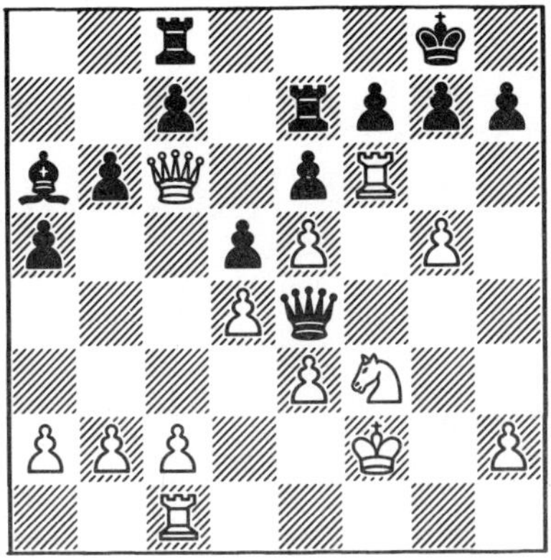

2 Torre-Petrosian Attack: Rare lines after 3 ... c5

1	d4	♘f6
2	♘f3	e6
3	♗g5	c5

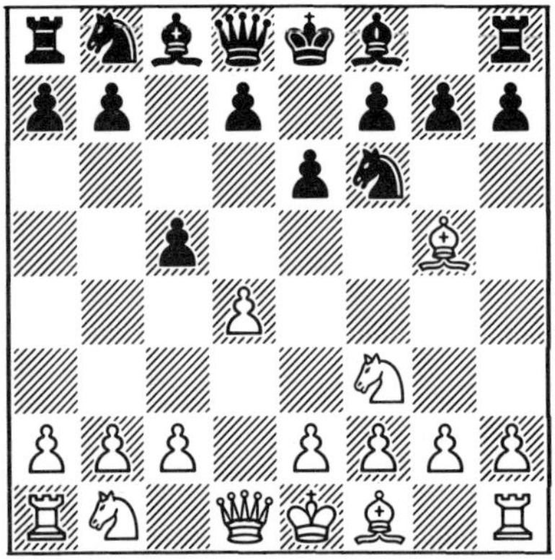

The variations presented in this chapter are seldom encountered in present-day tournament practice, yet they are likely to come into fashion again sooner or later.

Considering that throughout the Torre-Petrosian Attack White's worst weakness is b2, he always has to keep in mind the possibility of the ... ♕b6 threat. The natural response to this is 4 e3, dealt with in Chapter 3.

Prior to analysing the main lines in this chapter (4 e4?! and 4 c3) let us go through the other possibilities:

(a) 4 ♗xf6? (Illogical at a glance; compared with 3 ... h6 4 ♗xf6 it gives away a tempo to the opponent.) 4 ... ♕xf6 5 e3 (5 e4?! cxd4 6 ♕xd4 – 6 ♘xd4?! ♗c5 7 c3 ♘c6 ∓ – 6 ... ♘c6 7 ♕xf6 gxf6 8 c3 b6 9 ♘bd2 ♗b7 10 ♗d3 ♖c8 11 ♘c4 ♖g8 ∓ Wahltuch-Capablanca, London 1922) 5 ... ♘c6 6 c3 ♗e7 7 ♗d3 d5 8 ♘bd2 0-0 9 ♕e2?! (9 dxc5 ♗xc5 10 e4 =) 9 ... e5! 10 dxe5 ♘xe5 11 ♘xe5 ♕xe5 ∓ Wahltuch-Rubinstein, Illustrative Game No 10.

(b) 4 dxc5?! (Contradicting general principles. Capturing is better delayed until ... ♗e7 is played, e.g. 4 e3 ♗e7 5 dxc5!?.) 4 ... ♗xc5 5 e3 0-0 (5 ... d5 =) 6 a3 b6 (6 ... ♗e7 7 ♗d3 d5 8 ♘c3 ♘bd7 9 0-0 b6 10 e4 dxe4 11 ♘xe4 ♗b7 =

Tapasztó-Sándor, Budapest 1955.) 7 ♘c3 ♗b7 8 ♗d3 d5 9 0-0 ♗e7 10 ♖e1?! ♘bd7 11 ♕e2 ♘c5 ∓ Gy. Szilágyi-Spasov, Varna 1971.

(c) 4 d5?! (Interesting yet hardly sufficient.) 4 ... ♕a5+ (4 ... exd5!? 5 e3 ♗e7 6 ♘c3 ♕a5 7 ♗e2 h6 8 ♗xf6 ♗xf6 9 0-0 ♗xc3 10 bxc3 0-0 11 ♕xd5 ♕xc3 ∓ Tarashevich-Ronchenko, USSR 1964) 5 ♗d2 ♕b6 6 c4 ♕xb2 7 ♘c3 ♕b6 (Owing to the passive bishop on d2 White seems to have less compensation for the sacrificed pawn than in the 4 e3 ♕b6 5 ♘bd2 ♕xb2 line.) 8 e4 d6 9 ♖b1 ♕d8 10 ♕a4+ ♗d7 11 ♕c2 b6 12 e5 dxe5 13 ♘xe5 ♗d6 ∓ Shamkovich-Antoshin, USSR 1961.

2.1

4 e4

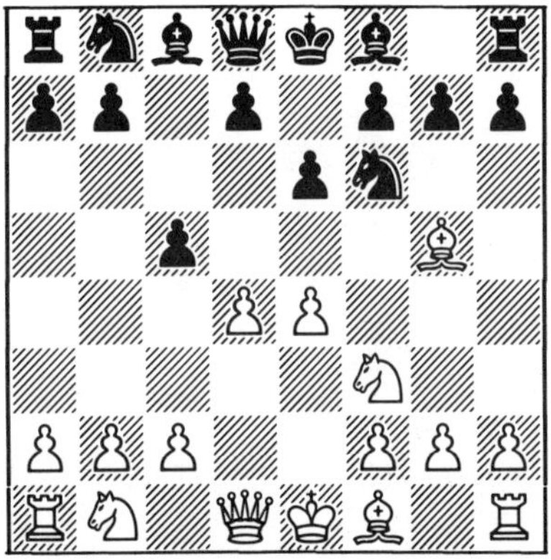

Common sense? In fact, with his undeveloped queenside and insecure centre, White's action is premature.

2.11

4 ... ♕b6?!

Riskier than after 4 e3 since White is better developed in this line. Also inadequate are the following continuations:

(a) 4 ... h6? 5 ♗xf6 ♕xf6 6 e5 ♕d8 7 d5! exd5 (7 ... d6 8 ♗b5+ ♗d7 9 ♗xd7+ ♕xd7 10 0-0 ±) 8 ♕xd5 ♗e7 9 ♘c3 0-0 10 0-0-0 ♘c6 11 ♕e4 d6 Malich-Zaitsev, Berlin 1968; 12 ♗d3! g6 13 ♗c4 ♗f5 14 ♕e3 ± (Uhlmann).

(b) 4 ... ♕a5+?! (Forcing the queen swap, but Black's development does not advance.) 5 ♕d2! ♕xd2+ (5 ... ♕b6!? 6 ♘c3!) 6 ♘bxd2 cxd4 7 ♘xd4 a6 8 e5 ♘d5 9 ♗c4 ♘c6 10 ♗xd5 ♘xd4 11 ♗e4 d5 12 exd6 ♗xd6 13 ♘c4 ♗c7 14 ♗e3 ± Grau-Coria, Buenos Aires 1931.

5 ♘bd2 cxd4

5 ... ♕xb2? 6 ♘c4 ♕b4+ 7 c3 ♕xc3+ 8 ♗d2 ±±.

6 e5 ♘d5
7 ♗d3

7 ♘c4 ♕c7?! 8 ♘xd4 a6 9 ♘f5! exf5 10 ♕xd5 ±; 7 ... ♕b4+ 8 ♗d2 ♕c5 9 a3 ∞.

7 ... h6

7 ... ♘c6 8 0-0 ♕c7 9 ♖e1 d6 10 ♘c4 dxe5 11 ♘3xe5 b5 Basman-Conroy, England 1967; 12 ♗e4! ±±.

8 ♗h4 ♘c6

8 ... ♘f4!? 9 0-0 ♘xd3 10 cxd3 d5 ∞.

9 0-0 ♕c7
10 ♖e1 ♘db4
11 ♗e4 d5
12 exd6 ♕xd6
13 c3!

Better developed, White's position is superior, e.g. 13 ... ♘d5 (13 ...dxc3 14 bxc3 ♘a6 15 ♗xc6+ ♕xc6 16 ♘e5 ♕c7 17 ♘e4 ±) 14 cxd4 ♗e7 15 ♘c4 ± Basman-Anoshin, Sinaia 1965.

2.12

4 ... cxd4!
5 e5

No matter which piece captures at d4 Black has a comfortable game: 5 ♕xd4 ♘c6; 5 ♘xd4 ♕a5+ 6 ♕d2 ♗b4. Alternatively: 5 ♘bd2 ♘c6 6 e5 h6 7 ♗h4 g5 8 ♗g3 ♘h5 (8 ... ♘d5!?) 9 ♗b5 (9 ♘e4? ♕a5+!) 9 ... g4 10 ♗h4 (10 ♗xc6 dxc6 11 ♘e4 ♗b4+! 12 ♔f1 gxf3 13 ♕xf3 ♘xg3+ -+) 10 ... ♕b6 (10 ... ♕c7!?) 11 ♗xc6 ♕xc6 12 ♘xd4 ♕xg2 13 ♖f1 ♕xh2 14 ♕xg4 ♕xe5+ 15 ♔d1 ♘f6! 16 ♕f3 ♗e7 -+ Malich-Adamski, Leipzig 1977.

5 ... h6
6 ♗h4 g5
7 ♗g3

7 exf6 (7 ♘xg5? hxg5 8 ♗xg5 ♕a5+!) 7 ... gxh4 8 ♕xd4 h3 9 g3 ♘c6 10 ♕h4 ♕b6 (10 ... ♖g8!?) 11 b3?! ♗c5 -+.

7 ... ♘e4

7 ... ♘h5 8 ♕xd4 ♘c6 9 ♕e4 ♗g7 10 ♗b5 (10 ♘c3 d5 11 exd6 ♗xc3+ 12 bxc3 ♘xg3 ∓) 10 ... ♕c7 11 ♗xc6 ♕xc6 12 ♕e2 ♕c5 13 0-0 ♘xg3 14 hxg3 g4 15 ♘fd2 ♕xe5 16 ♕xg4 ♕xb2 ∓ Marshall-Nimzowitsch, Berlin 1928.

8 ♕xd4 ♘xg3
9 hxg3 ♘c6
10 ♕e4 ♕b6!

Better than Bogolyubov's 10 ... ♗g7 11 ♘c3 ♕a5 12 ♗b5 d5, etc.

11 ♘bd2 ♕xb2 ∓

White has not got enough compensation for the pawn. E.g. 12 ♖b1 ♕c3 13 ♖b3 ♕a5 14 ♗d3 g4! etc, Apschenek-Kashdan, Illustrative Game No 10.

2.2

4 c3

A natural response: White attempts to play e4. The undeniable shortcoming of the move is that it somewhat slows down White's development.

2.21

4 ... ♕b6

Another natural reaction.

If Black ignores the e4 threat he will end up with an inferior game:

(a) 4 ... b6?! 5 e4! (5 e3 ♗e7 6 ♗d3 ♗a6 7 ♗xa6 ♘xa6 8 ♗xf6 ♗xf6 9 ♘bd2 0-0 10 0-0 ♕c7 11 ♘e4 ♗e7 12 d5!? ♕b7 13 d6 ♗d8 14 ♕d3 ± Tipary-Navarovszky, Budapest 1955) 5 ... h6 6 ♗xf6 ♕xf6 7 ♗d3 ♕d8 8 0-0 ♗a6 9 ♗xa6 ♘xa6 10 d5 ♘b8 11 ♘e5!? ♗d6 12 ♘xf7 ♔xf7 13 dxe6+ ♔e7 14 e5 ♗xe5 15 ♕f3 ± Lutikov-Velimirović, Sukhumi 1966.

(b) 4 ... h6 5 ♗xf6 ♕xf6 6 e4! ♘c6 (6 ... ♕d8 7 d5 ♕c7 8 ♘a3! ± Alekhine-Steiner, Illustrative Game No 12; or 6 ... d6 7 ♗d3 e5 8 ♘a3 ♗e7 9 dxe5 dxe5 10 ♗b5+ ± Vidmar-Kostić, Yugoslavia 1922) 7 ♗e2! (7 a3 cxd4 8 cxd4 d6 9 ♘c3 a6 10 ♗e2 ♗e7 11 ♕d2 0-0 = Michell-Vajda, Semmering 1926) 7 ... ♕g6?! 8 d5 ♘e7 9 0-0 ♕xe4 10 c4 exd5 11 ♘c3, etc. White's better development is ample compensation for the pawn (analysis).

2.211

5 ♕b3

(a) 5 ♕c2 cxd4 (5 ... ♘c6 6 ♗xf6 gxf6 7 dxc5 ♗xc5 8 e4 ♖g8 9 g3 ♕c7 10 ♘bd2 b6 11 ♘b3 ♗e7 12 ♗d3 ♗b7 13 ♕e2 a6 14 a4 h5 15 ♖f1 ♖g4 = G.Garcia-Gipslis, Jurmala 1983) 6 cxd4 (6 ♘xd4?! ♘c6! ∓ Marshall-Capablanca, Illustrative Game No 13) 6 ... ♘c6 7 e3 (7 ♗xf6 gxf6 8 e3 d5 9 ♗e2 ♗d7 10 ♘c3 ♗e7 11 0-0 0-0 12 ♘a4 ♕c7 13 ♘c5 ♖fe8 14 ♘xd7 ♕xd7 15 ♕a4 ♘e5 = Larsen-Portisch, Tilburg 1980) 7 ... d5 8 ♘c3 ♗d7 9 ♗e2 (9 ♗b5!? ♘e4! 10 0-0 ♘xc3 11 ♗xc6 ♕xc6 12 ♘e5 ♕a4 13 ♕xc3 ♖c8 =) 9 ... ♖c8 10 0-0 =.

(b) 5 ♕c1 ♘e4 6 e3 (6 ♗h4 or 6 ♗f4 leads to Chapter 3, best is 6 ... cxd4 and 7 ... ♗b4+.) 6 ... ♘xg5 d5 =.

5 ... ♘c6

(a) 5 ... cxd4 6 cxd4 ♘e4 7 ♗f4 ♘c6 8 e3 ♗b4+ 9 ♘fd2 =; 9 ♘bd2?? g5! 10 ♗xg5 ♗xd2+ 11 ♘xd2 ♕a5 0-1 Sangla-Karpov, Riga 1968.

(b) 5 ... ♘e4 6 ♗f4 ♘c6 7 e3

♗e7 8 ♗d3 (8 ♘bd2 ♘xd2 9 ♘xd2 d5 10 ♕xb6 axb6 11 ♗c7 ♗d8 = Klarić-Suba, Sochi 1977) 8 ... d5 9 ♗xe4 dxe4 10 ♘fd2 f5 11 ♘c4 ♕d8 12 ♘ba3 g5 13 ♗e5 0-0 14 0-0-0 cxd4 15 ♗xd4 ♘a5 16 ♘xa5 ♕xa5 17 ♘c4 ♕a6 ∞ Sokolov-Karpov, USSR 1977; 6 ♗h4!? ♘c6 7 e3 ♗e7 ∞.

6 e3 d5

6 ... ♕xb3 7 axb3 d5 8 ♘bd2 ♗d6 9 ♗e2 0-0 10 0-0 ♗d7 11 dxc5 ♗xc5 12 b4 ♗b6 13 ♗xf6 gxf6 14 e4 ± Trifunović-Zuidema, Belgrade 1964; 6 ... h6 7 ♗xf6 gxf6 8 ♕c2 ∞.

7 ♘bd2

7 ♕xb6 axb6 8 ♘bd2 ♗e7 9 ♗d3 c4 10 ♗c2 b5 11 ♘e5 b4! =.

7 ... ♗d7

7 ... ♗e7 8 ♗e2 0-0 9 0-0 h6 10 ♗h4 ♖e8 11 ♘e5 ♘d7 12 ♗xe7 ♖xe7 13 f4 cxd4 14 ♕xb6 ♘xb6 15 exd4 ♗d7 16 ♘b3 ♗e8 17 ♘c5 f6 = Lutikov-Karpov, USSR 1971.

8 ♗e2 cxd4
9 ♕xb6

9 exd4? ♗d6 10 0-0 h6! 11 ♗h4 ♘h5 ∓ Kostić-Capablanca, Illustrative Game No 14.

9 ... axb6
10 ♘xd4 ♘xd4
11 exd4 =

2.212

5 ♘bd2!?

A bold sacrifice of a pawn based on White's better development. Its only flaw is the inadequate c3 move.

5 ... ♕xb2

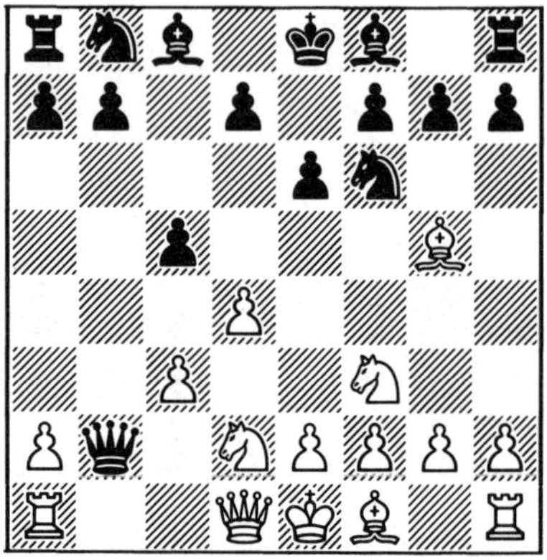

6 ♘c4! ♕b5

White was lucky enough to "lag behind" in development. His task is easier without e3: 6 ... ♕xc3+?? 7 ♗d2! ♕xc4 8 e4!.

7 e4 ♕c6
8 d5! exd5
9 ♘ce5

9 exd5 ♕xd5 10 ♗d3 ♕e6+ (10 ... ♔d8? 11 0-0 d6 12 ♕c2 ♔c7 13 ♘e3 ♕c6 14 ♖ab1 ± Rytov-Osulj, Sevastopol 1978) 11 ♔d2 d5! 12 ♗xf6 ♕xf6 13 ♘e3 ♗e6 14 ♕b3 d4 15 ♕xb7 dxe3+ ∞ Sokolov-Muratov, USSR 1971.

9 ... ♕c7
10 exd5 d6
11 ♕a4+ ♗d7

11 ... ♔d8? 12 ♕f4! ♕e7 13 0-0-0 ± Sokolov-Dobosz, Illustrative Game No 14.

12 ♘xd7 ♘bxd7
13 ♗xf6 gxf6
14 ♘h4

White has a strong counterplay for the pawn.

2.22

4 ... cxd4!

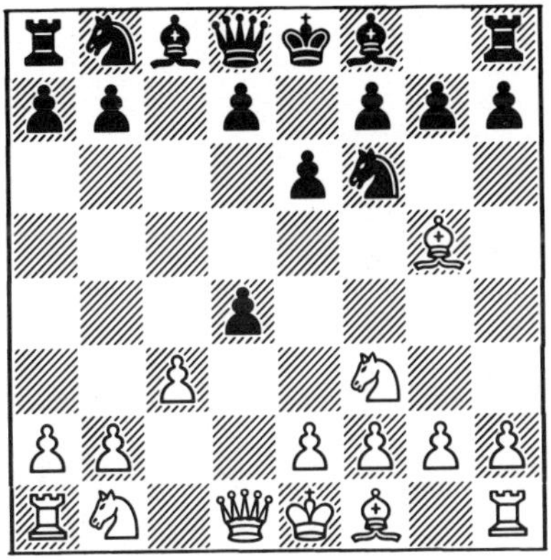

Probably the safest.

5 cxd4

A natural reply. Some artificial attempts:

(a) 5 ♘xd4 d5 (5 ... ♗e7 6 g3 ♘c6 7 ♗g2 0-0 8 0-0 h6 9 ♗xf6 ♗xf6 10 e3 d5 11 ♘a3 ♗d7 12 ♘b3 ♕e7 13 ♖c1 ♖fd8 14 ♕e2 ♖ac8 15 ♖fd1 ♘e5 ∓ Averbakh-M.Kovács, Budapest 1970) 6 ♘bd2 ♘bd7 7 e4 dxe4 8 ♘xe4 ♗e7 9 ♘xf6 ♗xf6 10 ♗xf6 ♘xf6 = Trifunović-Pirc, Amsterdam 1970.

(b) 5 ♗xf6 ♕xf6 (5 ... gxf6 6 cxd4 ♕b6 7 ♕d2 d5 8 ♘c3 ♗d7 9 e3 ♘c6 10 ♗d3 f5 11 0-0 ♗d6 12 ♖fc1 ♘e7 13 ♕e2 0-0 14 ♗b5 ♗c8 15 ♘a4 ± Tipary-Kluger, Budapest 1958) 6 cxd4 d5 7 ♘c3 ♘c6 8 e3 ♗d6 9 ♖c1 ♕e7 10 ♗e2 0-0 =.

5 ... ♕a5+

This check is the point of the previous exchange. Also playable here are:

(a) 5 ... d5 6 ♘c3 ♗e7 7 e3 0-0 8 ♗d3 b6 9 ♘e5 ♘fd7 10 ♘xd7 ♕xd7 11 ♗xe7 ♕xe7 12 ♕e2 ♘c6 13 a3 ♗b7 14 0-0 ♖fc8 = Tukmakov-Kapengut, USSR 1972.

(b) 5 ... ♘c6 6 ♘c3 d5 7 e3 ♕b6 8 ♖b1 (8 ♕c2!?) 8 ... ♗d7 9 ♗xf6 gxf6 10 ♗d3 ♗e7 11 0-0 ♖c8 12 ♘d2 f5 13 ♕h5 ♕d8 14 ♖bc1 ♗d6 15 f4 ♕f6 16 ♘f3 ♗e7 = Trifunović-Darga, Sarajevo 1962.

(c) 5 ... ♕b6!? 6 ♕c1 (6 ♕c2!? ♘c6 7 ♗xf6 gxf6 8 e3 d5 9 ♘c3 ♗d7 10 ♗e2 ♗e7 11 0-0 0-0 12 ♘a4 ♕c7 13 ♘c5 ♖fc8 14 ♘xd7 ♕xd7 15 ♕a4 ± Larsen-Portisch, Tilburg 1980; or 6 ♘bd2 ♘c6 7 e3 d5 = Duz Khotimirsky–Bogoljubow, Illustrative Game No 15) 6 ... ♘c6 7 e3 ♗e7 8 ♘c3 0-0 9 ♗e2 h6 10 ♗h4 d6 11 0-0 ♗d7 12 ♕d2 ♕d8 13 ♖fd1 d5 14 ♘e5 ♗e8 15 ♖ac1 ♖c8 = Hort-Korchnoi, Wijk aan Zee 1971.

6 ♗d2 ♕b6
7 ♘c3 d5

8	**e3**	**♘c6**
9	**a3**	

9 ♘a4 ♕d8 10 ♖c1 ♗d6 11 ♗d3 0-0 12 0-0 ♘e4 = Sakov-Zaitsev, USSR 1959.

9	**...**	**♗d6**
10	**♗e2**	**0-0**

White has not made any headway. Lechtinsky-Yudasin, Trnava 1983.

ILLUSTRATIVE GAMES

1 d4 ♘f6 2 ♘f3 e6 3 ♗g5 c5

10) **Wahltuch-Rubinstein**
London 1922

4 ♗xf6?! ♕xf6 5 e3 Relatively better than the opening of the position by 5 e4. **5 ... ♘c6 6 c3 ♗e7 7 ♗d3 d5 8 ♘bd2 0-0 9 ♕e2?! e5! 10 dxe5 ♘xe5 11 ♘xe5 ♕xe5 12 0-0-0?** Castling into it! **12 ... b5!** Offering a pawn to open a file. **13 ♘f3 ♕c7 14 ♗xb5 ♖b8 15 ♗d3 ♕a5 16 ♗b1 ♗f6 17 ♖d2 ♗a6 18 ♕d1**

(diagram)

18 ... ♗xc3! This destructive sacrifice forces the issue. **19 ♗xh7+ ♔h8** 19 ... ♔xh7? 20 ♕c2+!. **20 ♕c2 ♖xb2 21 ♖xd5** Desperate. **21 ... ♕xa2 22 ♖h5 ♕a1+ 23 ♕b1 ♖xb1+ 0-1**

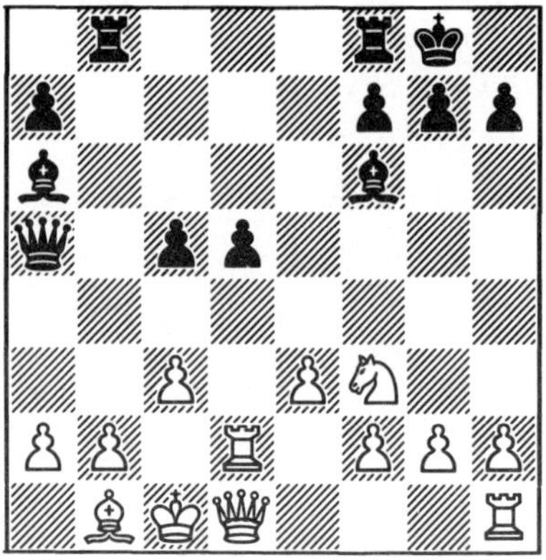

11) **Apschenek-Kashdan**
Hamburg 1930

4 e4 cxd4 5 e5 h6 6 ♗h4 g5 7 ♗g3 ♘e4 8 ♕xd4 ♘xg3 9 hxg3 ♘c6 10 ♕e4 ♕b6! The b2 pawn is the eternal dilemma of the Torre-Petrosian Attack. **11 ♘bd2 ♕xb2 12 ♖b1 ♕c3 13 ♖b3 ♕a5 14 ♗d3?** For better or worse, 14 ♗b5! was necessary to maintain the e5 outpost. **14 ... g4! 15 ♖b5?** An oversight. Nevertheless, 15 ♕xg4 ♘xe5 undoubtedly favours Black. **15 ... ♕a3!** Better than 15 ... ♕xa2 for now 16 ... ♕c1+ is a lethal threat. **16 ♘g1 a6 17 ♖b3 ♕c1+ 18 ♔e2 ♕a1 19 c3 ♘a5 20 ♖b1 ♕xc3 21 ♕xg4 ♘c6 22 ♘e4?** Some activity at last? **22 ... ♕xd3+! 0-1**

12) **Alekhine-E.Steiner**
Kemeri 1937

4 c3 h6?! 5 ♗xf6 ♕xf6 6 e4 ♕d8?! Black won't be able to make up for the lost tempi. **7 d5 ♕c7 8 ♘a3! a6 9 ♘c4 b5 10 ♘e3 e5 11 a4!** The better developed side should open files! **11 ... bxa4 12 ♕xa4 ♗e7 13 ♖d1 0-0? 14 d6! 1-0** 14 ... ♗xd6 15 ♘f5.

13) **Marshall-Capablanca**
New York 1927

4 c3 ♕b6 5 ♕c2 cxd4 6 ♘xd4?! ♘c6 7 e3 d5 8 ♘d2 ♗d7 9 ♘2f3?! 9 ♖c1 ♖c8 10 ♕b1 = (Alekhine). **9 ... ♘e4 10 ♗f4?** Looking for complications, Marshall will face more than enough. 10 ♗h4! **10 ... f6! 11 ♗d3?** The great tactician goes astray.

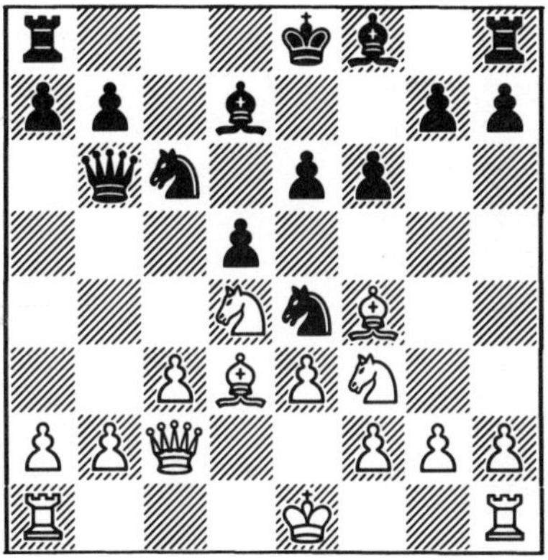

11 ... e5! 12 ♗xe4 12 ♘xc6 ♗xc6 13 ♗g3 ♘xg3 14 hxg3 e4. **12 ... dxe4 13 ♕xe4 0-0-0** White loses a piece since 14 ♘xc6 ♗xc6 15 ♕f5+ ♗d7 cannot save the game. **14 ♗g3 exd4 15 0-0 dxe3 16 a4 ♖e8 17 ♕d3 exf2+ 18 ♔h1 ♕e3 19 ♕d1 ♗g4 20 ♖xf2 h5 21 ♕f1 ♗xf3 22 ♖xf3 ♕e2 23 ♕g1 h4 24 ♖e1 hxg3 25 ♖xe2 ♖xe2 26 ♖xg3 ♗d6 27 ♕f1 ♖he8 28 ♕f5+ ♔b8 29 ♖f3 ♖8e5 30 ♕d3 ♖e1+ 31 ♖f1 ♖d5 32 ♕f3 ♘e5 33 ♕f2 ♖xf1+ 34 ♕f1 ♘g4 0-1**

14) **Kostić-Capablanca**
New York (match) 1919

4 c3 ♕b6 5 ♕b3?! ♘c6 6 e3 d5 7 ♘bd2 ♗d7 8 ♗e2 cxd4! 9 exd4?! Weakens f4. **9 ... ♗d6 10 0-0 h6 11 ♗h4** Better is 11 ♗e3 ♘g4 12 c4, whereas after 11 ♗xf6 gxf6 the two bishops and the safe centre would favour Black. **11 ... ♘h5! 12 ♕xb6 axb6 13 ♖fe1 g5 14 ♗g3** 14 ♘e5? ♗xe5 15 ♗xh5 ♗f4!. **14 ... ♘xg3 15 hxg3 f6!**

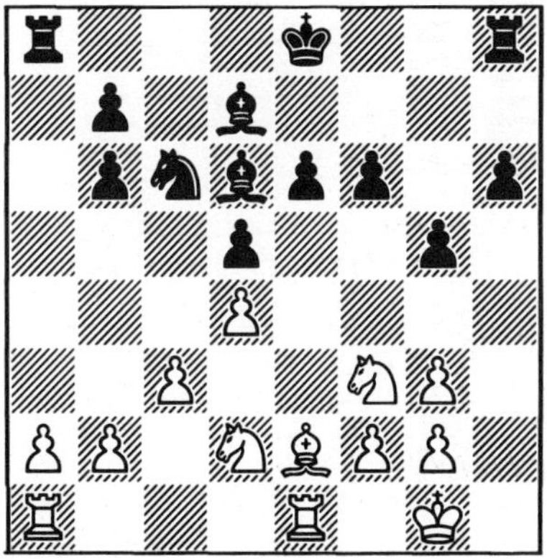

Black's advantage lies in the mobility of his pawns. **16 g4**

♔f7 17 ♘h2 ♘a5! 18 ♘hf1 b5 19 a3 Hindering 19 ... b4. **19 ... ♘c4 20 ♘xc4 bxc4 21 ♘e3 ♖a6! 22 g3 ♖b6 23 ♖a2 ♖a8 24 ♗f3!** The only defence. **24 ... ♖a5! 25 ♔g2 ♖ab5 26 ♖e2 ♗e8 27 ♖d2 ♔g7 28 ♗d1 ♗g6 29 ♗a4 ♖a5 30 ♗c2 ♗xc2 31 ♖xc2 ♔g6 32 ♖e2 ♖ab5 33 ♘d1 ♗f8 34 ♖a1 h5 35 f3?** 35 gxh5+ ♔xh5 36 ♖c1 ∓. **35 ... hxg4 36 fxg4 f5 37 gxf5+?** 37 ♔f3!. **37 ... exf5 38 ♖c1 ♖f6 39 ♖1c2 ♗d6 40 ♖e8 ♔f7! 41 ♖e1** 41 ♖2e2 f4!. **41 ... f4 42 g4**

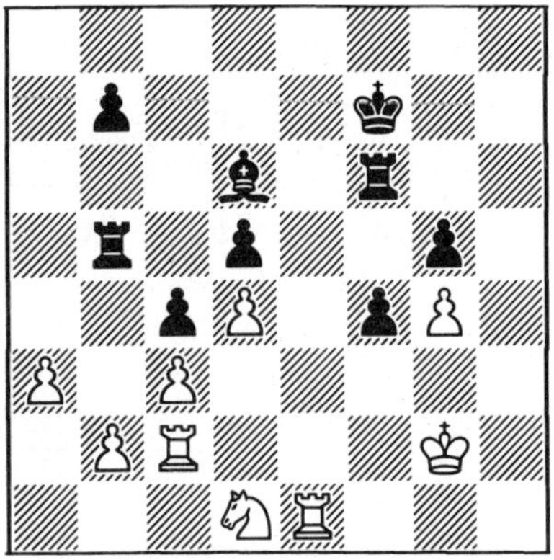

42 ... f3+! Preparing a pawn sacrifice. **43 ♔f2 ♖h6! 44 ♔xf3 ♖h3+ 45 ♔e2 ♖h2+ 46 ♘f2 ♗g3 47 ♖f1?** 47 ♔f1! ♖xf2+ 48 ♖xf2+ ♗xf2 49 ♔xf2 ♖xb2+ 50 ♖e2 ♖b3 51 ♖e5! was the last chance. **47 ... ♖b6! 48 ♔f3 ♗h4 49 ♔e2 ♖f6 50 ♔e3 b5 51 ♖d2 ♔e7!** The threat is the king's march to b3. **52 b4 cxb3 53 ♘d3 ♖xd2 0-1**

15) **Sokolov-Dobosz**
Primorsko 1970

4 c3 ♕b6 5 ♘bd2! ♕xb2 6 ♘c4! ♕b5 7 e4 ♕c6 8 d5 exd5 9 ♘ce5 ♕c7 10 exd5 d6 11 ♕a4+ ♔d8? 12 ♕f4! A witty sacrifice. **12 ... ♕e7 13 0-0-0 dxe5 14 ♘xe5 ♘bd7** The threat was 15 ♘c6+!. **15 ♘c6+! bxc6 16 dxc6 c4** 16 ... h6 17 ♗xf6 ♕xf6 18 c7+ ♔e8 19 ♕xf6 ♘xf6 20 ♖d8+ ♔e7 21 ♗b5 ++. **17 ♗xc4 ♕a3+ 18 ♔b1 ♕xc3** 18 ... ♗e7 19 ♗xf6 gxf6 20 c7+ ♔e8 21 ♕f3 ♕c5 22 ♕xa8 ♕xc7 23 ♗b5 ++. **19 c7+ ♔e8 20 ♖he1+ ♗e7 21 ♕d6 ♕xc4 22 ♕xe7 mate!**

16) **Duz Khotimirsky-Bogoljubow**
USSR Championship 1924

4 c3 cxd4 5 cxd4 ♕b6 6 ♘bd2 ♘c6 7 e3 d5 8 ♗d3 Unquestionably consistent yet 8 ♕b1 is more cautious. **8 ... ♕xb2!? 9 0-0 ♗e7 10 ♕e2 0-0 11 a3 ♕b6** According to Tarrasch, two tempi are worth a pawn in an open position. In the text, Black has lost several tempi for the pawn but the position is no more than half-open. At all events, White has seized the initiative. **12 ♘e5 ♕d8 13 f4 ♘d7!** Properly timed! Dubious is 13 ... ♖e8 14 ♕f3 ♘d7 15 ♗xh7+ ♔xh7 16 ♕h5+ ♔g8 17 ♕xf7+ ♔h8 18 ♖f3!. **14 ♗xh7+?** Unfortunately, not all sacrifices are correct. 14 ♕h5! f5 15 ♘df3 followed by g2-g4 gave White a sound game. **14 ... ♔xh7 15 ♕h5+ ♔g8 16 ♖f3 ♘dxe5 17 dxe5 f6 18 ♖h3 fxg5 19 fxg5**

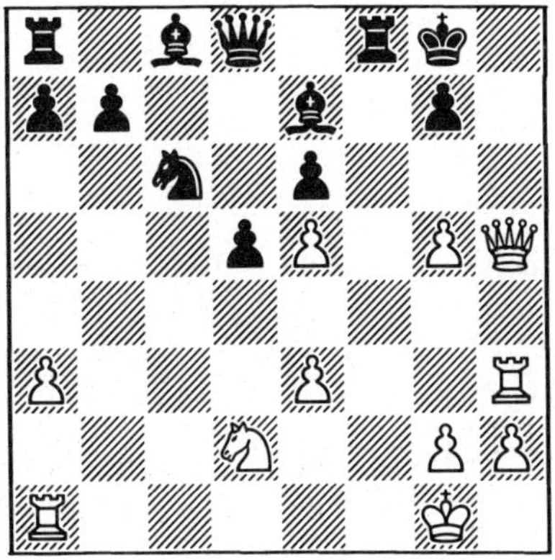

19 ... ♖f5! Cool-headed defence. 19 ... ♗xg5 20 ♕h7+ ♔f7 21 ♖f1+ gives better chances to the offensive side. **20 g4 ♗xg5?** 20 ... ♖f8? 21 g6 ±±; 20 ... ♖xe5? 21 ♖f1±±; 20 ... ♖xg5! ∓, though to see over the board that Black escapes after 21 ♕h7+ ♔f7 22 ♖f1+ ♖f5! 22 ♕h5+ g6! 23 ♕h7+ ♔e8 24 ♕xg6+ ♔d7 requires both a strong nerve and good chess vision. **21 gxf5 exf5 22 ♖g3?** 22 ♘f3 ♗xe3+ 23 ♔h1 ♗d7 24 ♖g1 ♗xg1 25 ♘g5 ♕xg5 26 ♕xg5 ♗d4 27 ♕h5 ♖e8 28 ♕h8+ ♔f7 29 ♕h5+ drawn. 23 ... ♗h6!? 24 ♖g1! ♔f8 ∞. **22 ... ♗h4 23 ♖h3 ♕g5+ 24 ♕xg5 ♗xg5 25 ♔f2 ♘xe5 26 ♖g3 ♘g4+ 27 ♔e2 ♗d7 28 ♖b1 ♗c6 29 h3 ♗h4 0-1**

3 Torre-Petrosian Attack: The Gambit Variation

1	**d4**	**♘f6**
2	**♘f3**	**e6**
3	**♗g5**	**c5**
4	**e3**	**♕b6**

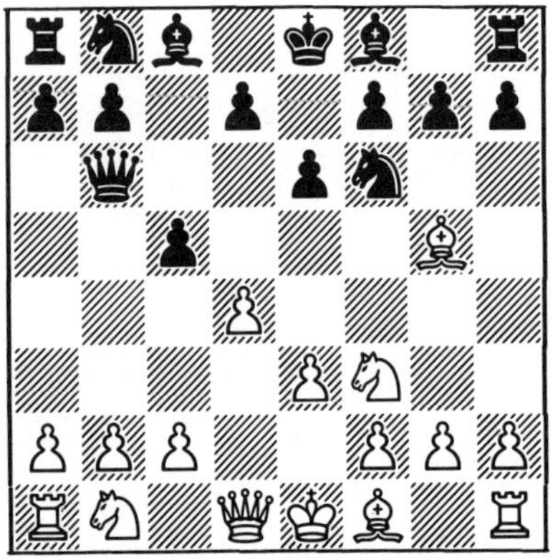

This is the first chapter on the main line introduced by 4 e3.

Legend has it that once a millionaire bequeathed his legacy to his heir on condition the heir never captured the b2 pawn with the queen – even if it was a correct move! In this position, however, this is just what Black is up to, and the protection of this pawn is quite an annoying task for White; should he leave it *en prise* and let it be taken, he will gain an advantage in development, yet this advantage is rather laborious to make good due to the relatively closed position. The final word about the gambit has not yet been said so those in favour of playing a defensive game ought not to choose this line when Black.

5 ♕c1 and 5 ♘bd2 are regarded as main lines, the first declining and the latter accepting the complications of a gambit.

5 ♗xf6 gxf6 is usually no more than a change in the order of moves compared to the main variations but it also provides the opponent with an unclear alternative: 5 ... ♕xb2 6 ♗xg7!? ♗xg7 (6 ... ♕xa1? 7 ♗xh8 ♕xa2 8 ♗d3 ±) 7 ♘bd2 cxd4 8 exd4 ♗xd4 (8 ... ♘c6!?) 9 ♖b1 ♕c3 10 ♖b3 ♕c5 11 ♗b5 ♗g7 12 ♘e4 ♕d5 ∞ Kamenets-Kuznetsov, USSR 1978.

5 b3 is not at all attractive, whereas 5 ♘c3?! has proved to be over-sharp, e.g. 5 ... ♕xb2 (5 ... d5!?) 6 ♘b5 ♕b4+! 7 c3 (7 ♕d2

♕xd2+ 8 ♘xd2 ♘a6 9 dxc5 ♗xc5 10 ♗xf6 gxf6 11 ♘e4 ♗e7 12 ♘ed6+ ♗xd6 13 ♘xd6+ ♔e7 ∓ Kostić-Vajda, Budapest 1921) 7 ... ♕a5 8 ♘d2 a6 9 ♘c4 ♕xb5! 10 ♘d6+ ♗xd6 11 ♗xb5 axb5 ∓ Bisguier-Sherwin, New York 1954/55.

3.1

5 ♕c1

Cautious yet not as modest as it may seem: White's queen can easily be activated whereas the c8 bishop gets stuck for a long while. The following variations illustrate some of the struggles for the e5 square which are quite characteristic of the main variations.

3.11

5 ... ♘c6
6 c3

6 ♗xf6 gxf6 7 c3 d5 8 ♘bd2 ♗d7 9 ♗e2 ♖c8 10 0-0 cxd4 11 exd4 ♗h6 12 ♕b1 0-0 (12 ... ♘e7 13 ♖e1 ♘g6 =; 14 a4!? a5 15 ♖a3 ♕c7 ∞ Kholmov-Anikayev, USSR 1976) 13 ♘b3 ♘e7 14 ♘c5 ♗c6 15 g3 ∞ Kogan-De Firmian, USA 1985.

6 ... d5
7 ♘bd2

7 ♗d3 ♗d6 (7 ... ♘d7?! 8 e4!) 8 ♘bd2 cxd4 9 exd4 ♘h5 10 ♘f1 h6 11 ♗d2 ♕c7 12 ♘g3 (12 g3!?) 12 ... ♘f4 13 ♗xf4 ♗xf4 14 ♕d1 g6 15 0-0 h5 16 ♖e1 0-0 17 ♕e2 = Vidmar-Nimzowitsch, Carlsbad 1929.

7 ... ♗d7

Preparing for counterplay along the c-file. 7 ... ♗d6 8 ♗d3 e5!? is worth considering here. 7 ... ♗e7 looks natural, but Black must beware a tempo loss after White's capture on c5, e.g. 8 ♗e2!? ♕c7 9 dxc5 ♗xc5 (the bishop has moved twice) 10 c4 ♗e7 11 0-0 0-0 12 a3 ♗d7 13 cxd5 ♘xd5 14 ♗xe7 ♘dxe7 15 ♕c5 ± Kovačević-Podlesnik, Ljubljana 1989.

8 ♗d3

8 ♗e2 ♖c8 9 ♕b1 ♗d6 (9 ... ♗e7!?) 10 0-0 0-0 11 ♗xf6 gxf6 12 dxc5 ♗xc5 13 e4 ± Larsen-Popel, USA 1972.

8 ... ♖c8

8 ... cxd4 9 exd4 ♗e7 10 0-0 ♖c8 11 ♕b1 h6 12 ♗h4 ♘h5?! Kurtenkov-Arnason, Plovdiv 1986; 13 ♗xe7! ♘xe7 14 ♘e5 ±.

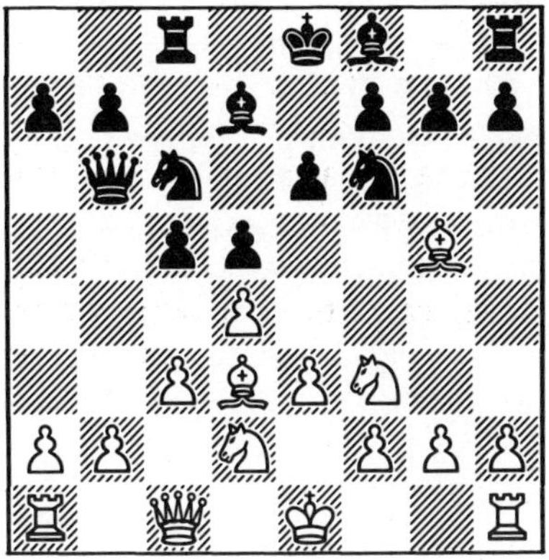

9 ♕b1

9 0-0!? ♗e7?! 10 dxc5 ♕xc5 11 e4! h6 12 ♗xf6 ♗xf6 13 ♕e1 d4 14 ♘b3 ♕d6 15 cxd4 ♗xd4 ± Barlov-Agzamov, Sochi 1985. Probably better is Capablanca's simplifying manoeuvre: 9 ... h6!? 10 ♗f4?! (10 ♗xf6!) 10 ... cxd4 11 exd4 ♘b4! 12 ♗e2 ♗b5! = Prokeš-Capablanca, Illustrative Game No 17.

9 ... h6
10 ♗h4 ♗e7
11 0-0

11 ♘e5? cxd4 12 exd4 ♘xe5 13 dxe5 ♘e4! 14 ♘xe4 dxe4 15 ♗xe7 exd3 16 ♗h4 ♖c4! ∓∓ Lutikov-Geller, Kislovodsk 1966.

11 ... 0-0

11 ... cxd4 12 exd4 a5? 13 a4 ♕c7 14 ♕e1! 0-0 15 ♘e5 ♗e8 16 f4 ± Varnusz-Gottardi, Balatonbereny 1981. 12 ... g5! 13 ♗g3 ♘h5 14 ♗e5 ♖g8 15 ♗h7 ♖f8 16 h3 (16 ♗g6!?) 16 ... ♘xe5 17 ♘xe5 ♗b5 18 ♖e1 ♘f6 ± Botterill-Plaskett, London 1980, or 14 ... ♘xe5 15 ♘xe5 ♘f4 16 ♘xd7 ♔xd7 = Kavalek-De Firmian, US Championship 1986.

12 ... ♘h5, in Capablanca style, does not quite equalise: 13 ♗xe7 ♘xe7 14 a4 0-0 15 ♘e5 ♕d6 16 g3 ♗e8 17 f4?! f5! ∞/± Varnusz-Pálkövi, Budapest 1989.

12 a3!

The threats are 13 dxc5 and 14 b4, or 13 ♘e5 and f2-f4 with a freer game for White.

3.12

5 ... ♘e4

Black tries to hinder White's development.

3.121

6 ♗h4

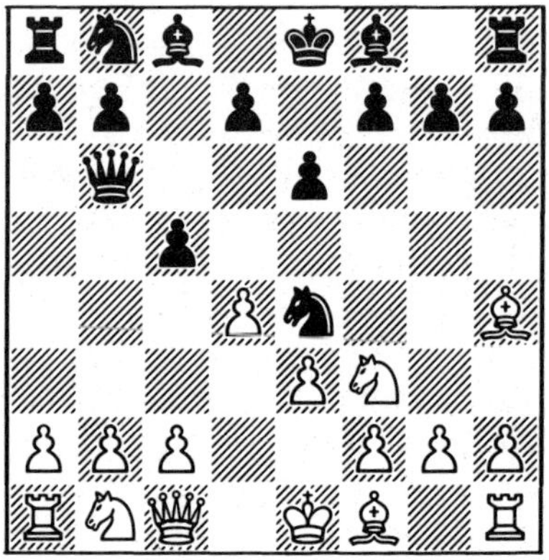

In principle, more appealing than retreating to f4 since ♗h4 thwarts ... ♗e7. There is little to be gained by relinquishing the bishop pair, e.g. 6 c3 ♘xg5 7 ♘xg5 ♗e7 8 ♘f3 d5 9 ♗d3 ♘c6 10 0-0 ♗d7 11 ♘bd2 ♖c8 12 ♕b1 g6 13 h4 0-0 = Kogan-Yusupov, Lone Pine 1981.

6 ... ♘c6

6 ... cxd4 7 exd4 g5? 8 ♗d3! ♕a5+ 9 c3 ♘xc3 10 ♘xc3 gxh4 11 ♘xh4 ± (Kovačević).

7 c3 d5

8 ♗d3

(a) 8 ♘bd2 f5 9 ♘xe4?! (Letting Black set up a dangerous outpost.) 9 ... fxe4 10 ♘d2 cxd4 11 exd4 ♗d6 12 ♗e2 (12 f3? 0-0!) 12 ... 0-0 13 0-0 ♗f4! 14 ♗g3 e5 15 dxe5 ♗xg3 16 hxg3 ♘xe5 17 ♘b3 ♗g4 ∞. White has got a more attractive pawn structure yet his king's position is dubious (Petrosian-Olafsson, Stockholm 1962).

(b) 8 ♘fd2?! f5 9 ♘xe4 fxe4 10 ♗g3 ♗d7 11 ♗e2 ♖c8 12 ♕d2 ♗e7 13 0-0 0-0 14 f4 exf3 15 ♗xf3 ♗g5 ∓ Quinteros-Ljubojević, Las Palmas 1974.

8 ... ♗d7

8 ... ♗d6? 9 ♗xe4! dxe4 10 ♘fd2 f5 11 ♘c4 ♕c7 12 ♘1a3! ♗e7 13 ♘b5! ♕d7 14 ♗xe7 ♔xe7 Shirazi-Saidy, USA 1982; 15 0-0! ±.

9 ♘bd2	**f5**
10 ♗g3	**♘xg3**
11 hxg3 ±	

Lobron-Korchnoi, Illustrative Game No 18.

3.122

6 ♗f4	**♘c6**

6 ... d5 7 ♗d3 (7 c3 ♘c6 8 ♗d3 ♗d6? 9 ♗xe4! ♗xf4 10 dxc5 ♕xc5 11 ♗xd5! ± ± Alekhine-Steiner, Dresden 1926; 7 ... ♗d7! 8 ♘bd2 ♘xd2 9 ♕xd2 ♗b5 =; 7 ... ♗d6! 8 ♗xd6 ♕xd6 9 ♘bd2 ♘c6 =) 7 ... ♘d7 (7 ... f5 8 c3 ♗e7 9 ♘bd2 ♘c6 10 h3 0-0 11 0-0! ±) 8 0-0 ♗d6 9 ♗xd6 ♕xd6 10 c4! 0-0 11 ♕c2 ♘ef6 12 cxd5 exd5 13 dxc5 ♘xc5 14 ♘c3 ± Alekhine-Spielmann, Semmering 1926.

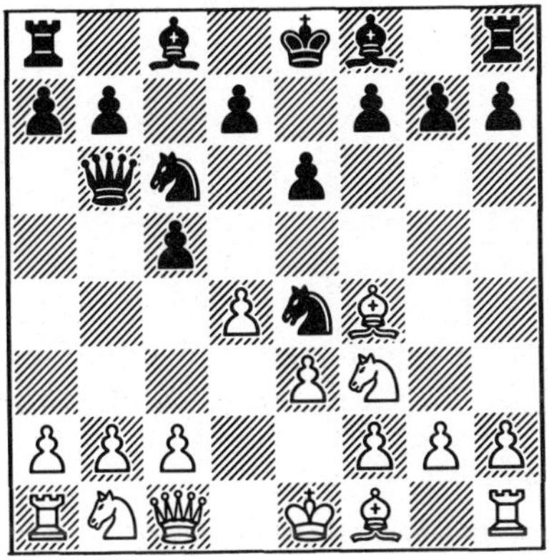

7 c3	**♗e7**

7 ... d5 8 ♘bd2 ♗e7 9 ♗d3 f5 10 h4 0-0 11 ♘e5 ♘xe5 12 ♗xe5 ♗d7 13 f3 ♘d6 14 dxc5 ♕xc5 15 ♗d4 ♕c7 16 f4 ♗b5 = Petrosian-Cherepkov, Moscow 1961. A more effective plan of development for White is 8 ♗d3 ♗e7 (8 ... ♗d7 9 0-0 ♖c8 10 ♘bd2 f5 Hort-Sosonko, Amsterdam 1979, and now 11 ♘e5! ±) 9 h3! ♗d7 10 0-0 f5 11 ♘e5 ♘xe5 12 ♗xe5 ♗f6 13 ♗xf6 gxf6 14 ♗xe4 fxe4 15 f3 ♗b5 16 ♖f2 ± Dreyev-Agzamov, Sevastopol 1986. The stonewall method does not quite seem to equalise.

8 ♘bd2	**f5**
9 ♗e2	**0-0**
10 0-0	**d5**
11 ♘e5	**cxd4**

12 exd4 ♘xe5
13 ♗xe5 ♗d7

White has a very slight advantage. E.g. 14 ♕c2 ♗b5! 15 ♗xb5 ♕xb5 16 ♘f3! ♖ac8 17 ♘e1! ♕c4 18 ♘d3 b5 19 f3 ± Spassky-Chandler, London 1985.

3.2

5 ♘bd2

The bold sacrifice was already mentioned at the beginning of this chapter. Some say it should neither be offered nor accepted.

3.21

5 ... cxd4

White ought to look out for this exchange in the 5 ... ♕xb2 lines as well. 5 ... d5 is also interesting, e.g. 6 ♗xf6 gxf6 7 c4 (7 ♕b1!? ♘c6 8 c3 cxd4 9 ♘xd4 e5 10 ♘4b3 ♗e6 11 a4 a6 12 a5 ♕a7 13 ♗e2 f5 14 0-0 ♗e7 15 c4 dxc4 ± Taimanov-Gipslis, Tallin 1980; 7 ♗e2 cxd4 8 exd4 ♘c6 9 ♘b3 ♗h6 10 0-0 0-0 11 ♖e1 ♗d7 12 c3 ♘e7 13 ♗d3 ♗b5 14 g3 ♗xd3 15 ♕xd3 a5 = Hug-Keller, Zürich 1984) 7 ... cxd4 8 exd4 ♘c6! (8 ... dxc4? 9 ♗xc4 ♘c6 10 0-0 ♗d7 11 d5 ♘a5? 12 ♖c1 e5 13 ♕e2 ♗g7 14 ♗d3 ± Tolush-Flohr, Illustrative Game No 19; 11 ... exd5 12 ♗xd5! 0-0-0 13 ♗xf7 ±) 9 cxd5 exd5 10 ♗d3 ♗e6 11 0-0 ♗d6 12 ♖c1 ± Plachetka-Hardicsay, Stary Smokovec 1982. 6 ♖b1 ♘c6 7 c3 is worth considering, see Chistiakov-Batiev, Illustrative Game No 20.

6 exd4

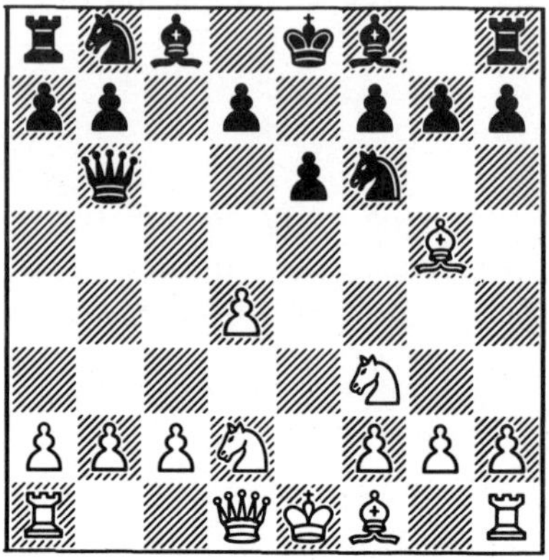

6 ♘xd4?! ♕xb2 7 ♘b5 ♘a6 8 ♖b1 ♕e5 9 ♗f4 ♕c5 10 ♘c4 ♗e7 11 ♘cd6+ ♔f8 12 ♗e2 ♘b4 13 0-0 ♘bd5 ∞ Alexeyev-Tolush, USSR 1962.

6 ... ♕xb2
7 ♗d3 d5

(a) 7 ... ♕b6 8 0-0 ♗e7 9 ♖e1 ♕c7 10 c4 b6 11 ♖c1 d6 12 ♗b1 ♘bd7 13 ♘f1 h6 14 ♗h4 ♗b7 15 ♘e3 0-0? 16 ♘d5! ± Nei-Mikenas, Moscow 1967; 15 ... ♕d8! ∞.

(b) 7 ... ♕c3 8 0-0 d5 9 ♖e1 ♗e7 10 ♖e3 ♕c7 11 ♘e5 ♘c6 12 c3 ∞ Spassky-Osnos, Illustrative Game No 21.

(c) 7 ... ♘c6 8 ♖b1 ♕c3 (8 ... ♕xa2 9 ♘c4 ♕a4) 9 ♖b3 ♕a5 10 0-0 ♗e7 11 ♘c4 ♕c7 12 ♘e3! d5?! 13 c4 ♘a5 14 ♖c3 ♘e4 15 ♗xe4 dxe4 16 ♗e7 ± Larsen-Stern, USA 1970.

8 0-0 ♕c3
9 ♖b1 ♗e7
10 ♖b3 ♕c7
11 ♕b1

11 ♘e5? ♘c6 12 ♘df3 ♘xd4 ∓ Hoi-Shamkovich, Illustrative Game No 22.

11 ... ♘c6
12 c4 ∞ (Shamkovich)

3.22

5 ... ♕xb2
6 ♗d3

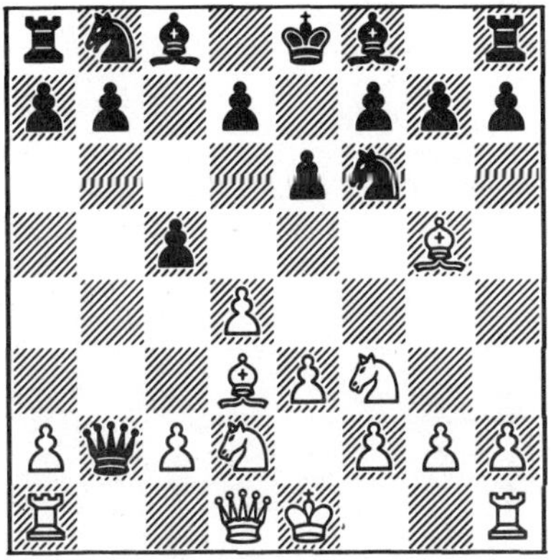

The main line, aiming for quick development. The alternatives are also dangerous:

(a) 6 ♗xf6 gxf6 7 ♗e2 ♕b6 (7 ... cxd4 8 ♘xd4 a6 9 0-0 ♕b6 10 ♖b1 ♕c7 11 ♗h5 ♖g8 12 ♕f3 ♗e7 13 ♕h3 ♘c6 14 ♘xc6 bxc6 15 f4 d5 16 e4 ♕a5 ∓ Garcia-Karpov, Leningrad 1977. Golubenko claims 8 ♖b1! as a major improvement, for example 8 ... ♕c3 9 0-0! ♕c7 10 ♘e4, Golubenko-Dragomaretsky, USSR 1988, and now 10 ... ♗e7 11 ♕xd4 ♕d8 12 ♘d6+ ♗xd6 13 ♕xd6 ♕e7 14 ♕g3 ±. Or 8 ... ♕a3 – 8 ... ♕xa2? 9 ♘c4 – 9 ♘xd4 ♘c6 10 ♘b5 ♕a5 11 0-0 d5 12 c4 a6 13 cxd5 ±. 7 ... ♘c6 steers a mid-course between pawn-snatching and retreat: 8 0-0 cxd4 9 ♘c4 ♕b4 10 ♖b1 ♕e7 11 exd4 d5 12 ♘e3 ♗h6 13 c4 dxc4 14 ♗xc4 0-0 15 ♕e2 ♖d8 16 ♖fd1 f5 17 ♗b5 ♗xe3 18 ♕xe3 = Hug-E.Torre, Zürich 1984) 8 0-0 ♗e7 9 c4 ♘c6 10 d5 ♘e5 11 ♘e1 f5 12 f4 ♘g6 13 ♗d3 d6 14 ♖b1 ♕a5 15 ♕c2 ♗f6 16 e4 ♘e7 ∞ Malaniuk-Oll, USSR 1986.

(b) 6 ♖b1 ♕xa2 (or 6 ... ♕a3 7 ♖b3 ♕a5 8 ♖b5 ♕xa2 9 ♗xf6 gxf6 10 ♘e4 a6 11 ♖xc5! ♗xc5 12 dxc5 ♕a5+ 13 ♘fd2 f5 14 ♘d6+ ♔e7 15 ♕h5 ∞ Kopec-De Firmian, USA 1986) 7 ♗xf6 gxf6 8 ♗c4 ♕a5 9 d5 a6 10 ♖a1 ♕c7 11 0-0 b5! 12 ♗xb5 ♗b7 = (Shamkovich). A recent practical test was 6 ♗xf6 gxf6 7 ♖b1 ♕xa2 (7 ... ♕c3; 7 ... ♕a3) 8 ♘c4 ♕a4 (9 ... ♕a6? 10 d5 exd5 11 ♕xd5 ♕c6 12 ♕h5 ± Ye Rongguang) 9 d5 b5! 10 ♘cd2 a6 11 ♖a1 ♕b4 12 c4! ♗b7 13 e4 ∞ Ye Rongguang-Chandler, Manila 1990.

3.221

6 ... d5

Black immediately gains space in the centre. For the pinning move 6 ... ♕c3 see 3.22. Other alternatives:

(a) 6 ... ♘c6 7 0-0 ♕b6 (7 ...
d5 8 ♗xf6 gxf6 9 c4 ♘b4 ∞, I.
Sokolov-Kir.Georgiev, Illustrative
Game No 23) 8 c4 (8 ♖b1 ♕d8
9 e4 cxd4 10 e5 h6 11 ♗h4 g5 12
♗g3 ♘d5 13 ♘e4 ♘c3 ∞; 8 ♘c4
♕c7 9 ♗f4 ♕d8 10 ♘d6+ ♗xd6
11 ♗xd6 cxd4 12 exd4 b6 13 ♖e1
♗b7 14 c4 ♘e7 15 d5 0-0 16 ♘d4
a6 ∞ Haik-Britton, Hastings 1978/
79) 8 ... d6 9 ♖b1 ♕c7 10 d5 ♘b4
11 ♗xf6 gxf6 12 ♘e4 ± Grünfeld-
J.Horváth, Belfort 1982.

(b) 6 ... ♕b6 7 0-0 d6 (7 ... ♘c6
transposes into (a); 7 ... cxd4
transposes into Nei-Mikenas, 3.21)
8 dxc5 dxc5 9 e4 h6 10 ♗h4 ♘c6
11 ♘c4 ♕c7 12 ♕b1 ♘h5 13 ♕b2
♗e7 14 ♗xe7 ♕xe7 15 ♘fe5
± Bondarevsky-Antoshin, Sochi
1964.

7 ♗xf6

7 c4 ♕c3 8 ♔e2 (8 ♘e5? ♘c6! 9
♖c1 ♕a3 10 ♘xc6 bxc6 11 ♕c2
♖b8 ∓ Spassky-Miles, Tilburg
1978) 8 ... ♘bd7 9 ♕a4 ∞.

7 0-0?! is slow: 7 ... c4 8 ♗e2
♗e7 9 ♘e5 ♘c6 10 ♖b1 ♕a3 11
♘xc6 bxc6 12 e4 0-0 13 ♖e1 c3!?
14 ♖b3 cxd2 15 ♖xa3 dxe1 = ♕+
16 ♕xe1 ♗xa3 ∓ Kristensen-Sher,
Hastings 1989/90.

7	...	gxf6
8	c4	♕c3!
9	♗e2	♘c6!

9 ... dxc4? 10 0-0 ♕a5 11 ♘xc4
♕c7 12 ♖c1 ♘c6 13 ♘cd2!? ♗e7!

Vaganian-Razuvaev, USSR Ch.
1983; 14 dxc5! ±; 13 e4!? cxd4 14
♘xd4 a6 15 ♘xc6 bxc6 16 e5! ±
(Vaganian) 9 ... cxd4? 10 ♖c1
♕a5 11 cxd5 ♘a6 12 ♘xd4 ♕xd5
13 0-0 ♗e7 14 ♗f3 ♕d7 15 ♘c6
0-0 16 ♕e2 ± Salov-de la Villa,
Szirák 1987.

10	♖c1?!	♕a3
11	cxd5	exd5
12	dxc5	♗xc5
13	0-0	♗e6
14	♘b3	♗b6

McCambridge-Browne, USA
1985.

15 ♘fd4

The position is unclear.

3.222

| 6 | ... | ♕c3 |

| 7 | 0-0 | d5 |
| 8 | ♗xf6 | |

8 ♖e1 and now:

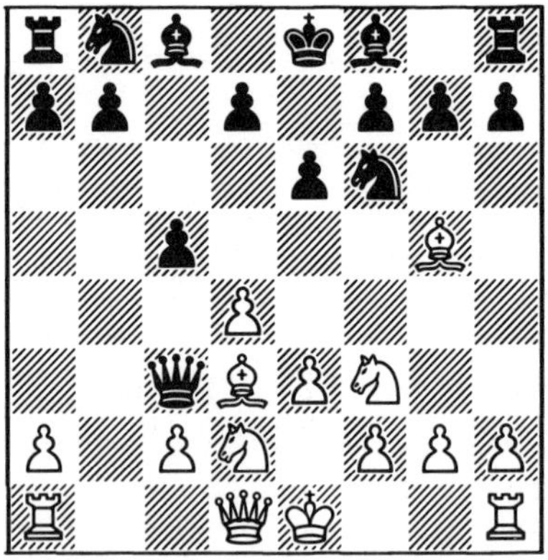

(a) 8 ... c4?! 9 ♗f1 ♘c6 10 ♗xf6 gxf6 11 e4 ♔d8? 12 ♖b1 ♗h6 13 exd5 exd5 14 ♖b5 ± Alexeyev-Balashov, Illustrative Game No 24.

(b) 8 ... cxd4! 9 ♘xd4 a6 10 ♘4f3 ♘c6 11 e4 ♗e7 12 exd5 ♘xd5 13 ♘e4 ♕a3 14 c4 ♘c3 15 ♕d2 ♘xe4 16 ♗xe4 f6 17 ♗f4 e5 18 ♖ad1 ♗g4 = Salov-Psakhis, Irkutsk 1986.

8 ... gxf6
9 dxc5

9 e4 c4 10 ♗e2 ♗e7 11 ♖e1 ♘c6 12 exd5 exd5 13 ♗xc4!? dxc4 14 ♘e4 ♕a5 15 d5 ♘e5 16 ♘xe5 (16 d6 ♗d8 17 ♘xe5 fxe5 18 d7+ ♗xd7 19 ♘d6+ ♔f8 20 ♘xf7 ∞ Shabalov) 16 ... fxe5 17 ♕f3 ♔f8 18 ♖ad1 ♗d7 19 ♕h5 ♖g8 20 ♕xh7 ♗g4 21 ♕h6+ ♖g7 with a perpetual, Balashov-Oll, Sverdlovsk 1987.

9 ... ♗g7

(a) 9 ... f5 10 ♖b1 ♘c6 11 ♖b3 ♕g7 12 c4 d4 13 exd4 ♘xd4 14 ♘xd4 ♕xd4 15 ♘f3 ♕f6 16 ♖e1 ♗xc5 17 ♗xf5!? ♕xf5 18 ♖e5 ♗xf2+ 19 ♔xf2 ♕f6 20 ♕d4 ∞ (±) Kamsky-De Firmian, Reykjavik 1990.

(b) 9 ... ♕xc5 10 c4 ♗g7 11 cxd5 ♕xd5 12 ♕c2 ♘c6 13 ♖ab1 ♕d7 14 ♘c4 h6 15 ♖fd1 ∞ K.Rodriguez-De Firmian, Reykjavik 1990.

10 ♖b1 ♕xc5
11 e4 dxe4
12 ♘xe4 ♕c7
13 ♗b5+ ♔f8
14 ♕d2 a6
15 ♗e2 ♘c6
16 ♖fd1 h5

The position is unclear. J. Benjamin-Yudasin, New York 1990).

ILLUSTRATIVE GAMES

1 d4 ♘f6 2 ♘f3 e6 3 ♗g5 c5 4 e3 ♕b6

17) **Prokeš-Capablanca**
Budapest 1929

5 ♕c1 ♘c6 6 c3 d5 7 ♗d3 ♗d7 8 ♘bd2 ♖c8 9 0-0 h6 10 ♗f4?! cxd4 11 exd4

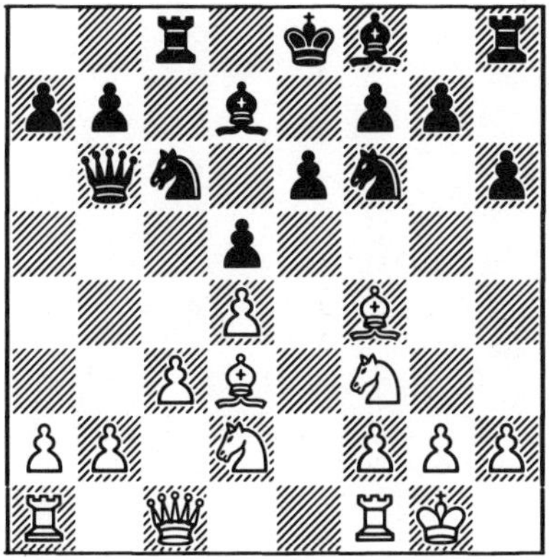

11 ... ♘b4! 12 ♗e2 ♗b5 13

♗xb5+ ♕xb5 14 ♘e5 ♘c6 15 ♘xc6 Meek. **15 ... ♖xc6 16 ♕c2 ♗e7 17 ♖fe1 0-0 18 ♖e3 ♘h5 19 ♗e5 ♗g5 20 ♖ee1 ♖fc8 21 ♔h1 ♗e7 22 ♖e3 ♗g5 23 ♖ee1 ♖b6! 24 ♖ab1 ♘f4 25 ♗xf4 ♗xf4 26 g3 ♗g5 27 ♘f3 ♗f6 28 ♘e5? ♗xe5 29 ♖xe5** Overlooking the loss of a pawn. 29 dxe5 d4! ∓. **29 ... ♕c4! 30 ♕c1 ♕xa2 31 ♖e1 a5! 32 ♔g2 a4 33 h4 ♕c4 34 ♖a1 ♖b3 35 ♖e3 ♕b5 36 ♖a2 ♕c4 37 ♕a1 ♖a8 38 ♔h2 ♕b5 39 ♖e1 ♖a6 40 ♔g2 ♕c4 41 ♖e3 ♖bb6 42 ♖a3 ♕c6 43 ♔g1 ♕b5 44 ♖a2 ♕e8 45 ♕e1 ♖b3 46 ♕a1 ♕a8 47 ♕d1** While manoeuvring, Black has been threatening to play . . . a3! for quite a long time. **47 ... ♕a7 48 ♔g2 ♕b6 49 ♕d2?! ♕b5 50 ♖e1**

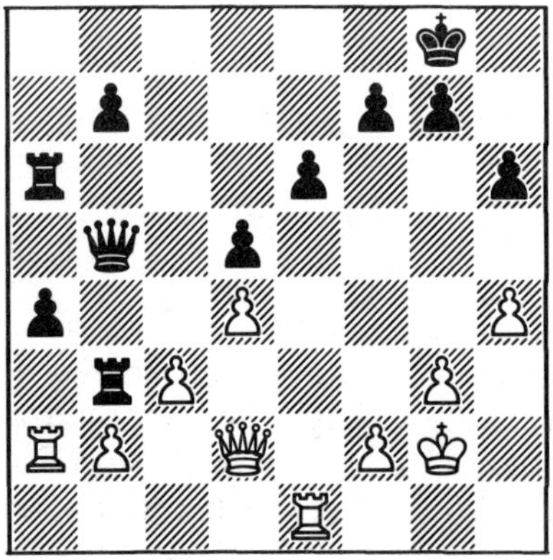

50 ... ♖b6! 51 ♖e2 ♕c4 52 ♕d1 ♖3b4! At last! **53 cxb4 ♕xa2 54 ♕c1 ♕c4 55 ♖c2 ♕xd4 56 ♖c8+ ♔h7 57 ♖f8 ♕e4+ 58 ♔g1 ♖c6 59 ♕a1 ♕f5 60 ♖a8 ♖c2 61 ♕f1 ♖xb2 0-1**

18) **Lobron-Korchnoi**
Biel 1984

5 ♕c1 ♘e4 6 ♗h4 ♘c6 7 ♗d3 d5 8 c3 ♗d7! 9 ♘bd2 f5 10 ♗g3! ♘xg3?! In fixed positions, a knight is worth more than a bishop. However, 10 ... ♗e7 11 ♗f4 0-0 12 h4! is not quite equal either. 11 ... g5!?. **11 hxg3 g6?!** Weakening rather than reinforcing Black's kingside. **12 g4! ♖c8** 12 ... fxg4? 13 ♘g5!. **13 gxf5 gxf5 14 ♗e2** 14 ... cxd4 15 exd4 ♘b4! and ... ♗b5 was the threat. **14 ... ♗e7 15 ♘b3!? c4 16 ♘bd2 ♕c7 17 g3 b5 18 ♘h4** Having crossed Black's queenside plans, White can seize the initiative on the opposite flank. **18 ... 0-0 19 a3 ♖f7 20 ♘g2! a5 21 ♘f4 b4 22 axb4 axb4 23 ♔f1! ♕b7** 23 ... ♗d6 24 ♖h6 ♗xf4 25 exf4 and Black would lose control of the dark squares. **24 ♘f3 ♖a8 25 ♔g2 bxc3 26 bxc3 ♗f6 27 ♖h6**

(diagram)

27 ♖h5! is more accurate. Both sides dominate a file but White's actions are more dangerous since he can get closer to the opponent's king. We see a bit of manoeuvring first.

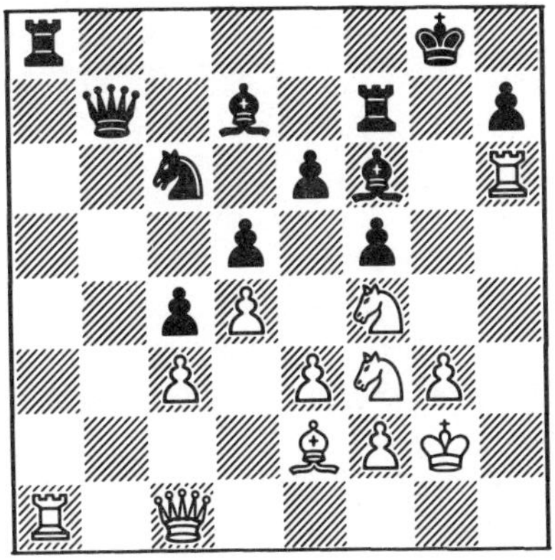

27 ... ♗g7 28 ♖h1 ♗f6 28 ... h6!. **29 ♖h5 ♖xa1 30 ♕xa1 ♘a7?!** 30 ... ♘d8 then ... ♗c8 and ... ♕a7 is passive but solid. **31 ♕h1! ♗c8** 31 ... ♖g7 32 ♖h6 ♖f7 33 ♕h5 ±; 31 ... ♘b5 32 ♘g5 ♗xg5 33 ♖xg5+ ♖g7 34 ♕h6 +−. **32 ♘g5 ♖e7 33 ♗f3!** Preparing the sacrifice. **33 ... ♘b5 34 ♕a1 ♗d7** 34 ... ♗xg5 35 ♖xg5+ ♖g7 36 ♕a5!. **35 ♕a5 ♗e8** 36 ♘gxe6! and ♗xd5 is indefensible. **36 ♘gxe6! ♗xh5 37 ♗xd5 ♕a7 38 ♕d8+ ♗e8 39 ♘c7+ ♔h8 40 ♘xe8 ♕d7 41 ♕xd7 1-0**

19) **Tolush-Flohr**
Pärnu 1947

5 ♘bd2 d5 6 ♗xf6 gxf6 7 c4 cxd4 8 exd4 dxc4? 9 ♗xc4 ♘c6 10 0-0 ♗d7 11 d5 ♘a5? 12 ♖c1 e5 13 ♕e2 ♗g7 13 ... 0-0-0 14 ♗b5+ ♔b8 15 ♗xd7 ♖xd7 16 ♘xe5! ♖e7 17 ♕g4 +−. **14 ♗d3** Black has a miserable game: he is behind in development, his pawn structure is ruined and there is a hole on f5. **14 ... ♕xb2** Snatching a pawn to compensate for his inferior position is cold comfort for Black. 14 ... 0-0 15 ♘h4!. **15 ♖c2 ♕b6 16 ♖b1 ♕d6 17 ♘e4 ♕e7 18 ♘g3 ♔d8** A desperate effort to secure the black king. **19 ♗f5 ♖c8 20 d6! ♕e8** 20 ... ♕xd6 21 ♖d1!. **21 ♖xc8+ ♔xc8** 21 ... ♗xc8 22 d7! ♗xd7 23 ♖d1.

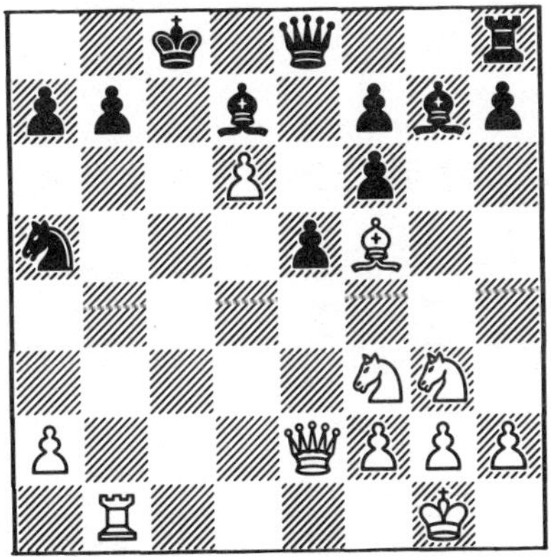

22 ♕b5! 1-0

20) **Chistiakov-Batiev**
USSR 1949

5 ♘bd2 d5 6 ♖b1!? However small in number are the games, this move might be the best antidote to 5 ... d5. **6 ... ♘c6 7 c3 ♗d7 8 ♗d3 ♗e7 9 0-0 h6 10 ♗h4 0-0 11 ♘e5!** White has achieved everything he wishes for in this opening. **11 ... ♖ad8 12 f4 ♖fe8?!** 12 ... ♗c8; 12 ... ♗e8. **13 ♗xf6! ♗xf6** On 13 ... gxf6? either 14 ♘xf7 or 14 ♕g4+ ♔f8 15 ♘xf7

♔xf7 16 ♕g6+ would win. **14 ♕h5! ♗xe5** 14 ... ♖f8 15 ♘g4 ♗e7 16 ♘xh6+ gxh6 17 ♕xh6 f5 18 ♕g6+ ♔h8 19 ♖f3 ±±. **15 fxe5 ♖f8 16 ♖f3! cxd4 17 exd4 ♗e8?** 17 ... ♘e7! was the last resort for the defensive side. **18 ♖g3 ♔h8**

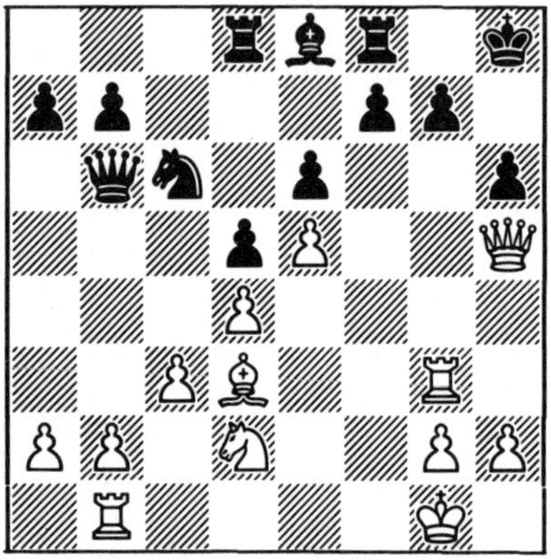

19 ♖xg7!! A typical demolishing sacrifice yet one of the most beautiful of its kind as the triumphant QR is still a long way away. **19 ... ♔xg7 20 ♕g4+ ♔h8 21 ♕f4 f5 22 exf6 ♖d7** 22 ... ♖f7 23 ♕xh6+ ♔g8 24 ♘f3, or alternatively 24 ♖f1 ♘xd4 25 ♔h1 ♘f5 26 ♗xf5 exf5 27 ♖xf5, would be decisive. **23 ♕xh6+ ♔g8 24 ♕g5+ ♔h8 25 ♖f1 ♕c7 26 ♕h6+ ♔g8 27 ♖f4 ♗h5 28 ♕g5+ ♖g7 29 fxg7! ♖xf4** 29 ... ♕xf4 30 gxf8 = ♕+!. **30 ♗h7+! 1-0**

21) **Spassky-Osnos**
USSR Championship 1963/64

5 ♘bd2 ♕xb2 6 ♗d3 cxd4 7 exd4 ♕c3 8 0-0 d5 9 ♖e1 ♗e7 10 ♖e3! ♕c7 11 ♘e5 ♘c6 12 c3 ♘xe5 More cautious is 12 ... ♗d7 and 13 ... ♖c8. **13 dxe5 ♘g8** Black hopes that this retreat is only temporary. **14 ♘f3 h6 15 ♗f4 ♗d7 16 ♘d4! ♗g5** 16 ... ♕xc3? 17 ♘xe6!. **17 ♗xg5 hxg5 18 ♕g4 ♕xc3! 19 ♘b3 ♘h6 20 ♕xg5 ♕b4 21 ♖g3!** 21 ♕xg7 0-0-0! **21 ... ♕f8?** Black should have returned the pawn by 21 ... ♕e7 22 ♕xg7 0-0-0. Now he is heading for a combination. **22 ♖c1! f6 23 ♕e3 f5** Apparently the ... f5-f4 threat gives Black time to complete his development.

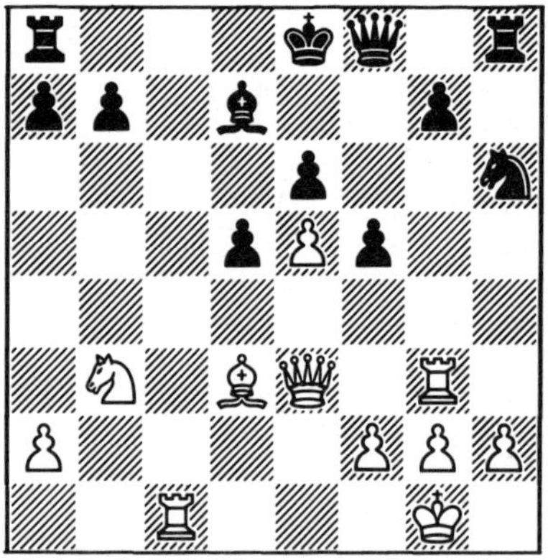

24 ♘c5!! f4 25 ♗g6+ ♔e7 26 ♕a3! 1-0

22) **Hoi-Shamkovich**
Esbjerg 1982

5 ♘bd2 cxd4 6 exd4 ♕xb2 7

♗d3 ♕c3 8 0-0 d5 9 ♖b1 ♗e7 10 ♖b3 ♕c7 11 ♘e5? The knight will not be able to hold this outpost. 11 ♕b1! ♘c6 12 c4 ∞. **11 ... ♘c6 12 ♘df3** 12 ♗f4 ♗d6 ∓. **12 ... ♘xd4! 13 ♘xd4 ♕xe5 14 ♗b5+ ♔f8** White obviously does not have sufficient compensation for the two pawns, nevertheless, his opponent's task of defending passively is not too appealing either. **15 ♗h4 ♘e4! 16 ♗xe7+ ♔xe7 17 ♖e1 ♕g5 18 ♘f3** 18 f3 ♘d6 19 ♖be3 ♖d8 20 ♖e5 ♕f6 21 ♖xd5 ♔f8 ∓. **18 ... ♕f6 19 ♕c1 ♖d8 20 ♕a3+ ♘d6 21 c4!?** 21 ♘e5 ♔f8 22 ♖f3 ♕e7 ∓. **21 ... dxc4 22 ♗xc4 ♔g8 23 ♗f1 ♕e7 24 ♖d1 f6!** Slowly but surely, Black gets the upper hand. **25 ♖bd3 ♘f7 26 ♖xd8+ ♘xd8 27 ♕d3 g6 28 ♘h4?** 29 h4 then h5 was the last practical chance. **28 ... ♗d7 29 ♘xg6?! hxg6 30 ♕xg6+ ♕f7 31 ♕h6 ♔e7 32 ♗e2 ♗e8 33 ♖d3 ♖c8 34 ♖g3 ♕f8 35 ♕e3 ♗f7! 36 ♗b5 ♘c6 37 h3 ♕d8 38 ♖g7 ♕d1+ 39 ♗f1 ♖d8 40 ♕g3 ♖d7 0-1**

(Notes based on Shamkovich's)

23) **I.Sokolov-Kir.Georgiev**
Palma de Mallorca 1989

5 ♘bd2 ♕xb2 6 ♗d3 ♘c6 7 0-0 d5 8 ♗xf6 gxf6 9 c4 ♘b4 9 ... cxd4 10 cxd5 **10 ♗e2** Avoiding exchanges, but 10 ♘b3!? could also be considered, the tactical justification being 10 ... ♘xd3 11 ♕xd3 b5? 12 cxd5 c4 13 ♕e4 cxb3 14 dxe6 ♖b8 15 ♕c6+ ±±. **10 ... ♕a3** 10 ... ♕c2!? 11 ♕e1 ♕g6!?; 11 ♕xc2 ♘xc2 12 ♖ac1 ♘b4 13 a3 ♘a6 ∞. **11 e4** White, a pawn down but better developed, must clear lines for attack before the Black king can escape! **11 ... dxe4 12 ♘xe4 ♗e7 13 ♕d2** Such attacks have to be played carefully, as premature sacrifices tend to encourage counter-sacrifices with the direction of the initiative being reversed, for example 13 d5 f5 14 d6 fxe4 15 ♘e5 ♕b2! 16 d7+ ♗xd7 17 ♕xd7+ ♔f8 18 ♕xb7 ♕xe5! 19 ♕a8+ ♔g7 and Black is better. **13 ... ♗d7 14 ♕f4 0-0-0 15 ♘xf6 cxd4 16 ♘xd4 ♗c6 17 ♘b5 ♕a5** 17 ... ♗xb5 leaves Black too open.

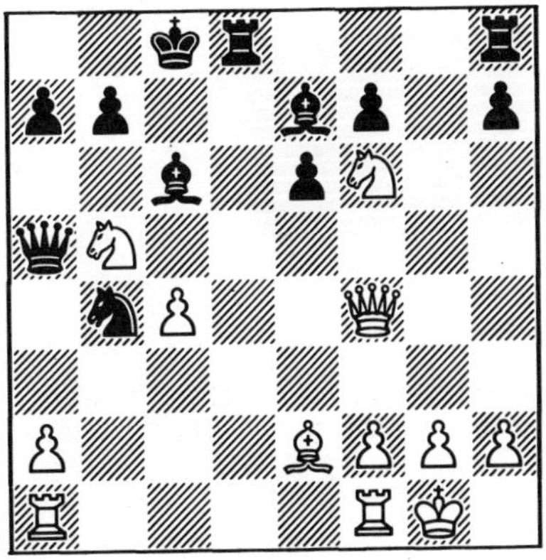

Black could be forgiven for thinking that he is safe here. Yet White has a beautiful positional sacrifice here, leaving him with complete and decisive control of the centre. **18 ♘e4! ♗xe4 19 ♕xf7!! ♖d7 20 ♕xe6 ♗c6 21 ♗g4** And Black is in a knot. **21 ... h5 22 ♗h3 ♗d8 23 ♖ad1 ♖h7 24 a3!** Attractively cruel. **24 ... ♘c2 25 ♕g6 ♖e7 26 ♕xc2 a6 27 ♘a7+ 1-0** Splendid use of long open lines.

(Notes based on Sokolov's)

24) **Alexeyev-Balashov**
USSR 1972

5 ♘bd2 ♕xb2 6 ♗d3 ♕c3 7 0-0 d5 8 ♖e1 c4 9 ♗f1 ♘c6 10 ♗xf6 gxf6 11 e4 ♔d8 12 ♖b1! ♗h6 13 exd5 exd5 14 ♖b5 ♗xd2 15 ♖xd5+ ♔c7 16 ♘xd2 ♗e6 17 ♘e4 ♕b2 18 ♖d6! f5 18 ... ♖ad8 19 d5! **19 d5! fxe4 20 dxe6 fxe6 21 ♖d7+ ♔b6 22 ♕d6 ♖ac8 23 ♗xc4 ♕xc2 24 ♕a3! ♖hf8 25 ♕e3+ 1-0**

4 Torre-Petrosian Attack Main Line without an early ... d5

1	d4	♘f6
2	♘f3	e6
3	♗g5	c5
4	e3	

After an early ... d7-d5 move Black's position loses its flexibility, and he will have no choice of pawn structures. The systems looked at in this chapter are flexible and useful in practice, except for the first variation. The lines are 4 ... b6?!, 4 ... ♘c6, 4 ... cxd4, 4 ... ♗e7 and 4 ... h6.

4.1

4 ... b6?!

Seemingly logical but Petrosian's reply shows how dubious it really is.

5 d5!

(diagram)

Blocking the long diagonal and, in most cases, upsetting Black's

pawn formation.

5 ... exd5

(a) 5 ... h6 6 ♗xf6 ♕xf6 7 ♘c3 a6?! (7 ... ♗b7! 8 e4 ♕d8 9 e5 ± Kavalek-Brunner, Solingen 1986; 7 ... ♕d8 8 dxe6!? dxe6 9 ♕xd8+ ♔xd8 10 ♘e5 ♔e7 11 ♗e2 ♗b7 12 0-0-0 ♗xg2 13 ♖hg1 ♗c6 14 ♗h5! g5 15 ♘xf7 ♖g8 16 h4 ± Z.Varga-Cs.Horváth, Budapest 1989. 7 ...

d6 8 ♗b5+ ♗d7 9 0-0 e5 10 ♘d2! ♕d8 11 f4 exf4 12 ♕g4 ± Manor-Quillan, Oakham 1990) 8 ♘a4! (8 a4 d6 9 ♘d2 e5 10 ♗d3 ♕d8 11 0-0 ♗e7 12 ♘c4 ± Petrosian-Peterson, USSR 1960) 8 ... exd5 (8 ... ♕d8 9 dxe6 fxe6 10 ♘e5!) 9 ♕xd5 ♘c6? (9 ... ♖a7! improves, but not by enough: 10 0-0-0 ♗b7 11 ♕d2 ♗e7 12 ♘c3 0-0 13 ♗c4 b5 14 ♗d5 ± Zaichik-Gipslis, Berlin 1988) 10 0-0-0 ♖b8 11 ♗xa6! +− Varnusz-Felméri, Budapest 1982.

(b) 5 ... d6 6 dxe6 (6 ♗xf6 ♕xf6 7 ♘c3 a6 8 ♘d2 ♕d8 9 a4 ♗e7 10 ♗e2 0-0 11 0-0 ♘d7 12 ♘c4 ♘f6 13 e4 ♖b8 14 dxe6 fxe6 15 e5 ± Barlov-Andersson, Haninge 1988) 6 ... ♗xe6 7 ♗b5+ ♘bd7 8 ♘c3 a6 9 ♗xd7+ ♗xd7 10 ♘d5 ♗e7 11 ♗xf6 ♗xf6 12 ♘xf6+ ♕xf6 13 ♕d5 ♔e7 14 0-0-0 +− Yusupov-Fries Nielsen, Skien 1979.

6 ♘c3 ♗b7

6 ... ♗e7 7 ♘xd5 ♗b7 8 ♗c4 (8 ♗xf6 ♗xf6 transposes into the next note) 8 ... 0-0 9 c3 ♘c6 10 h4 ♘a5 11 ♘xf6+ ♗xf6 12 ♗d5 ♗xd5 13 ♕xd5 ♕e7 14 ♗xf6 ♕xf6 15 ♕xd7 ♖fd8 ∞ Plaskett-Grószpéter, Sochi 1984.

7 ♘xd5 ♗xd5

7 ... ♗e7 8 ♗xf6 ♗xf6 9 c3 ♘c6 10 ♕c2 ♘e5?! (10 ... 0-0 11 ♕f5) 11 ♘xe5 ♗xd5 12 0-0-0 ♗e6 13 ♘xd7 +− Barlov-Ostermeyer, Biel 1985. 9 ... 0-0 is sounder, but still good for White, e.g. 10 ♗e2 d6 11 0-0 ♘a6 12 a4 ♘c7 13 ♗c4 ♖b8 14 ♕d3 ⩲ Piket-Farago, Wijk aan Zee 1988, or 10 ♗c4 a6, and now 11 a4! with a spatial advantage might well improve on the 11 0-0 ⩲ of Yusupov-Karpov, Illustrative Game No 25.

8 ♗xf6 ♕xf6
9 ♕xd5 ♘c6

9 ... ♕xb2? 10 ♖d1 ♕b4+ 11 c3! ♕xc3+ 12 ♖d2 ♕c1+ 13 ♔e2 +−.

10 0-0-0

10 ♗c4 ♗e7 11 0-0-0 ♖d8 12 ♖d2 ± Petrosian-Kozma, Illustrative Game No 26.

10 ... ♖d8
11 ♗b5! ♗e7
12 ♗xc6!

The simplest, although 12 ♕e4 0-0 13 ♖d2 ♘b8 14 ♖hd1 is also good.

12 ... dxc6
13 ♕e5 0-0
14 c3 +− (Tseitlin)

4.2

4 ... ♘c6

Active and flexible, this move has a slight shortcoming: the knight will block the diagonal of the b7 bishop.

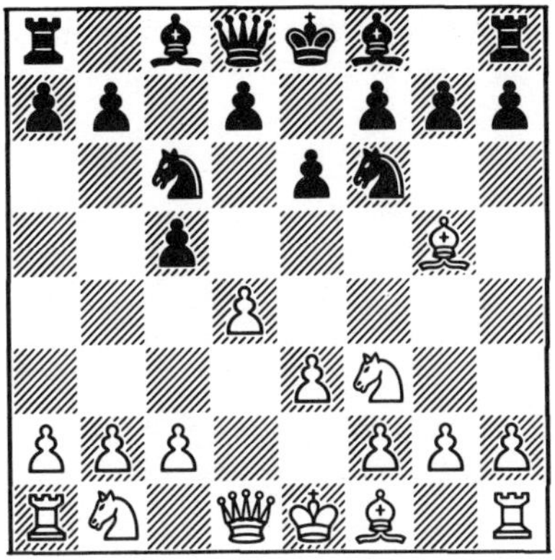

5 ♘bd2

5 c3 is only a change in move order, as 5 ... ♕b6 leads to Chapter 3.

5 ... b6

5 ... d5 6 c3 (6 ♗d3 ♕b6!? 7 ♗xf6 gxf6 8 dxc5 ♕xb2 9 0-0 ♕b4 10 c4 ♕xc5 11 ♖c1 ♗e7 12 cxd5 ♕xd5 13 ♗e4 ∞ Gusev-Novikov, USSR 1983) 6 ... ♕b6 (6 ... ♗e7 7 ♗d3 h6 8 ♗h4 ♕b6?! 9 ♖b1 0-0 10 ♘e5 ♖e8 11 f4 ♘d7 12 ♕h5! ± Varnusz-Kormányos, Kecskemét 1984) 7 ♖b1?! cxd4 8 exd4 e5!? 9 ♘xe5 ♘xe5 10 ♕e2 ♘g4 11 dxe5 ♗c5 12 ♗h4 0-0 13 h3 ♘xe5! 14 ♕xe5 ♕g6 ∞ Bisguier-I.Ivanov, USA 1986.

Definitely inaccurate is 5 ... h6? 6 ♗xf6 ♕xf6 7 ♘e4 ♕d8 8 d5! ± Sideif Zade-Vitolins, Borzhomi 1984.

6 c3 ♗b7

6 ... ♗e7 7 ♗d3 0-0?! 8 h4 cxd4 9 exd4 h6 10 ♗xf6 ♗xf6 11 g4! g6 12 g5 hxg5 13 ♘xg5 d5 14 f4 ♔g7 15 ♕f3 ♖g8 16 0-0-0 ♕c7 17 ♔b1 ♗d7 18 h5 ± Zaid-Yuferov, Erevan 1984. Premature castling.

7 ♗d3

4.21

7 ... cxd4

The exchange of the pawns was feasible earlier too.

8 exd4 ♗e7

9 0-0

9 ♘c4 ♕c7 (9 ... 0-0? It is unwise to castle before White does so! 10 ♕c2 h6 11 h4! ± Janowski-Sämisch, Illustrative Game No 27.) 10 ♕d2 ♖c8 11 0-0 h6 12 ♗f4 d6 13 ♖fe1 = C.Torre-Sämisch, Moscow 1925.

9 ... 0-0
10 ♖e1

10 ♕e2? ♘d5! 11 ♗xe7 ♘cxe7 12 ♖fe1 (12 ♕e5? f5 ∓ Krasnov-Averkin, Illustrative Game No 28.) 12 ... ♘f4 13 ♕f1 =.

10 ... ♘d5
11 ♗xe7 ♘cxe7
12 ♗f1 f5

Active, but loosens the pawn structure. 12 ... d6!?.

13 c4

13 ♘e5 ♕c7 14 ♖c1 ♖ae8 15 c4 ± Petrosian-Taimanov, Illustrative Game No 29.

13 ... ♘f6
14 b4 ♘e4
15 ♕b3

White's advantage in space is considerable, e.g. 15 ... ♔h8 16 ♖ad1 ♘g8 17 d5 ± Balashov-Lebredo, Cuba 1975.

4.22

7 ... ♗e7
8 0-0

8 a3!? 0-0 9 e4 d6 10 h3 cxd4 11 cxd4 e5 12 d5 ♘b8 13 ♗e3 ♘bd7 14 b4 ♖c8 15 ♖c1 ♘h5 16 0-0 ± Seirawan-Andersson, Skelleftea 1988.

8 ... 0-0

8 ... h6 9 ♗h4 0-0 10 a3 ♘h5 11 ♗xe7 ♕xe7 12 b4 cxd4 13 cxd4 ♖fc8 14 ♕e2 ♖c7 15 g3 d6 16 e4 ♖ac8 17 ♖ac1 ♘f6 and Black is very close to equality, Hort-Adorjan, Reykjavik 1988.

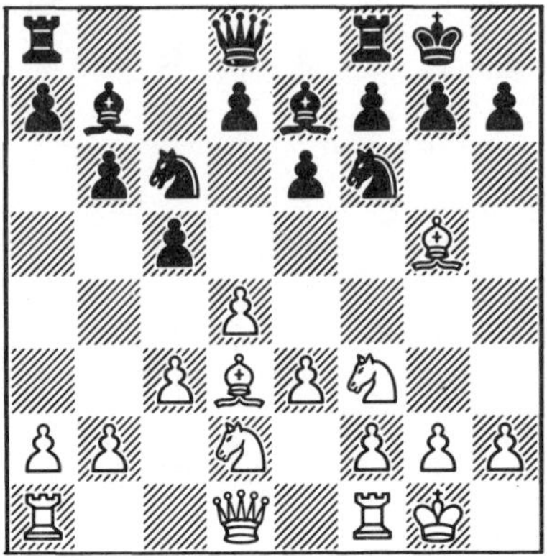

9 e4

White is at the crossroads: should he make this move immediately or only after some preparation?

Others:

(a) 9 dxc5 bxc5 10 e4 d6 = Kan-Keres, Illustrative Game No 30.

(b) 9 ♕e2 ♘d5! (or, a move later, 9 ... cxd4 10 exd4 ♘d5 11 ♗xe7 ♘cxe7 12 g3 ♘f6 13 ♗a6 ♕c8 14 ♗xb7 ♕xb7 = Spassky-Andersson, Clermont-Ferrand 1989). 10 ♗xe7 ♕xe7 (10 ... ♘cxe7 11 g3 f5 12 e4 fxe4 13 ♗xe4 ♖b8 14 ♖ae1 ∞ Rechlis-D.Gurevich, Jerusalem 1986) 11 ♗a6 ♗xa6 12 ♕xa6 ♘c7 13 ♕e2 d5 14 e4 cxd4 = Marshall-Capablanca, Bad Kissingen 1928.

(c) 9 ♖e1 d5 (9 ... ♖c8 10 ♖c1 ♘h5 11 ♘e4 f6 ∞ Balashov-Miles, Novi Sad 1975) 10 a3 ♕c7

11 ♕b1 h6 12 ♗h4 ♖fd8 = Petrosian-Averkin, USSR 1969.

(d) 9 a3 cxd4 (9 ... ♘d5 10 ♗xe7 ♕xe7 11 ♖e1 d6 12 g3 ♖fd8 13 ♕e2 ♘f6 14 e4 ± Kochiev-Kärner, Tallinn 1987; 9 ... h6 10 ♗h4 cxd4 11 exd4 ♘d5 12 ♗g3?! d6 ∞; 11 ... ♘h5?! 12 ♗g3 f5 13 d5 exd5 14 ♘b3 f4 15 ♗g6 ♘xg3 16 fxg3 fxg3 17 ♗c2 ± Epishin-Smirin, Vilnius 1988) 10 cxd4!? ♘d5 11 ♗xe7 ♕xe7 12 ♖e1 f5 13 e4 ♘f4 14 ♗f1 fxe4 15 ♘xe4 ± Varnusz-Végh, Eger 1983.

9 ... cxd4
10 ♘xd4

10 cxd4?! h6 11 ♗xf6 (11 ♗h4 ♘h5! =; Black should not be tempted by 11 ... ♘b4?! 12 ♗b1 ♗a6 13 ♖e1 d5? 14 ♗xf6 ♗xf6 15 ♕a4 dxe4 16 ♗xe4 ± Guseinov-Mochalov, Moscow 1983. 11 ♗e3?! ♘b4! ∓) 11 ... ♗xf6 12 e5 ♗e7 13 a3 d6 14 ♗e4 b5 ∓ Barlov-Adorján, New York 1985.

10 ... d5?!

10 ... d6! is similar to the Sicilian. There would be chances for both sides.

11	**♘xc6!**	**♗xc6**
12	**e5**	**♘e4**
13	**♗xe7**	**♕xe7**
14	**♘f3**	**f6?!**
15	**♕e2**	**♗b7**
16	**exf6**	**♕xf6** ±

Yusupov-Hmadi, Tunis 1985.

4.3

4 ... cxd4

Exchanging pawns in the centre is better done before c2-c3 to deprive White of the alternative recapture with the c-pawn. The drawback of the early exchange is that White can change his mind and transpose to a well-known variation of the Nimzo-Indian.

5 exd4 b6

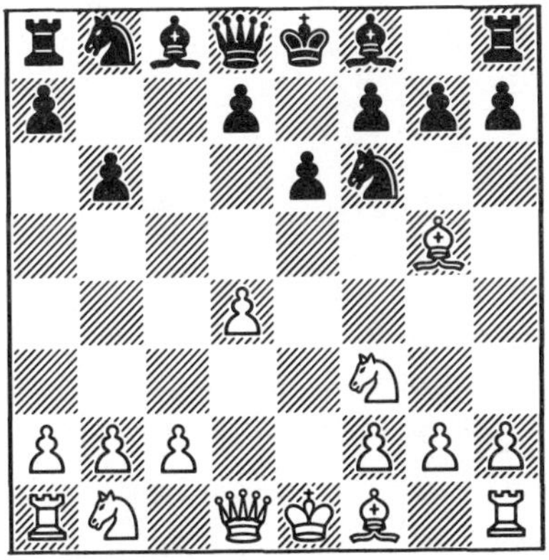

5 ... ♗e7 6 ♘bd2 b6 7 c3 = (±!?) C.Torre-Lasker, Illustrative Game No 31.

6 ♗d3

6 a3 (before c4) is an unnecessary precaution: 6 ... ♗e7 7 c4 0-0 8 ♘c3 ♗b7 9 ♗d3 d5 10 ♗xf6 ♗xf6 11 cxd5 exd5 12 0-0 ♘c6 = I. Ivanov-D.Gurevich, US Championship 1989.

6 ... ♗b7

7 ♘bd2

7 0-0 ♗e7 8 c4 0-0 9 ♘c3 d6 10 ♖e1 is familiar from the Nimzo-Indian. Due to the possible b2-b4 and d4-d5, White's game is a bit better.

Interesting is 9 ... d5 10 ♗xf6 ♗xf6 11 cxd5 exd5 12 ♕b3 ♘c6! (12 ... ♘a6? 13 ♘b5 ♖e8 14 ♖ac1 g6 15 ♖c3 ♕e7 16 ♖e1 ♕b4 17 ♖xe8+ ♖xe8 18 ♕c2 ♕e7 19 a3 ♕d8 20 ♘xa7 ± Yusupov-Portisch, Linares 1990) 13 ♖ad1 ♘a5 14 ♕c2 g6 15 ♖fe1 ♖e8 16 ♖xe8+ ♕xe8 17 h3 ♖c8 ∞ Yusupov-Brunner, Munich 1990.

7 ... ♗e7

4.31

8 c3

A minor trap in case Black should castle prematurely.

8 ... d6

(a) 8 ... 0-0 (Castling into the attack) 9 h4! ♘e8 10 g4 f5 11 gxf5 exf5 12 ♕b3+ ♔h8 13 0-0-0 ♘d6 14 ♖de1! ±± Kovačević-Minić, Illustrative Game No 32.

(b) 8 ... ♘d5 9 ♗xe7 ♕xe7 10 0-0 0-0 11 ♖e1 f5?! (Otherwise White pushes his pawn to c4. Yet Black is conceding too many weaknesses with this pawn thrust. 11 ... d6 is more circumspect, when we have transposed into the Timman-Andersson game in section 4.32) 12 ♗f1 ♘f6 13 a4 ♘c6 14 ♘c4 ♖ac8 15 a5 ♘d5 16 axb6 axb6 17 ♕b3 ± Trifunović-Pfeiffer, Yugoslavia-Germany match, 1954.

9	0-0	0-0
10	♖e1	♘bd7
11	a4	

11 ♘c4 ♖e8 12 ♕e2 ♕c7 13 ♖ad1 ∞ Torre-Lasker, Illustrative Game No 31.

11	...	a6!
12	h3	♖e8
13	♗f4	♕c7
14	♗h2	

14 ♖c1!?; 14 c4!?.

14 ... ♗f8 =

Spassky-Portisch, match 1977.

4.32

8 0-0 0-0

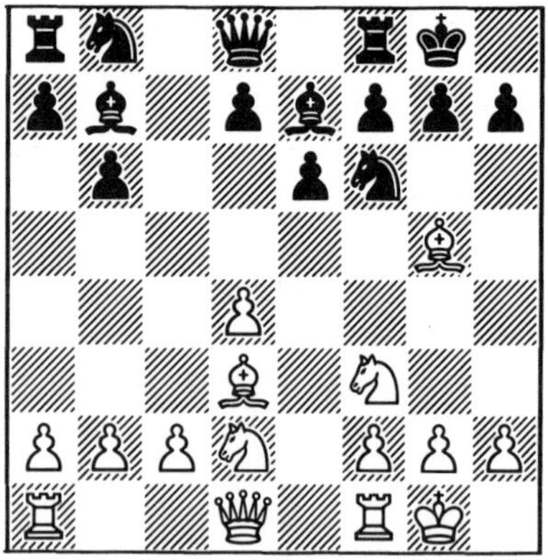

9 ♖e1

9 c3 ♘d5 10 ♗xe7 ♕xe7 11 ♖e1 d6 12 a4 ♘d7 13 a5 ♘7f6 14 ♕b3

(14 ♗f1!?) 14 ... ♕c7 15 ♕a3 ♖ab8 16 ♗f1 b5! 17 ♗xb5 ♘xc3 18 ♕xc3 ♕xc3 19 bxc3 ♗xf3 = Timman-Andersson, Brussels 1988.

9 ♗xf6 ♗xf6 10 c3 ♘c6 11 ♘e4 ♗e7 12 ♖e1 ♕c7 13 ♕e2 ♖ac8 14 ♖ad1 ♘a5 15 ♘g3 d6 = Piket-Lautier, Cannes 1990.

9 ... d6
10 a4

10 c3 ♘bd7! 11 a4 a6 12 ♘f1 ♖e8 13 ♘g3 ♘f8 14 ♗d2 ♕d7 15 ♘g5 h6 16 ♘h3 ♕c6 = Spassky-Portisch, Reggio Emilia 1987.

10 ... ♘c6?!

Probably better is 10 ... a6, then ♘bd7. For example, 10 ... a6 11 c3 ♘bd7 12 ♘c4 (12 ♘f1 is Spassky-Portisch, previous note) 12 ... b5!? 13 axb5 axb5 14 ♖xa8 ♕xa8 15 ♘a3 b4 16 cxb4 h6 17 ♗f4 ♘b6 18 b5 ♖c8 19 ♕e2 ♕a4 ∞ Zsu.Polgar-Petursson, Reykjavik 1988.

11 c3 ♘d5
12 ♗xe7 ♘cxe7?!
13 a5! bxa5
14 ♕a4 ♘f4
15 ♗e4

White has seized the initiative. Spassky-Beliavsky, Montpellier 1985.

4.4

4 ... ♗e7

A reliable move, quite often played after 2 ... e6 3 ♗g5.

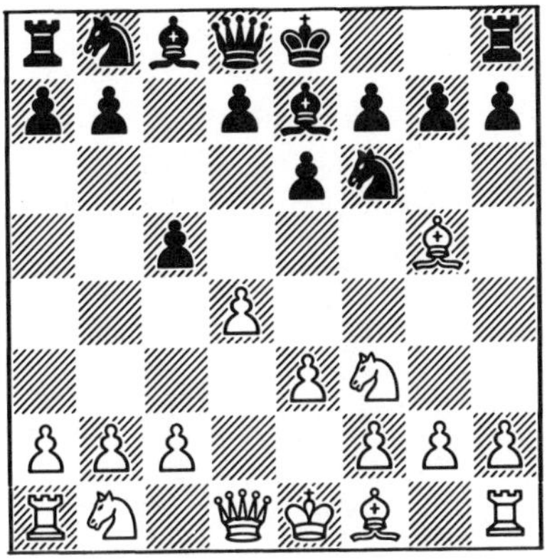

4.41

5 dxc5!?

Not characteristically Anti-Indian. White would like to exploit the tempo Black needs to recapture the pawn.

5 ... ♗xc5

5 ... ♕a5+ 6 ♘bd2 ♕xc5 7 c4 b6 8 ♗d3 ♗b7 9 0-0 h6 10 ♗h4 ♕c7 11 ♖c1 d6 12 b4 ♘bd7 13 ♘d4 ♖c8 14 f4 ± Varnusz-Palko, Budapest 1986. 7 ♗d3 is also promising, e.g. 7 ... d5 8 0-0 0-0 9 c4 ♘c6 10 ♖c1 ♕b6 11 cxd5 exd5 12 ♘b3 ♗g4 13 ♗e2 ± Hodgson-F.Rayner, Blackpool 1990. Black can insert 7 ... h6 but this does not change the essential nature of the position.

6 ♗e2

6 c4 ♗b4+! 7 ♘bd2 (7 ♘c3

♗xc3+ 8 bxc3 d6 ∞) 7 ... b6 8 ♗d3 ♘c6 10 0-0 ♗e7 11 ♕e2 0-0 12 ♖fd1 ♕c7 13 ♗f4 d6 = Yusupov-Karpov, 5th match game 1989. 6 ... 0-0 allows White a smoother development: 7 ♘c3 ♗e7 8 ♗d3 ♘c6 9 0-0 h6 10 ♗h4 b6 11 ♖c1 ♗b7 12 ♕e2 d6 13 ♖fd1 ♖c8 14 ♗b1 ♖e8 15 ♘b5 ⩲ Hodgson-Franzoni, Lucerne 1989.

6	**...**	**♗e7**
7	**c4**	**b6**
8	**♘c3**	**♗b7**
9	**0-0**	**0-0**
10	**♕c2**	**♘a6**
11	**♖fd1**	**♘c5**
12	**♖d4!** ⩲	

Hort-Adorján, Illustrative Game No 33.

4.42

5 c3

This is sometimes only a change in move order, but occasionally it really gives a different line from the main variation.

5 ♘bd2 0-0 (5 ... b6 6 ♗d3 cxd4 7 exd4 ♗a6 8 ♗xf6 ♗xf6 9 ♘e4 ♗e7 10 d5! ± Salov-Cebalo, Yugoslavia 1985) 6 ♗d3 b6 7 ♕e2 cxd4 8 exd4 ♘d5?! 9 h4! f5 10 c4 ♗xg5 11 hxg5 ♘f4 12 ♕f1 ♘c6 13 0-0-0 ± Lerner-Chekhov, Illustrative Game No 34.

5	**...**	**b6**
6	**♘bd2**	**♗b7**
7	**♗d3**	

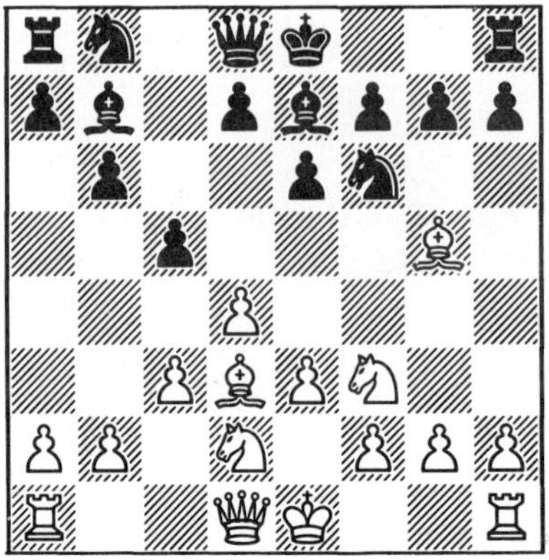

7 dxc5?! bxc5 8 e4 d5! 9 exd5 exd5 = Damjanović-Rohde, New York 1987.

7 ... cxd4

7 ... h6 8 ♗xf6 ♗xf6 9 0-0 ♘c6 10 ♕e2 a6 11 ♖ad1 ♕c7 12 ♖fe1 d6 13 a3 0-0 14 ♘e4! ♗e7 15 ♘g3 b5 16 ♗b1! ± Mohrlok-Larsen, Büsum 1969. 7 ... ♘c6 8 a3 0-0?! 9 e4 = Seirawan-Andersson, Skelleftea 1989; 8 ... ♘d5 =.

8 cxd4!?

8 exd4 ♘d5 9 ♗xe7 ♕xe7 10 g3 ♗a6 11 ♗xa6 ♘xa6 12 ♕e2 ♘ac7 13 ♘e5 d6 14 ♘d3 0-0 = Kamsky-Sax, Manila 1990. 10 0-0, as in the Trifunović-Pfeiffer game in 4.31, is probably more accurate.

8 ... ♘d5

(a) 8 ... 0-0 9 0-0 d6 10 ♖c1 ♘bd7 11 a3 ♖c8 12 ♕e2 ♖xc1 13 ♖xc1 ♕b8 14 e4 ♖c8 15 ♖d1! ⩲

Bronstein-Alster, Vienna 1957.

(b) 8 ... ♘c6 9 a3 0-0 10 0-0 ♘d5 11 ♗xe7 ♕xe7 (11 ... ♘cxe7 12 ♖c1 ♖c8 13 ♕e2 ♖xc1 14 ♖xc1 ♕b8 15 ♘e5 ♘f6 16 ♘g4 ♘xg4 17 ♕xg4 f5 18 ♕g3 ♕xg3 19 hxg3 ± Estevez-Lebredo, Cuba 1984) 12 ♕e2 (12 ♖e1 f5 13 ♖c1 ♘d8 14 ♗f1 ♘f7 15 ♘e5 ♘g5 16 g3 ± Costa-Brunner, Biel 1990) 12 ... ♖ac8 13 ♖ac1 ♘b8 14 ♖fe1 f5 15 ♕f1 ♘f6 ∞ Hort-Larsen, Linares 1983.

9 ♗xe7

9 ♘c4?! 0-0 10 h4!? f5 (10 ... f6 11 ♕b1!) 11 a3 ♘f6 12 ♕e2 ♗d5 13 ♖c1 = Spassky-Portisch, match 1977.

9	**...**	**♕xe7**
10	**0-0**	**f5**
11	**♖e1**	**0-0**
12	**e4**	**♘f4**
13	**♗f1**	**fxe4**
14	**♘xe4**	**♘c6 ±**

15 g3 ♘d5 16 ♗g2 ♖ad8 ± Timman-Andersson, Indonesia 1983.

4.5

4	**...**	**h6**
5	**♗xf6**	

For 5 ♗h4 Black has all the alternatives he had prior to 4 ... h6 and can also play ... g7-g5. This line can be regarded as an improved version of the 3 ... h6 variation although ... c7-c5 is sometimes inconvenient. A recent example where Black develops quietly: 5 ... ♗e7 6 ♘bd2 cxd4 7 exd4 b6 8 c3 ♗b7 9 ♗d3 d6 10 0-0 0-0 11 ♖e1 ♘h5 12 ♗xe7 ♕xe7 13 a4 ♘d7 14 a5 ♘f4 15 ♗f1 ♖fc8 = Lonov-Kholmov, Klaipeda 1988.

5 ... ♕xf6

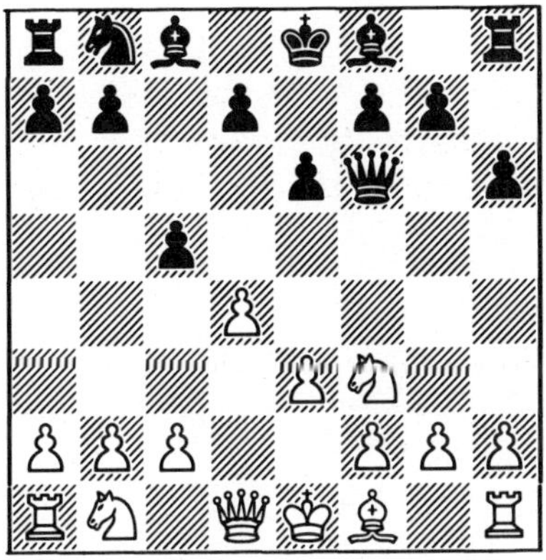

6 ♘bd2

6 c4!? cxd4 7 exd4 ♗b4+ 8 ♘bd2 (8 ♘c3?! ♗xc3+!) 8 ... b6 9 ♗e2 (9 ♗d3 ♗xd2+ =) 9 ... ♗b7 10 0-0 0-0 11 ♘e5! ♗xd2 12 ♕xd2 d6 13 ♘g4 ♕g6 14 ♘e3 ♘c6 15 f4 ♘e7 ± E.Torre-Cebalo, Novi Sad 1984.

6 ... cxd4

6 ... ♕d8 7 ♗d3 b6 8 ♕e2 ♗e7 9 c3 ♗b7 10 e4 (10 ♗e4!?) 10 ... 0-0 11 0-0 d6 12 ♖fe1 ♘d7 13 a3 ♖c8 14 d5 ± Varnusz-Cserna, Budapest 1986.

7	**exd4**	**♘c6**
8	**c3**	**d5**
9	**♗d3**	

9 ♗b5 ♗d6 10 0-0 a6!? 11 ♗xc6+ bxc6 12 c4 0-0 13 c5 ♗f4 14 ♖e1 ♕e7 15 ♕c2 f6 ∞ Sideif Zade-Dautov, Budapest 1989.

9	**...**	**♗d6**
10	**0-0**	**0-0**
11	**♖e1** ⩲ (Kogan)	

ILLUSTRATIVE GAMES

1 d4 ♘f6 2 ♘f3 e6 3 ♗g5 c5 4 e3

25) **Yusupov-Karpov**
match (5) 1989

4 ... b6 5 d5 exd5 6 ♘c3 ♗e7 7 ♘xd5 ♗b7 8 ♗xf6 ♗xf6 9 c3 0-0 10 ♗c4 10 ♗e2 is also good, e.g. 10 ... d6 11 0-0 ♘a6 12 a4 ♘c7 13 ♗c4 ± Piket-Farago, Wijk aan Zee 1988. White's grip on the weakened light squares is formidable. **10 ... a6 11 0-0** 11 a4!? **11 ... b5 12 ♗b3** Despite the final result, White is not really making the best of his chances, and in the next few moves Black reaches near-equality. Sharper is 12 ♘xf6+! ♕xf6 13 ♗d5 ♘c6 14 ♕d2 (14 a4!? Taimanov) 14 ... d6 15 ♖fd1 ♖fd8 16 a4 ±. **12 ... d6 13 ♕d2 ♘d7 14 ♖fd1 ♗xd5!** Paradoxically, despite the weakness of his light squares, it is the light-squared bishop that Black wants to exchange for the dominant knight. Black intends to place everything on dark squares! **15 ♗xd5 ♖b8 16 ♕c2 ♘b6 17 ♖d2 g6 18 ♖ad1 ♕c7?!** 18 ... ♕e7!. **19 ♕e4 ♔g7 20 h4 ♕e7 21 ♕f4 ♗e5 22 ♘xe5 dxe5 23 ♕g3 ♖bd8 24 h5 ♖d7 25 b3 ♖fd8 26 e4 g5** 26 ... f5!? **27 ♕e3 h6 28 c4 ♖c7 29 ♖d3 ♘d7!?** 29 ... ♖d6 was a more cautious defence.

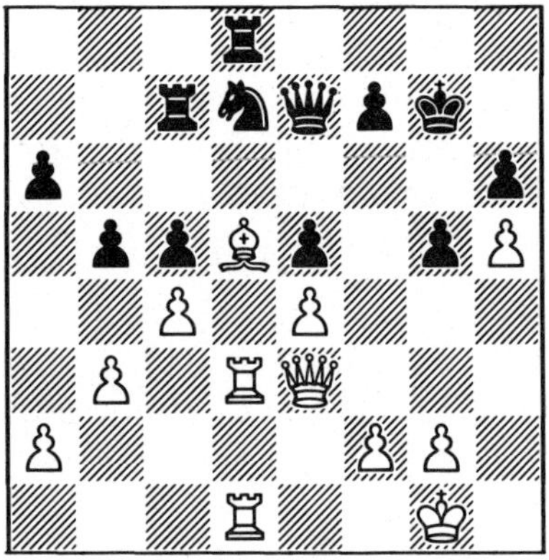

30 ♗xf7!! A 'discovered pin'! While Black is wondering how to untangle himself on the d-file, White invades. A memorable sacrifice. **30 ... ♔xf7** If 30 ... ♕xf7 31 ♕h3 followed by ♖d6 etc. **31 ♕d2?!** Taimanov gives 31 ♖d6! as an outright win, citing the variations 31 ... ♖cc8 32 ♖xh6 ♘f8 33 ♖d5! and 32 ... ♖dc8 33 ♕f3+ ♔e8 34 ♕f5 ♘f8 35 ♖1d5. In either case Black is in a complete bind. Surprisingly Yusupov does not mention this very logical possibility in his own notes. **31 ... ♔e8 32 ♕a5 bxc4 33 bxc4 ♖cc8?** In time trouble Black instinctively unpins, but this is a mistake. 33 ... ♖c6! keeps the game alive; White should then try 34 ♖d5. **34 ♕a4!** A fresh pin on the knight. Black can struggle into a lost endgame with 34 ... ♖b8 35 ♖d6 ♖b1! 36 ♖xd7 ♕xd7 37 ♕xd7+ ♖xd7 38 ♖xb1, but instead finds a way to lose more promptly. **34 ... ♖c7? 35 ♕xa6 ♖b8 36 ♕g6+ ♔f8?** 36 ... ♔d8 also loses after 37 ♖d6 (Yusupov) or 37 ♕xh6 (Taimanov), but less quickly. **37 ♖f3+ 1 0** The most famous Torre Attack of recent years. For a move like 30 ♗xf7!! you could easily forgive a few inaccuracies.

(Notes by Crouch, based on those of Yusupov and Taimanov)

26) **Petrosian-Kozma**
Munich 1958

4 ... b6 5 d5! exd5 6 ♘c3 ♗b7 7 ♘xd5 ♗xd5 8 ♗xf6 ♕xf6 9 ♕xd5 ♘c6 10 ♗c4 ♗e7 11 0-0-0 ♖d8 Holding the d5 square gives White a considerable yet only slowly exploitable advantage. **12 ♖d2 0-0 13 c3** Hindering 13 ... b5!. **13 ... ♘a5 14 ♗e2 ♕e6 15 ♖hd1 ♕xd5 16 ♖xd5 d6 17 ♘d2! f5** White has forced this weakening by threatening 18 ♘e4. **18 f4 g6 19 g3 ♖f6 20 e4 fxe4 21 ♘xe4 ♖e6 22 ♗f3 ♔g7?** The best chance to draw is 22 ... ♘c4 23 ♖5d3 d5! 24 ♖xd5 ♖xd5 25 ♖xd5 ♘d6. **23 b3 ♘c6 24 ♖5d3 ♘b8 25 ♘f2 h5** preventing 26 ♗g4.

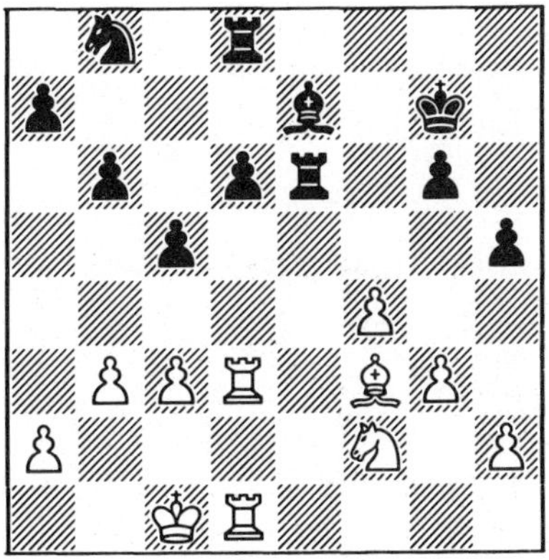

26 ♔d2! To achieve the ideal set-up, the king heads for f3. **26 ... ♗f8 27 ♗d5 ♖e7 28 ♘e4 ♘a6 29 ♔e3 ♘c7?** 29 ... c4! 30 ♗xc4 ♘c5 31 ♖d4 d5 or 30 bxc4 ♘c5 ±. **30 ♔f3 ♘xd5?! 31 ♖xd5 ♖de8 32 ♖e1! ♖e6 33 ♖e2 b5 34 h3 a5 35 g4 hxg4+ 36 hxg4 ♗e7 37 f5 ♖e5 38 ♖xe5 dxe5 39 ♖d2 ♖f8 40 ♖d7 ♖f7 41 ♖xe7 1-0**

27) **Janowski-Sämisch**
Marienbad 1925

4 ... ♘c6 5 ♘bd2 b6 6 c3 ♗b7 7 ♗d3 cxd4 8 exd4 ♗e7 9 ♘c4 0-0? Black should have waited for White to castle first. **10 ♕c2 h6 11 h4!** The commencement of the attack! **11 ... ♕c7 12 ♕d2! ♘g4! 13 ♗f4 d6 14 ♘e3 ♘xe3** 14 ... h5!? **15 ♕xe3 h5** White threatened 16

♗xh6. **16 ♖h3! e5?** Intending to slow down the attack, this pawn sacrifice actually accelerates it. 16 ... ♗f6 ±. **17 dxe5 ♘xe5 18 ♘xe5 dxe5 19 ♗xe5 ♗d6**

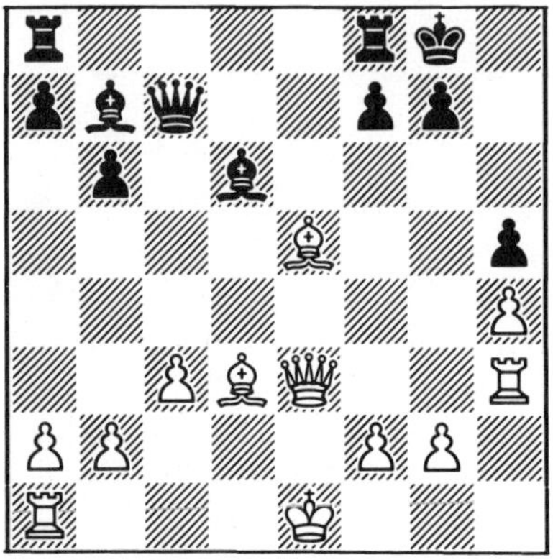

20 ♕h6!! 1-0

20 ... f5 21 ♗c4+! ♖f7 22 ♕xg7+ mate!

28) **Krasnov-Averkin**
USSR 1969

4 ... ♘c6 5 ♘bd2 b6 6 c3 ♗b7 7 ♗d3 cxd4 8 exd4 ♗e7 9 0-0 0-0 10 ♕e2?! Encouraging Black's counterplay against f4. 10 ♖e1!. **10 ... ♘d5! 11 ♗xe7 ♘cxe7 12 ♕e5?** The queen's wandering about helps Black to launch the attack. White should have tried 12 ♖fe1 ♘f4 13 ♕f1. **12 ... f5! 13 ♕d6 ♘g6 14 ♖fe1 ♖f6!** Threatening 15 ... e5!. **15 ♘e5 ♘xe5 16 dxe5** After 16 ♕xe5 d6! or 16 ♖xe5 ♘f4 17 ♗f1 ♗xg2!, the weakness of g2 is fatal. **16 ... ♖g6** The attack on the king has unrolled incredibly fast. **17 g3 ♘f4 18 ♔f1** 18 ♗f1 ♕h4! (the threat is 19 ... ♕xh2+) 19 ♗g2 ♘xg2! 20 ♕xd7 (20 gxh4 ♘e3+ mate) 20 ... ♘xe1 21 ♕xb7 ♖d8 22 ♔f1 ♕h6 ∓∓. **18 ... ♗g2+ 19 ♔g1**

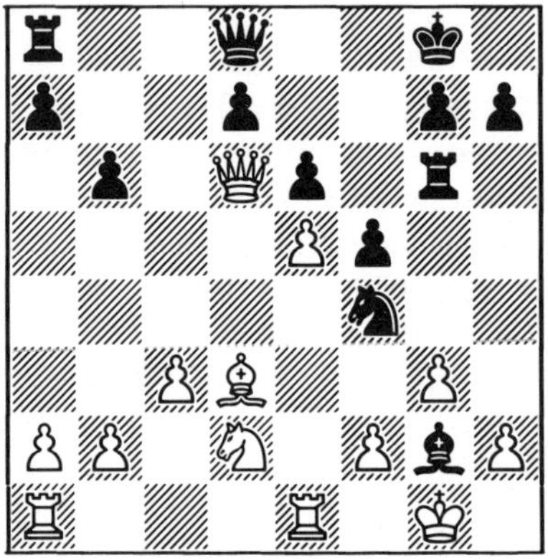

19 ... ♕h4!! 0-1

20 ... ♕xh2+ with mate threatens. 20 f3 ♖xg3! 21 hxg3 ♕xg3 22 ♘f1 ♗xf1+ 23 ♔xf1 ♕g2+ mate.

29) **Petrosian-Taimanov**
Leningrad 1960

4 ... ♘c6 5 ♘bd2 b6 6 c3 ♗e7 7 ♗d3 0-0 8 0-0 cxd4 9 exd4 ♘d5 10 ♗xe7 ♘cxe7 11 ♖e1 ♗b7 12 ♗f1 f5 13 ♘e5 ♕c7 14 ♖c1 ♖ae8 15 c4 ♘f6 16 ♕b3 Typically, White gets hold of the centre later than in other openings, but he can control it rather convincingly. Black's problems have been increased by ... f7-f5 yet without this disruption of his pawn structure he would not have chances for counterplay. **16 ... d6 17 ♘ef3 ♘g6 18 c5! ♗d5 19 ♕a3 dxc5 20 dxc5 ♘e4** 20 ... e5 21 cxb6 ♕xb6 22 ♘c4 ♗xc4 23 ♗xc4+ ♔h8 24 ♕a6 ±. **21 ♘xe4 fxe4?!** In exchange for his weak pawns Black hopes for an attack along the f-file. **22 ♘d2 ♕f4 23 ♕e3 bxc5 24 ♖xc5 ♕f6 25 ♖c2 ♘e5 26 ♕g3** 26 ♘xe4 ♕g6! is all too unclear **26 ... ♕f5 27 ♖c7 ♖f7 28 ♖xf7 ♘xf7 29 b3 ♘e5 30 f3! e3 31 ♖xe3 ♘c6 32 ♘e4 ♖f8**

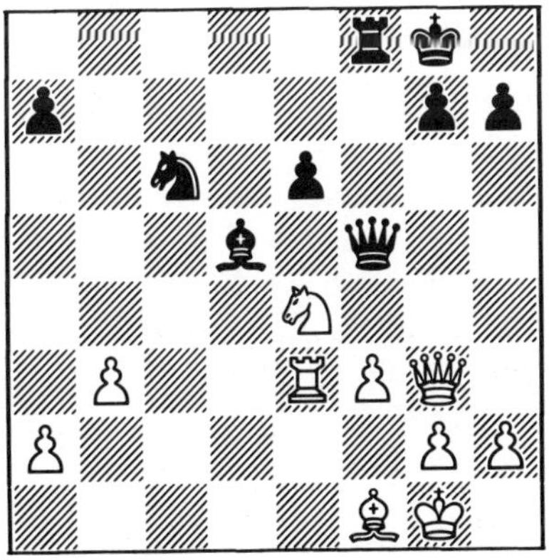

33 ♘g5! A decisive blow. **33 ... ♕f6 34 ♘xe6! ♖e8 35 ♘xg7 ♖xe3 36 ♘f5+ ♔f8 37 ♘xe3 ♕d4 38 ♕f2 ♗f7 39 h3 ♘b4 40 a3 ♘a2 41 ♘c4 ♕xf2+ 42 ♔xf2 ♘c1 43 b4 ♘a2 44 ♔e3 1-0**

30) **Kan-Keres**
USSR Championship 1952

4 ... ♘c6 5 ♘bd2 b6 6 c3 ♗b7 7 ♗d3 ♗e7 8 0-0 0-0 9 dxc5 bxc5 10 e4 d6 The position reminds us of the Sicilian Defence. **11 ♕e2 ♖b8 12 ♖ad1 ♘h5?!** Aggressive! **13 ♗e3 g6 14 ♖fe1 ♕c7 15 ♗h6 ♖fe8 16 ♘f1 ♗f8 17 ♗xf8 ♖xf8 18 ♕e3 ♕e7 19 h3?!** White has just missed the right moment for e5: Black's pawn formation would be weakened after both 19 ... dxe5 or 19 ... d5 20 ♕h6! f6 21 exf6. **19 ... ♔g7 20 ♘1h2 ♘f6 21 e5** Too late, because White's pieces are too far from the queenside. **21 ... dxe5 22 ♘xe5 ♘d5 23 ♕g3 ♘xe5 24 ♕xe5+ ♕f6 25 ♘g4 ♕xe5 26 ♘xe5 ♘b6 27 b3?!** 27 ♗c2! **27 ... ♖fd8 28 ♗e2 ♔f6 29 ♘g4+ ♔e7 30 ♘e3**

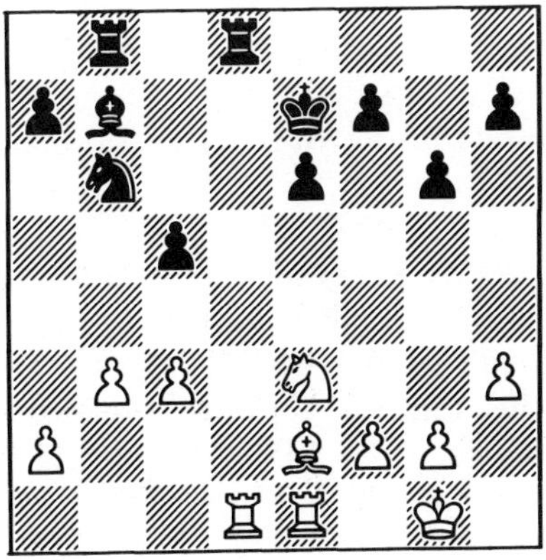

30 ... a5! A minority attack! **31 ♖xd8 ♖xd8 32 ♖d1 ♘d5! 33 ♘xd5 ♗xd5 34 c4?** Fixing his own pawns on white squares is a mistake. Black's two queenside pawns can hold White's three, while Black has an important extra pawn on the other wing. **34 ... ♗e4! 35 ♖xd8 ♔xd8 36 ♗d1** To prevent 36 ... ♗b1 37 a3 ♗c2. This permanent threat keeps White's hands tied and seals his fate. **36 ... ♔c7 37 ♔f1 ♔d6 38 f4** Otherwise the king would penetrate. **38 ... e5 39 g3 ♗b1 40 a4 exf4 41 gxf4 ♔e6 42 ♔f2 ♔f5 43 ♔e3 h5 44 ♔f3 h4! 45 ♔e3 ♔e6! 46 ♗g4+ ♗f5 47 ♔f3 ♔f6 48 ♗xf5 ♔xf5 49 ♔e3 f6 0-1**

31) **Torre-Lasker**
Moscow 1925

4 ... cxd4 5 exd4 b6 6 ♘bd2 ♗e7 7 c3 ♗b7 8 ♗d3 d6 9 0-0 0-0 10 ♖e1 ♘bd7 11 ♘c4 ♖e8 12 ♕e2 ♕c7 13 ♖ad1 ♘f8 14 ♗c1 Having completed his development White looks for an offensive plan.

14 ... ♘d5 15 ♘g5?! *Iuventus ventis!* 15 ♘a3!. **15 ... b5! 16 ♘a3 b4 17 cxb4 ♘xb4 18 ♕h5?!** 18 ♗b1!. **18 ... ♗xg5 19 ♗xg5 ♘xd3 20 ♖xd3 ♕a5!** Dr Lasker was famous for his aggressive defence. **21 b4!** Attempting to eliminate the horizontal pressure; 21 ... ♕xb4?? 22 ♖b1 **21 ... ♕f5?!** Analysts later proved that 21 ... ♕d5! gave Black quite an acceptable game. **22 ♖g3 h6 23 ♘c4! ♕d5?** 23 ... hxg5! 24 ♘xd6 ♕g6 **24 ♘e3 ♕b5**

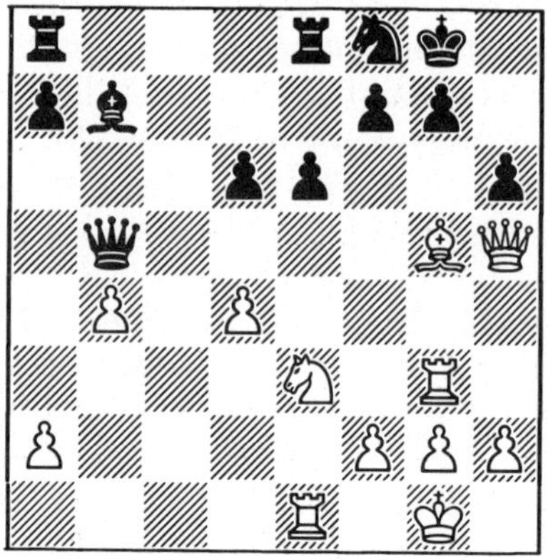

25 ♗f6!! Yes, this is the classic combination of Torre – the actual reason for calling the line the 'Torre Attack'. **25 ... ♕xh5 26 ♖xg7+ ♔h8 27 ♖xf7+ ♔g8 28 ♖g7+ ♔h8 29 ♖xb7+ ♔g8 30 ♖g7+ ♔h8 31 ♖g5+** Winning back his capital with compound interest. **31 ... ♔h7 32 ♖xh5 ♔g6 33 ♖h3 ♔xf6 34 ♖xh6+ ♔g5 35 ♖h3 ♖eb8 36 ♖g3+ ♔f6 37 ♖f3+ ♔g6 38 a3 a5 39 bxa5 ♖xa5 40 ♘c4 ♖d5 41 ♖f4 ♘d7 42 ♖xe6+ ♔g5 43 g3 1-0**

32) **Kovačević-Minić**
Karlovac 1977

4 ... cxd4 5 exd4 b6 6 ♗d3 ♗b7 7 ♘bd2 ♗e7 8 c3 0-0?! Once again: castling into the attack is not the safest policy! **9 h4! ♘e8?!** 9 ... d6 10 ♗xf6! ♗xf6 11 ♕c2 g6! (11 ... h6 12 g4!) 12 h5 ♕e8 ±. **10 g4 f5** 10 ... d6 11 ♕c2. **11 gxf5 exf5 12 ♕b3+ ♔h8?!** 12 ... d5 13

0-0-0 ♘d6 14 ♖de1 ±; 14 ... ♘e4? 15 ♗xe4 fxe4 16 ♖xe4 ±±. **13 0-0-0 ♘d6 14 ♖de1!** Forcing the opening of the h-file since 14 ... ♗f6 15 ♕a3! ♕c7 16 ♗f4 is unbearable. **14 ... ♗xg5 15 hxg5 g6** 15 ... ♘c6 16 ♘h4!. **16 d5! ♔g8** 16 ... ♘a6? 17 ♗xa6 ♗xa6 18 ♕a3 **17 ♕b4 ♘f7** 17 ... ♕c7 18 ♕h4 ♖f7 19 ♘e5 ♖g7 20 ♘xg6! hxg6 21 ♕h8+ ♔f7 22 ♖e7+ ♔xe7 23 ♕xg7+ ♘f7 24 ♖e1+. **18 ♕h4 h6** 18 ... h5 19 ♗xf5!. **19 ♖eg1 ♗xd5 20 ♕d4 1-0** (Kovačević)

33) **Hort-Adorján**
Reggio Emilia 1984/85

4 ... ♗e7 5 dxc5 ♗xc5 6 ♗e2 ♗e7 7 c4 b6 8 ♘c3 ♗b7 9 0-0 0-0 10 ♕c2 ♘a6! 11 ♖fd1 ♘c5 12 ♖d4! d5 13 ♖ad1 ♖c8 14 ♗f4 ♕e8!? 15 ♘e5 ♘fe4 16 ♘xe4 ♘xe4 17 ♖xe4! Simplifying to a favourable endgame. **17 ... dxe4 18 ♘d7 ♗c6 19 ♘xf8 ♕xf8 20 ♗e5 ♖d8 21 g3 f6 22 ♗c3 ♖xd1+ 23 ♕xd1 ♔f7 24 h4 ♗d6 25 ♗f1 ♕e7?** Some time during the last few moves, Black should have thwarted the mobilisation of white's queenside majority by ... a5. **26 ♕d2 ♕d7?! 27 b4! ♗f8 28 ♕c2 f5 29 a3 ♗a4 30 ♕e2 ♗d1 31 ♕b2 ♗g4 32 ♗d4 ♕a4 33 c5 e5?** 33 ... bxc5 34 bxc5 ♕d1 35 c6 ±. **34 ♗xe5 bxc5 35 ♕a2+ ♔e8 36 ♕e6+ 1-0** Black exceeded the allotted time in a hopeless position.

34) **Lerner-Chekhov**
USSR Championship 1984

4 ... ♗e7 5 ♘bd2 0-0 6 ♗d3 b6 7 ♕e2 7 c3 ♗a6! 8 ♗xa6 ♘xa6 9 a4 ♘b8 10 0-0 ♘c6 =. **7 ... cxd4 8 exd4 ♘d5?!** In trying to simplify the position prematurely, Black offers offensive possibilities to his opponent. 8 ... ♗b7 9 0-0 d6 was necessary. **9 h4!** The signal for the attack to begin. White allows the exchange of his powerful bishop, in return for which he will be able to open the h-file. 9 ♗xe7?! ♕xe7 10 0-0 ♘f4 11 ♕e4 ♘xd3 12 ♕xa8? ♘c6 13 cxd3 ♗a6 ∓. **9 ... f5** 9 ... h6 10 c4 ♘b4 11 ♗b1 hxg5 12 hxg5 g6 13 ♗xg6 fxg6 14 ♕e4 ±±; 9 ... ♗b7 10 c4 ♘b4 11 ♗b1 ±. **10 c4 ♗xg5 11 hxg5 ♘f4 12 ♕f1 ♘c6 13 0-0-0 b5!? 14 c5** White is not going to be led astray with 14 cxb5?!. **14 ... ♗a6** 14 ... ♕a5 15 ♗b1 ♗a6 16 g3 b4 17 ♘c4 ±. **15 g3 ♘xd3+ 16 ♕xd3 ♕a5 17 ♕b3** 17 ♔b1? ♕xa2+!. **17 ... ♕a4** Panicking, Black forces exchanges. However, the attack on the h-file is just as powerful without White's queen. **18 ♖h4! ♕xb3 19 ♘xb3 ♗b7**

(diagram)

20 d5! To unroll the attack, White has to block the diagonal of the opposing bishop. 20 ♖dh1?? ♘e7! **20 ... ♘d8** 20 ... exd5 21 ♖dh1 ±; 20 ... ♘e7 21 c6! dxc6 22

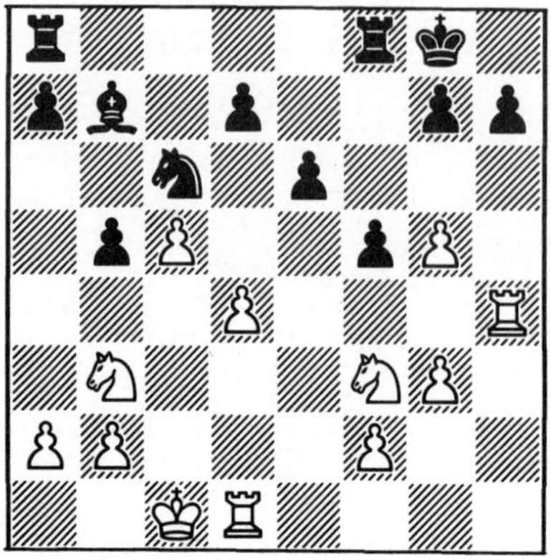

♘c5 ±. **21 c6! ♖c8 22 ♔b1 dxc6 23 ♖dh1! cxd5** 23 ... h6 24 gxh6 g6 25 h7+ ♔h8 26 ♘e5 ♖f6 27 ♖h6 ±±. **24 ♖xh7 ♘f7** Black wants to escape from the mating net: 24 ... ♔f7 25 ♘e5+ ♔e7 26 ♖xg7+ ♔d6 27 ♖d7+! ♔xe5 28 ♖e1+ mate! **25 g6 ♘h6 26 ♖1xh6 gxh6 27 ♖xb7 f4 28 ♘e5!** Black cannot avoid being checkmated, e.g. 28 ... fxg3 29 ♘g4!. **28 ... ♖f5 29 ♘g4 1-0**

(Notes based on Lerner's)

5 Torre-Petrosian Attack: Main Line without an early queenside fianchetto

1	d4	♘f6
2	♘f3	e6
3	♗g5	c5
4	e3	d5
5	♘bd2	

An eccentric idea is to keep the QN in reserve: 5 c3 ♗e7 6 ♗d3 ♘bd7 7 0-0 b6 8 ♘e5?! ♘xe5 9 dxe5 ♘d7 10 ♗f4?! ∞ Vaganian-Timman, Illustrative Game No 32.

5 ... ♗e7

A less common alternative to 5 ... ♗e7 is 5 ... ♘bd7 6 c3 ♗d6 7 ♗d3 h6 8 ♗h4 0-0 (8 ... e5? see Varnusz-Schepp) 9 0-0 b6 10 e4 dxe4 11 ♘xe4 ♗e7 12 dxc5 ♘xc5 13 ♘xc5 bxc5 14 ♕e2 ± Meister-Pigusov, Togliatti 1985.

6 c3

Black's set-up seems quite natural but he has problems owing to his idle bishop on c8. The saying 'a passive piece – a passive game' perfectly suits the black QB. So, eventually, Black will have to play ... ♗b7 or, to release his minor piece, ... e6-e5.

It should be noted that 5 ... ♕b6 leads to Chapter 3, whereas 5 ... ♘c6 is usually a simple transposition in move order, although 6 c3 may bring about significant deviations. E.g:

(a) 6 ... cxd4 7 exd4 ♗d6 8 ♗d3 ♗d7 9 0-0 ♖c8 10 ♖e1 ♕c7 11 ♕e2 h6 12 ♗h4 ♘h5 13 ♗g3 ♘xg3 14 hxg3 0-0 15 ♘e5 ♘xe5 16 dxe5 ± Tartakower-Sämisch, Vienna 1921.

(b) 6 ... ♕b6 7 ♕b3 ♗e7 8 ♗e2 0-0 9 0-0 ♖e8 10 ♖d1 cxd4 11 cxd4 ♘e4 12 ♗xe7 ♘xd2 13 ♖xd2 ♖xe7 14 ♗d3 ♕xb3?! 15 axb3 ♗d7 16 ♖a1 ± Trifunović-Averbakh, USSR v Yugoslavia 1961.

(c) 6 ... ♗d6 7 ♗d3 h6 8 ♗h4 0-0 (8 ... e5?! 9 dxe5 ♘xe5 10 ♘xe5 ♗xe5 11 ♘f3 ♗c7 12 ♗b5+ ♔e7 13 0-0 ±) 9 0-0 (9 ♕e2 e5 10 dxc5 ♗xc5 11 e4 d4 12 ♘b3 ± Tseitlin-Inkiov, Lódz 1980) 9 ... e5?! 10 e4 exd4 11 exd5 dxc3 12 ♘e4 cxb2 13 ♘xf6+ gxf6 14 ♕d2! ♔g7 15 ♖ae1 ± Tseitlin-Rogulj,

Lódz 1980.

(d) 6 ... h6 7 ♗h4 ♗e7 (7 ... ♗d6 8 ♗d3 e5? 9 dxe5 ♘xe5 10 ♘xe5 ♗xe5 11 ♘f3 ♗g4? 12 ♕a4+! ♗d7 13 ♗b5! a6 14 ♗xd7+ ♕xd7 15 ♕xd7+ ♘xd7 16 0-0-0 g5 17 ♘xe5 ♘xe5 18 ♗g3 +− Varnusz-Schepp, Pécs 1991) 8 ♗d3 0-0 9 0-0 ♘e8 10 ♗xe7 ♕xe7 11 dxc5 ♕xc5 12 e4 dxe4 13 ♘xe4 ♕e7 14 ♖e1 e5 15 ♘g3 ♘f6 16 ♗b5 ±, Trifunović-Velimirović, Yugoslavia 1963.

From the position shown in the diagram there are two common continuations, 6 ... ♘c6 and 6 ... ♘bd7. Rare lines are 6 ... 0-0 7 ♗d3 b6 8 ♘e5 ♗b7 (8 ... ♘fd7 9 ♕h5 g6 10 ♗xe7 ♕xe7 11 ♕h6 ♘xe5 12 dxe5 ♘c6 13 f4 f6 14 ♗b5 ♘d8 15 ♘f3 ⩲ Kiseliov-Ivanenko, Moscow 1984) 9 f4 (9 0-0 ♘bd7 – 9 ... ♘fd7 10 ♗xe7 ♕xe7 11 f4 ♗a6 12 ♗xa6 ♘xa6 13 ♕a4 ♘ab8 14 b4! ⩲ Spassky-Hübner, Montreal 1979 – 10 ♕a4 h6 11 ♗h4 ♘xe5 12 dxe5 ♘d7 13 ♗g3 ♕c7?! 14 ♘f3 ± Kavalek-Ravi, Illustrative Game No 41; 9 ♗xf6 ♗xf6 10 f4 ♗a6 11 ♗xa6 ♘xa6 12 ♘df3 ♘c7 13 ♕e2 ♘e8 = Platonov-Dolmatov, Tashkent 1980) 9 ... ♘e4 10 ♗xe7 ♕xe7 11 0-0 f6 12 ♘ef3 ♘d7 13 ♕c2 f5 14 ♗b5 ⩲ Petrosian-Gligorić, Illustrative Game No 36.

5.1

6	**...**	**♘c6?!**
7	**♗d3**	**♘d7**

This exchange does not free the bishop either. Other replies are not much better, though:

(a) 7 ... h6 8 ♗h4 cxd4 9 exd4 ♘h5 (9 ... ♕c7 10 0-0 0-0 11 ♖e1 ♘h5 12 ♗xe7 ♕xe7 13 ♘f1 f5? 14 ♗b5! ♘f6 15 ♗xc6 bxc6 16 ♘e5 ± Polugayevsky-Padevsky, Budapest 1965) 10 ♗xe7 ♕xe7 11 0-0 ♘f4 12 ♗c2 ♕f6 13 ♖e1 0-0 14 g3 ♘g6 15 ♕e2 b6 16 h4 ± Spassky-Matanović, Illustrative Game No 37.

(b) 7 ... ♕b6 8 ♖b1 ♗d7 9 0-0 a6 10 ♘e5 cxd4 11 exd4 ♘xe5 12 dxe5 ♘g8 13 ♕g4 ± Trifunović-Puc, Yugoslavia 1945. A more aggressive line for Black is 7 ... ♕b6 8 ♖b1 h6 9 ♗h4 cxd4 10 exd4 g5!? 11 ♗g3 ♘h5 (∞) 12 ♗e5? ♘xe5 13 ♘xe5 ♘f4 14 ♗f1 ♗d6 ⩱ Pecorelli-G.Garcia, Havana 1986.

(c) 7 ... ♕c7 8 0-0 0-0 9 dxc5!

Trifunović-Udovčić, Yugoslavia, 1948.

(d) 7 ... cxd4 8 exd4 h6 9 ♗f4?! ♘h5 10 ♗e3 ♘f6 11 ♘e5 ♘xe5 12 dxe5 ♘d7 13 ♗d4 ± Petrosian-Mecking, Illustrative Game No 38.

8 ♗xe7

8 ♗f4 0-0 9 0-0 ♗f6 ∞ O. Rodriguez-Beliavsky, 1984.

8	**...**	**♕xe7**
9	**0-0**	**0-0**
10	**♖e1**	**♕f6?!**
11	**♗b5!**	**♕d8**
12	**♖c1**	**♕b6**
13	**♗xc6 ±**	

Timman-Beliavsky, Illustrative Game No 39.

5.2

6	**...**	**♘bd7**
7	**♗d3**	

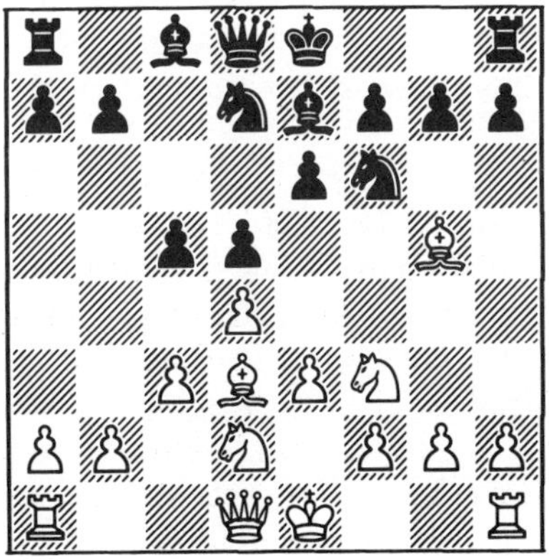

It is advisable to complete one's development instead of fighting an early close-range battle, the outcome of which is dubious: 7 ♘e5?! ♘xe5 8 dxe5 ♘d7 9 ♗f4 ♕c7 10 ♘f3 b6 (Here or on move move 9 better was ... h6 as in Spassky-Petrosian, Illustrative Game No 43, next chapter.) 11 ♗d3 ♗b7? 12 ♕e2 ♗c6 13 0-0 0-0 14 b4! ± Petrosian-Bouwmeester, Beverwijk 1960.

5.21

7	**...**	**a6?!**

Black should control e5 (see 5.22). Some other inferior lines:

(a) 7 ... h6?! (The drawback of this move is that White's bishop will be able to avoid exchange when necessary.) 8 ♗h4 0-0 (8 ... b6 may be better; see introduction to Chapter 6) 9 ♘e5 ♘xe5 10 dxe5 ♘d7 11 ♗g3! (The bishop has done it!) 11 ... f5 12 exf6 ♗xf6 13 ♕h5! ♕b6 (13 ... ♕e8?! 14 ♕xe8 ♖xe8 15 ♗g6 ±) 14 ♖b1 c4 15 ♗c2 ♘c5 16 0-0 ♗d7 17 ♕g6 ± Bronstein-Janošević, Belgrade 1954.

(b) 7 ... 0-0? (Castling into it.) 8 ♘e5! (More vigorous now than after White has castled.) 8 ... ♘xe5 9 dxe5 ♘d7 10 ♗f4! (The underlying tactical motif is 10 ... f6 11 ♕h5 g6? 12 ♗xg6! hxg6 13 ♕xg6+ ♔h8 14 h4! ±±.) 10 ... f5 11 h4! and Black has a cramped game, Petrosian-Lyublinsky, Illustrative Game No 40.

(c) 7 ... c4 is perhaps a bit too uncompromising! 8 ♗c2 b5 9 0-0 (9 e4?! dxe4 10 ♘xe4 ♗b7 =) 9 ... ♗b7 10 ♘e5! ♘xe5 11 dxe5 ♘d7 12 ♗f4 Grivas-P.Blatny, Haifa 1989; 12 ... ♕b6! ∞. White improves with 12 ♗xe7 ♕xe7 13 f4 ±; Black's pawns are slightly overextended.

8	**0-0**	**b5?**
9	**♘e5!**	**♗b7**
10	**f4**	**c4**
11	**♗c2**	**♘e4**
12	**♗xe7**	**♕xe7**
13	**♗xe4!**	**dxe4**
14	**♘xd7**	**♕xd7**
15	**b3!** ±	

White's game is superior since a knight is worth more than a bishop in a blocked position. 15 ... 0-0 16 bxc4 bxc4 17 ♕c2 ♕c6 18 ♖ab1 a5 19 ♖b2! ± Seirawan-Larsen, Linares 1983.

5.22

7	**...**	**♕c7!**

Keeping an eye on e5.

8	**0-0**	**0-0**

8 ... e5? 9 dxe5 ♘xe5 10 ♘xe5 ♕xe5 11 ♗b5+ ±.

9	**♕e2**	

9 e4 dxe4 10 ♘xe4 b6 (10 ... ♖e8!?) 11 ♕c2 h6 12 ♗h4 ± (Alekhine).

9	**...**	**b6**

9 ... e5?! releases the bishop but exposes Black's poor development: 10 e4! dxe4 11 ♘xe4 exd4 12 cxd4 b6 13 ♘xf6+ ♘xf6 14 ♖fe1 ±.

10	**e4**	

10 ♖ac1!? ♗b7 11 c4 leads to a Queen's Gambit type of position with a slight plus for White: 11 ... ♖fe8 12 dxc5 bxc5 13 ♖fd1 ♖ac8 14 cxd5 exd5 15 ♗f5 g6 16 ♗h3 ± Petrosian-Matanović, USSR v Yugoslavia 1956.

10	**...**	**dxe4**
11	**♘xe4**	**♗b7**
12	**♖ad1**	

12 dxc5 ♘xc5 13 ♘xc5 ♕xc5 14 ♗xf6 ♗xf6 = Tartakower-Capablanca, Nottingham 1936.

12	**...**	**♖fe8**

This type of position is familiar from the French and the Caro-Kann, with White having a small advantage in space, e.g. 13 dxc5 bxc5 (13 ... ♘xc5!? 14 ♘xf6+ ♗xf6 15 ♗xf6 gxf6 ±) 14 ♘g3 ♖ad8 15 ♖fe1 ♕c8 16 ♖d2 h6 17 ♗xf6 ♘xf6 18 ♘e5 ± Kholmov-Gipslis, USSR 1962.

ILLUSTRATIVE GAMES

1 d4 ♘f6 2 ♘f3 e6 3 ♗g5 c5 4 e3 d5 5 ♘bd2 ♗e7 6 c3

35) **Vaganian-Timman**
Tilburg 1983

5 c3 ♗e7 6 ♗d3 ♘bd7 7 0-0 b6 8 ♘e5?! White should not start his offensive before developing his queenside pieces. **8 ... ♘xe5 9 dxe5 ♘d7 10 ♗f4?!** 10 ♗xe7 =. **10 ... ♗b7 11 c4?!** The point of White's strategy. Still, the opening up of the position is in Black's favour. For 11 ♘d2 see Chapter 6. **11 ... dxc4 12 ♗xc4 ♕c7 13 ♗b5** There is no better. 13 ♕g4?? g5! 14 ♗g3 h5 ∓∓. **13 ... a6 14 ♗xd7+ ♕xd7 15 ♘d2 g5! 16 ♗g3 ♖d8 17 ♘f3 ♕c6 18 ♕e2 h5!**

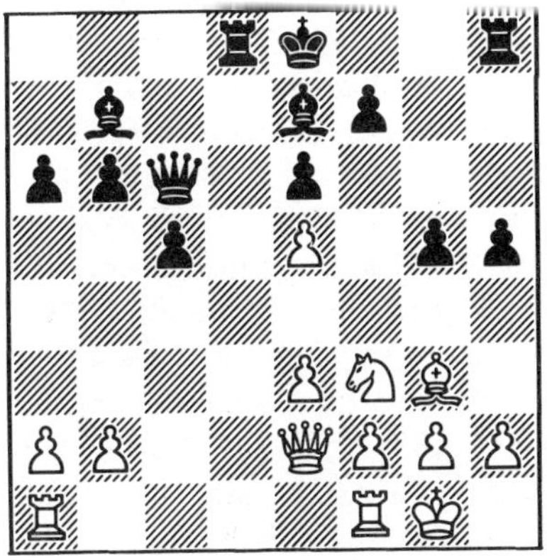

19 h3 g4 20 hxg4 hxg4 21 ♘e1 ♕e4 22 f3 gxf3 23 ♘xf3 23 ♕xf3 ♖h1+! 24 ♔f2 ♖xf1+ 25 ♔xf1 ♕xf3+ 26 ♘xf3 ♗xf3 27 gxf3 ♖d2 ∓∓. **23 ... ♕g4 24 ♗f4 ♖g8 25 ♖f2 ♖d7 26 ♘h2 ♕g6 27 ♘f3 ♕g4 28 ♘h2 ♕h3 29 ♔h1 ♗h4 30 e4 ♕d3** Black's offensive could not get through so he goes over to a favourable endgame. **31 ♕xd3 ♖xd3 32 ♖e2 ♖h8 33 ♔g1 ♖g8 34 ♔f1 ♗e7 35 ♖ae1 c4** A scattered pawn formation on one side, two bishops, activity and a queenside material surplus on the other. **36 ♘f3 ♖h8 37 ♔f2 b5 38 ♖d2?** An oversight in a lost position. **38 ... ♗b4! 39 ♖xd3 ♗xe1+ 40 ♘xe1 cxd3 41 ♘xd3 ♔d7 42 b4 ♖h1 43 ♘c5+ ♔c7 44 ♔g3 ♖a1 45 ♔h4 ♖xa2 0-1**

36) **Petrosian-Gligorić**
Nikšić 1983

6 ... 0-0 7 ♗d3 b6 8 ♘e5 With Black's queen's knight still on b8, White did not have to take any risks to reach the typical set-up. **8 ... ♗b7 9 f4** 9 ♕f3!? **9 ... ♘e4 10 ♗xe7 ♕xe7 11 0-0 f6 12 ♘ef3 ♘d7 13 ♕c2 f5** Theoretically speaking, White has emerged from the opening with a plus controlling e4 with his bishop while Black cannot hold e5 so firmly. **14 ♗b5!** The threat is already 15 ♗xd7, dominating e5. **14 ... ♘df6 15 ♘xe4 dxe4** 15 ... fxe4!?. **16 ♘e5 a6 17 ♗e2 ♘d5 18 ♕d2 cxd4 19 cxd4** 19 exd4 ±. **19 ... ♖ac8** 20 ... ♕b4 is threatened which was wrong just now because of the queen exchange and ♘d7!. **20 a3 g5?!** Very risky. 21 ... ♖c7! is practically =. **21 ♗c4** 21 g3? gxf4 22 gxf4 ♕g7+ 23 ♔h1 ♖c2! ∓.

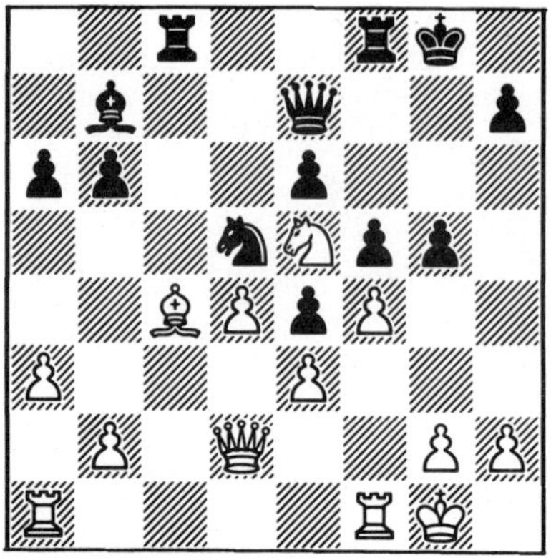

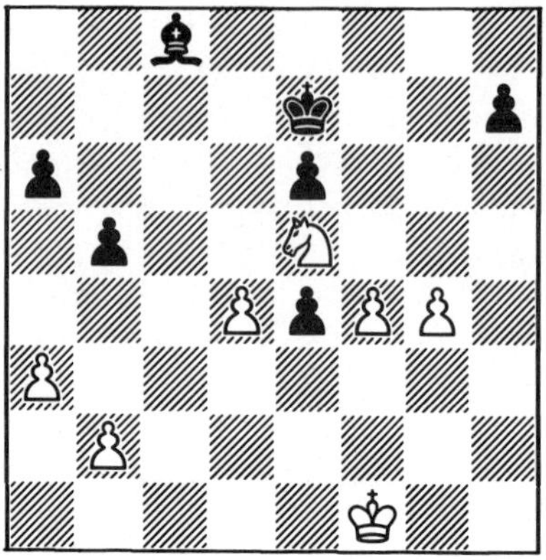

21 ... ♖xc4!? Gligorić sacrifices the exchange in Petrosian's style, not letting White obtain a good knight against a bad bishop after 22 ♗xd5. 21 ... gxf4?! 22 ♗xd5 fxe3 23 ♗xe6+ ♕xe6 24 ♕xe3 ±. **22 ♘xc4 b5!** 22 ... gxf4? 23 exf4 and ♘e3 ±. **23 ♘e5** 23 ♘a5? gxf4 24 exf4 ♗a8 =. **23 ... gxf4 24 ♖xf4!** Petrosian still aims for the good knight v. bad bishop motif and returns the exchange. 24 exf4 ♔h8! is dubious owing to the weakness of the long diagonal. **24 ... ♘xf4 25 exf4 ♖c8** 25 ... ♖d8!?. **26 ♖c1 ♖xc1+ 27 ♕xc1 ♕h4 28 h3!** The threat is 29 ♕c7!. **28 ... ♕d8 29 ♕c3 ♔f8 30 ♔f1 ♕c8 31 ♕c5+! ♔e8** Petrosian increases his advantage in his usual refined way. 31 ... ♕xc5? 32 dxc5 +−. **32 g4 fxg4 33 ♕xc8+ ♗xc8 34 hxg4 ♔e7?** 34 ... h6 defends better.

35 ♔e2? What a pity! 35 g5! would have blocked the h7 pawn and ♔e2-e3 then ♘g4-f6 would have been an easy win for White. **35 ... h6 36 ♔e3 ♗b7 37 ♘g6+?** Was this time trouble or was the Armenian grandmaster ageing too quickly? Blocking the a6 weakness by 37 b4! is still a likely win. **37 ... ♔f6 38 ♘h4 a5! 39 b4 axb4 40 axb4 ♗d5 41 ♔f2 ♗c6 42 ♔g3 e3 43 ♘g2 e2 44 ♘e1 ♗e8 ½-½**

45 ♔f2 h5 46 g5+ ♔f5 47 ♘d3 ♔e4 48 ♔xe2 ♔xd4 49 ♘e5 h4! 50 g6 ♗xg6 51 ♘xg6 h3 52 ♔f2 ♔c3 53 ♘f8 ♔xb4 54 ♘xe6 ♔c4 =.

(Notes based on Petrosian's)

37) **Spassky-Matanović**
Havana 1962

6 ... ♘c6 7 ♗d3 h6 8 ♗h4 cxd4 9 exd4 ♘h5?! The knight will now constantly be in search of a post for himself. **10 ♗xe7 ♕xe7 11 0-0 ♘f4 12 ♗c2 ♕f6 13 ♖e1 0-0 14 g3 ♘g6 15 ♕e2 b6 16 h4! ♖e8 17 ♘e5 ♘cxe5 18 dxe5 ♕e7 19 ♘f3 a5** Black has found a diagonal for his bad bishop at last but now there is a considerable difference between the power of the two knights. More important, the e5 outpost prevents Black from regrouping his pieces to aid his king. **20 ♘d4 ♗d7 21 ♗d3 ♖ab8 22 a4 ♘f8 23 f4 ♖ec8 24 ♔h2 ♕e8 25 g4! ♘g6 26 ♕f2 ♕e7 27 h5 ♘f8 28 ♖g1! f6 29 ♖ae1! ♗xa4 30 ♕g3 ♗e8 31 exf6 ♕xf6 32 ♖e5 ♕f7**

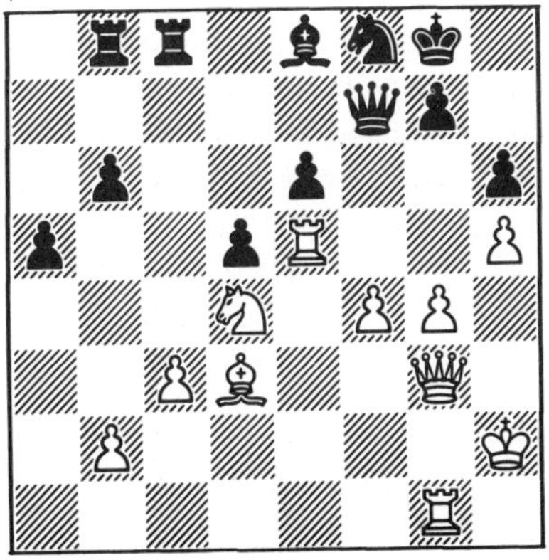

33 g5! Elegant! **33 ... ♕xh5+ 34 ♔g2 hxg5 35 fxg5 ♕f7 36 ♖f1 ♕e7 37 g6 ♖c4 38 ♖h5 ♖xd4 39 ♖xf8+!! 1-0**

39 ... ♕xf8 40 ♖h8+ ♔xh8 41 ♕h3+.

38) **Petrosian-Mecking**
Wijk aan Zee 1971

6 ... ♘c6 7 ♗d3 cxd4?! 8 exd4 h6 9 ♗f4!? ♘h5 10 ♗e3 ♘f6 11 ♘e5! ♘xe5 12 dxe5 ♘d7 A typical position. It is characterised by the e5 outpost, dividing Black's pieces and hindering their regrouping. **13 ♗d4 ♘c5 14 ♗c2 a5 15 ♕g4!** Preventing ... 0-0. **15 ... g6 16 0-0 ♗d7 17 ♖fe1 ♕c7 18 a4** Otherwise Black would gain space on this wing. The opening seemed to prepare an attack on the king but Petrosian is always Petrosian: he wants to squash Mecking positionally. **18 ... ♘a6 19 ♕e2 ♕f8 20 ♘f3 ♔g7 21 ♗e3 ♘c5 22 ♘d4 ♖a6 23 ♗c1 ♖aa8 24 g3 b6 25 h4! h5** Black ought not to be worried about actual threats, yet he has not got counterplay either. **26 ♕f3 ♕d8 27 ♗d2 ♕e8?** Losing his patience, Mecking weakens the dark squares around his king.

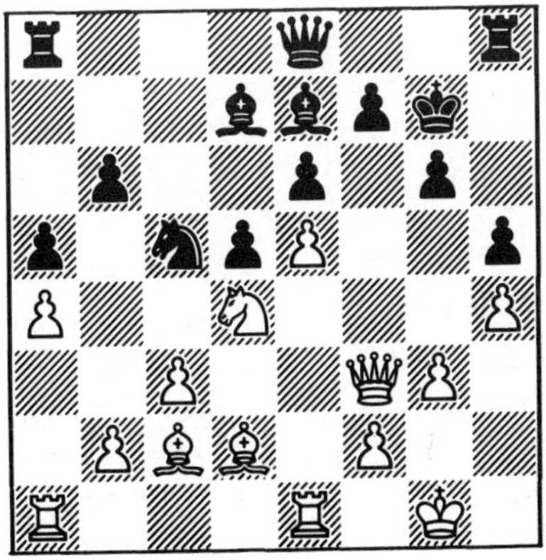

28 ♗g5! ♕d8 28 ... ♗xg5 29 hxg5 ♗xa4 30 ♗xa4 ♘xa4 31 ♖xa4! ♕xa4 32 ♘xe6+! fxe6 33 ♕f6+ ♔g8 34 ♕xg6+ ♔f8 35 ♕f6+ ♔g8 36 ♕xe6+ ♔g7 37 ♕f6+ ♔g8 38 ♕g6+ ♔f8 39 ♖e3 +−. **29 ♕f4 ♖c8 30 ♖e3! ♗xg5 31 hxg5** White's space advantage looks more and more threatening. **31 ... ♖a8 32 ♕f6+! ♕xf6 33 exf6+ ♔h7 34 ♔g2 ♖ae8 35 f4 ♖b8 36 ♖ee1 ♘b7 37 ♖h1 ♔g8 38 ♘f3 ♘d6 39 ♘e5 ♗e8 40 ♗d3 ♖c8 41 ♔f3 ♗c6 42 ♖h2 ♗e8 43 ♔e3 ♖c7 44 ♔d4 ♘b7 45 b4!** Slowly but surely! **45 ... ♘d8 46 ♖h4 ♘b7 47 ♖a2 ♘d6 48 ♖h1 ♘b7 49 b5! ♘c5 50 ♗c2 ♘d7 51 ♖a3 ♘c5**

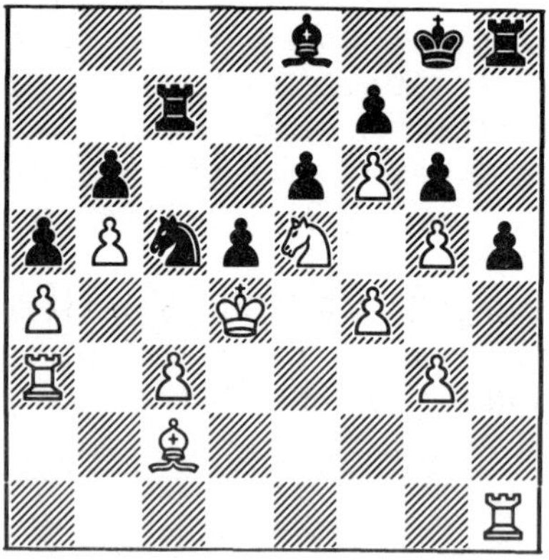

52 c4! Black's pieces are very passive. All that White needs is an open file. **52 ... ♘d7 53 ♖c3 ♘xe5 54 ♔xe5 dxc4 55 ♗e4! ♖c8 56 ♔d6! ♖c5 57 ♖hc1 h4 1-0**

Typically Petrosian! The final stage would have gone like this: 58 ♖xc4 ♖xc4 59 ♖xc4 hxg3 60 ♖c8 ♔h7 61 ♖c3 ♔g8 62 ♔e7! ♔h7 63 ♖xg3 etc. (Based on notes by Ivkov.

39) **Timman-Beliavsky**
Wijk aan Zee 1985

6 ... ♘c6 7 ♗d3 ♘d7 8 ♗xe7 ♕xe7 9 0-0 0-0 9 ... e5? 10 e4 dxe4 11 ♗xe4 cxd4 12 ♗xc6 bxc6 13 cxd4 0-0 14 ♖e1 ±. **10 ♖e1 ♕f6?!** 10 ... ♖d8! 11 ♕c2 h6 12 ♖ad1 ±. **11 ♗b5!** Preventing Black from freeing his pieces. **11 ... ♕d8 12 ♖c1** Also good is 12 dxc5 ♘xc5 13 b4 ♘d7 14 e4 ♘b6 15 ♕b3. **12 ... ♕b6** 12 ... a6 13 ♗xc6 bxc6 14 c4 ♕b6 15 ♘b3 ±. **13 ♗xc6 bxc6** 13 ... ♕xc6 14 c4!. **14 ♕c2 a5 15 ♘g5 g6** 15 ... ♘f6 16 ♘b3 c4 17 ♘c5 ±. **16 dxc5 ♕xc5 17 e4 ♗a6 18 e5 ♕e7 19 ♘gf3 f6?!** Black tries to break through the blockade but his pawns become very weak in the newly opened position. Somewhat better is 19 ... c5 20 c4 d4 21 ♘e4 ♗b7 22 ♕d2! ±. **20 c4! ♖ae8 21 ♕c3 ♕b4 22 exf6 ♖xf6 23 ♘e5 ♕xc3 24** ♖xc3 ♘xe5 25 **♖xe5 ♖b8 26 b3 a4 27 f3 axb3 28 axb3 ♔f7 29 ♖e1 ♗c8** The threat was 30 ♖a1!. The bishop remains passive throughout the game while White's knight will soon occupy the e5 stronghold.

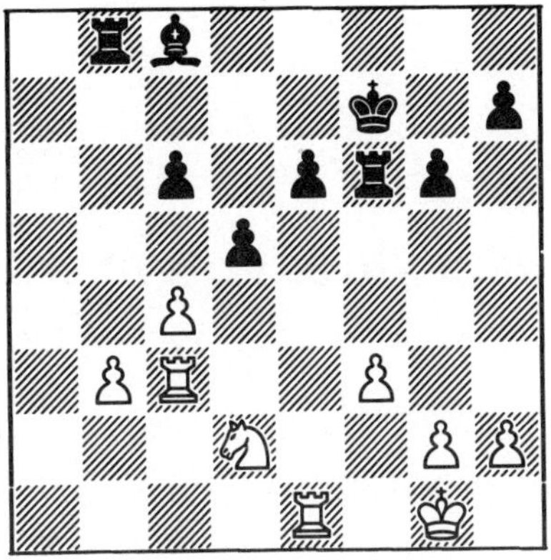

30 cxd5! exd5 30 ... cxd5 31 ♖c7+ ♔g8 32 ♖ec1 ♗b7 33 ♖e7 ±. **31 f4! ♖b6** 31 ... ♖xf4 32 ♖xc6 ♔g8 33 ♖d6 ±. **32 g3 ♖e6 33 ♖ec1 ♔e7** 33 ... ♖e2 34 ♘f3 ♖b2? 35 ♘d4 ±. **34 ♘f3 ♗d7 35 ♘e5 g5!? 36 ♘xd7 ♔xd7 37 fxg5 ♖e2?** 37 ... ♔d6 gave the last chance. **38 ♖f3 ♖a6 39 ♖f7+ ♔d6 40 ♖cf1 d4 41 ♖xh7 ♖aa2 42 g6 ♖g2+ 1-0**

(Mikhalchishin's notes included)

40) **Petrosian-Lyublinsky**
USSR Championship 1949

6 ... ♘bd7 7 ♗d3 0-0? 8 ♘e5! ♘xe5 9 dxe5 ♘d7 10 ♗f4! f5 11 h4! An important blockading move. **11 ... c4 12 ♗c2 b5?!** A bit better is 12 ... ♘c5! 13 ♘f3 ♗d7 14 ♘d4 ♕b6 15 ♗g5 ♖f7?! 16 ♗xe7 ♖xe7 17 ♕b1! ± Petrosian-Bannik, USSR 1951. **13 ♘f3 ♘c5 14 g4! b4 15 gxf5** 15 cxb4? ♘xd3+! is unclear. **15 ... exf5 16 ♘g5 g6?** 16 ... h6! would have avoided an immediate collapse: 17 ♕h5 ♘d3+ 18 ♗xd3 cxd3 19 ♕g6 hxg5 20 hxg5 ♕e8 21 ♕h7+ ♔f7 22 ♖h6 etc.

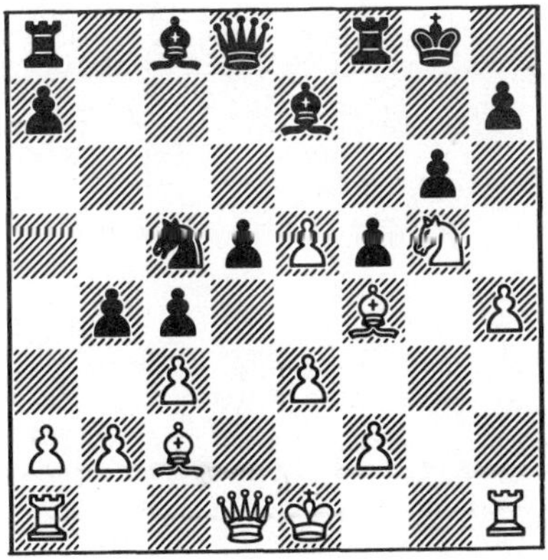

17 h5! ♘d3+ Winning a piece is forbidden since the d5 pawn is *en prise*. **18 ♗xd3 cxd3 19 hxg6 hxg6** 19 ... ♗xg5 20 ♖xh7!. **20 ♕xd3 bxc3 21 bxc3 ♗xg5 22 ♗xg5 ♕a5 23 ♗f6 ♖e8 24 ♕d4 ♔f7 25 e6+ ♖xe6 26 ♗d8 1-0**

6 Torre-Petrosian Attack: Main Line with a queenside fianchetto

1	**d4**	**♘f6**
2	**♘f3**	**e6**
3	**♗g5**	**c5**
4	**e3**	**d5**
5	**♘bd2**	**♗e7**
6	**c3**	**♘bd7**
7	**♗d3**	**b6**

When Black plays ... d7-d5 it is most advisable for him to activate his queen's bishop on the flank as soon as possible, but he should not hurry with castling since his castled king may be exposed to White's attack. Black does not have better prospects of equalising here than in the other variations.

Black can try throwing in ... h6, ♗h4 at some stage, but this is unlikely to be of positive assistance to him, and might be harmful as the g6 square will be weak after an eventual ... f6. Black was able to reach a playable position though in Yusupov-Speelman, Hastings 1989/90: 3 ... ♗e7 4 ♘bd2 h6 5 ♗h4 d5 6 e3 ♘bd7 7 c3 c5 8 ♗d3 b6 (compare with the diagram position) 9 ♘e5 (9 0-0!? looks more promising) 9 ... ♘xe5 10 dxe5 ♘d7 11 ♗xe7 ♕xe7 12 f4 ♗b7 13 ♕e2 0-0-0 14 0-0-0?! (14 0-0 ±) 14 ... f6 ∓.

8 0-0

Completing development is common sense. Other ideas:

(a) 8 ♘e5?! (This should be postponed until Black castles his king.) 8 ... ♘xe5 9 dxe5 ♘d7 10 ♗xe7 ♕xe7 11 f4 f6 (11 ... ♗b7 12 0-0 0-0-0 13 a4 f6 14 a5?! c4! 15

axb6 axb6 16 exf6 ♕c5! 17 fxg7 ♖g8 18 ♗e2 ♕xe3+ 19 ♔h1 ♖xg7 ∓ Rechlis-Arnason, Beer Sheva 1987) 12 ♕h5+ (After 12 ♘f3 fxe5, ineffective is 13 ♗b5 while 12 exf6 ♘xf6 gives an easy game for Black. This position was reached via 11 ... f5 12 exf6 ♘xf6 in Machulsky-Fernandez, Managua 1987, and White was slightly better after 13 0-0 0-0 14 e4 dxe4 15 ♘xe4 ♗b7 16 ♕e2; maybe 14 ... ♗b7 instead) 12 ... ♕f7 =.

(b) 8 ♕e2 (A natural move but it does not contribute to the success of a close-range fight after ♘e5.) 8 ... ♗b7 9 0-0 h6 10 ♗h4 0-0 11 ♗a6; see 6.1.

(c) 8 ♗b5 ♗b7 (8 ... a6 9 ♗c6 ♖a7 10 ♘e5 0-0 =) 9 ♘e5 0-0 10 ♘c6 ♗xc6 11 ♗xc6 ♖c8 =.

(d) 8 ♕a4 0-0 (8 ... h6 9 ♗xf6 ♗xf6 10 e4 ♗b7 11 e5 ♗e7 12 0-0 a6 13 dxc5 bxc5 14 ♕g4 ∞ Kharitonov-Novikov, USSR 1984) 9 ♘e5 ♗b7 (9 ... ♘xe5? 10 dxe5 ♘d7 11 ♗xh7+!) 10 ♘c6 ♗xc6 11 ♕xc6 a6! 12 ♕a4 b5 13 ♕d1 b4 14 c4 cxd4 15 exd4 dxc4 ∓ Slipak-Panno, Buenos Aires 1984.

The main lines here consist of 8 ... 0-0 and 8 ... ♗b7. A digression: 8 ... h6 9 ♗h4 0-0 10 ♘e5 ♘xe5 (10 ... ♗b7 11 f4 – 11 ♕f3?! ♘xe5! 12 dxe5 ♘e4! – 11 ... ♘e4 12 ♗xe7 ♕xe7 13 ♘df3 ♘df6 14 ♕e1 ±) 11 dxe5 ♘d7 12 ♗g3!? (The drawback of the early ... h6) 12 ... ♗b7 (12 ... ♗h4?! 13 ♗xh4 ♕xh4 14 f4 ♗b7 15 ♖f3 ♕e7 16 ♖g3 ♔h8 17 ♕h5 ± Tartakower-Keres, Kemeri 1937) 13 ♕g4 c4! (13 ... ♕c8? 14 ♗f4 ± Bronstein-Roizman, USSR 1963) 14 ♗e2 ♘c5 15 ♖ad1 ♘d3 16 ♗xd3 cxd3 17 ♘f3 ♗a6 ∞ Kavalek-De Firmian, USA 1985.

6.1

8 ... 0-0

6.11

9 ♕c2

(a) 9 ♕e2 h6 10 ♗h4 ♗b7 11 ♗a6 ♗xa6 12 ♕xa6 ♕c8 (12 ... ♕c7?! 13 a4 c4 14 ♗g3 ♕c8 15 ♕xc8 ♖fxc8 16 ♘e5 ♘xe5 17 ♗xe5 a6 18 ♗xf6 ♗xf6 19 e4 ± Mariotti-Beliavsky, Leningrad 1977) 13 ♕xc8 ♖fxc8 14 ♘e5 ♘xe5 15 dxe5 ♘e4 =.

(b) 9 ♕b1 h6 (9 ... ♗b7 10 b4 cxd4 11 cxd4 ♖c8 12 b5 h6 13 ♗h4 ♖c3 = Hübner Keene, Hastings 1969/70) 10 ♗h4 ♗b7 11 b4 (11 ♘e5? ♘xe5 12 dxe5 ♘g4! 13 ♗g3 ♗h4! 14 ♗xh4 – 14 ♗f4 g5! 15 ♕d1 ♘xf2! – 14 ... ♕xh4 15 ♘f3 ♕h5 ∓ Smyslov-Suetin, USSR 1971) 11 ... cxb4 12 cxb4 ♖c8 13 ♕b2 ♘e4 = Sigurjonsson-Weinstein, Wijk aan Zee 1975.

(c) 9 e4 dxe4 10 ♘xe4 ♗b7 11 ♘xf6+ (11 ♗xf6 ♘xf6 12 ♘xf6+ ♗xf6 13 dxc5 bxc5 14 ♕e2 ♖b8 = Knežević-Matulović, Yugoslavia 1965) 11 ... ♘xf6 12 dxc5 bxc5 13 ♖e1 ♕c7 14 ♘e5 ♖ad8 15 ♕c2 ∞.

(d) 9 ♕a4 ♗b7 10 ♘e5 a6 11 f4 c4?! 12 ♗e2 b5 13 ♕c2 ♘b6 14 ♗xf6 gxf6 15 ♘ef3 f5 16 h3 ♔h8 17 ♔h1 ± M.Piket-Deppe, Dinard 1987.

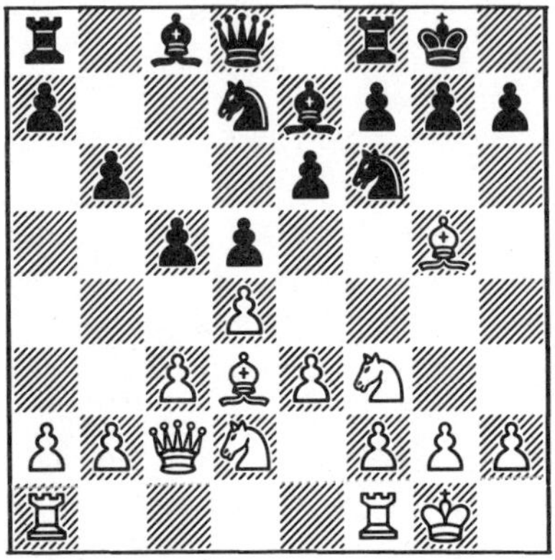

9 ... h6!

9 ... ♗b7?! 10 ♘e5! (10 ♖ae1 c4 11 ♗e2 b5! 12 ♘e5 ♘xe5 13 dxe5 ♘e4 14 ♗xe7 ♕xe7 15 f4 ♕c5 16 ♖f3 f5 17 exf6 ♘xf6 = E.Torre-Sokolov, Biel 1985) 10 ... h6 11 ♗xf6! ♘xf6 12 f4 ♗d6 13 ♖f3! ±.

10 ♗h4 ♗b7
11 ♖ae1 c4
12 ♗e2 b5 =

12 ... ♕c7?! 13 ♗g3 ♗d6 14 ♗xd6 ♕xd6 15 e4! ± Spassky-Reshevsky, Amsterdam 1964. The text line was Sokolov's original intention, but care needs to be taken with the move order.

6.12

9 ♘e5!

The basic idea of the opening!

9 ... ♗b7

After Black has castled, the swap is more troublesome though still playable: 9 ... ♘xe5 10 dxe5 ♘d7 11 ♗xe7 (11 ♗f4?! f5!) 11 ... ♕xe7 12 f4 ♗b7 (12 ... f5 13 exf6 ♖xf6 14 e4 ♗b7 15 e5 ♖f7 16 ♕g4 g6 17 ♖ad1 ♖d8 18 ♘g5 ± Trifunović-Filip, Varna 1962) 13 ♕h5 g6 14 ♕e2 f5 15 exf6 ♘xf6 16 e4 ± Gudmundsson-Matanović, Varna 1962.

10 f4

Once again a logical move, though other plans are also feasible:

(a) 10 ♕a4 h6 11 ♘xd7?! ♘xd7 12 ♗f4 a5 13 ♖fe1 ♖c8 14 ♖ac1 ♘f6 = Brahmeyer-Pietzsch, Weimar 1968. Better is 11 ♗h4! ♘xe5 12 dxe5 ± Kavalek-Ravi, Illustrative Game No 41.

(b) 10 ♕f3 h6 (10 ... ♘xe5 11 dxe5 ♘e4? 12 ♗xe7 ♘xd2 13 ♗xh7+!) 11 ♗f4 ♘xe5 12 dxe5 ♘h7 Trifunović-Filipćić, Yugoslavia 1945; 13 ♕g4! ±.

(c) 10 ♕b1 h6 11 ♗xf6 ♗xf6 12 ♘xd7 ♕xd7 13 f4 ♗c6 14 ♖f3 ♗b5 15 ♖h3 ♗xd3 16 ♕xd3 ♗e7 17 ♘f3 ♗d6 18 g4 ± Sokolov-Pisimeni, USSR 1974.

10 ... ♘e4

10 ... a6? 11 ♕f3 ♘xe5?! 12 fxe5 ♘d7 13 ♕h3 +− C.Torre-

Verlinsky, Illustrative Game No 42.

11 ♗xe7 ♕xe7
12 ♘xd7 ♕xd7

12 ... ♘xd2? 13 ♗xh7+! ♔xh7 14 ♘xf8+.

13 ♘f3 ±

6.2

8 ... ♗b7

Very popular these days. Black delays castling.

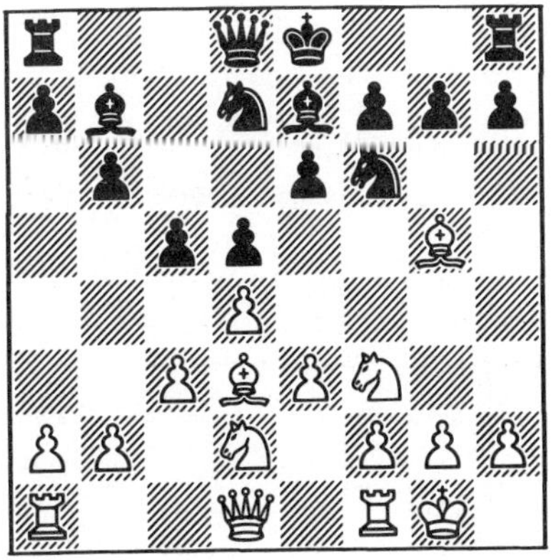

9 ♘e5

The 'patented' plan again. Other possible lines:

(a) 9 ♕b1 (Holding the diagonal and threatening b2-b4.) 9 ... h6! (9 ... ♕c7? 10 b4! ♖b8 11 c4! dxc4 12 ♗f4! ♗d6 13 ♗xd6 ♕xd6 14 ♘xc4 ♕e7 15 e4 ± Tukmakov-Schüssler, Helsinki 1983) 10 ♗h4 ♕c7 11 b4 ♗d6 12 bxc5 bxc5 13 e4 =.

(b) 9 a4 a6 10 ♕b1 h6 11 ♗f4 (11 ♗h4 0-0 12 ♖e1 ♕c7 13 e4 dxe4 14 ♘xe4 ♖fe8 15 dxc5 bxc5 16 ♘xf6+ ♗xf6 17 ♗g3 ♕c8 18 ♘d2 ♗e7 19 ♘c4 ♗d5 20 ♕c2 ♕b7 = Hodgson-Razuvayev, Sochi 1987) 11 ... ♘h5 12 ♗e5 0-0 13 h3 (13 b4!?) 13 ... c4 14 ♗h7+ ♔h8 15 ♗c2 b5 16 b3 ♗c6 17 axb5 axb5 18 ♕b2 ♕b6 = Hort-Kir.Georgiev, Thessaloniki 1984.

(c) 9 ♕c2, see 6.11. 9 ... h6 is the most accurate reply.

9 ... ♘xe5
10 dxe5 ♘d7
11 ♗xe7

Black has not castled yet so 11 ♗f4?! would take too many risks: 11 ... g5!? (11 ... ♕c7!? 12 ♘f3 h6 ∓ Spassky-Petrosian, Illustrative Game No 43.) 12 ♗g3 h5 13 f4 h4 14 ♗e1 gxf4 15 exf4 ♕c7 16 ♕g4 0-0-0 17 ♕h3 ♖dg8 ∓ Klarić-Geller, Sochi 1977.

11 ... ♕xe7
12 f4 f6

For 12 ... 0-0-0?! see Hébert-I.Ivanov, Illustrative Game No 44. 12 ... 0-0 is, as one would expect, risky: 13 ♕h5 g6 14 ♕h6 ♖fd8 15 ♖f3 ♘f8 16 ♖h3 f6 17 exf6 ♕xf6 18 ♖f1 ♕g7 19 ♕h4 d4 20 cxd4 cxd4 21 e4 ± Estevez-Sikeiro, Torrelavega 1984.

13 exf6

Or 13 ♕h5+!? ♕f7 14 ♕e2

0-0-0 (14 ... f5!? 15 a4 a5 16 ♘f3 h6 17 h3 ♘b8 18 ♗b5+ ♘c6 19 ♖fc1 ⩲ Hulak-Polajzer, Portoroz 1987. Again, kingside castling is doubtful: 14 ... 0-0 15 exf6 ♘xf6 16 ♘f3 ♕h5 17 ♕e1 ♘g4?! 18 h3 ♘f6 19 g4! ± A.Sokolov-Ivanchuk, Biel 1989) 15 e4 fxe5 16 exd5 exd5 17 fxe5 ♕e7 18 ♘f3 ♔b8?! (18 ... ♘f8 ⩲) 19 ♖ae1 d4 20 ♗e4 ± Hulak-van der Sterren, Wijk aan Zee 1987.

Interesting is 13 ♘f3!? 0-0-0 (13 ... fxe5? 14 ♗b5!) 14 ♗b5 ♔b8 15 a4 ♘f8?! (15 ... a6! 16 ♗xd7 ♖xd7 17 a5 b5 18 b4?! d4! ∞) 16 b4! a6 17 ♗d3 fxe5 18 ♘xe5 ♘d7 19 ♕h5 ± Dreyev-Novikov, USSR 1984.

13	**...**	**gxf6**
14	**e4**	**0-0-0**

14 ... 0-0 15 ♖f3! d4 16 ♖h3 e5 17 f5 ±.

15	**♕e2**	**d4**

15 ... ♘b8!? 16 a4 ♕d6 17 e5 fxe5 18 fxe5 ♕e7 19 a5 ♖hg8 20 axb6 axb6 21 ♘f3 ♖g7 ⩲ Nenarokov - Konstantinopolsky, USSR 1932.

16	**a4**	**e5**

16 ... a5?! 17 ♖a3! and 18 ♖b3 ±.

17	**f5**	**♘b8**
18	**a5**	**♘c6**

White has taken the initiative. Spassky-A.Sokolov, Bugojno 1986.

ILLUSTRATIVE GAMES

1 d4 ♘f6 2 ♘f3 e6 3 ♗g5 c5 4 e3 d5 5 ♘bd2 ♗e7 6 c3 ♘bd7 7 ♗d3 b6

41) **Kavalek-Ravi**
Dubai 1986

8 0-0 0-0 9 ♘e5 ♗b7 10 ♕a4 h6 11 ♗h4 ♘xe5 12 dxe5 ♘d7 13 ♗g3 ♕c7?! The e5 outpost gives White a small but distinct plus. 13 ... c4 14 ♗b1 ⩲ was better. **14 ♘f3 a5 15 ♖ad1 ♖fd8** 15 ... ♗a6? 16 ♗xa6 ♖xa6 17 e4! ±. **16 ♗b1 b5?! 17 ♕g4 ♕c6 18 ♗f4 f5** 18 ... ♔f8 19 ♗h7!. **19 exf6 ♘xf6 20 ♕h3** 20 ♕g6? ♕e8!. **20 ... ♗f8 21 ♘e5 ♕b6 22 ♗g6** Black's camp is full of holes. **22 ... ♗c8 23 ♗f7+ ♔h7**

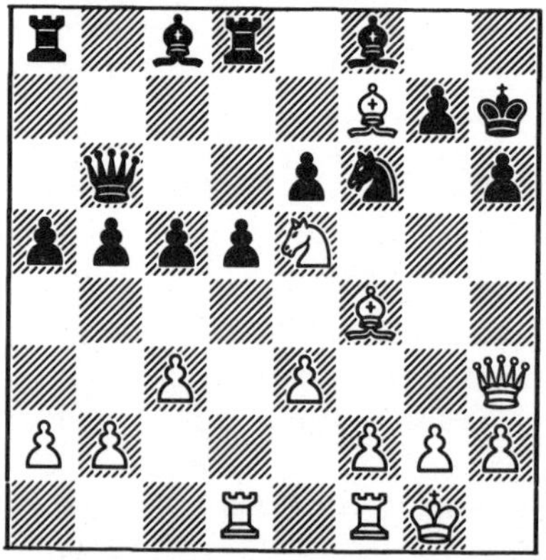

24 g4! The last storm! **24 ... ♖a7 25 g5 ♘d7?** 25 ... ♖xf7 26 g6+ +−; 25 ... ♘g8 26 ♗g6+ ♔h8 27 gxh6 +−. **26 g6+ ♔h8 27**

♘xd7 ♗xd7 28 ♗e5! 1-0
(Notes based on Kavalek's)

42) **C.Torre-Verlinsky**
Moscow 1925

8 0-0 0-0 9 ♘e5 ♗b7 10 f4 a6?! 11 ♕f3! ♘xe5? The knight should have been exchanged earlier! **12 fxe5 ♘d7?!** 12 ... ♘e8 gives a really cramped game but does not lose straight away. **13 ♕h3 g6** 13 ... h6 14 ♗xh6!. **14 ♗h6 c4** On the intended 14 ... ♖e8 White wins by 15 ♖xf7! ♔xf7 16 ♖f1+. **15 ♗c2 b5 16 ♖f2 ♕b6 17 ♖af1!?** Preferring the offensive to the winning of the exchange. **17 ... f5 18 exf6 ♖xf6 19 ♘f3 ♖e8 20 ♕g3 ♘f8 21 ♘e5 ♕d8 22 h4! ♖f5 23 ♗xf5 ♗xh4** The point of the defence. White, however, has seen further. **24 ♗xg6! ♗xg3** 24 ... ♘xg6 25 ♖f7!. **25 ♗f7+!** 25 ♖f7? ♗xe5!. **25 ... ♔h8 26 ♗xe8 ♗xf2+ 27 ♖xf2 1-0**

43) **Spassky-Petrosian**
match (7) 1966

8 0-0 ♗b7 9 ♘e5 ♘xe5 10 dxe5 ♘d7 11 ♗f4? The bishop is exposed to constant harassment here and White will have to spoil his kingside to parry all this. **11 ... ♕c7 12 ♘f3 h6! 13 ♗g3** 13 h4 g5!. **13 ... g5 14 b4! h5!** Hindering White's attack. 14 ... cxb4? 15 cxb4 ♗xb4 16 ♘d4! is exciting. **15 h4 gxh4 16 ♗f4 0-0-0 17 a4?!** Now Black will blockade the queenside and will have a free hand on the other wing. 17 bxc5!. **17 ... c4! 18 ♗e2 a6 19 ♔h1 ♖dg8 20 ♖g1 ♖g4 21 ♕d2 ♖hg8 22 a5 b5 23 ♖ad1 ♗f8 24 ♘h2**

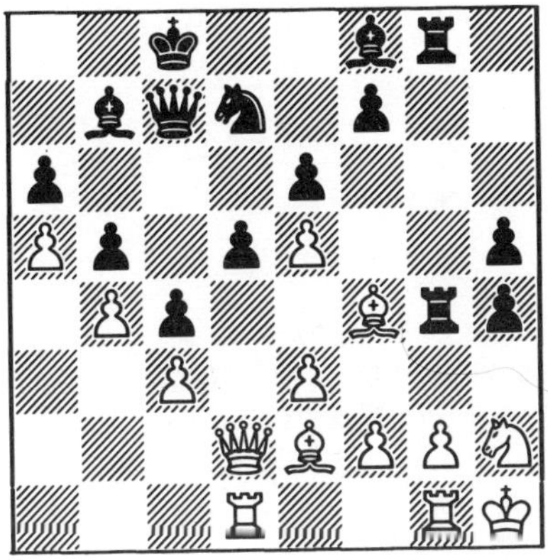

24 ... ♘xe5! Petrosian was famous for his delicate sacrifices of the exchange, and deservedly so! **25 ♘xg4 hxg4 26 e4! ♗d6** 26 ... dxe4? 27 ♗xe5 ∓∓. **27 ♕e3 ♘d7** 27 ... g3!? 28 f3!. **28 ♗xd6 ♕xd6 29 ♖d4?** Overlooking Black's breakthrough in the centre. 29 f4!. **29 ... e5 30 ♖d2 f5! 31 exd5** 31 exf5 h3!. **31 ... f4 32 ♕e4 ♘f6 33 ♕f5+ ♔b8 34 f3 ♗c8 35 ♕b1 g3** Weaving a mating net. **36 ♖e1 h3 37 ♗f1** 37 gxh3 g2+ 38 ♔g1 ♕d7!. **37 ... ♖h8 38 gxh3 ♗xh3 39 ♔g1 ♗xf1 40 ♔xf1 e4!** The steamroller gets under way! **41 ♕d1 ♘g4! 42 fxg4 f3 43 ♖g2 fxg2+ 0-1**

44) **Hébert-I.Ivanov**
Montreal 1983

8 0-0 ♗b7 9 ♘e5 ♘xe5 10 dxe5 ♘d7 11 ♗xe7 ♕xe7 12 f4 0-0-0?! 13 ♕e2 13 ♘f3! f6 14 ♗b5!. **13 ... f6 14 exf6 ♘xf6** 14 ... gxf6!?. **15 ♘f3 c4?** A gross positional blunder.**16 ♗c2 ♔b8 17 ♕d2! ♘d7 18 ♕d4 ♖de8**

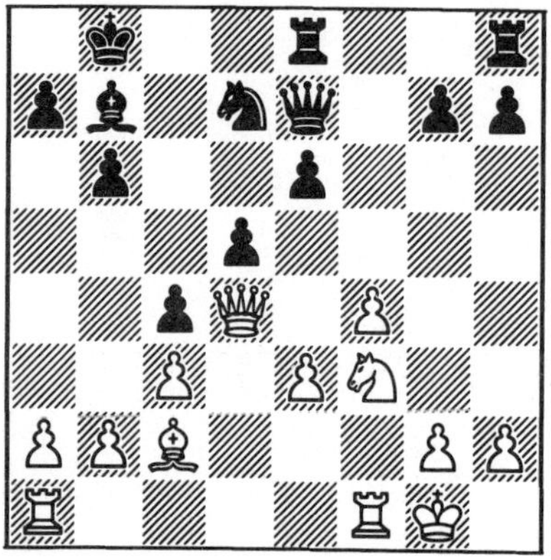

19 ♗a4! Forcing the exchange of this bishop for the black knight, thus obtaining a strong knight against a bad bishop. **19 ... ♖ef8 20 ♗xd7 ♕xd7 21 a4** 21 ♘e5 ♕e7 22 ♖f3 is also satisfactory here. **21 ... ♕c7 22 a5 bxa5 23 ♘e5 ♔a8 24 ♖a2 ♕b6 25 ♖fa1 ♕xd4 26 cxd4 ♖c8 27 ♖xa5 a6 28 ♘f7 ♖hf8 29 ♘g5! ♖c6 30 ♘xh7** With no counterplay in Black's grasp, White can afford to go pawn-snatching. **30 ... ♖b8 31 ♖b5! c3 32 ♖b3!** 32 bxc3? ♖xc3 33 ♔f2 ♖h8. **32 ... c2 33 ♖c1 a5 34 ♘g5 a4 35 ♖b4 ♗a6 36 ♖xb8+ ♔xb8 37 ♘f3 ♗e2 38 ♘e5 ♖c7 39 ♔f2 ♗d1 40 ♔e1 ♖b7 41 ♘d3 ♔c7 42 ♘c5 ♖b4?** 42 ... ♖xb2 43 ♘xa4 ♖b3 44 ♔d2 ±±. **1-0** (43 ♘a6+)

7 Torre-Petrosian Attack: Queen's Indian Variation

1	d4	♘f6
2	♘f3	b6
3	♗g5	

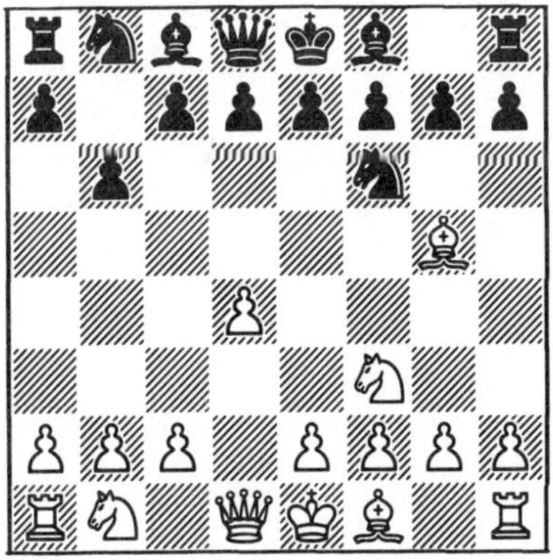

The Queen's Indian Variation is rarely played in its original form, as in most cases it transposes into one of the other lines of the Torre-Petrosian Attack.

This sequence of moves is not more risky for Black than the ones dealt with in the previous chapters, since the fianchettoing of his queen's bishop suits his plans.

The two main lines here are 3 ... ♗b7 and 3 ... ♘e4. 3 ... e6 4 e4 h6 5 ♗xf6 is Chapter 1.

7.1

3 ... ♗b7

A natural developing move.

4 ♘c3!?

Adding a special flavour to the line. Other possibilities are:

(a) 4 ♘bd2 e6 5 e4 h6 once again leads to Chapter 1. Yet 4 ... c5 5 ♗xf6 gxf6 6 e3 e6 7 ♗d3 ♘c6 8 0-0 d5 9 dxc5!? (9 c3 c4! 10 ♗c2 f5) 9 ... ♗xc5 10 a3 f5 11 b4 ♗d6 12 c4 ♘e5! ∞ Kochiev-Veingold, Illustrative Game No 45, is worth considering.

(b) 4 e3 e6 leads to Chapter 4, except for 5 ♗d3 ♗e7 6 ♘bd2 d6 ∞ Keres-Petrov, Illustrative Game No 46. Quite original is 4 ... h6 5 ♗xf6 (5 ♗h4 d6 6 ♘bd2 g5! 7 ♗g3 ♘h5 8 e4 ♗g7 ∞) 5 ... exf6 6 ♗d3 g6 (6 ... d5!?) 7 c4 ♗g7 8 ♘c3 f5 9 0-0 0-0 10 ♖c1 ♘c6?! 11 ♖e1 ♖e8 12 ♗f1 ♔h8 13 g3 ♖b8 14 ♗g2 a6 15 h4 ± Bronstein-Osnos, USSR 1965.

(c) 4 ♗xf6 exf6 5 d5! (5 g3? ♕e7! 6 ♗g2 ♕b4+ 7 ♘bd2 ♕xb2 8 0-0 ♕a3 9 ♘c4 ♕a4 10 ♕d3 ♘a6 11 ♕e3+ ♗e7 12 c3 d5 ∓ Stean-Korchnoi, Beer Sheva 1978) 5 ... g6 (5 ... c5!?; 5 ... ♗c5!?) 6 g3 ♗g7 7 ♗g2 f5 8 c3 0-0 9 0-0 ♖e8 10 a4 c5 Bronstein-Shmit, USSR 1970; 11 ♘a3 ±.

4 ... g6

4 ... d5? 5 e3 ♘bd7?! (5 ... e6 6 ♘e5 ♗e7 7 ♗b5+ c6 8 ♗d3 ♘bd7 9 f4 a6 10 ♕f3 c5 11 0-0 ♕c7 12 ♕h3 ⩲ Gereben-O'Kelly, Torremolinos 1962) 6 ♘e5! ♘xe5 7 dxe5 ♘e4 8 ♘xe4 dxe4 9 ♕g4 ♕c8 (9 ... ♕d5!?) 10 e6! ♕xe6 11 ♕xe6 fxe6 ± Petrosian-Golombek, Bucharest 1953.

4 ... h6!? 5 ♗xf6 exf6 6 e4 (6 a3!?) 6 ... ♗b4 7 ♗d3 0-0 8 0-0 ♗xc3 9 bxc3 d5 10 exd5 ♗xd5 11 ♘h4 ♕d7 12 ♘f5 ♕e6 13 ♘e3 = Klaman-Taimanov, USSR 1950.

4 ... e6 5 e4 h6 6 ♗xf6 ♕xf6 leads back to Chapter 1 (1.122).

5 e3 ♗g7

5 ... d5?! 6 ♗b5+ c6 7 ♗d3 ♗g7 8 e4 0-0 9 e5 ♘fd7 10 ♘e2 ± Petrosian-Nievergelt, Illustrative Game No 47.

6 ♗d3

More active is 6 ♗c4! since 6 ... d5 would cede White the e5 square.

6 ... c5
7 0-0 d6
8 ♕e2 0-0
9 ♖fd1 a6

Chances are practically equal, e.g. 10 dxc5 (10 e4 cxd4 11 ♘xd4 ∞) 10 ... bxc5 11 e4 ♘fd7 12 ♘d5 ♘c6 13 c3 ♖e8 = Füstér-Csom, Siegen 1970.

7.2

3 ... ♘e4

Attempting to hinder White's development.

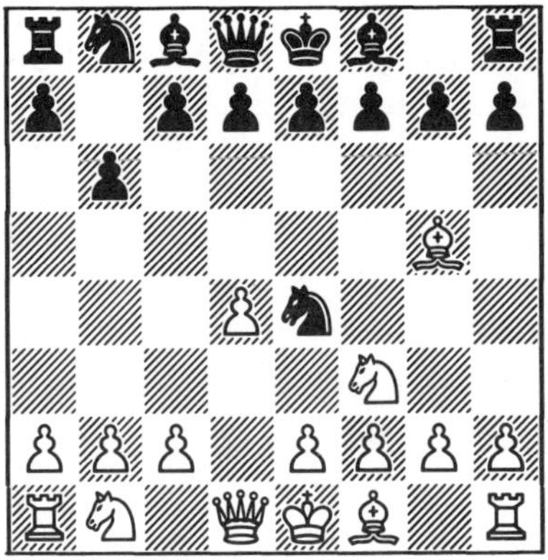

4 ♗h4

Less troublesome for Black is 4 ♗f4, e.g. 4 ... ♗b7 5 ♘bd2 ♘xd2 (5 ... e6 6 ♘xe4 ♗xe4 7 e3 ♗d6 – 7 ... ♘c6 8 c3 ♗e7 9 ♗e2 0-0 10 h4 h6 11 ♗d3 d5 12 g4 ♗d6 13 ♗xd6 ♕xd6 14 ♗xe4 dxe4 15 ♘d2 ⩲ Hulak-Miralles, Haifa 1989 – 8 ♗d3?! ♗xd3 9 ♕xd3 ♗xf4 10 ♕e4 ♘c6 11 ♕xf4 ♘b4! ∓ Duz-Khotimirsky–Kan, USSR 1933) 6 ♕xd2 e6 7 g3 ♗e7 8 ♗g2 c5 9 c3 0-0 10 0-0 d5 11 ♘e5 ♘d7 = Fred-

Szukszta, Munich 1958.

4 ... ♗b7

(a) 4 ... g6 5 ♘bd2 ♘xd2 6 ♕xd2 ♗b7 7 0-0-0! ♗g7 8 e4! 0-0 (8 ... ♗xe4?! 9 ♖e1 d5 10 ♗d3 f5 11 ♘g5 ♗h6 12 ♗f1! ±±) 9 e5 ± Timman-Sunye, Amsterdam 1985.

(b) 4 ... d5?! 5 ♘bd2! (5 e3?! ♕d6! 6 a3 ♕h6 7 ♕d3 g5 8 ♗g3 ♘xg3 9 fxg3 ♗g7 10 ♘c3 c6 11 0-0-0 ∞ Kochiev-Lysenko, USSR 1981; 6 ♗d3!?) 5 ... ♗b7 6 e3 ♘d7?! (6 ... g6!) 7 c4 ♘df6 8 ♖c1 e6 9 cxd5 ± Tseitlin-Popov, Illustrative Game No 48.

5 ♘bd2

5 e3 h6 6 ♘bd2 g5 7 ♗g3 ♘xg3 8 hxg3 e6 9 c3 d6?! (9 ... c5!) 10 ♕a4+! c6 11 ♘e4 g4 12 ♘h4 ♘d7 13 0-0-0 ♖g8 Bogoljubow-Alekhine, match 1934; 14 ♘d2! ±.

7.21

5 ... ♘xd2

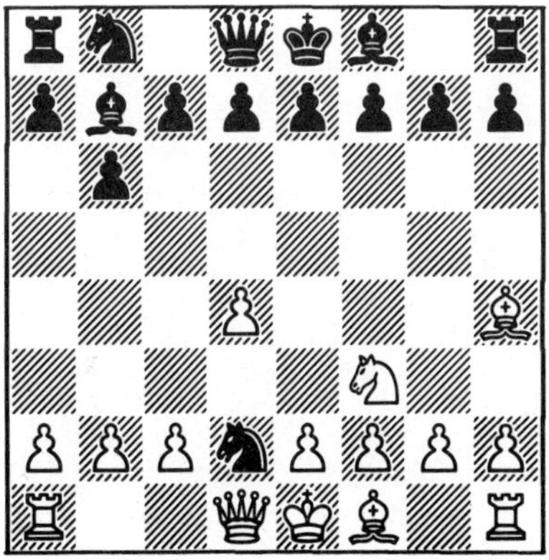

Apart from 5 ... g6 the following lines have been played in tournaments:

(a) 5 ... f5 6 e3 g6 7 ♘xe4 fxe4 8 ♘d2 ♗g7 9 c4! ♗f6 10 ♗g3! c5 11 d5! ♗xb2 12 ♘xe4 d6?! (12 ... ♗xa1 13 ♕xa1 0-0 14 h4 ♖f5 15 ♗d3) 13 ♖b1 ± Larsen-Szabó, Lugano 1970.

(b) 5 ... c5 5 e3 g6 7 ♘xe4 ♗xe4 8 ♗c4 f6!? 9 0-0 ♗b7 10 e4! ♗xe4?! 11 ♖e1 d5 12 ♗b5+ ♔f7 13 dxc5 ± Konstantinopolsky-Tolush, Moscow 1936.

(c) 5 ... d5 6 e3 ♘d7 7 ♘xe4 dxe4 8 ♘d2 ♕c8 9 ♗c4 ♘f6 10 0-0 g6 11 ♗b5+ c6 12 ♗c4 c5 13 c3 ♗g7 14 ♕a4+ ± Liskov-Cherepkov, Moscow 1945.

6 ♕xd2

6 ♘xd2 c5! gives Black a comfortable game.

6 ... g6

6 ... ♗xf3?! 7 exf3 c6 8 ♗d3 ♕c7 9 f4 ♕d6 10 0-0-0 ♕xd4 11 ♖he1 e6 12 c3 ♕d6 13 f5 ♗e7 14 ♗g3 ♕d5 15 ♔b1 ♗f6 16 ♕e2 ± Romanishin-Savon, USSR 1979.

7	**♗g5**	**h6**
8	**♗f4**	**d6**
9	**d5**	**♗g7**
10	**c4** ±	

Guimard-Bolbochan, Mar del Plata 1946.

7.22

5 ... g6

Black reconciles himself to the domination of the centre by White, hoping that his two bishops will take control later.

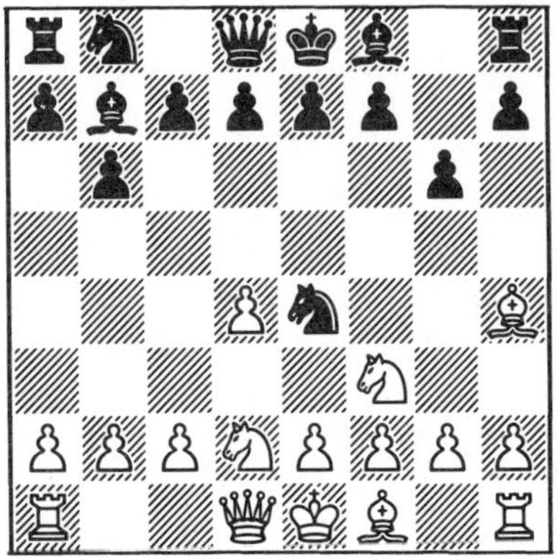

6	**♘xe4**	**♗xe4**
7	**♘d2!**	**♗b7**
8	**e4**	**♗g7**
9	**c3**	**0-0**
10	**♗c4**	**d5**
11	**exd5**	**♗xd5**
12	**0-0**	**♘c6!**

12 ... ♗xc4? 13 ♘xc4 ♕d5 14 ♘e3 ♕e4 15 ♗g3 ± Trifunović-Nikolac, Yugoslavia 1953.

13	**♖e1**	**♗xc4**
14	**♘xc4** ±	

Trifunović-Bolbochan, Mar del Plata 1950.

ILLUSTRATIVE GAMES

1 d4 ♘f6 2 ♘f3 b6 3 ♗g5

45) **Kochiev-Veingold**
Tallinn 1985

3 ... ♗b7 4 ♘bd2 c5 5 ♗xf6 Deviating from the Torre-Petrosian Attack. **5 ... gxf6 6 e3 e6 7 ♗d3 ♘c6 8 0-0 d5 9 dxc5 ♗xc5 10 a3 f5 11 b4 ♗d6 12 c4 ♘e5! 13 ♗e2 ♖g8!?** Black has equalised in the opening and has fine prospects for the middle game but he strives for more . . . **14 ♖c1 d4!? 15 exd4**

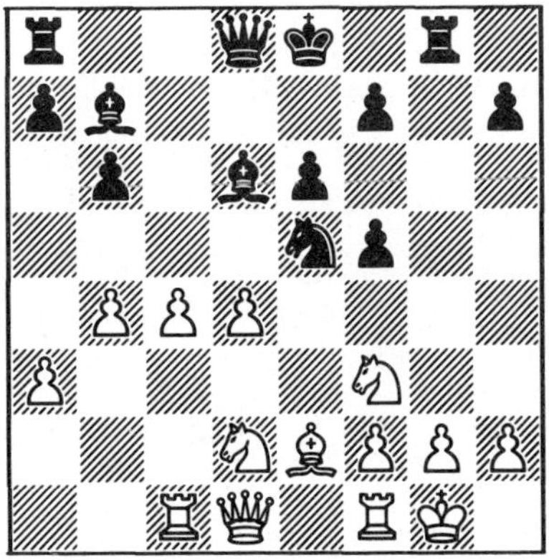

15 ... ♖xg2+!? An extraordinarily bold sacrifice, causing grave problems for White. **16 ♔xg2 ♕g5+ 17 ♔h1 ♕h6** After 17 ... ♘xf3 18 ♘xf3 ♗xf3+ 19 ♗xf3 ♕f4 20 ♗c6+ and 21 ♕h5, or 19 ... ♕h4 20 ♗c6+ and 21 f4, White wins. **18 d5** 18 dxe5? ♗xe5 19 ♔g1 ♕g6+ 20 ♔h1 ♕h5 21 ♔g1 ♕g4+ 22 ♔h1 ♕h3 23 ♔g1 ♔e7! ∓∓. **18 ... ♘g4 19 h4!** 19 ♔g2 ♕g7 20 ♔h1 ♕h6 =. **19 ... 0-0-0?** After 19 ... exd5? 20 c5!

and White wins, but if Black had played 19 ... ♗f4!, the outcome would have been in doubt. **20 c5! ♗xd5 21 cxd6+ ♔b8 22 ♕c2 ♖g8** 22 ... ♕xh4+ 23 ♔g1 is curtains but there are lethal threats after the text move. However, White has a vital tempo to hand. **23 ♕c7+ ♔a8 24 ♕c8+! ♖xc8 25 ♖xc8+ ♔b7 26 ♖c7+ ♔b8 27 ♗a6 1-0**

(Kochiev's notes included)

46) **Keres-Petrov**
Semmering-Baden 1937

3 ... ♗b7 4 e3 e6 5 ♗d3 ♗e7 6 ♘bd2 d6 7 0-0 ♘bd7 8 e4 e5 9 ♖e1 Allowing Black to exchange his passive bishop. 9 h3!. **9 ... ♘g4! 10 ♗xe7 ♕xe7 11 ♘c4 0-0 12 ♕d2 ♖ae8?** 12 ... exd4 13 ♘xd4 ♘ge5 14 ♘f5 ♕f6 gives equal chances, whereas after the text the rook will be missed on the queenside. **13 h3 ♘gf6 14 a4! a6 15 ♕c3! g6 16 ♘cd2!** Introducing an original strategy. **16 ... ♖c8 17 ♗c4 ♘h5?** This manoeuvre fails because f4 is only a temporary post for the knight. 17 ... exd4!. **18 ♗d5!? c6 19 ♗c4 ♘f4 20 ♗f1 c5?**

(diagram)

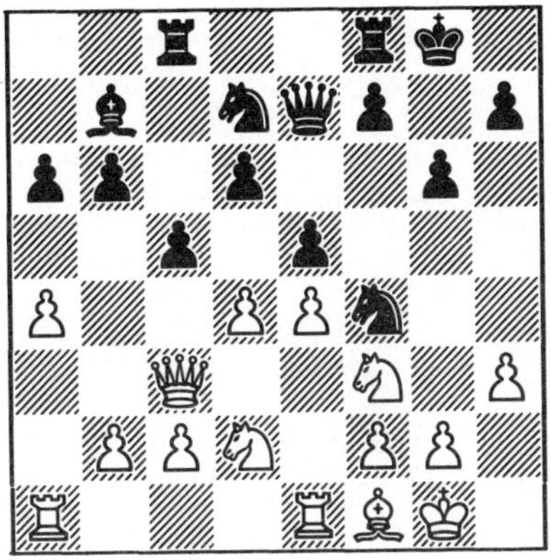

21 dxe5! After 21 d5 the b7 bishop would have been hemmed in temporarily but Black's defence would have been more or less airtight, whereas now White can exploit Black's weaknesses. **21 ... ♘xe5** 21 ... dxe5 22 ♘c4 f6 (22 ... ♖fe8 23 ♖ad1 ±±) 23 ♕b3 ±±. **22 ♘xe5 dxe5 23 ♘c4 ♖c6 24 g3 ♘h5 25 ♘xe5 ♖d6 26 ♘c4 ♖e6 27 e5 f6 28 exf6 ♕xf6 29 ♕xf6 ♖exf6 30 ♖e2 a5 31 ♗g2! ♗a6 32 ♗d5+ ♔h8 33 ♖ae1 ♖f5 34 ♗e6 ♖5f6 35 b3 ♘g7 36 ♗d5 ♘f5 37 ♖e6 ♘d4 38 ♖xf6 ♖xf6 39 ♖e8+** White has parried Black's counterplay and finishes the game on the offensive. **39 ... ♔g7 40 ♘e5** Amongst other things, 41 ♖g8+ ♔h6 42 ♘g4+ is threatened. **40 ... h5 41 ♖e7+ ♔h8 42 ♘f7+ ♔g7 43 ♘g5+ ♔f8** 43 ... ♔h6 44 h4. **44 ♖a7 1-0**

47) **Petrosian-Nievergelt**
Belgrade 1954

3 ... ♗b7 4 ♘c3 g6 5 e3 d5?! 6 ♗b5+! c6 7 ♗d3 ♗g7 8 e4! 0-0? 9 e5 ♘fd7 10 ♘e2 f6 11 exf6 exf6 12 ♗e3 ♘a6 13 h4! ♘b4 14 h5 ♘xd3+

15 ♕xd3 ♕e8 16 hxg6 hxg6 16 ... ♕xg6 17 ♘f4 ±. **17 ♘f4 ♘e5?!** 17 ... f5 18 0-0-0 ±. **18 dxe5 fxe5 19 ♕xg6 exf4 20 ♕h7+ ♔f7 21 ♖h6! ♕e7** 21 ... fxe3 22 ♘g5+. **22 ♕g6+ ♔g8 23 ♘g5 1-0**

48) **Zeitlin-Popov**
USSR 1982

3 ... ♘e4 4 ♗h4 d5?! 5 ♘bd2! ♗b7 6 e3 ♘d7?! 7 c4 ♘df6 8 ♖c1 e6 9 cxd5! Opening the c-file and the f1-a6 diagonal at the same time. **9 ... ♕xd5** 9 ... ♘xd2 10 ♕a4+! ±±; 9 ... exd5 10 ♕a4+! c6 11 ♖xc6 ♕d7 12 ♗b5 a6 13 ♖xe6+! ±±. **10 ♖xc7 ♘xd2** 10 ... ♗d6 11 ♗c4!. **11 ♘xd2 ♗d6 12 ♕a4+ ♔f8 13 e4!** Driving the queen away from the defence of the b7 bishop. **13 ... ♘xe4** 13 ... ♕h5 14 ♖xb7 ♕xh4 15 e5 ♗xe5 16 ♕a3+. **14 ♗c4 ♕xd4 15 ♖xf7+!** Another fine point. 15 ... ♔xf7 is met by 16 ♗xe6+. **15 ... ♔g8 16 ♘f3 ♕xb2 17 0-0 ♘c5 18 ♗xe6! ♘xe6 19 ♖xb7 b5 20 ♕e4 ♕xa2 21 ♖d7 ♗xh2+** Black loses a piece anyway. **22 ♔xh2 ♖f8 23 ♖e1 ♘c5 24 ♖xg7+! ♔xg7 25 ♕g4+ 1-0**

Part II: Countering the King's Indian and the Grünfeld 1 d4 ♘f6 2 ♘f3 g6

Introduction to Chapters 8-16

The King's Indian and the Grünfeld Defences are two of the most popular openings these days. It is therefore very important to have a simple and rather easily accessible weapon at hand to counter them successfully. The following chapters offer three main variations for this purpose.

In each of them, White postpones the c2-c4 move, otherwise the three lines represent three different ideas.

In the first one, White's queen's bishop goes to g5 and his pawn formation is supposed to paralyse Black's king's bishop while White's dark squared bishop is a more dynamic one. The system, called in this book the 'queen's bishop line', gives a practical, rather than a positionally established, advantage to White. Black has very promising chances to equalise either by ... d7-d6 or by ... d7-d5. (Chapters 8-11)

White has even less to hope for in the 'wait-and-see' variation, introduced by ♗f4. No wonder this line is seldom encountered in tournament practice. It is worth mentioning, however, that theoretically under-educated players, have always had a liking for this natural continuation. (Chapters 12-13).

The third variation, the king's bishop line, is concerned with fianchettoing the bishop. White exerts positional pressure on Black's set-up and sets a difficult defensive task. (Chapters 14-16)

8 Countering the King's Indian and the Grünfeld: QB Line, rare alternatives on move 3

1	d4	♘f6
2	♘f3	g6
3	♗g5	

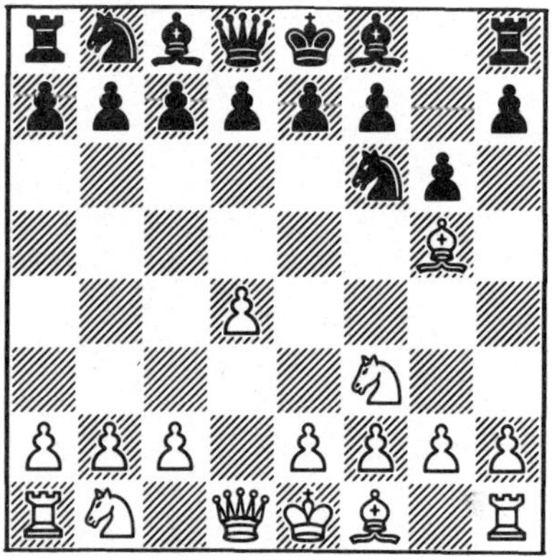

A natural developing move, preparing ♘b1-d2 and indirectly pinning Black's knight. The special pawn formation of the line was mentioned in the Introduction. It should be noted that **3 c3** is only a change in move order in most cases, although an immediate ... d7-d5 will prevent White from playing c2-c4. A few independent variations: 3 ... ♗g7 4 ♗g5 (4 ♕c2 0-0 5 e4 d6 6 ♗d3 ♘c6 7 ♘bd2 ♘d7 8 ♘c4 e5 9 ♗g5 ♕e8 10 d5 ♘e7 = Ed.Lasker-Yates, New York 1924) 4 ... d6 5 h3 0-0 6 ♘bd2 h6 7 ♗f4 ♘c6 8 e4 e5! 9 dxe5 ♘h5 10 ♗e3 dxe5 11 ♕c2 ♕f6 12 ♘b3 ♖d8 13 ♘fd2 b6 = Cebalo-Vukić, Yugoslavia 1981.

3	...	♘e4

An original handling of the opening, although some variations remind us of the Grünfeld.

(a) 3 ... d6 4 ♘bd2 h6 (4 ... ♘bd7 5 e4 h6 6 ♗h4 g5?! 7 ♗g3 ♘h5 8 ♘c4! ♗g7 9 c3 e6 10 ♘fd2! ♘xg3 11 hxg3 ♕e7 12 ♘e3 ♘f6 13 ♕b3! c6 14 0-0-0 e5?! 15 dxe5 dxe5 16 ♘dc4 ± Salov-Smirin, USSR 1988) 5 ♗h4 g5 6 ♗g3 ♗f5?! 7 h3 ♘bd7 8 e3 c6 9 ♗d3 ♗xd3 10 cxd3 ♕a5?! ± Yusupov-Kapengut, Illustrative Game No 49.

(b) 3 ... h6 4 ♗xf6 exf6 5 e3 b6 6 ♗d3 f5 7 ♘bd2 ♗g7 8 c3 ♗b7 9 0-0 0-0 10 ♖e1 d6 11 a4 ± Müller-Flesch, Beverwijk 1965.

(c) 3 ... c5 4 ♗xf6 exf6 5 dxc5 ♗xc5 6 e3 ♕b6 7 ♕c1 d5 8 ♗e2 0-0 9 0-0 ♖d8 10 ♖d1 ± Kholmov-Taimanov, USSR 1963.

(d) 3 ... d5?! (It is unwise to give White a second option. 3 ... ♗g7 and 4 ... d5 – see Chapter 4) 4 ♗xf6 exf6 5 e3 ♗g7 6 c4 0-0 7 ♘c3 ±.

In the main variation the bishop can retreat to h4 or f4, but ♗h4 seems a bit better.

8.1

4 ♗h4 d5

4 ... c5 5 ♘bd2 (5 c3 ♗g7 6 ♘bd2 ♘xd2 7 ♕xd2 cxd4 8 ♘xd4 d5 =; 6 ... d5!?) 5 ... d5 6 dxc5?! ♘xc5 7 ♘b3 ♘c6 8 ♘xc5 ♕a5+ 9 c3 ♕xc5 10 e3 ♗g7 11 ♗e2 0-0 12 0-0 e5 13 ♖c1 a5 = E.Torre-Ermenkov, Thessaloniki 1984; 6 e3! ♗g7 7 c3 ♗g4? 8 ♕b3 ♗xf3 9 ♕xb7 ♘xd2 10 ♗b5+ ♘d7 11 ♗xd7+ ± Psakhis-Konopka, Erevan 1986.

5 e3 ♗g7

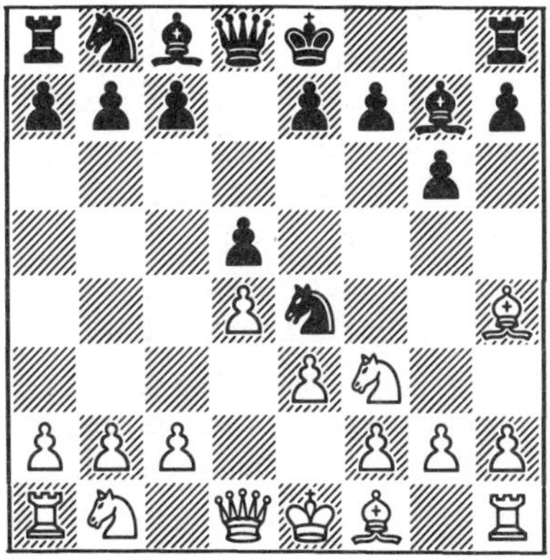

6 ♘bd2

(a) 6 ♗d3 0-0 7 c4 ♗f5 8 ♘c3 ♘xc3 9 bxc3 dxc4 10 ♗xc4 c5 11 0-0 ♘c6 12 ♗d3 ♗xd3 13 ♕xd3 ♕d7 14 ♖fd1 cxd4 15 cxd4 e6 16 ♖ab1 ♖fc8 17 ♘d2! f5 18 ♕b5 ± Filip-Stein, Stockholm 1962.

(b) 6 c4 c6 7 ♘c3 0-0 8 ♕b3 (8 ♗d3 ♘xc3 9 bxc3 dxc4 10 ♗xc4 ♘d7 ±; 10 ... ♗g4 ±) 8 ... dxc4 9 ♗xc4 ♘d6 (9 ... ♘xc3!? 10 bxc3 b5 11 ♗e2 ♗e6 ±) 10 ♗d3 ♗e6 11 ♕c2 ♘f5 12 ♗g5 ♘d7 13 0-0 ♘f6 ± Tartakower-Petrov, Lodz 1938.

6 ... c5

6 ... ♘d6 7 c3 (7 ♗d3 ♗f5 8 ♕e2 ♗xd3 9 ♕xd3 c6 10 0-0-0 Kan-Averbakh, USSR 1947; 10 ... 0-0 =. White can avoid this simplification with 7 ♗e2 c6 8 0-0 ♘d7 9 c4 ♘f5 10 ♗g5 f6 11 ♗f4 g5 12 ♗g3 h5 13 ♗d3 ♘f8 14 ♕c2 ± Meduna-Robatsch, Trnava 1987). 7 ... c6 8 ♗e2 (8 ♗d3 ♗f5) 8 ... ♘bd7 9 0-0 ♘f5 10 ♗g5 f6?! 11 ♗f4 g5?! 12 ♗d3! e6 13 ♗xf5 exf5 14 ♗d6 ± Petrosian-Furman, Illustrative Game No 50.

7 c3 cxd4

7 ... ♘xd2 8 ♕xd2 b6 (8 ... ♕a5?! 9 b4 cxb4 10 cxb4 ♕b6 11 ♖c1 ♗g4 12 ♗e2 ♘d7 13 a4 ♗f6 14 ♗g3 0-0 15 a5 ± Malaniuk-Semeniuk, USSR 1986) 9 ♘e5 0-0 10 f4!? ♗b7 11 ♗d3 ♘d7 12 0-0 ♘f6 13 ♖ad1 ∞ Gereben-Trincardi, Reggio Emilia 1963/64.

8 exd4 ♘xd2

Less convincing is 8 ... ♘c6 9 ♘xe4 dxe4 10 ♘g5 ♗f6 11 d5 ± Filip-Molnár, Lyon 1955 or 8 ... 0-0 9 ♘xe4! dxe4 10 ♘d2 f5 11 ♗c4+ ♔h8 12 ♗g5 ♕e8 13 h4! e5 14 dxe5 ♘c6 15 h5 ♘xe5 16 hxg6 ♕xg6 17 ♕h5 ♕xh5 18 ♖xh5 ♘xc4 19 ♘xc4 ♗e6 20 ♘d6! ± Spassky-Berezhnoi, USSR 1963.

9 ♕xd2 0-0

White has slightly the freer game.

8.2

4 ♗f4

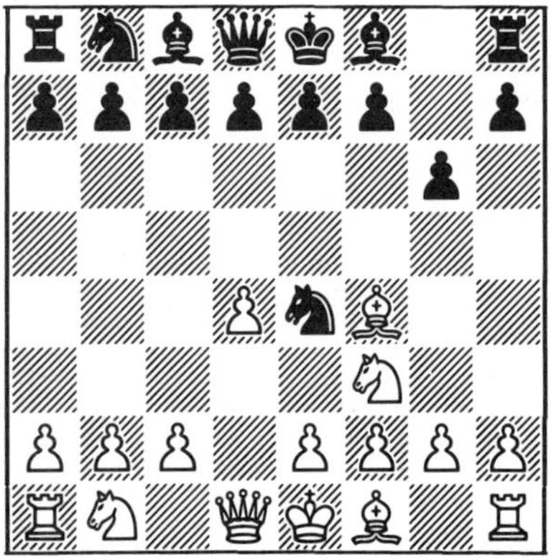

4 ... d5

4 ... c5 or 4 ... ♗g7 is usually a simple switch in move order, but if Black is unwilling to play ... d7-d5 he is going to be unable to hold the centre: 4 ... c5 5 c3 ♗g7 6 ♘bd2 ♘xd2?! 7 ♕xd2 cxd4 8 cxd4 ♕b6?! 9 e3 d6 10 ♗e2 0-0 11 0-0 ♗g4 12 h3 ± Sakharov-Kolpakov, Tashkent 1964 or 4 ... ♗g7 5 ♘bd2 ♘xd2 6 ♕xd2 d6 7 ♗h6 0-0 8 h4! ± Lemaire-Thibault, Brussels 1951.

5 e3 ♗g7

5 ... c5 is a mere change in the sequence, except for 6 ♘bd2 (6 ♗e5!? f6 7 ♗xb8 ♖xb8 8 ♗b5+ ♔f7 9 ♗d3 ♕b6 10 ♕c1 ♗g4 11 dxc5 ♘xc5 12 ♗e2 e5 ∞ Bronstein-Aronin, Sochi 1959) 6 ... ♘c6 7 c3 ♕b6 (7 ... cxd4?! 8 ♘xe4! dxe4 9 ♘xd4 ♕b6 10 ♘xc6 ♕xc6?! 11 ♕b3 a6 12 ♗c4 e6 13 ♗e5 ± Ritov-Vaganian, Tallinn 1979) 8 ♘xe4?! dxe4 9 ♘d2 ♕xb2 10 ♖c1 ♗g4! 11 ♖c2 ♗xd1 12 ♖xb2 ♗a4 13 ♖xb7 cxd4 14 exd4 f5 15 ♘c4 ♘d8 16 ♖b4 ± Soloviev-Aronin, USSR 1963.

6 ♘bd2

6 ♗e2 (6 ♗d3 0-0 7 h3 c5 8 c3 ♕b6 9 ♕c1 ♘c6 =) 6 ... c6 7 0-0 ♘d7 8 c4 ♘df6 9 ♘c3 ♘h5 10 ♗e5 f6 11 ♗g3 ♘xg3 12 hxg3 ♗e6 13 ♘xe4 dxe4 14 ♘d2 f5 15 g4 0-0 = Rossetto-Levy, Lone Pine 1975.

6 ... c5

(a) 6 ... ♗g4?! 7 ♘xe4!? dxe4 8 h3 ♗xf3 9 gxf3 exf3 10 ♕xf3 c6 11 ♗c4 0-0 12 h4 h5 13 ♖g1 e6 14 0-0-0 ± Solmundarsson-Ogaard, Siegen 1970.

(b) 6 ... 0-0 7 ♘xe4 (7 c3 b6 8

♘xe4 dxe4 9 ♘d2 ♗b7 10 ♕c2 f5 11 h4 e6 12 0-0-0 ♘d7 13 g4! ♘f6 14 gxf5 gxf5 15 ♘c4 ± Doda-Honfi, Kecskemét 1968) 7 ... dxe4 8 ♘d2 f5 9 ♗c4+ ♔h8 10 h4 c5 11 c3 cxd4 12 cxd4 ♘c6 13 h5 ♕e8 14 hxg6 ♕xg6 15 ♕h5 ± Mikenas-Stein, USSR 1965.

7 c3

7 ♗b5+ ♗d7 8 ♗xd7+ ♘xd7 9 c3 ♘xd2 10 ♕xd2 0-0 11 0-0 ♖e8 12 b4 cxb4 13 cxb4 ♘b6 14 b5 ♕d7 15 ♕b4 ♖ec8 16 ♖fc1 f6 17 ♘d2 Böhm-van der Sterren, Holland 1975; 17 ... ♗f8 ∞.

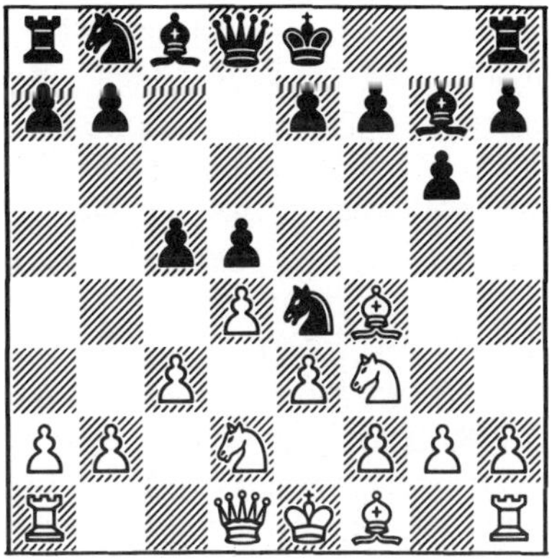

7 ... ♘c6

Another natural move.

(a) 7 ... ♕b6 8 ♕b3 (8 ♕c1 ♘xd2 9 ♕xd2 0-0 10 ♗d3 ♘c6 ∞) 8 ... ♘xd2 9 ♘xd2 c4 10 ♕xb6 axb6 11 ♗xb8 ♖xb8 12 e4 e6 13 ♗e2 b5 14 e5 ♖a8 15 0-0 ♗f8 16 a3 ♗e7 ± Kovačević-Bertok, Zagreb 1969.

(b) 7 ... ♘xd2 8 ♕xd2 cxd4 (8 ... ♘d7 9 0-0-0 c4 10 e4! ♕a5 11 a3 dxe4 12 ♘g5 ♕d5 13 ♖e1 ♘f6 14 f3 exf3 15 ♖e5 ± Slepoi-Korsakov, USSR 1963) 9 exd4 ♘c6 10 ♗e2 0-0 11 ♗h6 ♗g4 12 0-0 e6 Gy.Szilágyi-Gereben, Budapest 1952; 13 ♗xg7 ♔xg7 14 ♘e5 ♘xe5 15 dxe5 ±.

(c) 7 ... 0-0 8 ♘xe4! dxe4 9 ♘d2 cxd4 10 exd4 f5 11 f3 exf3 12 ♗c4+ ♔h8 13 ♘xf3 ♘c6 14 ♕e2 ♗d7 15 h4 ± Rodriguez-Westerinen, Alicante 1980.

8 ♘xe4

8 ♗e2 (8 ♗d3 ♗f5 9 ♗xe4 dxe4 10 ♘g5 cxd4 11 exd4 e5! ∞) 8 ... 0-0 9 0-0 h6 10 ♘xe4 dxe4 11 ♘d2 cxd4 12 cxd4 ♗f5 13 g4 e5! = Oblikov-Sakharov, USSR 1963.

8 ... dxe4
9 ♘g5 cxd4
10 exd4 ♕d5
11 ♕b3 e6

Both sides have chances. Keres-Botvinnik, Illustrative Game No 51.

ILLUSTRATIVE GAMES

1 d4 ♘f6 2 ♘f3 g6 3 ♗g5

49) **Yusupov-Kapengut**
USSR 1981

3 ... d6 An unusual move order.

4 ♘bd2 h6 5 ♗h4 Doubling Black's pawns would not be worth surrendering the two bishops. **5 ... g5 6 ♗g3 ♗f5?!** That is what Black had up his sleeve! Now he manages to develop his own bishop, but he forgets to exchange his opponent's menacing bishop. 6 ... ♘h5! would have led back to the main variations. **7 h3 ♘bd7 8 e3 c6 9 ♗d3! ♗xd3 10 cxd3 ♕a5?** The queen's sortie is premature. 10 ... ♗g7 ±. **11 ♕b3?!** White wants to punish it immediately, only to create problems for himself. 11 0-0 ±. **11 ... ♘b6 12 0-0 ♕a4! 13 ♕c3!?** Rather losing a tempo than swapping the queens. **13 ... ♘fd5 14 ♕c1 ♕b5** 14 ... ♘b4 15 ♘e1 ♕b5 16 ♕b1 ±. **15 ♘c4!? ♘b4 16 ♕d2!?** White's last few moves have prepared a pawn sacrifice, aimed at taking advantage of his better development. 16 ♕c3 ♘4d5 17 ♕c2 ♘b4. **16 ... ♘xc4** 16 ... ♘xd3?? 17 ♘a3. **17 dxc4 ♕xc4 18 ♖fc1 ♕b5 19 a4 ♕b6** 19 ... ♕a5?? 20 ♖c4 c5 21 dxc5 bxc5 22 ♕c3 ±±. **20 a5 ♕b5 21 e4 e6?** Black neglects development. 21 ... ♗g7!. **22 d5! e5** Otherwise 23 ♘d4! would cost a piece!.

(diagram)

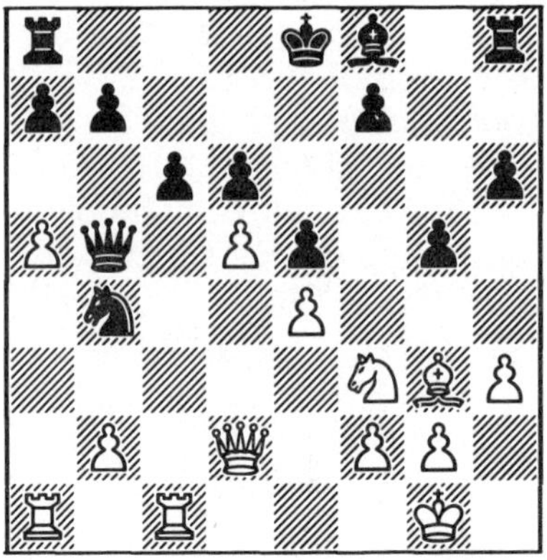

26 a6! Witty! **23 ... ♘xa6?** This knight on the edge of the board will permanently burden Black. 23 ... c5! 24 axb7 ♕xb7 25 ♕e2 and ♘d2-c4-e3 is more tolerable. **24 ♖a5!** Exploiting the clumsy set-up of Black's queenside pieces. **24 ... ♕b4** 24 ... ♕b6 25 dxc6 bxc6 26 ♘xe5! dxe5 27 ♖xe5+ ♗e7 28 ♖xe7+! ♔xe7 29 ♕xd6+ ♔e8 30 ♕e5+ ♔d7 31 ♖d1 ±± etc. **25 dxc6 ♕xd2** 25 ... ♖c8? 26 ♖xe5+! dxe5 27 ♕d7 mate! **26 ♘xd2 ♖c8 27 ♖c4! ♘b8 28 cxb7 ♖xc4 29 ♘xc4 a6 30 ♘xe5! f5 31 ♘g6 f4 32 ♘xh8 fxg3 33 ♖a4 d5 34 exd5 ♗c5 35 ♖c4 gxf2+ 36 ♔f1 ♗a7 37 ♘g6 ♔d7 38 ♘e5+ ♔d6 39 ♘c6 1-0**

(Notes based on Yusupov's)

1 d4 ♘f6 2 ♘f3 g6 3 ♗g5 ♘e4

50) **Petrosian-Furman**
USSR Championship 1958

4 ♗h4 d5 5 e3 ♗g7 6 c3 c6 7 ♘bd2 ♘d6 8 ♗e2 ♘d7 9 0-0 ♘f5

10 ♗g5 f6?! 11 ♗f4 g5?! 11 ... e5 12 dxe5 fxe5 13 ♗g5 and 14 e4!. **12 ♗d3! e6 13 ♗xf5 exf5 14 ♗d6 ♘f8 15 ♗a3 ♗e6 16 ♖c1! ♘g6 17 c4 ♔f7**

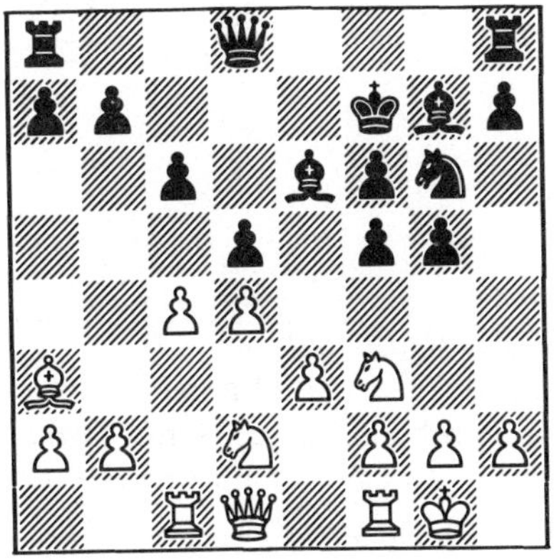

18 ♘e1! The knight heads for c5 to paralyse Black's queenside. **18 ... ♖c8 19 ♘d3 ♖c7! 20 ♘c5 ♗c8 21 cxd5 cxd5 22 ♕a4! b6** Weakening the queenside was inevitable but perhaps 22 ... a6 was the lesser of two evils. **23 ♘a6 ♗xa6 24 ♕xa6 ♕c8 25 ♖xc7+ ♕xc7 26 b3 ♕d7 27 ♖c1 ♖d8 28 ♕a4!** Accepting doubled pawns to dominate the c-file. **28 ... f4 29 ♕xd7+ ♖xd7 30 g4! ♗f8 31 ♗xf8 ♔xf8** In spite of the exchanges, control of the c-file is a decisive advantage for White. **32 ♔f1 ♔e7 33 ♔e2 fxe3 34 fxe3 ♘h4 35 ♘f3 ♘xf3 36 ♔xf3 ♔d6 37 ♖c8 ♖f7 38 ♖d8+ ♔e6 39 e4 dxe4+ 40 ♔xe4 ♔e7 41 ♖a8 ♔e6 42 d5+ ♔d6 43 ♖e8 ♖c7 44 ♖e6+ ♔d7 45 ♖c6! 1-0**

51) **Keres-Botvinnik**
Budapest 1952

4 ♗f4 ♗g7 5 ♘bd2 d5 6 e3 c5 7 c3 ♘c6 8 ♘xe4 dxe4 9 ♘g5 9 ♘d2 cxd4 10 exd4 f5 11 ♗c4 e5!. **9 ... cxd4 10 exd4** No better is 10 cxd4, owing to the coming ... e5 threat. **10 ... ♕d5! 11 ♕b3 e6 12 ♕c2** 12 ♗c4?! ♕f5!. **12 ... f5 13 f3 0-0!** 13 ... exf3?! 14 ♘xf3 e5 15 dxe5 ♘xe5 16 ♘xe5 ♗xe5 17 ♖d1 ±. **14 fxe4 fxe4 15 g3 e5** 15 ... ♗xd4? 16 ♖d1 e5 17 ♗e3 ±±. **16 dxe5 ♘xe5 17 ♕xe4 ♕xe4 18 ♘xe4 ♗g4 19 ♗xe5! ½-½**

9 Countering the King's Indian and the Grünfeld: QB Line, offshoots on move 4

1 d4 ♘f6
2 ♘f3 g6
3 ♗g5 ♗g7

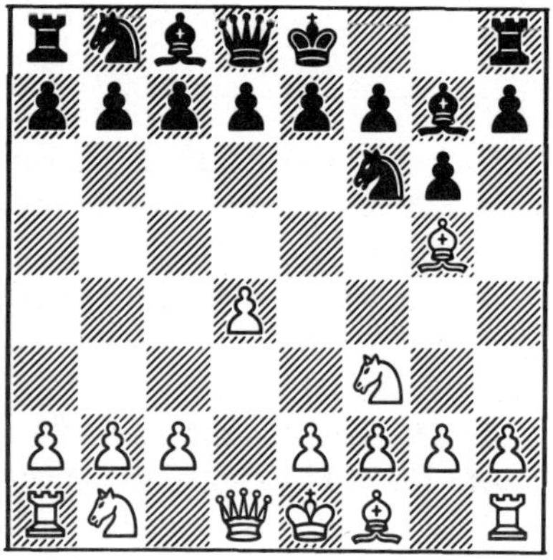

Black refrains from close-range fighting at the beginning of the game. Instead, he continues his development and keeps his plans secret.

This chapter looks first of all at the variations in which Black plays the Benoni-like ... c7-c5, although there will be other ideas to be found in the subvariations.

9.1

4 c3

This logical move attempts to prevent the 4 ... c5 counter-blow. As will be seen, the other main line here 4 ♘bd2, is much more popular. All possibilities other than 4 ♘bd2 are listed below:

(a) 4 e3 0-0 (4 ... c5 5 ♘bd2 b6 6 c3 ♗b7 7 ♕a4 0-0 8 ♗e2 d6 9 0-0 ♘bd7 10 b4! ♕c7 11 bxc5 bxc5 12 ♖ab1 ± Kovačević-Larsen, Illustrative Game No 52; 4 ... d6 5 h3 0-0 6 ♗e2 ♘bd7 7 0-0 h6 8 ♗f4 ♕e8! 9 c4 e5 10 ♗h2 ♘e4! 11 dxe5 ♘xe5 12 ♘xe5 ♗xe5 13 ♗xe5 ♕xe5 = Keres-Gheorghiu, Petropolis 1973) 5 ♗e2 (5 ♗c4 d5 is Chapter 11 with an extra tempo for Black. 5 c3 c5? 6 ♗xf6! ♗xf6 7 dxc5 ♕c7 8 ♕d5 a5 9 ♘bd2 a4 10 ♘d4 ♖a5 11 b4 ± Petrosian-Hort, Hamburg 1965) 5 ... d6 6 0-0 h6 7 ♗h4 g5 8 ♗g3 ♘h5 etc, see Chapter 10.

(b) 4 h4?! (Premature!) 4 ... d5 (4 ... c5!?) 5 ♗xf6 ♗xf6 6 h5 c5 7 hxg6 hxg6 8 ♖xh8+ ♗xh8 9 c3 ♕b6 10 ♕d2 ♗f5 ∓ Roux-Onat, Havana 1966.

(c) 4 ♗xf6 ♗xf6 5 e4 (This may be in some ways quite logical, but does not seem too good) 5 ... d6 6 c3 0-0 7 h4 h5 8 ♗e2 e5 9 dxe5 dxe5 10 ♘a3 ♕xd1+ 11 ♖xd1 ♗e6 12 ♘c4 ♘d7 ∓ Solmundarsson-Andersson, Reykjavik 1972.

4 ... b6

Moves like 4 ... d6, 4 ... h6 or 4 ... d5 are dealt with in the forthcoming chapters.

5 ♘bd2 ♗b7
6 e3

Probably better is 6 a4! c5 7 e3 h6 8 ♗h4 ♘c6 9 ♗d3 0-0 10 0-0 d6 11 ♕b1! leading to Ribli-Gheorghiu, 9.22.

6 ♗xf6!? ♗xf6 7 e3 c5 8 ♗d3 ♗g7 9 0-0 0-0 10 b4 cxb4 11 cxb4 ♘c6 12 a3 f5 13 ♕b3+ e6 14 ♖ac1 ♔h8 15 ♘c4 d6 16 b5 ♘e7 17 ♘g5 ♗d5 ∞ Bronstein-Suetin, USSR 1964.

6 ... d6
7 ♗b5+ ♘bd7
8 0-0 a6! ±

White's ♖e1, ♗f1 set-up must be prevented, otherwise White obtains a small but secure advantage: 8 ... 0-0?! 9 ♖e1! a6 10 ♗f1 e5 11 dxe5 ♘xe5 12 ♘xe5 dxe5 13 e4 ± Larsen-Iskov, Gellerup 1975.

9.2

4 ♘bd2

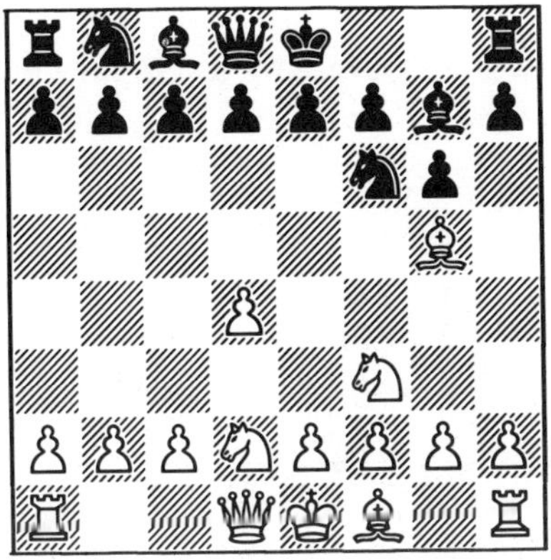

More frequent than 4 c3, this move offers a great bulk of theoretical material. The intention is 5 e4, so Black has to reveal his intentions as regards his set-up. What are his alternatives? 4 ... c5 and 4 ... 0-0 are the main lines; 4 ... d5 is looked at in another chapter. 4 ... h6 5 ♗h4 leads to Chapter 10. One has to bear in mind that 5 ... c5?! 6 ♗xf6 ♗xf6 7 ♘e4 ♗xd4 is a variation of 9.212, when the insertion of ... h6 is to Black's disadvantage (see move 10 of the quoted sentence).

Another possibility is 6 ... exf6 7 dxc5 ♘a6 8 ♘b3 ♘xc5 9 ♘xc5 ♕a5+ 10 c3?! ♕xc5 11 ♕d4 ♕e7 = Trifunović-Janošević, Yugoslavia

1951. Better is 10 ♕d2! ♕xc5 11 e4 ±. The following plan is also worth considering: 4 ... h6 5 ♗xf6 ♗xf6 6 c3 (6 e4 d6 7 ♗c4 e5 8 dxe5 dxe5 9 0-0 0-0 10 ♖e1 ♕e7 11 a4 a5 = Guimard-Quinteros, Argentina 1967) 6 ... d6 7 e3 0-0 8 ♗c4 ♗g7 9 0-0 c5 10 b4 cxd4 11 cxd4 ♘c6 = Damjanović-Gheorghiu, Varna 1971.

9.21

4 ... c5

A plan familiar from a number of openings: Black wants to take the initiative on the long diagonal, aided by his g7 bishop. White can either remain cautious (5 c3) or pick up the gauntlet (5 ♗xf6!?). For 5 e3 see 9.22.

9.211

5 c3?!

No longer popular; the drawback of this move is that after the exchange and the opening of the c-file the proper post of knight would be c3.

5 ... cxd4!

The most consistent move. Still, 5 ... 0-0 is acceptable as well: 6 ♗xf6 exf6 (6 ... ♗xf6 7 ♘e4 ♕b6 8 ♘xf6+ exf6 9 ♕d2 d6 10 e3 ♘bd7 = Ostrovsky-Nezhmetdinov, USSR 1963) 7 dxc5 f5 8 e3 f4 9 exf4 b6! (The better developed side wants to open files!) 10 ♗e2 bxc5 11 0-0 d5 12 ♘b3 ♕d6 13 ♘e5 ♘c6 14 ♘xc6 ♕xc6 15 ♗f3 ♗e6 = Trifunović-Spassky, Varna 1962.

6 cxd4 0-0

6 ... ♘c6 7 e3 0-0 8 ♗d3! (8 ♗e2 d6 9 0-0 ♗f5 10 ♕b3 ♖b8 11 ♖ac1 ♗e6 = Trifunović-Tan Beverwijk 1963; 8 a3?! h6 9 ♗h4 d6 10 ♗c4 ♗f5 = Bisguier-Fischer, Illustrative Game No 53) 8 ... d6 9 0-0 ♗d7 (9 ... h6 10 ♗xf6 ♗xf6 11 ♕b3 ± Trifunović-Pavlov, Halle 1963) 10 a3 ♘d5 11 ♕b3 ♘b6 12 ♖ac1 ♗e6 13 ♕d1 ♖c8 14 b4 ± Marshall-Bogoljubow, Bad Kissingen 1928.

7 e3 d5!

The simplest, giving the Slav-Grünfeld type of structure mentioned in the introduction to chapters 8-16. 7 ... b6?! 8 ♗e2 ♗b7 9 0-0 d6 10 ♖c1 ♘bd7?! 11 ♗b5! ± Neikirch-Bobotsov, Sofia 1962.

Black must be a bit careful with his planning: 7 ... ♘c6 8 ♗e2 d5?! (less appropriate with the bishop on e2 and the knight already committed to c6; 8 ... d6 transposes into Trifunović-Tan, previous note) 9 0-0 ♗f5 10 ♕b3 ♕b6 11 ♕xb6 axb6 12 a3 ♖fc8 Balashov-Hellers, Malmö 1987/88; 13 h3! ±.

8 ♗d3 ♕b6

8 ... ♘c6 9 0-0 ♕b6 10 a3 ♗g4 11 b4? e5! 12 b5 ♘xd4! ∓ Rakić-Gligorić, Yugoslavia 1957; 11

♖b1! =.

9	♖b1	♘c6
10	a3	a5
11	0-0	♗e6
12	♗xf6	♗xf6
13	♕a4	♗f5
14	♗xf5	gxf5 =

Trifunović-Bukić, Yugoslavia 1963.

9.212

5 ♗xf6!?

Introducing a sharp hand-to-hand fight.

5 ... ♗xf6

No one had ever recaptured with a pawn here until recently. 5 ... exf6 6 dxc5 (6 ♘e4!?) 6 ... 0-0 7 c3 b6 8 cxb6 ♕xb6 9 ♕b3 ♕c7 10 e3 ♘c6 11 ♗e2 ♖b8 12 ♕c2 d5 13 ♘b3 ♗f5 14 ♕d2 ± Plachetka-Velimirović, Stara Pazova 1988. The pawn sacrifice looks speculative.

4 ... h6 5 ♗h4 c5 6 ♗xf6 has also occurred in master play.

6 ♘e4 ♗xd4

6 ... ♕b6 7 ♘xf6+ ♕xf6 8 c3 (8 e3 b6!) 8 ... cxd4 9 cxd4 (9 ♕xd4 ♕xd4 10 ♘xd4 ♘c6 11 e3 d6 12 ♗e2 ♗d7 13 0-0-0 ♖c8 14 g4 ♘e5 15 ♖hg1 a6 16 h4 b5 ∞ E.Torre-Timman, London 1984) 9 ... d5 (9 ... ♘c6?! 10 e4 d6 11 h3 ♗d7 Varnusz-Szöllősi, Budapest 1982; 12 ♕d2! ±) 10 ♕b3! (10 e3 ♕b6! 11 ♕d2 ♘c6 =) 10 ... ♕d6 11 e3 ±.

7	♘xd4	cxd4
8	♕xd4	0-0

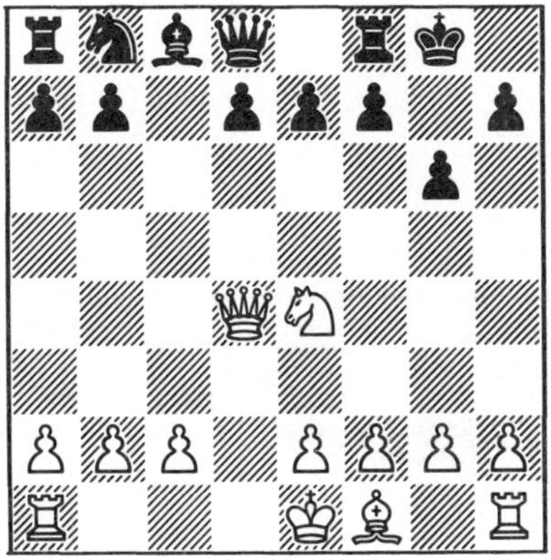

9.2121

9 0-0-0

9 ♕d2 usually transposes, e.g. 9 ... ♘c6 10 0-0-0, or 9 ... d5 10 0-0-0. For 9 ♕d2 ♘c6 10 ♘c3, see 9.2122.

9 ... ♘c6

9 ... ♕a5?! 10 ♘c3! (10 a3? ♘c6 11 ♕d5 ♕xd5 12 ♖xd5 f5! 13 ♘g5 f4 ∓ Sturua-Gulko, USSR 1981) 10 ... ♘c6 11 ♕d2 d6 12 h4 ♗e6 13 ♔b1 (13 h5 g5 14 e4 h6 15 ♔b1 ♖fc8 16 ♘d5 ± Lombard-Kochiev, Kapfenberg 1976) 13 ... ♖ac8 14 e4 ± Yusupov-Gorelov, USSR 1981.

10 ♕d2 d5!

This pawn sacrifice is considered Black's best chance so far. 10 ...

♕c7? 11 ♘c3 e6 12 e4 ± E.Torre-Vogt, Baku 1980.

11 ♘g3

11 ♕xd5 ♕c7 12 ♕c5!? (12 ♕g5 ♗f5 13 ♘c3 ♘b4 ∓) 12 ... b6! (12 ... ♗e6? 13 e3! ± Blees-Nijboer, AVRO 1989) 13 ♕c3 ♕f4+ 14 ♘d2 ♗f5 ∞.

11 ... ♗e6

11 ... d4 12 e3 ♕d5 13 b3 e5 14 ♗c4 ♕c5 15 ♔b2 b5 16 ♘e4 ∞.

12 e3 ♖c8
13 ♔b1 ♕b6
14 ♗d3

14 ♘e2? d4! 15 ♘c1 ♘b4 16 ♗d3 ♘d5 ∓ Agzamov-Loginov, USSR 1986.

14 ... d4
15 exd4 ♗xa2+

The counter-attack probably achieves a draw: 16 ♔xa2 ♘b4+ 17 ♔b1 ♕a5 18 c3 (18 ♕e3? ♕a2+ 19 ♔c1 ♕a1+ 20 ♔d2 ♕xb2 21 ♖c1 ♖c3 ∓) 18 ... ♕a2+ 19 ♔c1 ♕a1+ 20 ♗b1 ♘a2+ 21 ♔c2 ♘b4+ 22 ♔c1 = (22 ♔b3?? b5!).

9.2122
9 ♘c3

To eliminate the ... d5 sacrifice in the previous line.

9 ... ♘c6
10 ♕d2 ♕b6
11 h4

Again White is faced with the problem of what to do with the pawn on b2; 11 0-0-0?? ♕xf2. If 11 ♖b1 ♕d4! 12 ♖d1 ♕xd2+ 13 ♖xd2 d6 14 ♘d5 b5! ∓ Miles-Gulko, Philidelphia 1987. 11 b3 d6?! 12 ♘d5 ♕d8 13 e4 e6 14 ♘e3 ± Epishin-Tseitlin, USSR 1984. As usual, the sacrifice of the b-pawn will lead to a sharper game.

11 ... ♕xb2
12 ♖b1 ♕a3
13 h5 ∞ (Gulko)

9.2123
9 c4

Recently White, disappointed with the results of simple development, has turned to this move, aiming to create some pawn control in the centre.

9 ... ♘c6
10 ♕d2 d6

10 ... ♕a5 11 g3 b6 12 ♗g2 ♗a6 (12 ... ♗b7?! 13 ♘c3 d6 14 0-0 ♖ac8 15 ♖fd1 ♕e5 16 b3 ♖fd8 17 ♘d5 ± Wegner-Michalsen, West German Championship 1989) 13 b3 ♕xd2+ 14 ♔xd2 ♖ac8 15 ♖hd1 ♖fd8 16 ♘c3 ♔f8 17 ♔c2 ♗b7 18 ♔b2 ♘a5 19 ♗h3! ± Azmaiparashvili-Ye Jiangchuan, Beijing 1988.

11 ♘c3 ♗e6
12 e4 ♕b6!

12 ... ♕a5 13 ♗e2 a6 14 ♘d5

♕xd2+ 15 ♔xd2 ♗xd5 16 cxd5 and White has the better endgame, for example 16 ... ♘d4 17 ♗d3 ♖fc8 18 ♖ac1 ♔f8 (18 ... e5 19 ♖c3 ♖c5 20 ♖hc1 ♖ac8 21 ♖xc5 ♖xc5 22 ♖xc5 dxc5 23 ♔c3 ± Smyslov) 19 ♔e3 ♘b5 20 g4 h6 21 h4 ± Smyslov-Ernst, London 1988.

13 ♗e2

Or 13 ♘d5 ♗xd5 14 exd5 ♘d4! with the tactical idea 15 ♖d1 e5 16 dxe6 ♖ae8!! 17 ♕xd4 ♖xe6+ 18 ♗e2 ♖fe8 with near equality. 15 0-0-0 is unclear. 13 ♖d1? ♘e5! 14 b3 f5! ∓ Spiridonov-Kasparov, Illustrative Game 54.

13	**...**	**♘d4**
14	**0-0**	**♖ac8**
15	**b3**	

With a microscopic edge to White.

9.22

4 ... 0-0

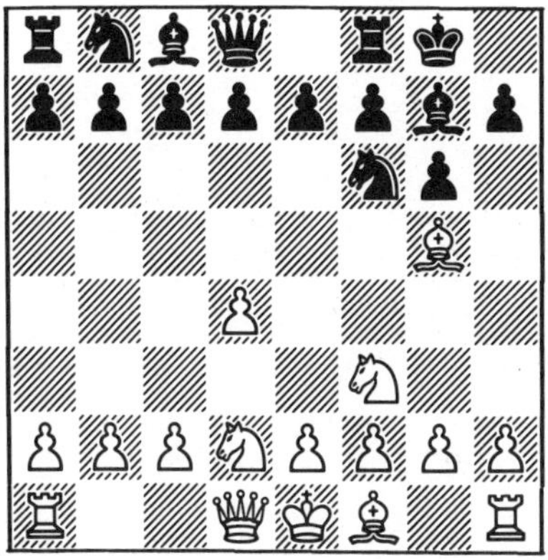

As we have mentioned, this move will be looked at in connection with ... c7-c5.

5 e3

For 5 c3 d6 6 e4 or 5 e4 d6 see the next chapter. The latter move order is dubious due to 5 ... c5!? 6 c3?! cxd4 7 cxd4 d5!. Rozentalis-Glek, Odessa 1988 continued instead 6 e5 ♘d5 7 dxc5 h6 8 ♘c4 (8 ♗h4 ♘f4 9 ♗g3 ♘e6 =) 8 ... hxg5 9 ♕xd5 g4 10 ♘fd2 ♘c6 11 c3 ♕c7 12 f4 gxf3 13 ♘xf3 b5! 14 cxb6 axb6 ∞. Also possible for Black is 5 ... d5 6 ♗d3 h6 7 ♗xf6 exf6!? 8 exd5?! ♖e8+ 9 ♗e2 ♗f5 10 ♘c4 ♕xd5 11 0-0 ♗e4 12 ♘e3 = Bezold-Veingold, Budapest 1989.

In the following we look at the ... c7-c5 set-ups, although the order of moves might change in some of the cases.

5 ... c5

5 ... h6 6 ♗h4 (6 ♗f4 d6 7 h3 ♘bd7 8 c3 b6 9 a4 ♗b7 10 ♗c4 e5! ∓ Smyslov-Padevsky, Havana 1964) 6 ... c5 7 c3 b6 8 ♗d3 ♗b7? 9 ♗xf6! exf6 10 dxc5 bxc5 11 ♗xg6! ± Basman-Ciocaltea, Bognor Regis 1964; 5 ... d6 6 ♗c4 = Alekhine-Blümich, Illustrative Game No 55.

6 c3

6 ♗xf6 ♗xf6 7 ♘e4 ♕b6! 8 ♘xf6+ ♕xf6 9 c3 d6 10 ♗e2 b6 11 0-0 ♗b7 12 a4 cxd4 13 exd4 a6 14

♖e1 ♘d7 = Taimanov-Gulko, USSR 1976; 6 ♗d3 cxd4 7 exd4 ♘c6 8 c3 (8 0-0 d6 9 ♖e1 h6 10 ♗xf6 ♗xf6 11 c3 ♗g7 12 ♗e4 ♖b8 = Johanessen-Olafsson, Bergendaa 1960) 8 ... d6 9 0-0 ♕c7! 10 ♖e1 e5 11 dxe5 dxe5 12 ♘c4 ♘e8 13 ♕e2 f6 14 ♗d2 ♗e6 ∓ Vizhmanavin–Lanka, USSR 1986.

6 ... b6

(a) 6 ... cxd4 7 exd4 (7 cxd4 d5 =) 7 ... d5 (7 ... d6 8 ♗d3 ♘c6 9 0-0 h6 10 ♗h4 ♘h5! 11 ♖e1 f5 12 d5 ♘e5 13 ♗c2 ♘f4 ∓ Timman-H.Olafsson, Malta 1980; 10 ♗xf6 ♗xf6 11 d5 ♘e5 12 ♘xe5 dxe5 13 ♕b3 ♗g7 14 ♖ad1 ♔h7 ∞ Filip-Olafsson, Varna 1962; 8 ♗c4!?) 8 ♗d3 ♘c6 9 0-0 ♕c7 10 ♖e1 ♘h5 11 ♘f1 ♘f4 12 ♗b5 e6 13 ♕d2 ♘h5 14 ♘g3 ♘xg3 15 hxg3 a6 16 ♗xc6 bxc6 17 ♗h6 ± Trifunović-Gligorić, Yugoslavia 1971.

(b) 6 ... d6 7 ♗e2 (7 ♗d3 ♘c6 8 0-0 ♗d7? 9 ♕e2 ♖c8 10 dxc5! dxc5 11 ♖fd1 h6 12 ♗h4 g5 13 ♗g3 ♘h5 14 ♘e4 Taimanov-Ojanen, Helsinki 1966; 8 ... b6!) 7 ... h6 8 ♗h4 ♘bd7 9 a4 ♕c7 10 ♕b1?! e5 11 0-0 ♖e8 12 dxe5 ♘xe5 13 ♘xe5 dxe5 ∓ Guimard-Keres, Buenos Aires 1964; 7 ♗c4 d5 8 ♗d3 =, see Chapter 11.

9.221

7 ♗d3

This stereotyped developing move does not necessarily secure a plus for White.

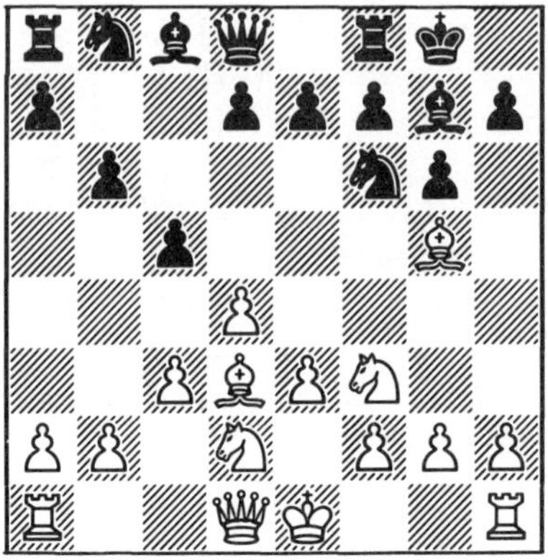

(a) 7 ♗c4 d5 8 ♗e2 ♗a6 9 0-0 ♕c8 10 a4 ♘c6 Möller-Ader, Moscow 1956 or 7 ... ♗b7 8 0-0 d6 9 h3 ♘c6 10 ♕e2 ♖c8 11 ♗a6? (11 a3!) 11 ... ♕c7 12 ♗xb7 ♕xb7 13 ♖fd1 ♘d8! 14 ♖ac1 ♘e6 15 ♗h4 ♖c7 ∓ Toran-Taimanov, Kapfenberg 1970.

(b) 7 ♗e2 ♗b7 (7 ... ♗a6?! 8 0-0 ♕c8? 9 h3 h6 10 ♗h4 ♗xe2 11 ♕xe2 ♕a6 12 ♖fe1 ♕xe2 13 ♖xe2 ♘c6? 14 ♗xf6! ♗xf6 15 dxc5 bxc5 16 ♘e4 ± Guimard-Taimanov, Buenos Aires 1960; 8 ... d6!?) 8 0-0 d6 9 a4 (9 ♖e1 ♕c7 10 a4 ♘bd7 11 ♗b1 e5?! 12 dxe5 dxe5 13 e4 a6 14 ♗c4 ♗c6 15 ♗xf6 ♘xf6 16 ♕e2 ♗b7 17 ♗d3 ♘e8 18 ♘f1 ♘d6 19 ♘3d2 ± Platonov-Sideif Zade, Tashkent 1980; 11 ... h6 12 ♗xf6 ♘xf6 13 e4 e6 =) 9 ... a6 10 b4 ♘bd7 11 ♕b1 (11 ♕b3 ♕c7 12 ♖fc1 e5 13 ♕d1 h6 14 ♗xf6 ♗xf6 15 dxc5 bxc5 16 e4 d5 17 exd5

♗xd5 18 ♘c4 ♗e6 ∓ Quinteros-Ribli, Amsterdam 1973) 11 ... cxd4?! 12 cxd4 ♖c8 13 ♖c1 ♖xc1+ 14 ♕xc1 ♕b8 15 ♕a3 ± Doda-Suba, Sandomierz 1976.

7 ... ♗b7

7 ... ♗a6 8 ♗xa6 ♘xa6 9 ♕a4 ♕c8 10 0-0 ♕b7 11 b4 d6 12 b5 ♘c7 13 ♕b3 a6 14 a4 axb5 15 axb5 = Liebert-Bednarski, Zinnowitz 1965.

8 0-0 d6
9 b4

9 ♕e2?! ♘c6 (9 ... ♘bd7 10 ♖fd1 ♖c8?! 11 a4! ♕c7 12 a5 ± Trifunović-Teschner, Dortmund 1961; 10 ... h6! 11 ♗h4 g5 12 ♗g3 ♘h5 13 ♗a6 ♗xa6 14 ♕xa6 f5 ∞ Konstantinopolsky-Zaitsev, Moscow 1966; 9 ... h6 10 ♗h4 ♘bd7 11 h3! ♘h5 12 ♘h2 cxd4 13 cxd4 ♗f6 14 ♗xf6 ♘dxf6 15 ♖ac1 ± Petrosian-Wade, Leipzig 1960) 10 ♖fd1 cxd4 11 cxd4 h6 12 ♗h4 ♘b4 13 ♗c4 a6 14 ♗b3 ♖c8 15 ♖ac1 b5 = Hort-Smyslov, Wijk aan Zee 1972.

9 ♕a4 ♘bd7: see Illustrative Game No 49.

9 ... ♘bd7
10 dxc5 bxc5
11 ♕a4

11 ♖b1 ♕c7 12 ♕a4 e5? (12 ... ♗c6) 13 dxe5 dxe5 14 e4! ♘b6 15 ♕a5 ♕d6 ± Miles-Watson, New York 1987.

11 ... ♘b6
12 ♕a3 ♕c7
13 ♖ab1 ♖fc8 =

Pietzsch-Smyslov, Havana 1965.

9.222
7 a4!

Better than the stereotyped developing moves. White wants to ruin Black's pawn formation by a4-a5.

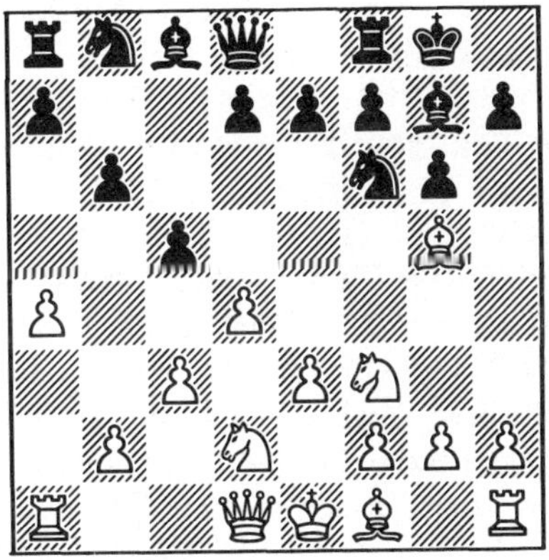

7 ... ♘c6

Thwarting the above mentioned threat, the knight will nevertheless block the bishop's way on the long diagonal.

8 ♗d3 ♗b7
9 0-0 h6
10 ♗h4 d6
11 ♕b1!

A delicate multi-purpose move, gaining an advantage in space: 11 ... ♖c8 12 ♖c1 cxd4 13 exd4 ♘d5

14 ♖e1 ♘f4 15 ♗c4 ♕d7 16 ♗g3 g5 17 ♗b5 a6 18 ♗f1 ± Ribli-Gheorghiu, Baile Herculane 1982 (but different order of moves).

ILLUSTRATIVE GAMES

1 d4 ♘f6 2 ♘f3 g6 3 ♗g5 ♗g7

52) **Kovačević-Larsen**
Bugojno 1984

4 e3 c5 5 ♘bd2 b6 6 c3 ♗b7 7 ♕a4!? 0-0 Due to the order of moves, this game was quoted at 9.1(a), yet the position now is already 9.1(b). **8 ♗e2** More active is 8 ♗d3! **8 ... d6** If 8 ... d5 9 0-0 ♘bd7 10 ♖fd1, then ♖ac1 and c4 ±. **9 0-0 ♘bd7 10 b4 ♕c7 11 bxc5 bxc5 12 ♖ab1 ♖fc8 13 ♕a3 ♘b6 14 ♗d3 e6** Black has equalised. Even simpler was 14 ... h6 15 ♗h4 g5 16 ♗g3 ♘h5 17 ♖fe1 ♘xg3 18 hxg3 e6. **15 ♖fe1 h6 16 ♗h4 ♘h5 17 ♘f1 cxd4** 17 ... g5 18 ♗g3 ♘xg3 19 ♘xg3 g4 20 ♘d2 cxd4 21 cxd4 ♕c3 =. **18 cxd4 ♗xf3?!** Black is going to miss his bishop. **19 gxf3 ♕c3 20 ♕a6!** Threatening a later advance of the a-pawn (a2-a4-a5). **20 ... ♗f6** 20 ... ♘d5? 21 ♗e4 ±. **21 ♗xf6 ♘xf6 22 ♔g2?!** Shilly-shallying! 22 ♘g3! then ♘e2 and ♖ec1 ±. **22 ... ♘e8! 23 ♗e2** 23 ♘g3? ♘c7!. **23 ... d5** 23 ... ♘c7 24 ♕d3 ♘cd5 =. **24 ♖ed1 ♘d6 25 ♘d2 ♘f5 26 ♘b3?! ♕c7 27 ♘d2** 27 ♖bc1 ♕e7 28 ♖xc8+?! ♖xc8 29 ♖c1 ♖xc1 30 ♘xc1 ♘xd4! ∓. **27 ... ♕e7 28 ♗d3 ♘h4+ 29 ♔f1! ♖c6** 29 ... ♕g5 30 a4!. **30 ♖dc1 ♖ac8 31 ♖xc6 ♖xc6 32 ♔e2 ♔g7 33 f4 ♕c7 34 ♕a5 ♖c3?** 34 ... g5!?. **35 ♖b5!** 36 ♖c5! is threatened. **35 ... ♘d7 36 ♕b4 ♘f5?** On 36 ... ♕c8 White's reply is 37 a4 then a5-a6 and ♖b7. **37 ♗xf5 gxf5 38 ♖b7 ♕c6 39 ♖xd7 1-0** (Kovačević)

53) **Bisguier-Fischer**
US Championship 1965/66

4 ♘bd2 c5 5 c3 cxd4 It is usually reasonable for Black to open the c-file, provided that White's knight is already posted to d2. **6 cxd4 ♘c6 7 e3 0-0 8 a3** White's concept seems harmless. **8 ... h6 9 ♗h4 d6** Obviously, 9 ... d5 is just as playable but Fischer wants to have a sharp game. **10 ♗c4 ♗f5 11 h3 ♖c8 12 0-0 e5 13 e4 ♗d7 14 dxe5 dxe5 15 ♗a2?!** 15 ♖c1!?; 15 ♗xf6!?. **15 ... g5 16 ♗g3 ♕e7 17 ♖e1** The White pieces are already just fiddling about, trying to find themselves proper posts. **17 ... ♖cd8 18 ♘h2 ♗e6 19 ♗xe6 ♕xe6 20 ♘hf1 ♖d3! 21 ♖e3?! ♖d7** Giving away a tempo to hinder the ♘f1-e3-f5 manoeuvre. **22 ♕b3 ♕e7! 23 ♘f3 ♖fd8 24 ♖ae1 ♘h5! 25 ♖c3 ♕f6 26 ♘e3?** For better or for worse, 27 ♗h2 should have been played to prevent the doubling of the pawns. **26 ... ♘d4! 27 ♘xd4 exd4 28 ♘g4 ♕g6 29 ♖d3 ♘xg3! 30 fxg3?** Playing 30 ♖xg3 d3! is in Black's favour still, it is the lesser of two evils. **30 ... ♖c7 31 ♘f2 ♖dc8 32 ♖e2 ♖c1+ 33 ♔h2 h5!** Weaving a mating net! **34 ♕xb7 ♗e5 35 ♕d5!** White wants to use his queen in the defence. **35 ... ♖1c5 36 ♕d7 h4 37 ♘h1** A ridiculous place for the knight, yet it seems to parry Black's offensive. **37 ... ♖c1 38 ♖f3?!** After 38 ♕g4! the agony lasts longer.

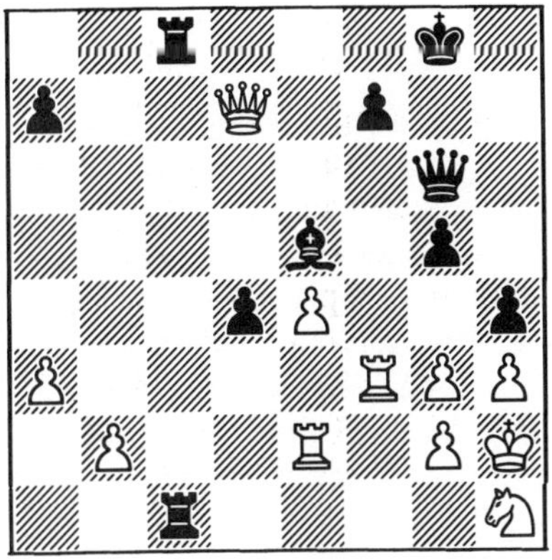

38 ... g4!! Revealing that not only is the g3 pawn in trouble, but also that mate is possible on the h-file. **39 ♕xg4 ♕xg4 40 hxg4 ♔g7!** The threat is 41 ... hxg3+ and 42 ... ♖h8+ mate. **41 ♖f5 ♖xh1+! 0-1**

Black threatens checkmate not only from his own back rank but also from White's: 42 ♔xh1 ♖c1+ etc.

54) **Spiridonov-Kasparov**
Skara 1980

4 ♘bd2 c5 5 ♗xf6 ♗xf6 6 ♘e4 ♗xd4 7 ♘xd4 cxd4 8 ♕xd4 0-0 9 c4 ♘c6 10 ♕d2 d6 11 ♘c3 11 e3 ♗e6 12 ♘c3 a6 13 ♗e2 ♕a5 14 0-0 ♖ab8 =. **11 ... ♗e6 12 e4 ♕b6! 13 ♖d1?** 13 ♘d5?! ♗xd5 14 exd5 ♘d4! 15 ♖d1 e5 16 dxe6 ♖ae8 17 ♕xd4 ♖xe6+ 18 ♗e2 ♖fe8 ±; 13 ♗e2! ♘d4 14 0-0 ♖ac8 15 b3 =. **13 ... ♘e5! 14 b3 f5! 15 ♗e2** 15 exf5 ♖xf5 16 f4 ♖af8 ∓; 16 ♘e4 ♖af8 17 ♗e2 ♖f4 ∓.

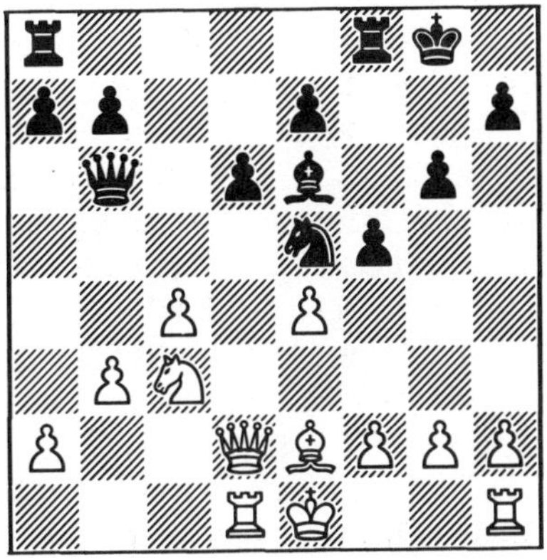

15 ... f4! The blockade has been completed and Black's strong knight on e5 is going to dominate the rest of the game. Positionally speaking, Black has won. **16 ♘d5 ♗xd5 17 ♕xd5+ ♔g7 18 0-0 ♖ac8?!** More accurate is 18 ... ♔f6!, e.g.

19 b4?! ♕xb4 20 ♖b1 ♕a3 21 ♖xb7 ♖ab8! ∓. **19 b4!? ♕xb4 20 ♖b1 ♕a3 21 ♖xb7 ♔f6! 22 h4!? h6** 22 ... ♕xa2? 23 ♗g4!. **23 ♖d1?** 23 ♕d2! g5 24 ♖b3! ♕c5 25 ♖b5 ∞. **23 ... ♖b8!** Getting hold of the open file again! A terrible trap was 23 ... ♕xa2?? 24 ♕xd6+!! exd6 25 ♖xd6+ mate! **24 ♖c7 ♖fc8 25 ♖xc8 ♖xc8 26 ♕b7 ♕c5 27 ♕b2?** 27 ♖b1!?. **27 ... ♕b6! 28 ♕c1 g5 29 ♖d5 e6 30 hxg5+ hxg5 31 ♖d1 ♔e7** 31 ... ♖h8!. **32 ♕c2** 32 ♕c3 ♖h8 ∓. **32 ... ♖b8 33 ♕a4 g4! 34 ♕a3 ♕c5! 35 ♕c3 g3 36 ♖f1 gxf2+ 37 ♖xf2 ♖b1+ 38 ♗f1 ♕e3! 39 ♕xe3 fxe3 40 ♖c2 ♘xc4! 0-1**
(Kasparov)

55) **Alekhine-Blümich**
Dresden 1926

4 ♘bd2 0-0 5 e3 d6 6 ♗c4 Once Pillsbury's favourite, this move provokes ... d6-d5 yet, to the best of our knowledge today, ... d5 gives Black a fair chance to equalise. See Chapter 10. **6 ... ♘c6** Apart from 6 ... d5, quite promising is 6 ... ♘bd7 too, e.g. 7 c3 e5 8 0-0 (8 ♘e4 ♕e8 9 ♘xf6+ ♗xf6 10 ♗xf6 ♘xf6 11 dxe5 dxe5 12 0-0 ♕e7 = Bukal-Matulović, Sarajevo 1969) 8 ... h6 9 ♗h4 ♕e8 10 dxe5 dxe5 11 a4 a5 Guimard-Najdorf, Havana 1962; 12 ♕e2 =. Bad is 6 ... c5?! 7 c3 ♘a6 8 0-0 ♘c7 9 ♕e2 ♕e8 10 ♖fd1 b5 11 ♗b3 ♗b7 12 a4! c4 13 ♗c2 a6 14 e4 e5 15 dxe5 dxe5 16 b3! ± Gy.Szilágyi-Tapasztó, Budapest 1955. **7 c3 a6?! 8 ♕e2 ♗g4?** 8 ... ♗d7!. **9 h3 ♗d7 10 ♘h2!** Unusual but very strong, threatening 11 ♘g4 and 11 f4 simultaneously. **10 ... ♕c8** 10 ... e5 11 ♘g4 ♗xg4 12 hxg4 exd4 13 cxd4 ±. **11 f4 e5?!** In a certain respect this can be seen as giving White a forced win, but without the attempt to escape, Black's game is unbearably cramped after 12 0-0 and e3-e4-e5. **12 fxe5 dxe5 13 0-0 ♘h5** If 13 ... ♘e8 14 d5, then 15 ♗e7 and White wins the exchange.

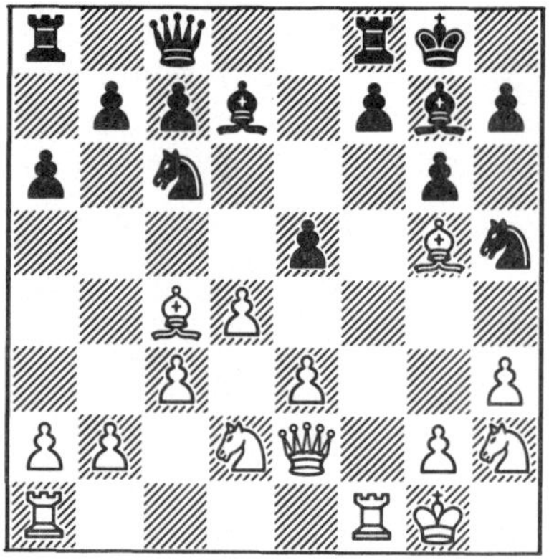

14 ♖xf7!!? Alekhine cannot suppress the artist in himself. In his analysis, however, he admits that the simple 14 ♕f3 (threatening 15 g4) would have been enough to win. E.g. 14 ... exd4 15 cxd4 ♘xd4 (forced!) 16 exd4 ♗xd4+ 17 ♗e3! ± ±. Still, chess is not only a sport, but an art as well, and the text move really meets our aesthetic needs. **14 ... ♖xf7 15 ♗xf7+ ♔xf7 16 ♕c4+ ♗e6** 16 ... ♔f8 17 ♖f1+ ♗f5 18 g4 ♘g3 19 ♖f3 +-. **17 d5 ♗xd5**

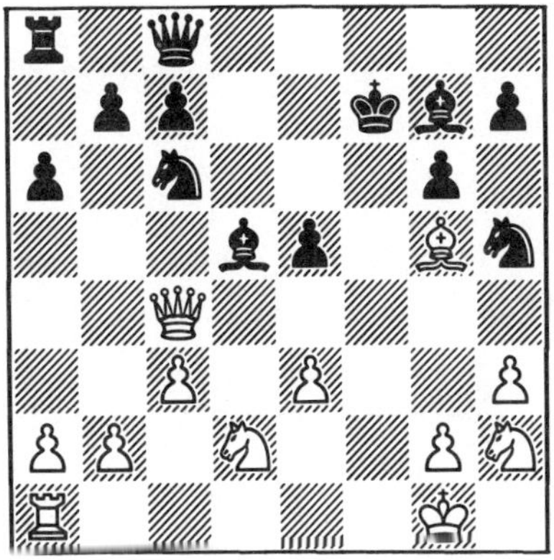

18 ♖f1+!! The point of the combination! For on 18 ... ♗f6 White's response is not 19 ♕xd5+ but 19 ♕h4!, e.g. 19 ... ♔g8 20 ♗xf6 ♘xf6 21 ♕xf6 ♕e6 22 ♘g4 +-. Real complications emerge after 18 ... ♔e6! 19 ♕g4+ ♔d6 20 ♘c4+ and now: (1) 20 ... ♔c5 21 b4+ ♘xb4 (21 ... ♔b5 22 a4+ ♔xa4 23 ♕d1+!) 22 ♗e7+ ♔c6 (22 ... ♔b5 23 a4+!) 23 ♘a5+ ♔b6 24 ♗c5+! etc; or (2) 20 ... ♗xc4! 21 ♕xc4 b5 22 ♖d1+ ♘d4 23 ♕e2 ♕f5 24 ♘f3 ♘g3 25 ♕e1 ♘e4 26 ♗h4 g5 27 ♗g3 +-. **18 ... ♘f6?! 19 ♕xd5+ ♕e6 20 ♕f3** 21 ♘g4 and 21 ♘e4 can not both be parried. **20 ... ♕f5 21 ♗xf6 1-0**

(Notes based on Alekhine's)

10 Countering the King's Indian and the Grünfeld: QB Line with Black playing the traditional King's Indian

1	**d4**	**♘f6**
2	**♘f3**	**g6**
3	**♗g5**	**♗g7**
4	**♘bd2**	**d6**

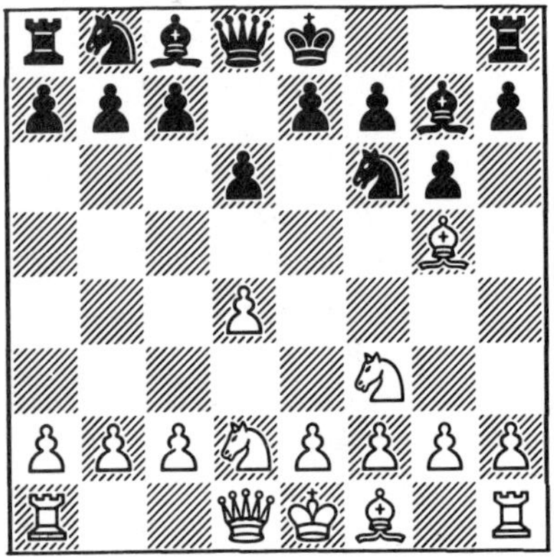

This chapter looks at the variations in which Black is determined to play ... d7-d6 (King's Indian or Flank). The latter may emerge from 1 e4 g6 as well. On the other hand, Black is free to choose either ... c7-c5 or ... e7-e5 and to time his castling.

5 e4

A logical consequence of the preceding move. 5 c3 is usually only a change in the order of moves although there are a few exceptions:

5 ... h6 (5 ... 0-0 6 e4 h6 7 ♗h4 ♕e8 8 ♗d3 e5 9 dxe5 dxe5 10 0-0 ♘bd7 11 ♖e1 ♘c5 12 ♗f1 ♗g4 13 ♕e2 ♘h5 14 ♕e3 ♘e6 15 ♘c4 ♘ef4 16 b4 b6 17 a4 ±. E.Torre-Gutman, Illustrative Game No 56; 7 ... ♘c6?! 8 ♗b5 ♗d7 9 0-0 a6?! 10 ♗c4! e5 11 dxe5 dxe5 12 ♖e1 ♕e8 13 a4 ♘h5 14 ♘b3! g5 15 ♗g3 ♖d8 16 ♘fd2 ± Smyslov-Nunn, Tilburg 1982; 7 ... c5?! 8 dxc5 dxc5 9 ♗c4 ♘c6 10 0-0 ♘a5 11 ♗e2 ♗e6 12 ♘e5 ♕c7 13 ♗g3! ♘xe4 14 ♘xe4 ♗xe5 15 f4 f5 16 fxe5 fxe4 17 ♕d2 ± T.Horváth-Perényi, Budapest 1982; 5 ... ♗f5!?) 6 ♗h4 g5 7 ♗g3 ♘h5 8 e3! (Original!) 8 ... ♘xg3 (8 ... e6 9 ♗d3 ♕e7 10 ♕e2 ♘c6 11 ♘b3 ♗d7 12 ♘fd2 ♘xg3 13 hxg3 0-0-0

± Kovačević-Ree, Plovdiv 1983) 9 hxg3 ♘d7?! 10 a4! Ribli-Adorján, Illustrative Game No 57.

Extravagant is 5 h3, e.g. 5 ... h6 6 ♗f4 b6 7 e4 ♗b7 8 ♗b5+ ♘bd7 9 ♕e2 a6 10 ♗d3 e5 11 dxe5 ♘h5 12 ♗h2 dxe5 13 0-0-0 ♕e7 14 ♖he1 0-0 = Smyslov-Larsen, Tilburg 1982.

A popular continuation is 5 e3, often leading into the variations of Chapter 9. 5 ... 0-0, and now:

(a) 6 ♗e2 ♘bd7 7 0-0 (7 c3 e5 8 0-0 h6 9 ♗h4 ♕e8 10 a4 e4 11 ♘e1 ♘h7 12 ♘c2 f5 13 f3 ♘df6 14 ♗xf6 ♘xf6 15 fxe4 fxe4 16 a5 c6 17 ♕e1 d5 ∓ Kovačević-Gligorić, Yugoslavia 1979; 7 ... b6 8 0-0 ♗b7 9 a4 a6 10 ♕c2 c5 11 ♖fd1 ♕c7 12 ♘e1 ♖ac8 13 ♗f3 ♖fe8 14 ♗xb7 ♕xb7 15 ♕d3 d5 = Klarić-Krogius, Sochi 1984) 7 ... e5 8 ♗h4 ♖e8 9 c4!? b6 10 ♖c1 h6 11 h3 ♗b7 12 d5 a5 13 b3 ♘c5 14 a3 g5 15 ♗g3 c6 16 b4 axb4 17 axb4 ♘ce4 ∞ Ye Rongguang-Dreyev, Manila 1990.

(b) 6 ♗d3 ♘bd7 (6 ... ♘c6 7 0-0 h6 8 ♗h4 g5 9 ♗g3 ♘h5 10 c3 e6 11 e4 f5 12 exf5 exf5 13 ♕b3+ ♔h8 14 h3 ♗d7 15 ♘c4 ♖b8 = Khalifman-Hodgson, Moscow 1985) 7 0-0 (7 ♕e2 h6 8 ♗xf6 ♘xf6 9 h3?! e5! 10 dxe5 dxe5 11 0-0-0 ♕e7 = Kamsky-Ermolinsky, USSR 1987) 7 ... b6 8 ♖e1 (8 c3 ♗b7 9 ♕e2 h6 10 ♗h4 ♕c8 11 e4 e5 12 dxe5 dxe5 13 ♖fe1 ♖e8 14 b4 ♘h5 15 ♕d1 ♗f6 = E.Torre-Nunn, Tilburg 1982) 8 ... c5 9 c3 ♗b7 10 a4 ♕c7 11 a5 e5 (Dreyev-Kr.Georgiev, Moscow 1985) 12 dxe5! dxe5 13 e4 =.

10.1

5 ... h6!?

It is quite a common opinion that the chasing of the white bishop is Black's best chance hence this move is played more frequently in master play than 5 0-0. The debate, however, is not at all 'finished'.

6 ♗h4

(a) 6 ♗xf6?! ♗xf6 7 e5 (7 ♗c4 e5 8 dxe5 dxe5 =; 7 c3 ♗g7 8 ♗c4 ♘d7 9 0-0 0-0 10 ♕e2 e5 11 dxe5 dxe5 12 ♖fd1 ♕e7 13 ♘f1 ♘c5 ∓ Simić-Vadász, Yugoslavia 1977) 7 ... ♗g7 8 ♗b5+ (8 ♗c4 0-0 9 ♕e2 ♘c6 10 c3 a6 11 e6 f5 12 d5 b5 13 dxc6 bxc4 14 0-0-0 ♖b8 15 ♘xc4 ♕e8 ∞ Thorbergsson-Taimanov, Reykjavik 1968) 8 ... c6 9 ♗d3 ♗e6 10 ♕e2 d5 11 0-0 ♘d7 12 c3 ♕b6 13 ♖ab1 c5 14 ♕e3 0-0-0 15 a4 ♔b8 16 b4 c4 ∞ Guimard-Rabar, Gothenberg 1955.

(b) 6 ♗e3?! ♘g4?! 7 ♗f4 e5 8 dxe5 ♘xe5 9 c3 ♘bc6 10 ♗b5 0-0 11 0-0 ♕f6 12 ♗g3 ♗g4 13 ♗e2 ♖fe8 14 ♘xe5 ♗xe2 15 ♕xe2 ♘xe5?! 16 f4 ± Johansson–Bobotsov, Havana 1966.

6 ... g5

6 ... 0-0 7 c3 ♘h5 8 ♗c4 ♘c6 9 0-0 ♘f4 10 ♖e1 g5 11 ♗g3 e5 12 dxe5 dxe5 13 ♘f1 ♕f6 14 ♘e3 ♘e7 = Ochoa-Karlkins, New York 1987.

7 ♗g3 ♘h5

In for a penny, in for a pound . . .

8 c3

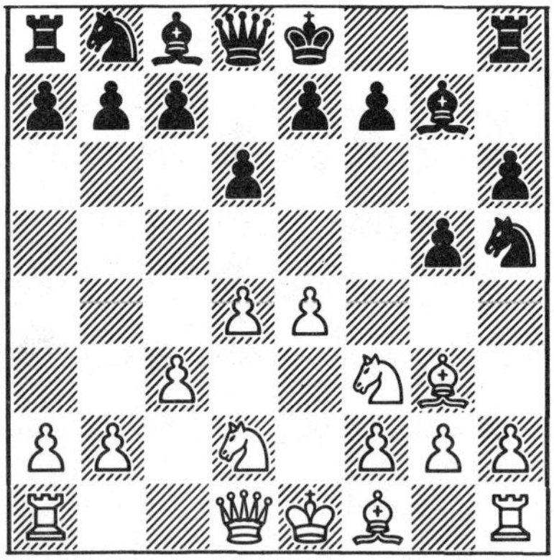

10.11

8 ... ♘d7

There is no 'last word' about the choice between this and 8 ... e6 (see 10.12), although the latter seems more flexible. Others:

(a) 8 ... c5?! 9 dxc5 ♘xg3 10 hxg3 dxc5 11 ♗c4! e6 12 g4 ♗d7 13 ♗e2 ♗c6 14 ♕c2 ♘d7 15 ♘c4 ♕c7 16 ♖d1 ♘e5 17 ♘fxe5 ♗xe5 18 ♕d3 ± Agzamov-Rashkovsky, USSR 1983. Much worse for Black is 11 ... ♘c6? 12 ♘xg5! hxg5 13 ♖xh8+ ♗xh8 14 ♕h5 ♗f6 15 f4 e6 16 e5 ♗g7 17 ♘e4 ± Trifunović-Damjanović, Yugoslavia, 1961.

(b) 8 ... ♘xg3 9 hxg3 c6 10 ♘c4 b5 11 ♘e3 ±.

(c) 8 ... 0-0 9 ♗c4 e6 10 e5 c5 11 ♘e4 d5 12 ♘fxg5! ♘xg3 13 hxg3 dxe4 14 ♘xe4 cxd4 15 ♕g4! ± Z.Nikolić-Martinović, Yugoslavia 1980. Or 9 ♘c4 c5 (9 ... e6 10 e5 ♘xg3 11 hxg3 ♘c6 12 ♕c2 ♖e8 13 ♘e3 dxe5 14 dxe5 ♘xe5 15 ♘xe5 ♗xe5 16 ♘g4 ♗g7 17 ♖d1 ♕e7 18 ♘xh6+ ♔f8 19 ♕h7 ♕f6 20 ♖d3 ± Balashov-Smirin, USSR 1987) 10 dxc5 ♘xg3 11 hxg3 dxc5 12 ♕c2 ♘c6 13 ♖d1 ♕c7 14 ♘e3 ± Ionov-Gusinov, USSR 1988.

9 ♘c4

(a) 9 ♗c4 e6 10 ♘f1!? ♘xg3 (10 ... ♕e7 11 ♘e3! ♘b6 12 ♗e2 ±; 10 ... f5?! 11 exf5 exf5 12 ♘e5 ♘hf6 13 ♘e3!? ♘b6 14 ♘f7 ♕e7 15 ♘xh8 ♗xh8 16 h4 ♗g7 ∞) 11 hxg3 g4 12 ♘h4! h5 13 f4 ♘f6 14 ♕d3!? c6 15 d5! exd5 16 exd5 cxd5 ± Dobosz-Jansa, Copenhagen 1981, or 10 ♕e2 a6! 11 a4 b6 12 ♘f1 ♗b7 13 ♘3d2 ♘f4 ∓ Simić-Ciocaltea, Yugoslavia 1977. Or 10 ♕c2 ♕e7 11 0-0-0 a6 12 a3 ♘b6 13 ♗d3 ♗d7 14 ♖he1 ♘xg3 15 hxg3 g4 16 ♘h2 h5 17 ♘hf1 ♕f6 18 ♖e2 0-0-0 19 ♘e3 ♕g5 ∞ Cifuentes-Hort, Amsterdam 1987.

(b) 9 ♗d3?! c5 10 d5 0-0 11 a4 ♘df6! ∓ Espig-Uhlmann, Illustrative Game No 58.

9 ... ♘xg3

(a) 9 ... ♘df6 10 ♕c2 ♘xg3 (10 ... ♗g4!?) 11 hxg3 e6 12 0-0-0 ♕e7 13 ♘e3 ♗d7 14 e5! ♘d5 15 ♘xd5 exd5 16 exd6 ♕xd6 17 ♖e1+ ♗e6 18 ♕a4+ c6 19 ♗d3 ± Spassky-Najdorf, Moscow 1967.

(b) 9 ... e6 10 ♘e3 (10 ♘fd2 ♘xg3 11 hxg3 ♕e7 12 ♘e3 ♘f6 13 f4 gxf4 14 gxf4 ♗d7 15 ♗d3 0-0-0 = Balashov-Tseshkovsky, Sochi 1975. Better is 13 ♕b3! c6 14 0-0-0 e5?! – 14 ... ♘d7 ⩲ – 15 dxe5 dxe5 16 ♘dc4 ± Salov-Smirin, USSR Championship 1988) 10 ... ♕e7 11 ♕c2 b6 12 0-0-0 ♗b7 13 ♗c4 0-0-0 14 ♖he1 ⩲ Kramer-Honfi, Wijk aan Zee 1969.

10 e6

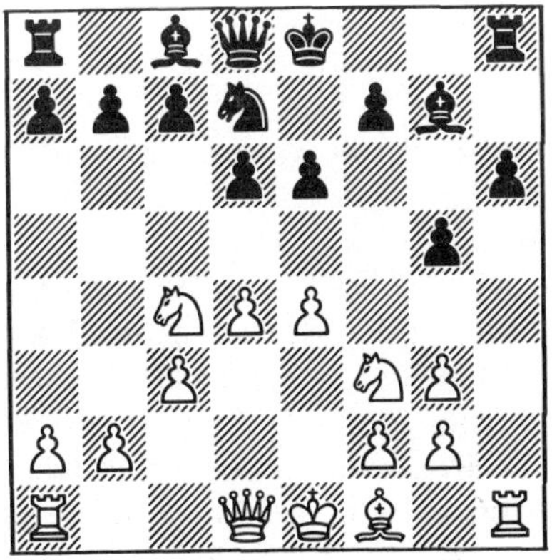

11 ♗d3 ♕e7
12 ♕a4?!

If there is improvement for White, it must be found somewhere around here.

12 ... a6
13 ♘e3 c6
14 ♕c2

Chernin-Short, Wijk aan Zee 1986; 14 ... b5! =.

10.12

8 ... e6

Probably more flexible than 8 ... ♘d7 since here Black has a choice where to develop his b8 knight.

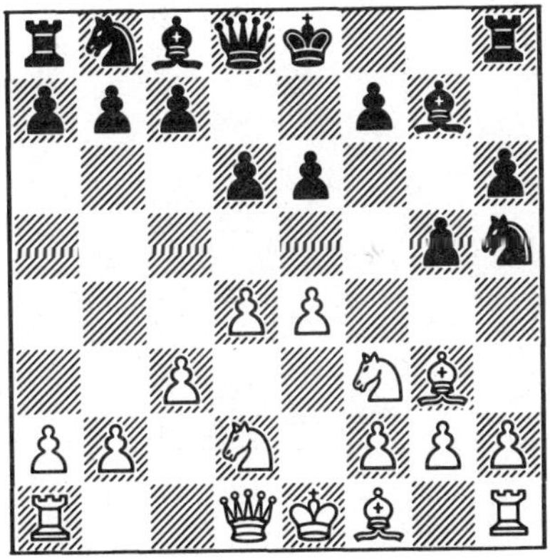

10.121

9 ♗d3

There are plenty of digressions from the main lines of 9 ♗d3 and 9 ♗c4:

(a) 9 ♘b3?! ♘d7 10 ♘fd2 ♘xg3 11 hxg3 0-0 12 ♗d3 a5! 13 a4 f5 ∓ Bronstein-Gufeld, Tallinn 1981.

(b) 9 e5!? ♘xg3 10 hxg3 g4?! (10 ... c5; 10 ... d5) 11 ♘h2 dxe5 12 ♕xg4 ♕g5 13 dxe5 ♕xe5+ 14 ♗e2 ⩲ Varnusz-Forgács, Budapest 1982.

(c) 9 ♕c2 ♘xg3 10 hxg3 ♘c6 11 ♘c4 ♗d7 12 0-0-0 g4 13 d5!? exd5 14 exd5 gxf3 15 dxc6 ♕g5+ 16 ♔b1 ♗xc6 17 ♖e1+ ∞ Morovic-Taylor, New York 1987.

9 ... 0-0

(a) 9 ... ♘d7 10 ♘c4 ♕e7 (10 ... ♘xg3 11 hxg3 ♕e7 leads to 10.11) 11 e5 ♘xg3 12 fxg3! (12 hxg3 g4 13 ♘fd2 f5 ⩱) 12 ... g4 13 ♘h4 dxe5 14 ♕xg4 0-0! 15 dxe5 ♘c5 16 ♗c2 b5 17 ♘e3 ♕g5! = Gofman-Tseitlin, USSR 1982.

(b) 9 ... ♕e7 10 0-0 (10 ♕e2 ♘c6 11 ♘b3 ♗d7 12 ♘fd2 ♘xg3 13 hxg3 0-0-0 14 ♘c4 ♔b8 15 0-0-0 f5 16 ♘ca5 ♘xa5 17 ♘xa5 ∞ Kovačević-Ree, Plovdiv 1983) 10 ... ♘d7 11 ♘c4?! (11 ♖e1) 11 ... 0-0 12 ♖e1 b6 13 a4 Varnusz-Halász, Budapest 1983; 13 ... a6! ∞,or 10 ... 0-0 11 ♖e1 ♘xg3 12 hxg3 ♘d7 13 g4 ♖d8 14 ♘f1 c5 15 ♘g3 cxd4 = Bisguier-R.Byrne, New York 1987.

10 0-0

10 ♘g1?! ♘xg3 11 hxg3 e5 12 dxe5 dxe5 13 ♕c2 ♘d7 14 ♖d1 ♕e7 15 ♘e2 ♘c5 ∞ Christiansen-Bouaziz, Szirák 1987.

10 ... b6!

10 ... ♘c6?! 11 ♘c4 f5 12 exf5 exf5 13 h3 f4 14 ♗h2 ♘f6 (14 ... ♗e6! 15 ♘h4 ♘f6 16 ♘f5 ♕d7 17 ♕c2 ⩲) 15 ♖e1 ♘e7 16 a4 ± Ribli-Schmidt, Illustrative Game No 59.

11 ♘c4 ♗b7
12 a4 a6
13 ♖e1 ♘d7
14 ♘fd2

White has a slight advantage in space (Chernin-Gavrikov, USSR 1985).

10.122

9 ♗c4 ♘d7

(a) 9 ... ♕e7 (9 ... f5?! 10 exf5 exf5 11 ♕b3 ♕e7+? 12 ♔d1 ±) 10 0-0 ♘xg3 11 hxg3 ♘d7 12 a4 h5!? 13 ♕e1! (13 ♕e2 g4 14 ♘h2 ♘f8 ∞) 13 ... ♘f8 14 e5! Psakhis-Zilberstein, Irkutsk 1983; 14 ... g4! 15 exd6 cxd6 16 ♘h4 ♗f6 17 d5! ⩲.

(b) 9 ... ♘c6 10 ♕e2 ♗d7 11 0-0-0 ♕e7 12 ♘e1 ♘xg3 13 hxg3 0-0-0 14 ♘c2 ♔b8 15 ♘b3 ⩲ Yusupov-Vasyukov, USSR 1981.

10 ♘f1

10 ♕c2 ♕e7 11 0-0-0 a6 12 a3 ♘b6 13 ♗d3 ♗d7 14 ♖he1 ♘xg3 15 hxg3 g4 16 ♘h2 h5 17 ♘hf1 ♕f6 18 ♖e2 0-0-0 19 ♘e3 ♕g5 ∞ Cifuentes-Hort, Amsterdam 1987.

10 ... ♘xg3
11 hxg3 g4

11 ... ♘f6 12 e5 dxe5 13 ♘xe5 ♕e7 14 ♘e3 ⩲.

12 ♘h4 h5
13 f4 ♘f6

14	**♕d3**	**c6**
15	**d5**	**exd5**
16	**exd5**	**cxd5**
17	**♗b5+**	**♔f8**
18	**♘e3**	

White stands slightly better (Dobosz-Jansa, Copenhagen 1981; 18 ... a6!? 19 ♗a4 ♘e4 20 ♘xd5 ♘c5 ±).

10.2

5 ... 0-0

For the assessment of this move, see 10.1.

10.21

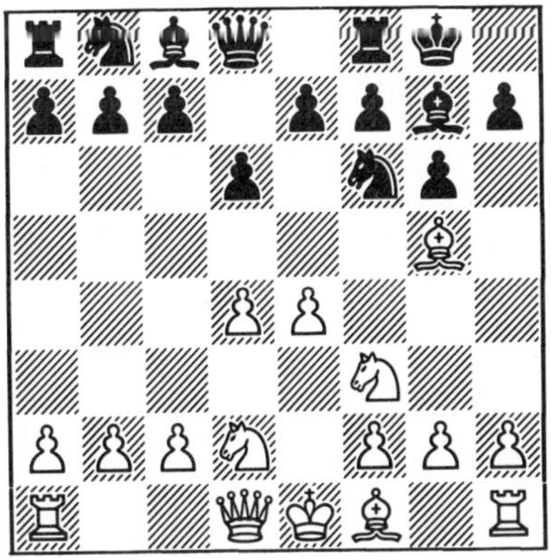

6 c3!

Thus the 'dragon' bishop is condemned to passivity by the c3-d4 pawn formation. Other lines are:

(a) 6 ♗c4?! ♘xe4 7 ♘xe4 d5 8 ♗d3 dxe4 9 ♗xe4 c5! 10 c3 cxd4 11 ♘xd4 ♕a5 12 ♗e3 e5 13 ♘b3 ♕c7 ∓ Guimard-García, Buenos Aires 1964.

(b) For 6 ♗e2 see 7 ♗e2.

(c) 6 h3 ♘c6! (6 ... h6 7 ♗e3! ♘bd7 8 ♗c4 e5 9 dxe5 dxe5 10 g4!? ♕e7 11 ♖g1! ♘c5 12 g5 hxg5 13 ♖xg5 ♘e6 14 ♖xe5 ♘d7 15 ♖xe6 fxe6 16 ♔e2 ∞ Gurevich-Tukmakov, USSR 1976 or 8 c3 e5 9 dxe5 dxe5 10 ♗e2 ♕e7 11 b4 b6 12 0-0 a5 13 a3 ♗a6 ∞ Kovačević-Tseshkovsky, Zagreb 1975) 7 c3 (7 ♗b5 ♗d7 8 0-0 h6 9 ♗e3 e5 10 dxe5 ♘xe5 11 ♗xd7 ♘exd7 12 ♗d4 ♖e8 = Johanessen-Petrosian, Varna 1962) 7 ... e5 8 dxe5 ♘xe5 (8 ... dxe5 9 ♗b5 h6 10 ♗h4 g5 11 ♗xc6 gxh4 12 ♗b5 ♘h5 13 ♘xe5 ♘f4 ∞ or 10 ♗xf6?! ♕xf6 11 ♕e2 ♘d8 12 ♕e3 ♕b6 13 ♕xb6 axb6 ∓ Kholmov-Boleslavsky, Moscow 1947) 9 ♘xe5 dxe5 10 ♗c4 h6 11 ♗e3?! (11 ♗h4!) 11 ... b6 12 0-0 ♘h5 13 ♘f3 ♕f6 14 ♔h2 ♘f4 ∓ Kovačević-Tukmakov, USSR 1975.

10.211

6 ... c5
7 dxc5!

Otherwise after the exchanges in the centre Black will have a comfortable game due to the passive knight on d2, e.g. 7 ♗d3?! cxd4 8 cxd4 ♘c6 =.

7 ... dxc5

A special position that may emerge from a wide range of openings.

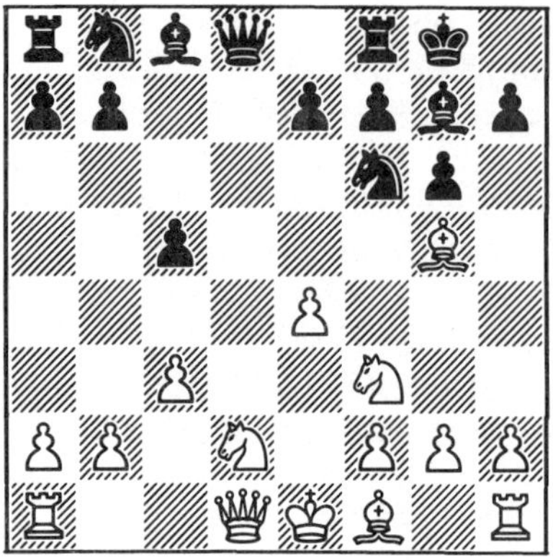

8 ♗c4 ♘c6

8 ... h6 9 ♗h4 ♘c6 10 0-0 ♗g4 11 ♕c2 g5 12 ♗g3 ♘h5 13 ♖fe1 ♘xg3 14 hxg3 e6 15 a4 ♕c7 16 ♗e2 ♗h5 = Korchnoi-Hansen, Jerusalem 1986.

9 0-0

9 ♕e2 h6 10 ♗e3 b6 11 h3 ♘a5 12 ♗d3 ♕c7 = Trifunović-Smyslov, Dortmund 1961. Perhaps 10 ♗h4 ♘h5 11 ♕e3 ♕c7 ∞ is better.

9 ... ♘a5!?

An interesting attempt to drive back White's forces.

(a) 9 ... ♗g4 10 h3 (10 ♕c2!?) 10 ... ♗xf3 11 ♕xf3 h6 12 ♗e3 ♕c7 (12 ... ♘e5!?) 13 ♕e2 ♖ad8 14 f4 ♘a5 15 ♗d3 ♘h5 16 ♖f3 e5 17 f5 ♕d6 18 ♗c4 ± Trifunović-Udovčić, Yugoslavia 1956 or 13 ... b6 14 f4 e6 15 e5 ♘d5 16 ♘e4 ♔h8 17 ♖ae1 ± Trifunović-Smailbegović, Yugoslavia 1957.

(b) 9 ... ♕c7 10 ♕e2 (10 ♖e1 h6! 11 ♗h4 ♘h5 ±; 10 ... e5?! 11 ♘f1 h6 12 ♗xf6! ♗xf6 13 ♘e3 ± Trifunović-Aaron, Beverwijk 1961) 10 ... ♘a5 (10 ... h6?! 11 ♗xf6! exf6 – 11 ... ♗xf6? 12 ♕e3! – 12 ♘h4! ♔h7 13 f4 ♗d7 14 ♕f2 ♘e7 15 ♖ae1 ± Trifunović-Bolbochan, Varna 1962) 11 ♗d3 h6 12 ♗xf6! exf6?! 13 ♘c4 ♗e6 14 ♘e3 ♖ad8 15 ♖fd1 a6 16 c4 ♖fe8 17 ♖ac1 ♘c6 18 ♗b1 ± Trifunović-Bannik, USSR v Yugoslavia 1963.

10	**♗e2**	**h6**
11	**♗f4**	**♗e6**
12	**h3**	**a6**
13	**a4**	**b6**
14	**♘e5**	**♕c8**

Chances are equal. Malaniuk-Yurtayev, USSR 1986.

10.212

6 ... ♘bd7

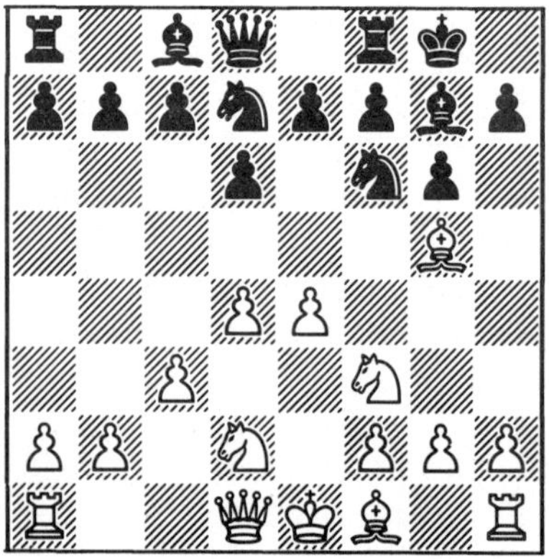

There are numerous alternatives apart from this and 10.211:

(a) 6 ... ♘a6?! 7 ♗e2 c5 8 0-0 ♘c7 9 dxc5 dxc5 10 ♕c2 ♘e6 11 ♗h4 ♘f4 12 ♗c4 ♕d7?! 13 a4 ♘6h5 14 ♖fe1 ♕g4 15 ♗g3 e5 16 ♖ad1 ♕d7 17 ♘f1 ♕c7 18 ♘e3 ♗e6 19 ♗xe6 ♘xe6 20 ♘d5 ± Kasparov-McNab, Dortmund 1980.

(b) 6 ... b6 7 ♗c4 (7 ♗e2) 7 ... ♗b7 8 ♕e2 c5 9 dxc5 bxc5 10 0-0 ♘c6 11 ♗a6 ♕b6 12 ♗xb7 ♕xb7 13 ♘c4 ♘d7 14 ♖fe1 ♖ab8 15 ♖ac1 ♕a6 16 b3 ♕b7 17 h4! ± Szily-Liptay, Budapest 1965.

(c) 6 ... ♘c6?! 7 ♗b5! (7 ♗d3 e5!) 7 ... a6 (7 ... ♗d7 8 0-0 e5 is already the Ruy Lopez! Alternatively, 7 ... h6 8 ♗h4 a6 [8 ... *♗d7 9 0-0 g5!? 10 ♗g3 ♘h5 11 ♖e1 e6 12 ♘f1 ♕e7 Kholmov-Glyanets, USSR 1989; 13 ♘3d2±*] 9 ♗a4 b5 10 ♗c2 ♘d7 11 0-0 ♖b8 12 ♖e1 ♕e8 13 a4 b4 14 a5 ♘a7 15 ♘c4 bxc3 16 bxc3 ♘b5 17 e5 ± Cifuentes-Douven, Wijk aan Zee 1988) 8 ♗a4 ♗d7 9 0-0 h6 10 ♗h4 ♕e8 (11 ... ♘xd4! is threatened. Even so, it is safer to switch to the Steinitz Variation of the Ruy Lopez with 10 ... e5 11 ♖e1) 11 e5! ♘h5 (11 ... dxe5 12 ♗xc6 ♗xc6 13 ♘xe5 ±) 12 ♖e1 ± Darga-Ciocaltea, Siegen 1970.

(d) 6 ... ♕e8!? (An improved version of (c), since the c6 knight is not so easily pinned now) 7 ♗e2 (7 ♗d3 ♘c6 8 0-0 e5 9 ♖e1 h6 10

♗h4 ♘h5 11 dxe5 ♘xe5 12 ♘xe5 dxe5 ± Torre-Romanishin, Leningrad 1987; 7 ♗c4!? e5 8 dxe5 dxe5 9 a4 ♘h5 10 0-0 ♘d7 11 ♖e1 ♘c5 12 ♗e3 ♕e7 13 b4 ♘e6 14 a5 a6 15 ♕c2 ± Korchnoi-Gutman, Wijk aan Zee 1987) 7 ... ♘c6 8 0-0 e5 9 dxe5 dxe5?! 10 ♕c2 ♘d8 11 ♗h4! ♘h5 12 ♖fe1 ♘e6 13 ♘c4 ♘f4 14 ♗f1 ± Salov-Romanishin, Leningrad 1987.

7 ♗e2

White has to be prepared to play dxe5, the only move promising an advantage:

(a) 7 ♗d3?! h6 (7 ... e5 8 0-0 ♕e8 9 dxe5?! dxe5 10 b4 h6 11 ♗h4 ♘h5 12 ♘c4?! – 12 ♖e1! ♘f4 13 ♗f1 ♘b6, Cvitan – 12 ... ♘f4 13 ♗c2 ♘b6 14 ♘a5?!, Mazulski-Cvitan, Sibenik 1987; and now 14 ... ♗g4! 15 ♘xb7 ♕c8 16 ♘c5 g5 17 ♗g3 ♖d8 ∓) 8 ♗h4 (8 ♗f4 e5! 9 dxe5 ♘h5) 8 ... e5 9 0-0 ♖e8 10 ♖e1 c6 11 ♕c2 ♕c7 12 ♖ad1 ♘f8 13 ♗g3 ♘h5 14 dxe5 dxe5 15 ♘c4 ♗g4 = Neikirch-Pachman, Amsterdam 1954.

(b) 7 ♗c4 e5 (7 ... c6 8 ♗b3 b5 9 0-0?! ♘b6 10 ♖e1 ♕c7 11 ♖c1 a5 12 a3 ♗a6 13 e5?! ♘fd5 14 exd6 exd6 15 ♘f1 ♘c4! = Gulko-Westerinen, Moscow 1966; 8 0-0!? ♘xe4 9 ♘xe4 d5 10 ♗d3 dxe4 11 ♗xe4 ♘f6 12 ♗d3 ♗g4 13 h3 ± Malaniuk-Gurevich, USSR 1980) 8 dxe5 (8 0-0 h6 9 ♗h4 ♕e7 10 ♖e1 g5 11 ♗g3 ♘h7 12 dxe5 dxe5 13 ♘f1 ±; 9 ... ♖e8 10 ♖e1 ♘f8 11 ♕b3 ♖e7 12 ♖ad1 ♕e8 13 ♗b5 c6 14 ♗d3 g5 15 ♗g3 ♘h5 16 ♘c4 ♗e6 17 ♕a3 ± Trifunović-Udovčić, Bled 1961) 8 ... dxe5 9 0-0 h6 (9 ... ♕e7 10 ♖e1 h6 11 ♗e3?! ♘g4 12 ♘f1 = Trifunović-Geller, Helsinki 1952; 11 ♗h4! g5 12 ♗g3 ±) 10 ♗h4 ♕e8 11 ♖e1 ♘h5 12 a4 ♗f6 13 a5! ♕e7 14 ♗xf6 ♕xf6 15 ♗f1 ± Petrosian-Jansa, Illustrative Game No 60.

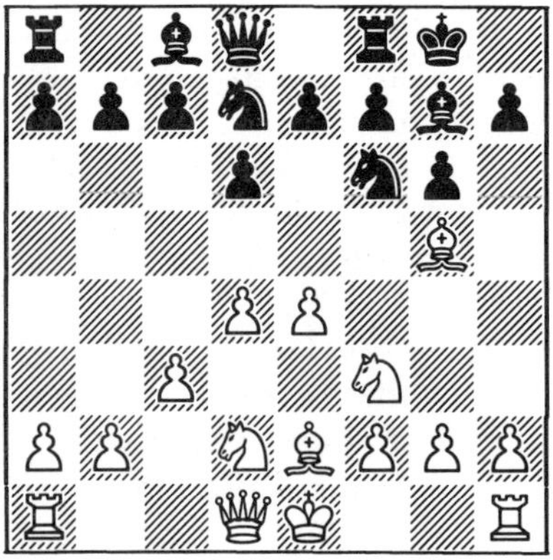

7 ... h6

7 ... e5 8 dxe5 dxe5 9 0-0 c6 10 ♕c2 ♕c7 11 ♖fe1 ♖e8 12 ♗f1 b6 13 a4 a5 14 ♘c4 ♗b7 15 ♖ad1 ♖e6 16 ♗xf6! ♘xf6 17 ♘g5 ♖e7 18 ♘d6 ♗a6?! 19 ♗xa6 ♖xa6 20 ♕b3! h6 21 ♘dxf7! ♖xf7 22 ♖d8+! ± Epishin-Kantsler, USSR 1989.

8 ♗h4 e5

(a) 8 ... ♘h5 9 0-0 ♘f4 10 ♗c4 c6 11 a4 g5? 12 ♘xg5!? hxg5 13 ♗xg5 ♘e6 14 ♗e3 ♘f6 15 ♗d3 ♘c7 16 h3 e5 17 f4 ± Rossetto-Penrose, Mar del Plata 1962.

(b) 8 ... g5 9 ♗g3 ♘h5 then 10 ... ♘xg3 and ... a6, ... ♕e7 has not been tried out in tournament practice yet.

9 dxe5!

Consistent! Also satisfactory is 9 0-0 ♖e8 10 ♕c2 g5?! 11 ♗g3 ♘h5 12 ♘c4 ♘f4 13 dxe5 ♘xe5 14 ♘fxe5 ♗xe5 15 ♖ad1 ♕e7 16 ♘e3 ♗e6 17 ♗g4 ± Balashov-Vukić, Bugojno 1978.

9 ... dxe5
10 0-0 ♕e7

After 10 ... ♕e8 Black can get rid of the pin without weakening his camp: 11 ♖e1 ♘h5 (11 ... ♘c5?! 12 ♕c2 ♘h5 13 ♘c4 ♘f4 14 ♗f1 ♗g4 15 ♘fd2 ±) 12 ♗f1 ♘f4 13 ♘c4 ♘b6 14 ♘e3 ♗e6 15 ♘d2 f5 16 f3 ± Petursson-Veröci, London 1980.

11 ♖e1 b6
12 ♕c2 ♗b7
13 ♗f1 ♖fd8

13 ... ♖fe8 14 b4! a6 (14 ... a5 15 a3 ♖a7 16 ♗d3 ♖ea8 17 ♕b2 ±) 15 ♘c4 ♖ac8? (15 ... ♕e6 16 ♘fd2 c5 17 ♘e3 ±) 16 a4! ± Kasparov-Martinović, Illustrative Game No 61.

14 ♘c4 ♕e6
15 ♘fd2 ♕g4
16 ♗xf6! ♗xf6

White has taken the initiative: 17 ♘e3 ♕e6 18 ♗c4 ♕d6 19 ♖ad1 c6 20 ♘f3 ♕e7 21 ♘g4 ♗g7 22 ♕d2 b5 (22 ... ♘f6 23 ♘xh6+! ♔h7 24 ♘g5+) 23 ♗b3 ♔h7 24 ♕d6! ♕xd6 25 ♖xd6 ♘c5 26 ♖xd8 ♖xd8 27 ♗xf7 etc, Balashov-Sax, Rio de Janeiro 1979.

ILLUSTRATIVE GAMES

1 d4 ♘f6 2 ♘f3 g6 3 ♗g5 ♗g7 4 ♘bd2 d6

56) **Torre-Gutman**
Biel 1985

5 c3 0-0 6 e4 h6 7 ♗h4 ♕e8 This novelty does not change the basic character of the opening. **8 ♗d3** 8 ♗c4 b5! would have been the point of Black's idea. **8 ... e5 9 dxe5 dxe5 10 0-0 ♘bd7** A typical set-up in this opening, with White having a tiny advantage in space. **11 ♖e1 ♘c5 12 ♗f1 ♗g4 13 ♕e2** 13 ♕c2. **13 ... ♘h5 14 ♕e3 ♘e6 15 ♘c4 ♘ef4 16 b4 b6 17 a4** Since the position is a typical one, this space-winning manoeuvre is worth remembering. **17 ... ♕e6 18 ♘fd2** With 18 a5? White would have fallen into a trap: 18 ... ♘xg2! 19 ♔xg2 ♗h3+. **18 ... g5** 18 ... ♗f6 and exchanging Black's very passive bishop might seem logical, yet after 19 ♗xf6! ♕xf6 20 g3! Black's remaining pieces will be in trouble. **19 ♗g3 ♕g6 20 a5 ♖ad8 21 axb6 axb6 22 ♖a7** At last, White has achieved something though Black is unlikely to go bankrupt as a result of the penetrating rook. **22 ... ♖d7 23 h3 ♗e6 24 ♘f3 f6 25 ♘b2** White wants to swap the light-squared bishops to exploit the weakness of f5 later on. **25 ... ♕f7 26 ♗b5 ♖e7 27 ♘h2 ♘g6** 27 ... f5!?. **28 ♘g4 ♘hf4 29 ♕d2!** Preparing ♘e3-f5. **29 ... ♘h4?! 30 ♗xh4 gxh4 31 ♘e3?!** It is not easy to tell how, but White has managed to increase his advantage – yet his last move is inaccurate. 31 ♔h2! ♕g6 32 ♗c4! was necessary. **31 ... ♕g6! 32 ♔h2 ♕xe4 33 ♗c4** The lost pawn is compensated for by the activity of the white pieces. **33 ... ♗xc4** 33 ... ♕g6 34 g3 hxg3+ 35 fxg3 ♗xc4 36 ♘bxc4 ♘e6 37 ♘xb6 f5 38 ♘bd5 ♖ef7 39 ♖a6!. **34 ♘bxc4 h5?**

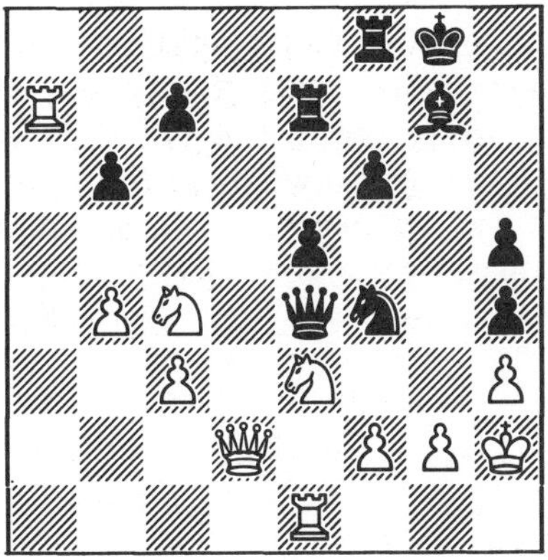

Black fails to notice the way White gets hold of f5, gaining a decisive positional advantage. 34 ... ♖ef7! 35 ♖a2! ♕c6 was the correct response.

35 ♘d6 ♕g6 36 ♘df5 ♖ef7 37 ♘xh4 ♕d3 38 ♕a2! ♕xc3 39 ♖d1 ♘d3 39 ... ♔h7 40 g3 ♘g6 41 ♘hf5 and ♕e2-h5 ±±. **40 ♘d5 ♕d4 41 ♘f5 ♕e4 42 f3! 1-0**

42 ... ♕xf5 43 ♘e7+!. (Torre's notes included)

57) **Ribli-Adorján**
Budapest 1981

5 c3 h6 6 ♗h4 g5 7 ♗g3 ♘h5 8 e3!? This is the way White can keep the a1-h8 diagonal closed. **8 ... ♘xg3 9 hxg3 ♘d7 10 a4!** This pawn is quite often used as a battering ram on the queenside. For better or for worse, Black should have replied 10 ... a5. **10 ... ♘f6?! 11 a5! ♗d7** 11 ... ♗f5!?. **12 ♗d3 e6 13 e4! g4?!** Black's first active move in the game but in vain: his defence is disintegrating and the centre is dominated by White. **14 ♘h2 h5 15 ♘hf1 ♗h6 16 ♕e2 e5 17 d5 c6! 18 c4 c5?** In the blockaded position, the knight's superiority will be decisive. 18 ... ♕c7 and 19 ... ♔e7 was more tolerable. **19 ♘e3 ♔f8**

(diagram)

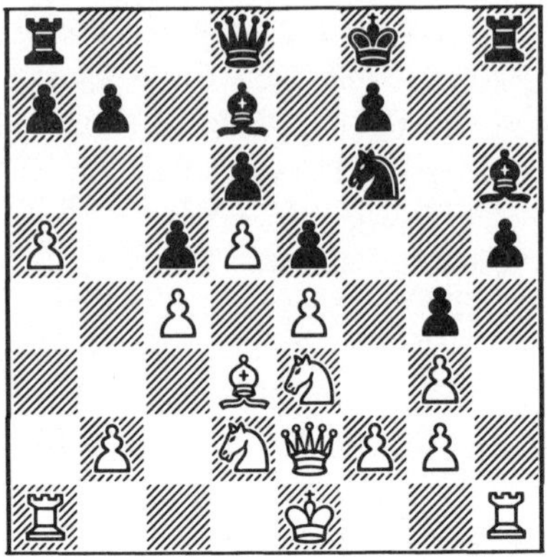

20 a6! Weakening the light squares on the queenside, which, together with the weakness of f5, will prove to be fatal. **20 ... b6?!** 20 ... ♕c7. **21 ♘b1! ♗g5** After 21 ... ♗xe3 22 ♕xe3 the kingside dark squares would be weak too. **22 ♘c3 ♖h7 23 ♔d1! ♕e8 24 ♗c2!** After the exchange of the light-squared bishops Black cannot hold the weak light squares. However, the game ends with another strategic twist. **24 ... ♔e7 25 ♘f5+! ♗xf5 26 exf5 ♔d8 27 ♗a4!** The bishop is sufficient to dominate the light squares. **27 ... ♕e7 28 ♗c6 ♖c8 29 ♗b7 ♖c7 30 ♘b5 e4!? 31 ♘xa7! ♕e5 32 ♘c6+ 1-0**

58) **Espig-Uhlmann**
GDR Championship 1983

5 e4 h6 6 ♗h4 g5 7 ♗g3 ♘h5 8 c3 ♘d7 9 ♗d3?! c5! 10 d5 0-0 11 a4 11 ♘xg5? ♘xg3 12 hxg3 ♘e5 13 ♗c2 hxg5 14 ♕h5 ♖e8 15 ♕xg5 e6 ∓. **11 ... ♘df6! 12 ♘c4 ♘xg3 13 hxg3 e6! 14 ♘e3 exd5 15 exd5 ♘g4! 16 ♘f5?** Castling is more important than the attempted domination of the f5 square. **16 ... ♖e8+ 17 ♔f1 ♕f6 18 ♘xg7 ♔xg7 19 ♕c2 ♗d7 20 ♔g1** 20 ♖e1 ♖xe1+ 21 ♔xe1 ♖e8+ 22 ♔f1 ♘e5 ∓. **20 ... ♖e7 21 ♘h2 ♘e5 22 ♗e4** 22 f3? ♘xd3 23 ♕xd3 ♖ae8 ∓∓. **22 ... ♘c4 23 f3** 23 ♗d3 ♘e5 24 ♗e4 ♖ae8 ∓. **23 ... ♖ae8 24 b3**

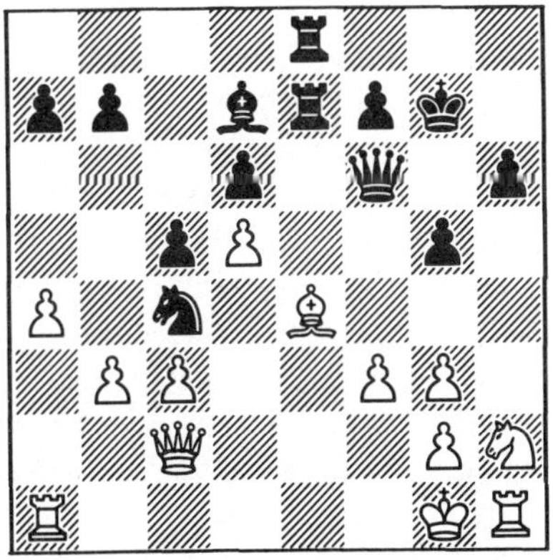

24 ... ♘a5! What an exception: the knight is posted best on the edge of the board! True, it is going to return to the main battle-field soon. **25 ♖d1 c4! 26 bxc4** 26 b4 ♘b3 27 a5 ♗f5!! 28 ♗xf5 ♖e2 29 ♕b1 ♕xc3 30 ♘f1 ♖b2 ∓∓. **26 ... ♘xc4 27 ♖d4 b5 28 axb5 ♘a3 29 ♕b2 ♘xb5 30 ♘g4 ♗xg4 31 ♕xb5 ♗f5! 32 ♗xf5 ♕xf5 33 ♔h2** 33 ♕d3 ♕xd3 34 ♖xd3 ♖e2 35 c4 ♖a2 ∓∓. **33 ... ♖e2 34 ♕d3 ♕f6! 35 ♖a4!** 35 ♖e4 ♖8xe4 36 fxe4 ♕f2 37 ♖g1 ♖e3 ∓∓. **35 ... ♖8e3 36 ♕d4 ♕xd4 37 cxd4 ♖xf3 38 ♖xa7** 38 ♖e1 ♖b2! 39 ♖b1! ♖ff2! 40 ♖xb2 ♖xb2 41 ♖a6 ♖b6 42 ♖xa7 ♖b5 ∓. **38 ... ♖ff2 39 ♖g1 ♖d2 40 ♖a6 ♖f6 41 ♖a4 g4! 42 ♖ga1 ♖ff2 43 ♖g1 ♔g6! 44 ♖a6 ♖f6 0-1**

59) **Ribli-Schmidt**
Baile Herculane 1982

5 e4 h6 6 ♗h4 g5 7 ♗g3 ♘h5 8 c3 e6 9 ♗d3 0-0 10 0-0 ♘c6?! 11 ♘c4 f5 12 exf5 exf5 13 h3 f4 14 ♗h2 Contradicting the saying 'A passive piece makes a passive game.' Apart from the lame bishop, White's pieces are remarkably well placed, while at the same time Black's light squares are weak. **14 ... ♘f6?** 14 ... ♗e6! 15 ♘h4! ♘f6 16 ♘f5 ♕d7 17 ♕c2 ±. **15 ♖e1 ♘e7 16 a4 a5 17 ♕b3 ♔h8** Apparently Black is alright . . .

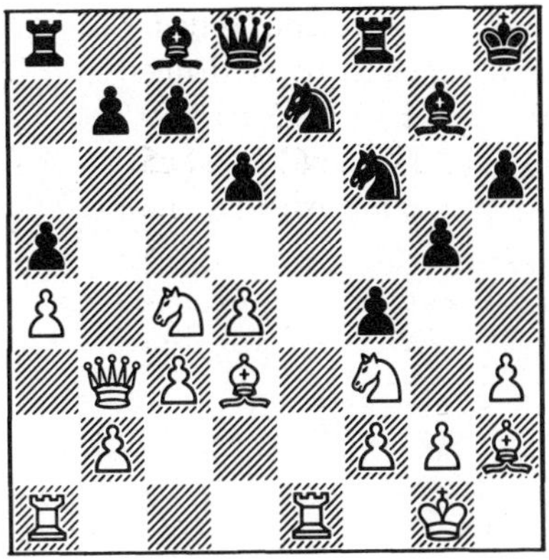

18 ♖xe7!! A bolt from the blue! White beautifully exploits the hidden weakness of the black king's position. **18 ... ♕xe7 19 ♘ce5 ♕e6** 19 ... dxe5 20 ♘xe5 ♕e6 21 ♘g6+ ♔g8 22 ♗c4. **20 d5! ♕e8** 20 ... ♕xd5 21 ♘g6+ costs a queen. **21 ♘g6+ ♔g8 22 ♖e1 ♕d8 23 ♘xf8 ♕xf8 24 h4!** The punishment for Black's disorderly pawn structure. **24 ... ♘g4** 24 ... g4 25 ♘d4 ♘h5 26 ♗g6 ±±. **25 hxg5 hxg5 26 ♘xg5 ♗e5 27 ♘f3 ♕g7 28 ♕c4 ♘xh2 29 ♔xh2 ♗d7 30 ♘xe5 dxe5 31 d6+ 1-0**

60) **Petrosian-Jansa**
Bar 1980

5 e4 0-0 6 c3 ♘bd7 7 ♗c4 e5 8 dxe5 dxe5 9 0-0 h6 10 ♗h4 ♕e8 11 ♖e1 ♘h5 12 a4 ♗f6! 13 a5! ♕e7 14 ♗xf6 ♕xf6 15 ♗f1! In order to stop Black's offensive. **15 ... ♖d8 16 ♕e2 ♘f4 17 ♕e3 g5** An inevitable weakening, otherwise after 18 g3 and 19 ♘c4 and Black is paralysed. **18 ♖ed1 ♖e8 19 g3 ♘g6 20 h3 ♘df8 21 ♘h2! h5?** So far some shortage of space has been all Black could complain about, but his last move weakens his kingside.

(diagram)

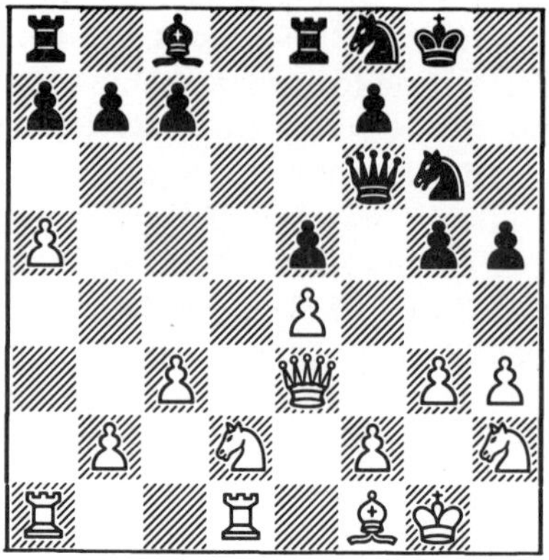

22 ♗e2! Aiming at g4, then to get hold of f5, e.g. 22 ... ♗xh3 23 ♗xh5. **22 ... h4 23 ♗g4! ♔g7 24 ♘df1 ♘h7 25 ♖d3 ♗e6 26 ♗xe6 ♕xe6 27 ♘g4 ♘f6** Leading to a hand to hand fight, but there is no better due to the ♕f3, ♘f1-e3-f5 threats. **28 ♕xg5 ♘xe4 29 ♕h6+ ♔g8 30 ♖ad1 ♘f6 31 ♘fe3 ♘xg4** 32 gxh4 then h4-h5 was threatened. 31 ... hxg3 would have failed to 32 fxg3 and play along the open f-file. **32 ♘xg4 hxg3 33 ♖xg3 ♖ad8 34 ♖e1 ♕f5 35 h4 ♖e6 36 h5 ♕f4 37 hxg6 1-0**

61) **Kasparov-Martinović**
Baku 1980

5 e4 0-0 6 c3 ♘bd7 7 ♗e2 h6 8 ♗h4 e5 9 dxe5 dxe5 10 0-0 ♕e7 11 ♖e1 b6 12 ♕c2 ♗b7 13 ♗f1 ♖fe8 14 b4! Gaining space! **14 ... a6 15 ♘c4 ♖ac8?** 15 ... c5? 16 ♖ad1 cxb4 17 ♘d6 ±; 15 ... ♕e6!. **16 a4 ♕e6 17 ♘fd2 ♘h5 18 f3 ♗f6?!** 18 ... ♗f8 gives a cramped yet solid game. **19 ♗f2 ♗g5 20 ♘e3 ♘df6?! 21 c4!** After a neo-romantic opening, Kasparov shifts to the style of the classics, securing his advantage in space by advancing a pawn. **21 ... c6** One weakness generates another. 22 ♘d5 can only be parried by the weakening of d6 and b6. **22 ♘b3 ♘d7 23 c5 b5 24 ♖ed1 ♗e7** 25 ♖d6 had to be thwarted but now the queen cannot return safely.

(diagram)

25 ♘c4! ♖c7 26 ♘d6 ♖b8 27 axb5 cxb5 27 ... axb5 28 ♖a7. **28 ♘xb7!** To reveal Black's weaknesses, White is ready to give his active knight for the poorly posted bishop. **28 ... ♖bxb7 29 ♕a2! ♘b8 30 ♘a5 ♕xa2 31 ♖xa2 ♖a7**

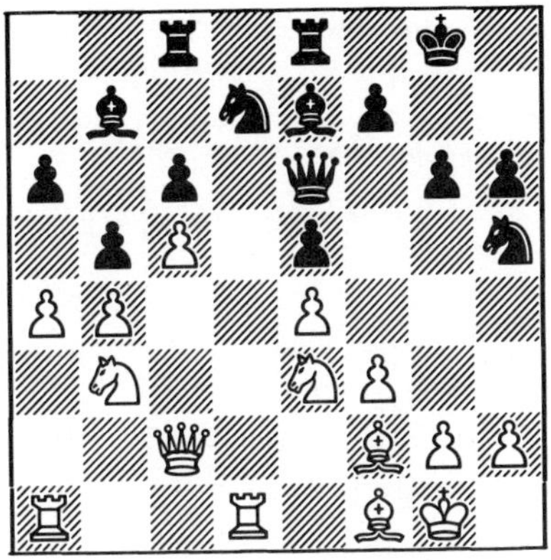

31 ... ♖d7 32 ♖d5! **32 c6!** A precisely calculated simplification! **32 ... ♖a8 33 ♖c2 ♗xb4 34 ♖d8+ ♔g7 35 ♗b6 ♗xa5 36 ♗xa5 ♖xc6 37 ♖xb8 ♖xb8 38 ♖xc6 b4 39 ♗c7 1-0**

11 Countering the King's Indian and the Grünfeld: QB Line with ... d5

1	d4	♘f6
2	♘f3	g6
3	♗g5	♗g7
4	♘bd2	d5

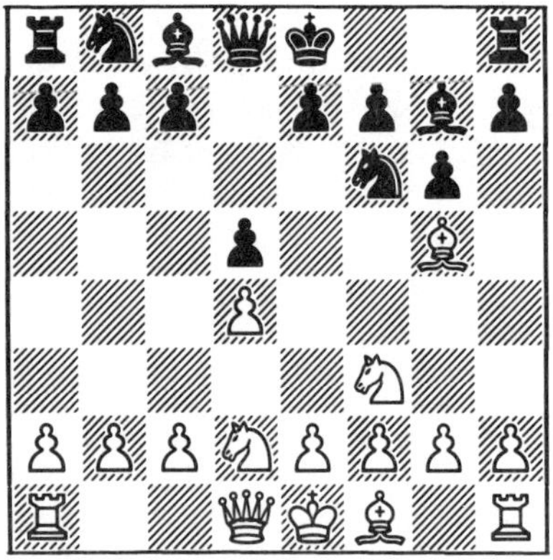

The simplest method to prevent e4 and to equalise. Black can develop his queen's bishop comfortably and if he can gain space by ... e7-e5 he will have a splendid game.

It is rather odd that some specialists in the King's Indian cling to ... d6 and refuse playing this solid and reliable system – out of sheer habit.

5 e3

Commonsense. In Keres-Toran, Bamberg 1968, White had a small plus after 5 c4 c6 6 e3 0-0 7 ♗e2 ♗e6?! 8 0-0 ♘bd7 9 ♖c1 ♕b6 10 ♕a4! a5 11 a3 ♖fc8 12 cxd5! ♗xd5 13 ♕c2 but Black's game can be improved by 5 ... c5!. Thus Black has a comfortable position since the white knight is misplaced on d2 in the Grünfeld-like set-up.

5 c3 is discussed under 6 c3.

5 ... 0-0

5 ... c5 might be more accurate because now 6 c3 or 6 b4 can hinder ... c5. For instance 5 ... c5 6 c3 and now:

(a) 6 ... ♕b6 7 ♕b3 ♘c6 8 ♗e2 0-0 9 0-0 ♗f5 10 dxc5 (10 ♗xf6?!) 10 ... ♕xc5 11 ♘d4 ♗c8 12 ♖fd1 e5 13 ♕b5 ♕d6 14 ♘4b3 a6 15 ♕d3! ♕e6 (15 ... e4?! 16 ♘xe4! ♘xe4 17 ♕xe4 ♕xh2+ 18 ♔xh2 dxe4 19 ♘c5 ±) 16 e4 ♘xe4 (16 ... ♖d8?! 17 exd5 ♖xd5 18 ♕g3! ± Lechtinsky-Stohl, Trnava 1989) 17 ♘xe4 dxe4 18 ♕xe4 ±.

(b) 6 ... cxd4 7 cxd4 0-0 8 ♗d3 ♘c6 9 ♕b3 ♕b6 10 0-0 ♖d8!? 11 ♖fc1 ♗f5 12 ♗xf5 gxf5 13 ♕a3 ♖dc8! (13 ... ♖ac8 14 ♘e5!) 14 ♘b3 e6 15 ♗xf6!? ♗xf6 16 ♘c5 ♕c7 Gelfand-Ernst, Tallinn 1987; 17 b4 ±.

11.1

6 c3

11.11

6 ... b6

Fianchettoing the bishop together with ... e7-e5 is natural and powerful although there are other promising moves as well. 6 ... ♘bd7 is considered under 1.12, while 6 ... ♗f5 is possible:

6 ... ♗f5 7 ♗e2 (7 ♕b3!?) 7 ... ♘bd7 8 0-0 (8 ♕b3 c5!? 9 0-0 ♕b6 10 ♖fc1 h6 11 ♗f4 ♕xb3 12 axb3 ♘h5 13 ♗e5 f6 14 ♗g3 ♗e6 15 dxc5 ♘xg3 16 hxg3 ♘xc5 17 b4 ♘e4 = Trifunović-Gufeld, Sarajevo 1964) 8 ... c6 (8 ... h6 9 ♗h4 c5 10 ♕b3 ♕a5?! 11 ♘e5 ♘xe5 12 dxe5 ♘d7 13 ♗xe7 ♖fe8 14 ♗d6 ♗xe5 15 ♗xe5 ♘xe5 16 ♕xb7 ♖ab8 17 ♕xd5 ± Lobron-London, Manhattan 1985; 8 ... c5 9 ♘h4 ♗e6 10 f4 cxd4 11 exd4 ♘e4 12 ♘xe4 dxe4 13 f5 ♗d5 14 fxg6 fxg6 15 ♕d2 ♖xf1+ 16 ♗xf1 ♘b6 17 b3 a5 ∞ Zhukovsky-Kotkov, USSR 1963) 9 ♕b3 ♕b6 10 ♖ac1 h6 11 ♗h4 ♖fe8 12 c4 e5 13 ♘xe5 ♘xe5 14 dxe5 ♖xe5 = Lein-Gufeld, USSR 1964.

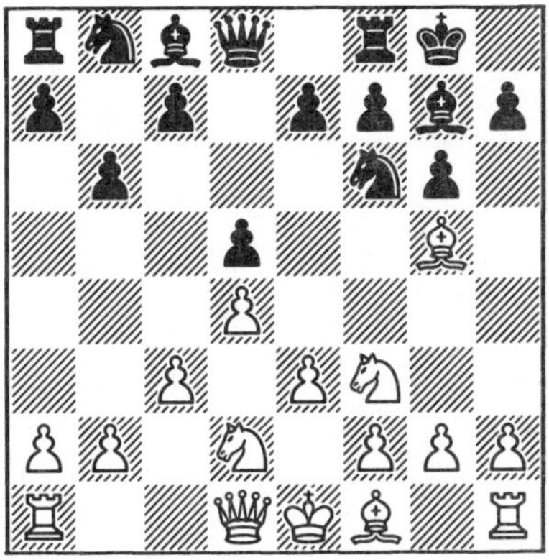

7 b4

The natural way of gaining space on the queenside. Others:

(a) 7 a4 a5 (7 ... ♗b7 8 a5 c5 9 b4 cxb4 10 cxb4 bxa5 11 bxa5 ♗a6 = Möller-Darga, Moscow 1956) 8 ♗d3 ♗b7 9 0-0 ♘e4 10 ♗f4 ♘d7 11 ♕c2 ♘xd2 12 ♕xd2 ♖e8 = Sloth-Kristiansen, Esbjerg 1978.

(b) 7 ♗e2 ♗b7 8 0-0 ♘bd7 9 b4 ♕e8 10 ♖c1 ♘e4 11 ♗f4 e5 12 dxe5 ♘xe5 = Larsen-Bilek, Teesside 1972.

(c) 7 ♗d3 ♗b7 (7 ... c5!? 8 0-0 ♘c6 9 a3 ♕c7 10 ♗f4 ♕b7 11 h3 ♘d7! 12 ♗e2 a5 ∞ Salov-Lputian, Moscow 1987) 8 0-0 (8 ♕b1 ♘bd7 9 0-0 c5 – 9 ... ♖e8!? – 10 b4 ♕c8 11 h3 ♖e8 12 ♖c1 e5 = Agzamov-Vogt, Postdam 1985) 8 ... ♘bd7!? (8 ... ♘e4?! 9 ♗f4 e6 10 ♕c2 f5 11 ♗e5 ♘d7 12 ♗xg7 ♔xg7 13 a4 a5 14 b4 ± Nielsen-Kristiansen, Esbjerg 1978) 9 a4 ♖e8 10 a5 e5 11

♗b5 e4 12 ♘e5 ♘xe5!? 13 ♗xe8 ♕xe8 14 dxe5 ♕xe5 ∞ Hartoch-Pelen, Amsterdam 1984.

7 ... ♘bd7

7 ... ♗b7 8 ♗e2 ♘bd7 9 0-0 ♘e4? 10 ♘xe4 dxe4 11 ♘d2 ± Kavalek-Browne, Illustrative Game No 59. Better is 9 ... ♕e8 10 ♗xf6!? ♗xf6 11 b5 a6 12 a4 e5 13 dxe5 ♘xe5 14 ♘xe5 ♗xe5 15 ♕b3 axb5 16 axb5 d4 17 cxd4 ♗xd4 18 ♖xa8 ♗xa8 19 ♗f3 ± Seirawan-Kudrin, US Championship 1988.

8 b5 ♕e8!

Here too, Black prepares ... e5. Other: 8 ... ♗b7 9 a4 ♖e8 10 ♗e2 e5 11 0-0 h6 12 ♗h4 c5 13 bxc6 ♗xc6 14 ♕b3 ♕e7 15 ♗b5 ♖ac8 = Torre-Zapata, Brussels 1986.

9	**♗e2**	**e5**
10	**0-0**	**♗b7**
11	**a4**	**♘e4**
12	**♖c1**	**a6**

Chances are equal. 13 ♗h4 axb5 14 axb5 ♖a7 etc, Torre-Kasparov, Brussels 1987.

11.12

6 ... ♘bd7

A simple and natural plan: with the queenside untouched, Black attempts to set himself free by ... ♖e8 and ... e5.

11.121

7 ♗e2

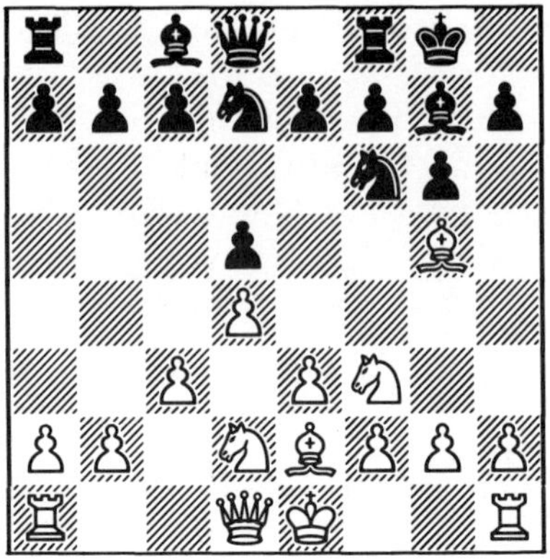

7 b4 a5 (7 ... ♖e8 8 ♗e2 e5 9 ♘b3 – 9 0-0 see 7 ♗e2 – 9 ... b6 10 ♗b5 e4 11 ♗c6 Vaganian-Beliavsky, Illustrative Game No 64; 11 ... exf3! =; 7 ... ♕e8 8 ♗f4 c6 9 ♗d3? ♘g4! 10 ♗e2 e5 11 ♗g3 f5 12 dxe5 ♘dxe5 13 ♘d4 g5! ∓ Torre-Vaganian, Leningrad 1987. Better is 9 ♗e2! ♘h5?! 10 ♗c7! ±) 8 ♗e2 (8 b5 a4 9 ♗e2 c5 10 bxc6 bxc6 11 0-0 c5 12 ♖b1 ♕a5 13 ♖b5! ♕a7 – 13 ... ♕xc3 14 ♘b1! – 14 ♕b1 ♗a6 15 ♖a5 ± Torre-Jansa, Biel 1985) 8 ... ♖e8 9 0-0 e5 10 ♘b3 axb4 11 cxb4 e4 12 ♘fd2 ♘f8 13 ♗h4 h5 14 ♕c2 ♗f5 15 ♖fc1 ♖e7 16 a4 ♘e6 ∞ Malaniuk-Dorfman, Lemberg 1988.

7	**...**	**♖e8**
8	**0-0**	

(a) 8 ♕b3 c6 9 c4 ♘b6 10 cxd5 ♕xd5 11 0-0 ♗f5 = Bronstein-W.Watson, London 1989.

(b) 8 b4 c6 9 0-0 e5 (9 ... a5 10 b5

a4 ∞ 9 ... h6 10 ♗h4 e5 11 ♘b3 g5 12 ♗g3 ♘e4 13 ♖c1 ♘xg3 14 hxg3 e4 15 ♘h2 f5 16 c4 ♗f8 17 b5 cxb5 18 cxd5 ♕b6 ∞ Torre-Uhlmann, Thessaloniki 1988) 10 ♘b3 ♕b6 11 ♗xf6! ∞ Petrosian-Korchnoi, Illustrative Game No 63. For 10 a4, see the main text.

8 ... e5
9 b4

9 c4 exd4 (9 ... e4 10 ♘e1 c5!? 11 ♘c2! cxd4 12 ♘xd4 ♘c5! 13 ♗h4 ± Ye Rongguang-Tseshkovsky, Belgrade 1988) 10 ♘xd4 ♘c5 11 cxd5 ♕xd5 12 ♗f4 c6 13 ♗f3 ♕d8 14 ♕c2 ♘e6 ± Torre-Sokolov, Biel 1989.

9 ... c6
10 a4

A recent try, gaining further space on the queenside. 10 ... h6 11 ♗h4 a5! 12 b5?! c5 ∓, Torre-Kasparov, Thessaloniki 1988, was encouraging for Black. 12 ♕b3 transposes into the text.

10 ... a5
11 ♕b3 h6
12 ♗h4 e4
13 ♘e1 g5!
14 ♗g3 h5

With a complicated position, Salov-Gelfand, Linares 1990. After 15 h4 ♘g4 16 hxg5 ♕xg5 17 ♗f4 ♕g6 18 f3 exf3, 19 ♗d3 fxg2 20 ♗xg6 gxf1 = ♕+ 21 ♘xf1 fxg6 ∞ (Kapengut-Gelfand) improves on 19 ♖xf3 ∓.

11.122
7 ♗d3

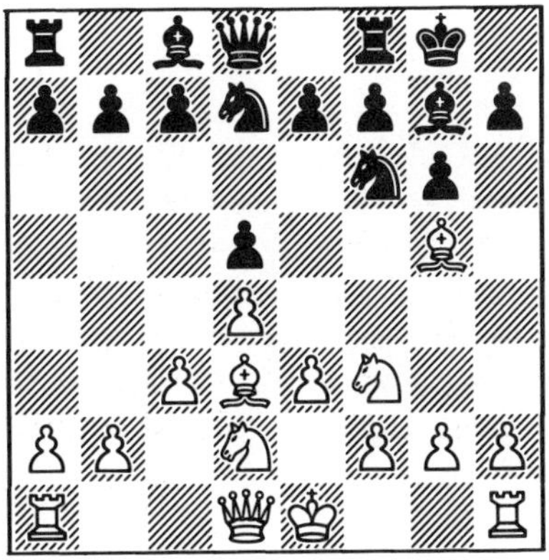

7 ... ♖c8

7 ... c5 8 0-0 (8 h3 b6 9 ♕e2 ♗b7 10 ♗a6 ♕c8 11 ♗xb7 ♕xb7 12 0-0 ♖fe8 13 ♗f4 a6 14 a4 e6 15 ♖fb1 ♖ac8 = Buchmann-Liutsko, USSR 1984) 8 ... b6 9 b4 ♗b7 10 ♕b1 cxd4 11 cxd4 ♖c8 12 a4 h6 13 ♗h4 g5 14 ♗g3 ♘h5 15 ♗e5 f6 16 ♗g3 ♘xg3 17 hxg3 (Malaniuk-Loginov, Tallinn 1982) 17 ... e6! ±.

8 ♗f4

To prevent ... e5. 8 ♕b3, however, seems more suitable for the purpose. See Petrosian-Krogius, USSR 1962. Others:

(a) 8 e4 dxe4 9 ♘xe4 ♘xe4 10 ♗xe4 c5 11 0-0 cxd4 12 cxd4 ♘f6 = Popov-Tukmakov, Moscow 1983.

(b) 8 h3 e5 9 dxe5 ♘xe5 10

♘xe5 ♖xe5 11 ♘f3 ♖e8 12 0-0 c6 13 ♖e1 ♕b6 14 ♗xf6 ♗xf6 15 ♕c2 ♗e6 = Smyslov-Kamsky, Manila 1990.

8 ... ♘h5!
9 0-0

9 ♗g5!? ♘hf6 10 ♕b3! c6 11 0-0 e5 12 e4! Petrosian-Krogius, USSR 1962; see 6 ♗d3 (11.2).

9 ... ♘xf4
10 exf4 c5
11 ♘e5 ♕b6
12 ♕b3 ♕xb3
13 axb3 cxd4
14 cxd4 f6 =

15 ♘xd7? ♗xd7 16 ♖a5 ♗h6 17 a3 e5 ∓ Yusupov-Vaganian, Moscow 1983; 15 ♘ef3! =.

11.2

6 ♗d3

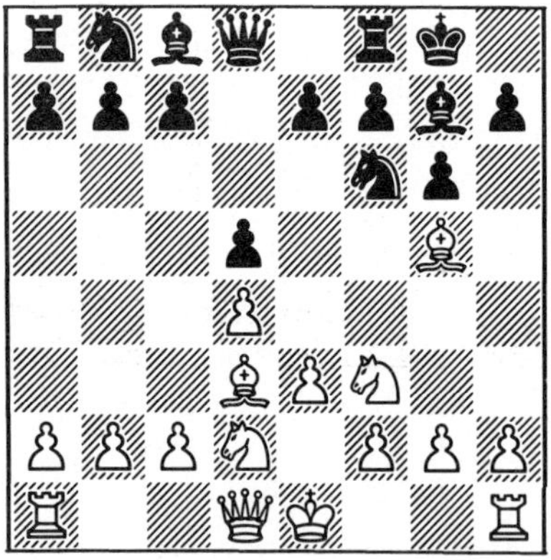

A sly move, maintaining the possibility of c2-c4 although the pawn is seldom pushed forward. Other possibilities (except for 6 c3):

(a) 6 b4 ♘bd7 (6 ... ♗g4 7 ♗e2 ♘bd7 8 h3 ♗xf3 9 ♗xf3 c6 10 0-0 e5 11 c3 a5 12 b5 ∞ Torre-Züger, Biel 1988) 7 c4! c6 8 ♖c1?! (8 ♗d3!) 8 ... ♘e4! 9 ♗h4? ♘df6 10 ♗e2 a5! 11 b5 cxb5 12 cxb5 ♗f5 13 0-0 ♕d6 ∓ Balashov-Rodriguez, Minsk 1982.

(b) 6 ♗e2 c5 7 c3 ♕b6 (7 ... b6 8 0-0 ♘bd7 9 ♕a4 ♗b7 10 ♗a6 ♕c8 11 ♗b5?! ♖d8 12 ♘e5 ♘xe5 13 dxe5 a6! ∓ Vaganian-Timoshchenko, Illustrative Game No 65; 7 ... ♘bd7 8 0-0 ♖e8 9 b4 cxb4 10 cxb4 ♕b6 11 ♕b3 e5 12 dxe5 ♘xe5 13 ♘xe5 ♖xe5 14 ♘f3 ± Rohrberg-Barrios, Siegen 1970; 7 ... cxd4 8 exd4 ♘c6 9 0-0 ♕c7 10 ♗d3 ♗f5 11 ♕e2 ♗xd3 12 ♕xd3 e6 13 ♖fd1 ♘d7 = Salov-Vaganian, Barcelona 1989) 8 ♕b3 ♘c6 9 0-0 ♗f5 10 ♗xf6 ♗xf6 11 ♕xd5 cxd4 12 cxd4 ♕xb2 13 ♖fc1 e5 = Vaganian-Ftačnik, Hastings 1982/83.

6 ... c5

6 ... ♘bd7 7 c3 ♖e8 8 ♗f4 (8 h3 e5!) 8 ... ♘h5 9 ♗g5 ♘hf6 10 ♕b3! c6 11 0-0 e5 12 e4! exd4 13 cxd4 dxe4 14 ♘xe4 ♕b6 15 ♘d6 ♖e6 16 ♘xc8 ♖xc8 17 ♗c4 ♖e7 18 ♕a3 ♖ee8 19 ♗d2! ± Petrosian-Krogius, USSR 1962. 7 h4 is too wild: 7 ... ♕e8! 8 ♗f4 c5 9 c3 ♘g4 10 h5 e5 ∓ Kamsky-H.Olafsson,

Reykjavik 1990.

6 ... ♘c6 7 c3 ♖e8 8 0-0 h6 9 ♗h4 ♗f5 10 ♗xf5 gxf5 11 ♗xf6 ♗xf6 12 ♔h1 e6 13 ♘e1 ♘e7 14 ♘d3 ♘g6 15 f4 b6 16 ♖f3 h5 17 ♖h3 h4 ∞ Lein-G.Fernandez, Saint John 1988.

7 c3

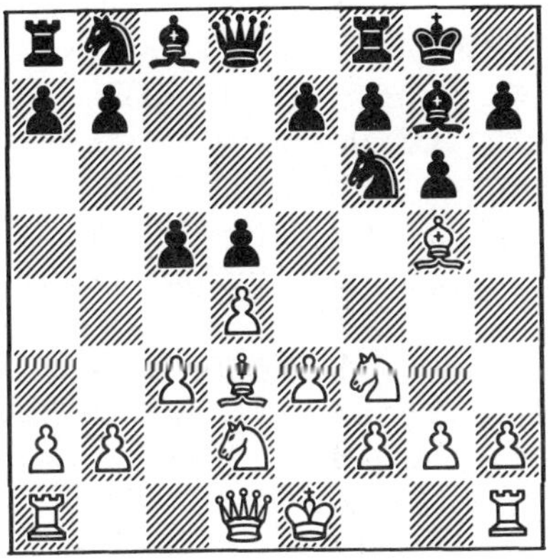

One of the basic positions of the variation, Black has good prospects of equalising. The main problem is whether the c5 pawn is safe or not. The important variations here are 7 ... cxd4, 7 ... ♘bd7, 7 ... ♕b6, and 7 ... b6. Others:

(a) 7 ... ♘fd7 8 0-0 ♘c6 9 ♖b1! h6 10 ♗h4 g5 11 ♗g3 f5 12 ♕c2 e6 13 ♗d6 c4! 14 ♗e2 ♖f7 15 b3 g4 16 ♘e1 Plachetka-Schmidt, Trnava 1985; 16 ... ♘f6! 17 ♗g3 b5 =.

(b) 7 ... ♘c6 8 0-0 (Keres mentions 8 dxc5 e5 9 e4! as a possibility. Better is 8 ... ♘d7 9 ♘b3 h6 10 ♗h4 g5 11 ♗g3 ♘a5) 8 ... ♘d7 (For 8 ... ♕b6 see 11.23 except for 9 ♕b1 e5! Keres-Shcherbakov, Illustrative Game No 66. Bad is 8 ... ♗g4 9 h3 ♗xf3 10 ♘xf3 ♘e4 11 ♗f4 cxd4 12 exd4 ♘b6 13 ♕e2 ♖c8 14 ♖fe1 a6 15 h4! e6 16 h5 ± or 8 ... ♖e8? 9 dxc5 ♘d7 10 ♘b3 h6 11 ♗h4 ♘de5 12 ♘xe5 ♘xe5 13 f4 ±) 9 ♖b1! (see (a). For neutral moves, Black can reply 9 ... ♕b6 and 10 ... e5.)

11.21

7	**...**	**cxd4**
8	**exd4**	

Of course not 8 cxd4 because the knight is poorly posted on d2 when the c-file is open.

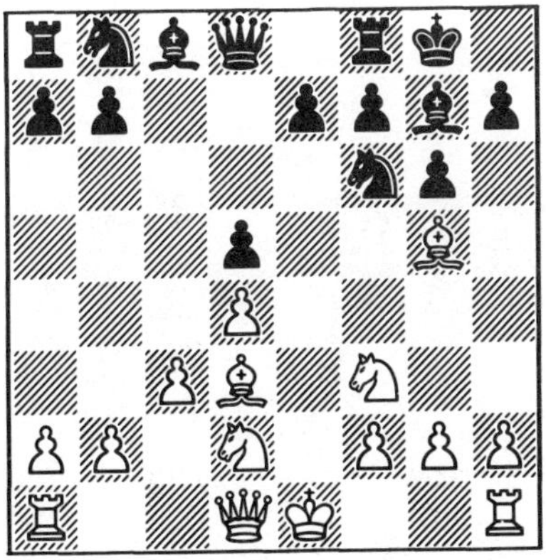

8	**...**	**♘c6**
9	**0-0**	

9 ♕e2 ♕c7 10 0-0 ♘h5 11 ♗e3 f5? (11 ... ♘f4 =) 12 ♘b3 a5 13 a4 b6 14 ♖fe1 ♗d7 15 ♗b5 ♖ae8 16 ♕d1 ± Benko-Kagan, Netanya

1971.

9 ... ♕c7

9 ... h6 10 ♗h4 ♘h5 11 ♖e1 ♕d6 12 ♗b5 g5 Schüssler-Vaganian, Tallinn 1983; 13 ♗xc6! ±; 9 ... ♗f5!?.

10	**♖e1**	**♘h5**
11	**♘f1**	**♘f4**
12	**♗b5**	**e6**
13	**♕d2**	**♘h5**
14	**♘g3**	**♘xg3**
15	**hxg3**	**a6**
16	**♗xc6**	**bxc6** ±

Trifunović-Gligorić, Yugoslav Championship 1951.

11.22

7 ... ♘bd7

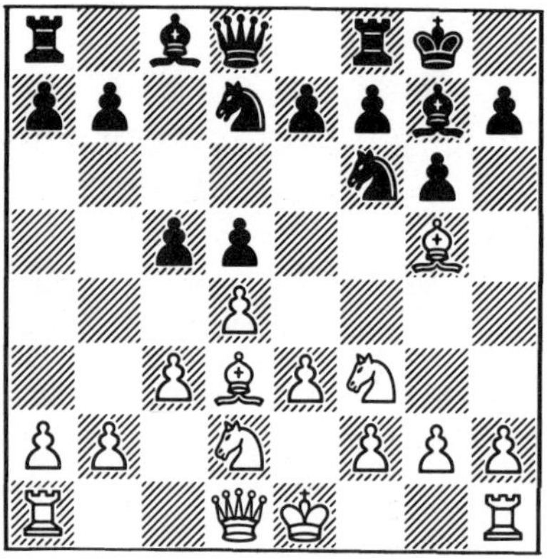

8 0-0 b6

For 8 ... ♕b6 see 11.23. An independent possibility: 9 ♕c2 ♖e8 10 c4! cxd4 11 exd4 ♕c7 12 ♖ac1 a6 13 ♖fe1 e6 14 ♗h4 b6 15 ♗g3 ♕c6 16 b4 dxc4 17 ♘xc4 ♗f8 18 ♕b2 ♕b5! ∞ Smyslov-Vaganian, USSR Championship 1988. Others:

(a) 8 ... ♕c7? 9 ♖e1! b6 10 ♗f4 ♕d8 11 h3 ♗b7 12 ♕b1 ♕c8 13 b4 ♗a6 14 ♗c2 ♗b7 15 a4 ♖e8 16 ♗h2 ± Trifunović-Bertok, Yugoslavia 1951.

(b) 8 ... ♘e8 (Unnatural.) 9 ♗h4 ♘d6 10 ♗g3 b6 11 b4 c4 12 ♗c2 ♘f6 13 a4 ♗g4 14 h3 ♗c8 15 ♗e5 ♗b7 16 ♕e1 ± Sokolov-Khodos, USSR 1966.

9	**♕e2**	**♗b7**
10	**♖ad1**	

10 ♗a6 ♕c8 11 ♗xb7 ♕xb7 12 ♖fe1 ♖fe8 13 h3 e5 = Palda-Primavera, Helsinki 1952.

10	**...**	**♘e4**
11	**♗f4**	**♕c8**

11 ... a6 12 ♘e5 (12 ♗xe4? dxe4 13 ♘g5 h6 14 ♘gxe4 f5 ∓) 12 ... ♘xe5 13 ♗xe5 ♗xe5 14 dxe5 ♘xd2 15 ♖xd2 ♕c7 16 f4 Lein-Savon, USSR 1967; 16 ... f5! = (Petrosian).

12	**h3**	**♖e8**
13	**♘e5**	**♘xe5**
14	**dxe5**	**♘xd2**
15	**♖xd2**	**f6!**

Chances are equal. Vlansky-Yudovich, correspondence 1967.

11.23

7 ... ♕b6

This counter-attack is Black's most active response.

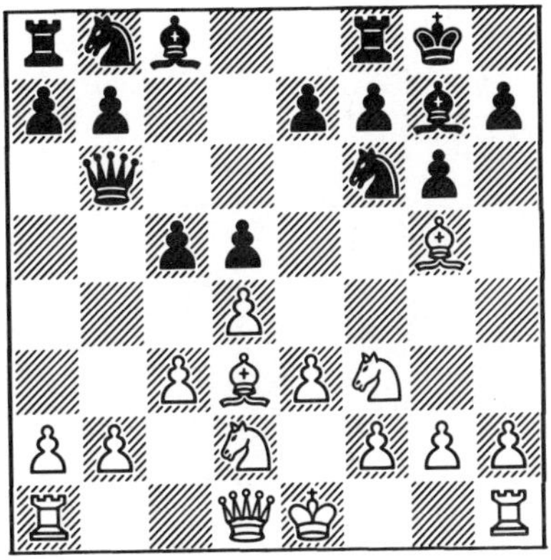

8 ♖b1

8 ♕c1 (8 ♕b1 ♘c6 9 0-0 e5 = Keres-Shcherbakov, Illustrative Game No 66) 8 ... ♘c6 9 0-0 ♗g4 10 h3 ♗xf3 11 ♘xf3 ♘e4 12 ♗f4 f5 = (13 c4? ♘b4 14 ♗e2 cxd4 15 exd4 ♗xd4 16 ♘xd4 ♕xd4 17 ♗e3 ♕f6 ∓ Johanessen-Gligorić, Belgrade 1962); 8 ♕b3 ♘c6 9 0-0 ♖e8 (9 ... c4 10 ♕xb6 axb6 11 ♗c2 ♗f5 =) 10 ♖fd1 ♕xb3 11 axb3 e5 ∞ Co.Ionescu-Ghinda, Timisoara 1987.

8 ... ♘bd7

8 ... ♘c6 (8 ... ♗d7?! 9 ♕e2! ♘c6 10 0-0 ♖ae8 11 b4 ⩲) 9 0-0 e5 10 ♗xf6! (10 dxe5 ♘g4!. It should be mentioned that 10 ♘xe5 ♘xe5 11 dxe5 ♘g4 12 ♘f3 leads to the main variation whereas 12 c4?! ♘xe5 13 cxd5 ♘xd3 14 ♘c4 ♕a6 15 ♕xd3 b5 ⩱ is Illustrative Game No 67) 10 ... ♗xf6 11 e4 ♗e6 (11 ... exd4 12 exd5! and the black knight is *en prise*, so its proper place is on d7!) 12 exd5 ♗xd5 13 ♗e4 ♖fd8 14 ♗xd5 ♖xd5 15 ♘c4! ♕a6 16 ♘e3 ♖dd8 17 d5 ±.

Better is 9 ... ♖e8! 10 b4 cxd4 11 cxd4 a5 (11 ... ♗g4 12 h3 ♗xf3 13 ♕xf3 a5 14 ♗xf6 ♗xf6 15 ♕xd5 axb4 16 ♘e4 ♖d8 17 ♕b3 ⩲ Tseitlin-Kurz, Budapest 1989) 12 ♕a4?! (12 b5!?) 12 ... ♗d7 13 bxa5 ♕xa5 14 ♕xa5 ♘xa5 ½-½ Spassky-Gligorić, Moscow 1967.

9 0-0

9 ♕a4 e5! 10 ♘xe5 ♘xe5 11 dxe5 ♘g4 12 ♗e7 ♘xe5 13 ♗e2 ♗d7 14 ♕a3 ♖fc8 = Malaniuk-Georgadze, Lemberg 1986.

9 ... e5!

If Black has this freeing move he can equalise. 9 ... ♖e8?! 10 ♕a4 ♕d8 11 ♕a3 ♕b6? 12 c4 e6 13 ♖fc1 ♗f8 14 dxc5 ♗xc5 15 b4 ♗f8 16 c5 ± Trifunović-Lindblom, Wageningen 1957.

10 ♘xe5

10 dxe5 (10 ♗xf6 ♗xf6 11 e4 exd4 12 cxd4 dxe4! 13 ♘xe4 ♗xd4 ∓) 10 ... ♘g4 11 c4?! (11 ♗e2!?) 11 ... ♘dxe5 12 cxd5 ♘xd3 13 ♘c4 ♘dxf2! 14 ♘xb6 ♘xd1 15 ♘xa8 ♘dxe3 16 ♗e7 ♘xf1 17 ♖xf1 ♗xb2 ∓ Yudovich-Aronin, USSR 1961.

10	**...**	**♘xe5**
11	**dxe5**	**♘g4**
12	**♘f3**	**♘xe5**
13	**♘xe5**	**♗xe5**
14	**f4**	**♗f6! ∞**

Better than 14 ... ♗g7? 15 f5! ±. An example of lazy play by White: 15 ♗h6? c4! 16 ♗xf8 cxd3 17 ♗a3 ♕xe3+ 18 ♔h1 ♗f5 ∓ Neverov-Sideif Zade, USSR 1987. Better is 15 ♗xf6 ♕xf6 16 f5 ♕e5 17 ♖f3 (17 ♕d2 ♗d7 18 f6 ♔h8 19 e4 d4 20 ♗c4 ♗e6 21 ♕h6 ♖g8 ∞ Dreyev-Khalifman, Moscow 1985) 17 ... ♗d7 (17 ... g5!?) 18 ♕d2 ♖ae8 19 f6 ♕g5 20 ♕f2 ♖e5 21 b4 c4 22 h4 ± Neverov-Glek, Lemberg 1985.

11.24

7 ... b6

The variations are often mixed with those of 7 ... ♘bd7 and 6 c3. Here we look at independent lines.

8 0-0 ♗b7

9 ♕b1

(a) 9 ♘e5 ♘fd7 (9 ... ♘e4?! 10 ♘xe4 dxe4 11 ♗c4 cxd4? 12 cxd4 ♘d7 Filip-Ghitescu, Marianské Lázné 1960; 13 ♘xf7! ♖xf7 14 ♕b3 ♕e8 15 ♖ac1 ±) 10 ♘g4 f6 11 ♗h6 ♗xh6 12 ♘xh6+ ♔g7 13 ♘f5+! gxf5 14 ♗xf5 ∞ Tsvetkov-Savon, USSR 1964.

(b) 9 a4 ♘e4 (9 ... ♘bd7 10 a5 ♗c6 11 c4 dxc4 12 ♘xc4 ♘e4 13 ♗f4 cxd4 14 exd4 bxa5 = Filip-Minev, Amsterdam 1954) 10 ♗f4 ♘d7 11 ♕e2 ♘xd2 12 ♘xd2 (12 ♕xd2 ♖e8 13 a5 e5 =) 12 ... e5 13 dxe5 ♗xe5 14 ♗xe5 ♘xe5 15 ♗a6 ♗xa6 16 ♕xa6 ♖e8 ∓ Malich-Stein, Kecskemét 1968.

(c) 9 ♕c2 ♘bd7 10 ♖ae1 ♖c8 (10 ... c4 11 ♗e2 b5 ∞) 11 ♕b1 ♖e8 12 ♗h4 ♕c7 13 ♗g3 ♕c6 14 ♘e5 ♘xe5 15 ♗xe5 ♘e4 16 ♗xe4 ♗xe5 17 ♗d3 ♗g7 18 f4 ± Rakić-Ostojić, Belgrade 1965.

(d) 9 ♗h4 ♘bd7 10 ♘e5 ♘xe5 11 dxe5 ♘e4 12 f4 ♘xd2 13 ♕xd2 f6 14 exf6 exf6 15 ♖ad1 ± Sokolov-Baikov, USSR 1974.

9 ... ♘c6

9 ... ♘bd7 10 a4 ♖e8 (10 ... ♕c8 11 h3 ♖e8 12 ♗f4 ♘h5 13 ♗e5 ♘xe5 14 ♘xe5 ♗xe5? 15 dxe5 ♕e6 16 f4 f5? 17 ♔h2 ± Sokolov-Zhenov, USSR 1973; 14 ... ♗a6! 15 b4! ±) 11 a5 ♕c8 12 b4 c4 13 ♗c2 b5 14 ♕b2 a6 15 ♖ae1 ♗c6 16 e4 dxe4 17 ♘xe4 ♗b7 18 ♗xf6 ♘xf6 19 ♘c5 ± Trifunović-

Robatsch, Beverwijk 1963.

10	**b4**	**cxd4**
11	**cxd4**	**♕d6**
12	**a3**	**♖fc8** ±

13 ♗f4 ♕e6 14 h3 ♘d8 15 ♕b2 ♘e4 16 a4 Agzamov-Loginov, USSR 1983.

ILLUSTRATIVE GAMES

1 d4 ♘f6 2 ♘f3 g6 3 ♗g5 ♗g7 4 ♘bd2 d5 5 e3 0-0

62) **Kavalek-Browne**
US Championship 1986

6 c3 b6 7 b4 ♗b7 8 ♗e2 ♘bd7 9 0-0 ♘e4?! Actually, this move will weaken Black's pawn structure. 10 ... ♕e8 or 10 ... ♖e8 and ... e5 would have suited the position. **10 ♘xe4 dxe4 11 ♘d2 h6 12 ♗h4 g5 13 ♗g3 f5 14 f3! f4?!** Far too optimistic; Black will expose his weaknesses after the exchanges. 14 ... ♘f6 15 ♗e5! is a bit better. **15 ♗f2 exf3 16 ♗xf3 ♗xf3 17 ♘xf3 fxe3 18 ♗xe3 e5** Otherwise the backward e7 pawn would give trouble. **19 ♕b3+ ♔h8**
(diagram)

20 ♕e6! Black's king is in danger! **20 ... ♕c8?** 20 ... ♕e8 21 ♕h3 ♔g8 22 ♖ae1 e4 23 ♘d2 ♖xf1+ 24 ♖xf1 ♘f6 25 ♕g3 ♕e7 26 h4 ±. **21 ♖ae1 ♖e8 22 ♕g6 e4? 23 ♘xg5! hxg5 24 ♖f7 1-0**
(Kavalek's notes included)

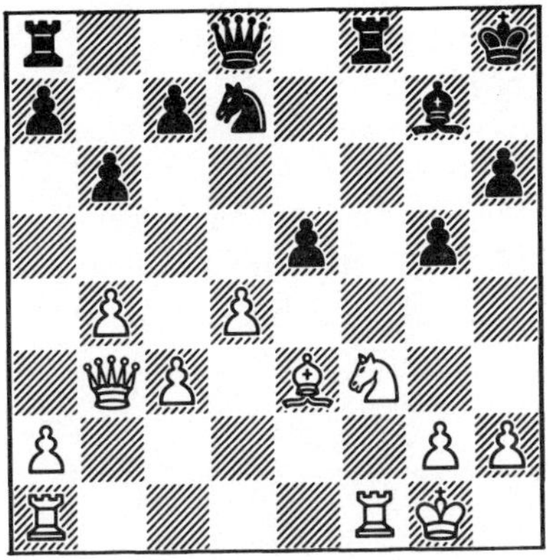

63) **Petrosian-Korchnoi**
match (2) 1974

6 c3 ♘bd7 7 ♗e2 ♖e8 8 h4 8 ♘e5? ♘xe5 9 dxe5 ♘d7 10 f4 f6 ∓. **8 ... c6 9 0-0 e5** 9 ... a5!? 10 b5 a4 ∞. **10 ♘b3 ♕b6 11 ♗xf6!** 11 ... ♘e4 and 11 ... exd4 were threatened. In the blockaded position the knight will be superior to the bishop. **11 ... ♗xf6 12 a3 ♕c7** 12 ... e4 13 ♘fd2 ♗g5 14 c4 f5 15 g3 ±. **13 ♖c1 e4 14 ♘fd2 b5!** Otherwise White takes the initiative by c3-c4. **15 a4! a6** 15 ... bxa4!?. **16 ♖a1 ♗b7 17 ♗g4 ♘b6 18 ♘c5 ♗g7?!** More precise is 18 ... ♗g5!, preventing f2-f4. After the text move White could have continued 19 a5! ♘c8 20 ♗xc8 ♗xc8 21 f4 ±. **19 axb5?! axb5 20 ♕e2 f5 21 ♗h3 ♘a4! 22 ♘db3!** 22 ♘xa4?! bxa4 23 c4 ♗a6 24 b5 cxb5 25 cxb5 ♗b7 ∓. **22 ... ♘xc3 23 ♕c2 ♘a4 24 ♘xa4**

bxa4 25 ♘c5 a3 26 ♕b3?! 26 ♖a2! was the last chance to outplay Black. **26 ... ♗a6!** Forcing the exchange of the active knight for the passive bishop. **27 ♘xa6 ♖xa6 28 ♖xa3 ♖xa3 29 ♕xa3 ♗f8 30 g3 ♖b8 31 ♖b1 ½-½**

31 ... ♕b6 32 ♕a4 ♗xb4 33 ♖c1 ♖c8 34 ♖b1 =.

(Notes based on Korchnoi's)

64) **Vaganian-Beliavsky**
USSR Championship 1975

6 c3 ♘bd7 7 b4 ♖e8 8 ♗e2 e5 9 ♘b3 b6?! 9 ... e4 leads to game No 60. **10 ♗b5 e4 11 ♗c6** 11 ♘e5? ♘xe5! 12 ♗xe8 ♘d3+. **11 ... ♖b8?** Very passive. 11 ... exf3! 12 ♗xa8 fxg2 13 ♖g1 h6 14 ♗h4 g5 15 ♗g3 ♘f8 16 ♗c6 ♗g4 17 ♕c2 ♖e6 18 ♗b5 ♗h3 = or 14 ♗xf6 ♘xf6 15 ♖xg2 ♗g4 16 ♖xg4 ♘xg4 17 ♕xg4 ♖xa8 =. **12 ♘fd2 ♗b7 13 ♗xb7 ♖xb7 14 b5!** Blockading the queenside! **14 ... a6!** The only chance. **15 a4 ♖a7 16 0-0 ♕e7** 16 ... ♕a8!?. **17 ♕e2 ♖ea8 18 a5 axb5 19 ♕xb5 bxa5 20 ♖xa5 ♖xa5 21 ♘xa5 c5?!** Black should have left the pawn where it was. **22 ♘c6 ♕f8 23 ♘b3 c4** Better is 23 ... cxd4 24 cxd4 ♕a3. The text demonstrates that Black is aiming at the weak pawn on c3.

(diagram)

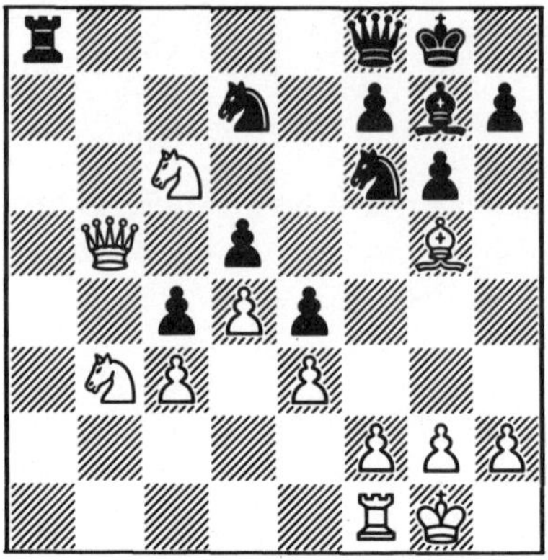

24 ♘c5! The doubled pawns are going to be a menace to Black! **24 ... ♘xc5 25 dxc5 h6 26 ♗h4 g5 27 ♗g3 ♕e8 28 ♗d6 ♗f8 29 ♕b7 ♕c8 30 ♘e7+ ♗xe7 31 ♕xc7 ♕e6** Is there any better? **32 ♕xe6 fxe6 33 ♖b1 ♘e8 34 ♗e5** The powerful bishop forces the issue. **34 ... ♖c8 35 ♖b6 ♔f7 36 c6 ♔g6 37 g4! ♘c7** 37 ... h5 38 c7!. **38 ♖b7 ♘a6 39 ♖g7+ mate 1-0**

(Ufimtsev's notes included)

65) **Vaganian-Timoshchenko**
USSR Championship 1978

6 ♗e2 c5 7 c3 ♘bd7 8 0-0 b6 9 ♕a4 ♗b7 10 ♗a6 ♕c8 11 ♗b5?! Unnatural, 11 ♗xb7 ♕xb7 12 b4 was necessary. **11 ... ♖d8 12 ♘e5?! ♘xe5 13 dxe5 a6!** An important move to interpose. **14 ♗e2?!** 14 exf6? exf6! 15 ♗xf6 ♗xf6 16 ♗e2 d4! ∓; 14 ♗d3! ♘g4! 15 ♗xe7 ♖e8 16 ♗h4 ♘xe5 ∓. **14 ... ♘e4 15 ♘xe4 dxe4 16 ♖fd1** 16 ♗xe7 ♖d2 17 ♖fe1

♗xe5 ∓. **16 ... ♗xe5 17 ♗xe7 ♖xd1+ 18 ♖xd1 ♗c6! 19 ♕c2 ♕c7 20 ♗h4 ♗xh2+ 21 ♔f1 ♗e5** More convincing is 21 ... h6! and the threat is 22 ... g5. **22 ♗c4!** Holding d5, White prevents Black from making good his extra pawn. **22 ... ♕b7 23 ♕d2 ♔g7** 23 ... h6!. **24 ♗d5 ♖e8 25 a4 b5** 25 ... h6!?. **26 ♗xc6 ♕xc6 27 ♕d5!** The only chance. **27 ... ♖e6 28 ♕xc6 ♖xc6 29 axb5 axb5 30 ♖d5 ♗d6 31 g4! f6 32 ♔g2 ♔f7 33 f3 exf3+ 34 ♔xf3 ♔e6 35 e4 b4 36 ♗f2 c4?** 36 ... b3! 37 c4 ♗e5 38 ♖d3 ♗xb2 39 ♖xb3 ♗d4 ∓. **37 cxb4 ♗xb4 38 ♖b5 ♗d6 39 ♗d4 ♖c8 40 ♖b6 ♖b8 41 ♖c6 ♖b3+ ½-½**

(Timoshchenko's notes included)

66) **Keres-Shcherbakov**
USSR Championship 1955

6 c3 c5 7 ♗d3 ♘c6 8 0-0 ♕b6 9 ♕b1 e5! 10 dxe5 10 dxc5 ♕xc5 11 e4 dxe4 =. **10 ... ♘g4 11 e4 ♘cxe5?** On the following moves Black underestimates the effect of the passed pawn on the d-file. 11 ... dxe4! 12 ♘xe4 ♘gxe5 13 ♘xe5 ♘xe5 =; 14 ♗e7? ♖e8 15 ♗xc5 ♕c6∓. **12 ♘xe5 ♘xe5 13 exd5 ♘xd3 14 ♕xd3 ♗f5** 14 ... ♕xb2 15 ♘e4 ∓. **15 ♘e4 ♕xb2** 15 ... ♖fe8 16 ♖ae1 ♕xb2 17 d6!. **16 d6!** The d-pawn is White's trump card. 16 ♗e7?! ♖fe8 17 d6 ♗xe4 18 ♕xe4 ♗f6! **16 ... ♕b6** 16 ... f6 17 ♗h4 b6 18 ♘xf6+! ♗xf6 19 ♕d5+ ♔g7 20 ♕b7+!. **17 ♖fe1** 17 ♗e7!? ♖fe8 18 ♖fe1. **17 ... ♕c6?!** 17 ... f6 18 ♕d5+ ♔h8 19 ♗h4 ±. **18 ♗e7! c4 19 ♕f3 ♗xe4** 19 ... ♖fe8 20 ♖ad1 ±. **20 ♖xe4 ♗xc3 21 ♖c1 f5 22 ♖e2 ♕xf3 23 gxf3 ♗g7 24 ♖xc4!** More convincing than 24 ♗xf8 ♗xf8. **24 ... ♖fb8 25 d7 ♗f8**

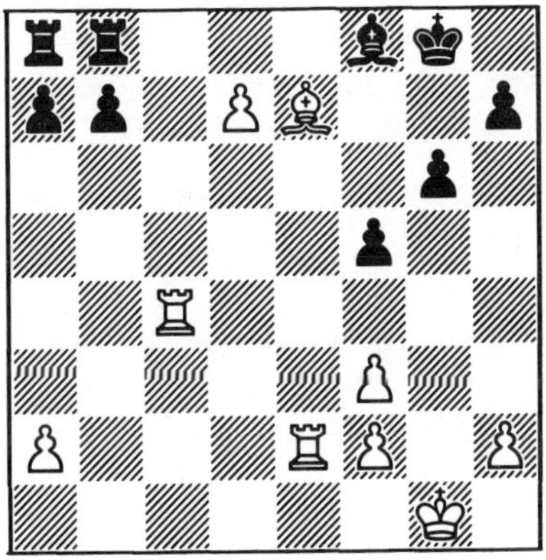

26 ♖ec2!! An elegant finish! **26 ... ♗xe7 27 ♖c8+ ♔f7 28 ♖xb8 ♖xb8 29 ♖c8! 1-0**

67) **Malaniuk-Romanishin**
USSR 1983

6 ♗d3 c5 7 c3 ♕b6 8 ♖b1 ♘c6 9 0-0 e5 10 ♘xe5?! 10 ♗xf6!. **10 ... ♘xe5 11 dxe5 ♘g4 12 c4?!** 12 ♘f3 =. **12 ... ♘xe5 13 cxd5 ♘xd3 14 ♘c4 ♕a6 15 ♕xd3 b5! 16 ♘d2** 16 ♘a3 c4 17 ♕c2 ♖e8 ∓. **16 ... c4 17 ♕c2 ♕xa2** Black has recaptured the pawn, his pieces are active and he threatens to play 18 ... c3!. **18 ♗e7 ♖e8 19 ♗b4**

c3! The exchange is in Black's favour: he will free his queen, and after further exchanges he will have a 'good' bishop and a queen-side pawn majority. **20 ♗xc3 ♗xc3 21 ♕xc3 ♕xd5 22 f3 ♕e5 23 ♕xe5 ♖xe5 24 e4 ♖e7 25 ♖fc1?!** Here or on the next move b2-b4 was necessary. **25 ... ♗e6 26 ♖c5?! ♖d8 27 ♘f1 b4 28 ♔f2 ♖d4 29 g4 ♖ed7 30 ♖a1 ♖d3 31 ♖c2 ♔g7 32 ♔e2 ♗b3 33 ♖d2** 33 ♖cc1 is much tougher.

(diagram)

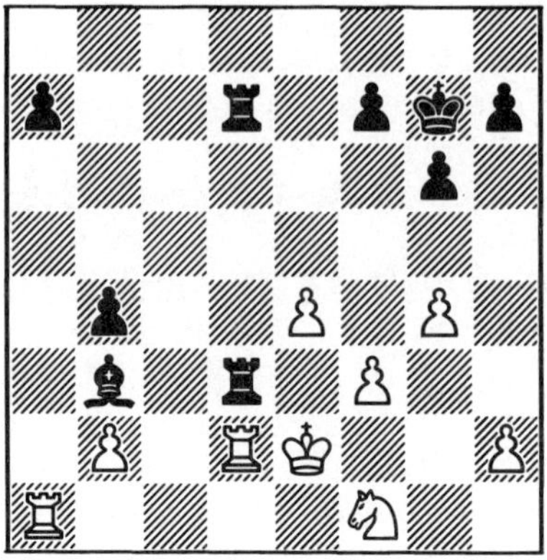

33 ... ♗c4! 34 ♖xd3 ♖xd3 35 ♔f2 ♖b3 36 ♖b1 36 ♖xa7 ♖xb2+ also loses straight away. **36 ... ♗xf1 37 ♖xf1 ♖xb2+ 38 ♔e3 a5 39 ♖d1 a4 0-1**

12 Countering the King's Indian and the Grünfeld: 'Wait and See' Variation, old-fashioned line

1 d4 ♘f6
2 ♘f3 g6
3 ♗f4

3 ♗f4 is a natural developing move, yet it does not hinder Black's development and (at least for the moment) does not threaten anything. Originally it was probably intended to prevent ... e7-e5 but tournament practice has proven that this plan is impossible to carry out. So it is no wonder that ever since the 1920's this line has never really been popular with top-class players, though it can still be encountered sometimes. Still, it was part of the repertoire of such immortals of the game as Capablanca, Alekhine, Keres, Smyslov, etc. – not to mention the theoretically less learned players with whom the line is quite popular even today.

As will be seen, White can hardly squeeze out any advantage from the opening but his practical chances are considerable. The emerging positions are rich: occasionally White's queen's bishop pressurises the h2-b8 diagonal and the game is very rarely simplified at an early stage. In short: the better player wins!

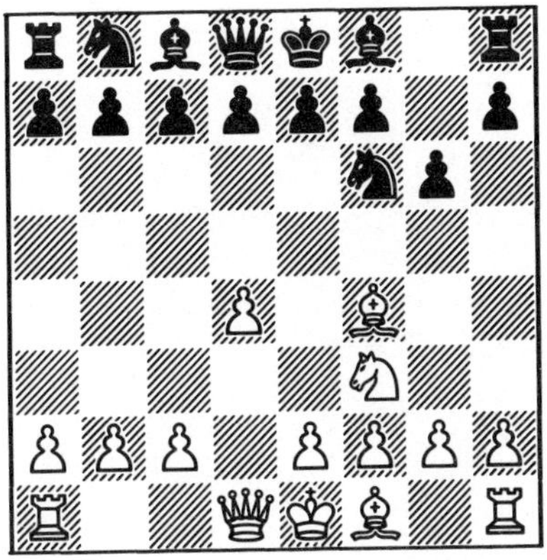

12.1

3 ... d5

We shall see that Black can successfully parry the 'Wait and See' variation by ... d6 but the text move is also satisfactory. Black can postpone ... d5. In fact, it may be better to wait for ♘b1-d2 since now White has the option to transpose into the Grünfeld by 4 c4 ♗g7 5 ♘c3 – although this may be just as well to Black's liking.

Our examples are not new ones as the variation is very seldom played these days.

Other deviations from 3 ... ♗g7, the main line:

(a) 3 ... d6 4 e3 (4 h3) 4 ... ♘h5! 5 ♗g5! (5 ♗g3 ♘xg3 6 hxg3 ♗g7 7 ♗c4 e6 = S.Nikolić-Ermenkov, Illustrative Game No 68) 5 ... ♗g7 6 ♗e2 h6 7 ♗h4 f5 (7 ... g5!?) 8 g4! fxg4 9 ♘fd2 g5 (9 ... ♘f6!?) 10 ♗xg4 ♗xg4 11 ♕xg4 ♘f6 12 ♕g2 ♘c6 13 ♘c3 ♕d7 14 0-0-0 0-0-0 ± Sapis-Kupreichik, Lemberg 1988.

(b) 3 ... c5 4 c3 (4 dxc5 ♘a6!) 4 ... b6 5 dxc5!? (Turning the tables!) 5 ... bxc5 6 e4 ♗b7? (6 ... ♘c6!) 7 ♗c4 e6 8 ♘bd2 ♘h5!? Plaskett-Razuvaev, Manchester 1983; 9 ♗e3! ±. Better is 8 ... ♘xe4! 9 ♘xe4 ♗xe4 ∞.

4 e3 ♗g7

4 ... c6 5 c3 ♗g7 6 ♘bd2 ♘bd7 7 ♗d3 ♘h5! 8 ♗g5 h6 9 ♗h4 g5 10 ♘e5? ♗xe5 11 ♕xh5 ♘f6 12 ♕e2 ♗xd4 ∓ Arkell-Speelman, England 1984.

5 ♘bd2

(a) 5 ♗d3 (5 c4 c5!? is worth considering) 5 ... ♘h5 6 ♗g5 h6 7 ♗h4 ♘d7 8 c4? g5 9 ♗g3 ♘xg3 10 hxg3 dxc4 ∓ Malaniuk-Vaganian, USSR 1983.

(b) 5 h3 0-0 6 ♗d3 c5 7 c3 ♕b6 8 ♕c1 ♘e4 9 ♘bd2 ♗f5 10 0-0 ♘g3! 11 ♗xg3 ♗xd3 12 ♖e1 ♘a6 13 ♘b3 ♖fd8 ∓ Mascarinas-Dorfman, Lvov 1981.

(c) 5 ♗e2 0-0 6 0-0 c5 7 c3 ♘c6 8 ♘e5 ♕b6 (8 ... ♘d7 9 ♘xd7 ♗xd7 10 dxc5 e5 11 ♗g3 ♗e6 ∞ Andruet-Kouatly, Royan 1988) 9 ♕b3 ♘e8 10 ♘xc6 bxc6 11 ♕a3 a5 12 ♘d2 cxd4 13 cxd4 c5 = Hansen-Birnboim, Jerusalem 1987.

5 ... 0-0

5 ... c5 6 c3 ♘bd7 (6 ... ♕b6?! 7 ♕b3! 0-0 8 ♕xb6 axb6 9 ♗c7 ♘fd7 10 ♗b5 ♘a6 11 ♗g3 ± Bronstein-Bertok, Vinkovci 1970) 7 ♗d3 0-0 then 8 ... b6 and 9 ... ♗b7 = (Recommended by Cvetković and Sokolov.)

6 ♗e2

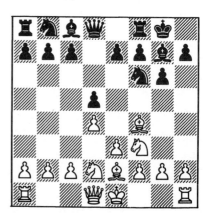

6 ♗d3 ♘bd7 (6 ... b6 7 c3 ♗b7 8 ♕e2 c5 9 0-0 ♘c6 10 ♘e5 ♘h5 11 ♘xc6 ♘xf4 12 exf4 ♗xc6 13 ♘f3 ♗b7 = Kulzinski-Andrić, Yugoslavia 1948) 7 c3 b6 8 ♘e5 ♗b7 9 h4?! ♘h5! 10 g4 ♘xf4 11 exf4 ♘xe5 12 fxe5 f6 Safvat-Badilles, Moscow 1956; 13 f4! =.

6	**...**	**c5**
7	**0-0**	**♘bd7**

7 ... cxd4?! 8 exd4 ♘c6 9 c3 ♘h5 10 ♗e3 ♕c7 11 ♖e1 ♗g4 12 ♘b3 ♘f4 13 ♗b5 ± Keres-Bronstein, Illustrative Game No 69.

8	**c3**	**b6**
9	**h3**	**♗b7**
10	**♘e5**	**♘xe5**

10 ... e6 11 ♘xd7 ♕xd7 12 ♗e5 ♖fc8 13 ♕e1 ♗c6 14 f4 ♗b5 = Flotow-R.Byrne, Lugano 1968.

11	**♗xe5**	**♘d7**
12	**♗xg7**	**♔xg7** =

13 f4 e6 14 ♗d3 ♘f6 15 ♕e2 ♕d6 16 ♖ad1 ♖fd8 = Doda-Hamann, Lugano 1968.

12.2

3	**...**	**♗g7**

Black has not revealed his intentions yet.

4 ♘bd2

This move has disappeared from tournaments, and understandably so: if White wants to play e2-e4

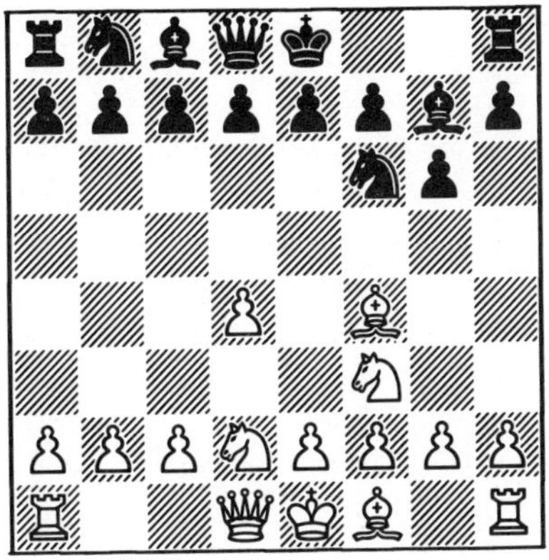

then ... e7-e5 will prove that ♗f4 was premature, and should White choose e2-e3, he will miss the possibility of c2-c4 and ♘c3. No wonder that 4 e3 (Chapter 13) is much more popular. Interesting is: 4 c3 and now:

(a) 4 ... 0-0 5 e3 d6 6 ♗e2 ♘fd7 7 e4 ♘c6 8 0-0 e5 9 dxe5 dxe5 10 ♗e3 ♕e7 11 ♘bd2 f5 12 exf5 gxf5 13 ♗g5 ∞ Dreyev-Yurtaev, Simferopol 1988.

(b) 4 ... d6 5 h3 0-0 6 ♘bd2 ♗f5 7 g4!? ♗d7 8 ♗g2 ♘c6 9 ♗g3 ♕e8 10 ♕c2 e5 11 dxe5 dxe5 12 ♘c4 ♘d5!? 13 ♘fxe5 ♘xe5 14 ♗xe5 ♘e3! 15 ♘xe3 ♕xe5 16 ♗xb7 ♖ab8 17 ♖d1 ♗e6 18 ♗d5 ♗h6 ∞ Korchnoi-Gulko, OHRA 1989.

(c) 4 ... b6 5 e3 ♗b7 6 h3 0-0 7 ♗e2 d6 8 0-0 c5 9 ♘bd2 ♘bd7 10 ♗h2 ♕c7 11 a4 a6 12 ♕b1 cxd4 13 exd4 ♘d5! 14 ♖e1 ♖fe8 15 ♕a2 ♗h6 ∞ Portisch-Gulko, Linares 1990 (see Chapter 13).

4 ... 0-0

(a) 4 ... d5 5 e3 0-0 6 c4 is a variation of the Slav, and it is harmless for Black. Better is 6 c3.

(b) 4 ... ♘h5?! 5 ♗e5! f6 6 ♗g3 d6 7 e4 ♘xg3 8 hxg3 e6 9 ♗d3 ♘d7 10 ♕e2 ♕e7 11 0-0-0 e5 12 c3 ± Keres-Taimanov, Tallinn 1975.

(c) 4 ... d6 5 e4 ♘c6 6 d5 e5 7 dxe6 ♗xe6 8 ♗b5 0-0 9 0-0 a6 10 ♗a4 b5 11 ♗b3 ♗xb3 12 axb3 ♕e8 = Taimanov-Vasyukov, USSR 1971.

(d) 4 ... c5!? 5 c3 (5 e3 d6 6 c3 ♘c6 ∞ Alekhine-Euwe, Illustrative Game No 70; 5 dxc5?! ♘a6!) 5 ... cxd4 6 cxd4 d5! 7 ♗xb8?! (7 e3 is the Slav again, now with chances for both sides. Pawn-snatching is premature) 7 ... ♖xb8 8 ♕a4+ ♗d7 9 ♕xa7 ♘e4 10 e3 ♘xd2 11 ♘xd2 e5! ∞ Keres-Fischer, Illustrative Game No 71.

12.21

5 e3

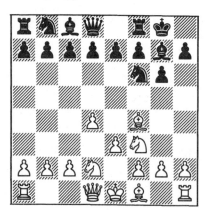

As mentioned before, White's e3 move should precede the development of the queen's knight.

5 ... d6

5 ... c5 (5 ... ♘h5? 6 ♗e5! f6 7 g4 ±) 6 c3 b6 (6 ... ♘c6? 7 dxc5 ♘h5 8 ♗g3 b6 9 cxb6 ♕xb6 10 ♕b3 ± Alekhine-Richter, Podebrady 1936) 7 ♗e2 (7 a4 d6 8 h3 ♗b7 9 ♗c4 ♘bd7 10 0-0 a6 11 ♕e2 h6 12 ♗h2 ♖e8 13 ♗a2 d5! = Moiseyev-Pribyl, Primorsko 1974) 7 ... ♘c6 (7 ... ♗a6 8 ♗xa6 ♘xa6 9 h3 d5 10 0-0 ♕e8 11 ♖e1 ± Barcza-Westerinen, Varna 1962, or 9 0-0 ♕c8 10 ♕e2 d5! 11 h3 ♕b7 12 ♘e5 ♖ac8 = Bondarevsky-Aronin, Illustrative Game No 72) 8 h3 ♗b7 9 0-0 d5 (for 9 ... d6 see Chapter 13) 10 ♖b1 ♘d7 11 b4 cxb4 12 cxb4 e5 13 dxe5 ♘dxe5 14 b5 ± Bisguier-Byrne, USA 1965/66. Probably better is 6 ... cxd4! 7 cxd4 (7 exd4 ♘c6 8 h3 d6 9 ♘c4 b5 10 ♘e3 b4 11 d5 bxc3! 12 dxc6 cxb2 13 ♖b1 ♘e4 14 ♗d3 ♕a5+ 15 ♔f1 ♗a6 ∓ Kotov-Petrosian, USSR 1952) 7 ... ♘c6 8 ♗e2 d5 9 0-0 ♕b6 10 ♕b3 ♕xb3 11 ♘xb3 ♗f5 = Ilivitzky-Geller, Illustrative Game No 73.

6 h3

Typical in this line. The bishop must retreat to h2 in safety.

6 ... c5

(a) 6 ... b6 7 c3 ♗b7 8 ♗c4 ♘fd7

9 ♗g3 ♘c6 10 0-0 h6 11 ♕c2 e5 = Weenink-Euwe, Holland 1928; 12 ♕xg6?? d5 13 ♗xd5 ♘e7 ∓∓.

(b) 6 ... ♘c6 7 ♗h2 ♕e8 8 ♗e2 e5 9 dxe5 ♘xe5 10 ♘xe5 dxe5 11 ♘c4 ♘d7 12 0-0 ♘b6 13 ♕d2 ♕e7 14 ♖fd1 ♗f5 = Smyslov-Gligorić, Vienna 1957.

(c) 6 ... ♘bd7 7 ♗c4 (7 ♗e2 b6 8 0-0 ♗b7 9 c3 e6! 10 ♗h2 ♕e7 11 ♘c4 ♘e4 12 ♕b3 ♗d5 13 ♖ad1 f5 14 ♕c2 h6 15 ♘fd2 ♘g5 ∓ Prameshuber-Hübner, Paignton 1970) 7 ... ♕e8 (7 ... e6 8 c3 ♕e7 9 e4?! e5 10 dxe5 dxe5 11 ♗e3 b6 12 ♕e2 a6 13 g4?! ♘c5 14 ♗g5 ♗b7 15 ♕e3 ♕e8! ∓ Vidmar-Flohr, Illustrative Game No 74; 9 0-0 e5 10 ♗h2 e4 11 ♘e1 ♘b6 12 ♗b3 ♗h6 13 ♘c2 ♗f5 14 g4!? ♗d7 15 f4 exf3 ∞ Bisguier-Langeweg, Beverwijk 1962) 8 0-0 e5 9 dxe5 dxe5 10 ♗h2 ♕e7 11 e4 ♘h5 12 ♕e2 ♘c5 13 ♕e3 c6 14 ♖fe1 b5 15 ♗f1 ♘a4 = Franklin-Ree, 1964.

7 c3

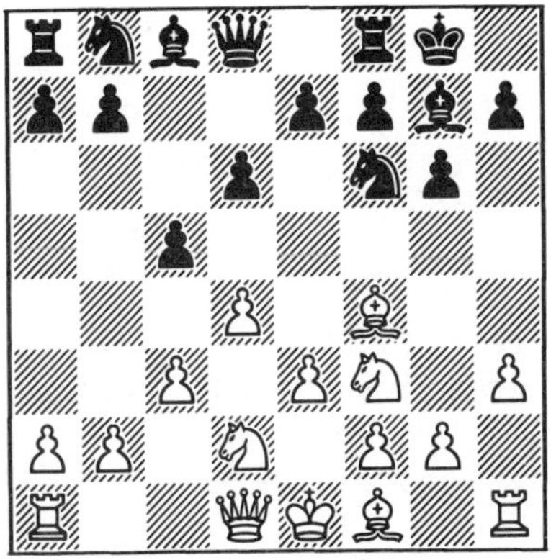

7 ♗e2 ♘c6 8 ♗h2 cxd4 9 exd4 ♗d7 10 0-0 ♖c8 11 ♖e1 a6 12 ♗f1 b5 13 c3 ♘a5 = Smyslov-Boleslavsky, Zürich 1953.

7 ... cxd4

There used to be a lot of different responses at this point:

(a) 7 ... ♘c6 8 ♗c4 a6 (8 ... ♖e8? 9 0-0 e5 10 dxe5 ♘xe5 11 ♗xe5! ± Alekhine-Euwe, Illustrative Game No 70) 9 a4 cxd4 10 exd4 (10 cxd4?! ♗f5! ∓) 10 ... e5 11 dxe5 (11 ♗e3 e4 12 ♘h2 d5 13 ♗a2 ♗e6 14 0-0 ♘e7 ∓ Kotov-Lambert, London 1977) 11 ... dxe5 12 ♗h2 e4 13 ♘e5 ∞ (Hort).

(b) 7 ... ♘bd7 9 ♗e2 a6 9 0-0 b5 10 a4 ♖b8 11 axb5 axb5 12 dxc5 ♘xc5 13 ♘d4 ♗d7 14 ♗h2 ♕b6 = Prameshuber-Golz, Budapest 1960.

(c) 7 ... b6 8 ♗c4 (8 ♗d3 ♗b7 9 0-0 ♘c6 10 ♕e2 a6 11 ♖ad1 cxd4 12 exd4 b5 13 ♘e4 ♘d5 14 ♗c1 ♕c7 15 ♖fe1 ♘d8 = Smyslov-Gligorić, Moscow 1947; 8 ♗e2 ♗b7 9 0-0 ♘c6 10 a4 ♖b8 11 ♘c4 ♕d7 12 ♕c2 ♖fc8 13 ♖fd1 ♘d5 14 ♗g5 h6 = Rossetto-Panno, Mar del Plata 1955) 8 ... ♗b7 (8 ... ♗a6 9 ♗xa6 ♘xa6 10 ♕e2 ♘c7 11 0-0 ♕d7 12 dxc5 bxc5 13 e4 e5 14 ♗e3 ♖ab8 15 b3 ♕c6 = Bondarevsky-Bronstein, Leningrad 1963; 9 0-0 ♗xc4 10 ♘xc4 ♘a6 11 ♕e2 ♘c7 12 ♖ad1 ♕c8 13 ♖fe1 ♕a6 = Bondarevsky-Gheorghiu, Sochi 1964) 9 0-0 ♘bd7 (9 ... ♘c6

10 ♕e2 a6 11 a4 ♕c7 12 ♖fd1 h6 13 ♖ac1 ♖fc8 = Taimanov-Smyslov, USSR 1968) 10 ♕e2 (10 ♖e1 a6 11 a4 d5 12 ♗f1 e6 13 ♗h2 ♕c8 14 ♘e5 ♖d8 15 ♕c2 ♗h6 = Novopashin-Simagin, USSR 1963; 10 a4 a6 11 ♗h2 ♘e8?! 12 ♕e2 ♘c7 13 e4 ♖b8 14 e5 d5 15 ♗d3 e6 16 ♗f4 ± Franklin-Lee, London 1977; 10 ... ♗d5!? 11 ♗a6 ♖b8 12 ♕e2 ♘e4 13 ♘xe4 ♗xe4 14 ♖ad1 ♗c6 15 ♗b5 ♕c8 = Bondarevsky-Ufimtsev, USSR 1947) 10 ... ♘e4 (10 ... ♕c7 11 ♗h2 ♖ae8? 12 e4 cxd4 13 cxd4 e5 14 ♖ac1 ♕b8 15 d5 ♖c8 16 ♗b5! ± Capablanca-Réti, Illustrative Game No 75) 11 ♖fd1 ♘xd2 12 ♖xd2 ♘f6 13 a4 ♘e4 14 ♖dd1 cxd4 15 cxd4 ♖c8 = Keres-Liberzon, USSR 1963.

8 cxd4

8 exd4 ♘c6 9 ♗e2 ♖e8 10 ♘c4 (10 ♗h2 e5 11 dxe5 dxe5 12 ♘c4 ♘d5 13 0-0 ♘f4 14 ♗xf4 exf4 15 ♕xd8 ♖xd8 16 ♖fd1 ♗e6 ∓ Taimanov-Gligorić, Vinkovci 1970) 10 ... ♗e6 11 0-0 ♖c8 (11 ... ♘d5? 12 ♗d2 ♖c8 13 ♘g5 ♗d7 14 ♕b3 h6 15 ♗f3 ± Janowski-Marshall, New York 1924) 12 ♗h2 ♗h6 13 ♖e1 ♘a5 = Kholmov-Gufeld, USSR 1959.

8 ... ♘c6

8 ... ♕b6 9 ♕b3 ♗e6 10 ♕xb6 axb6 11 ♘c3 ♘d5 = Hort-Velimirović, Reggio Emilia 1986/7.

9 ♗c4 ♗f5

9 ... e5!? 10 dxe5 dxe5 11 ♘xe5 ♘h5 12 ♘xc6 bxc6 13 ♗h2 ♗xb2 14 ♖b1 ♗c3 15 ♖b3 ♗a5 ∞ Bronstein-Gurgenidze, USSR 1957.

10	**0-0**	**♖c8**
11	**♕e2**	**♘a5**
12	**♗d3**	**♗xd3**
13	**♕xd3**	**♕b6**
14	**♖ab1**	**♘d5** =

Keres-Gheorghiu, Varna 1962.

12.22

5 e4

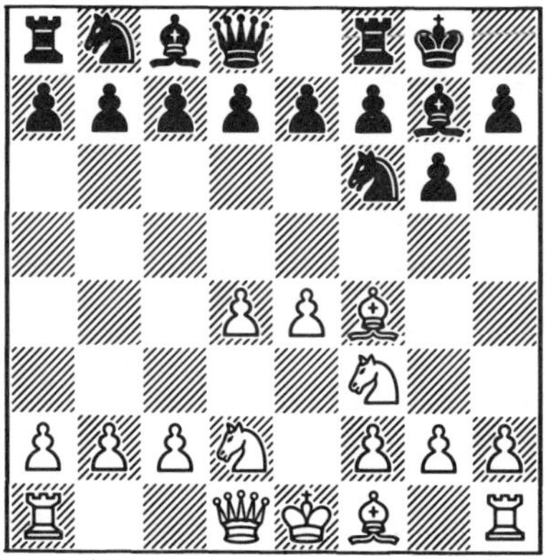

This might not be better than 5 e3 but at least it is consistent.

5 ... d6
6 c3

(a) 6 h3 c5?! (6 ... ♘bd7!) 7 dxc5 dxc5 8 e5 ♘d5 9 ♗h2 b6 10 ♗d3 ♗b7 11 0-0 ♘c7 12 ♕e2 ♘c6 13 ♖ad1 ± Bronstein-Savon, USSR 1961.

(b) 6 ♗c4 ♘c6 7 c3 ♘h5 8 ♗e3 e5 = (Euwe).

(c) 6 ♗d3 ♘bd7 7 h3 (7 0-0 ♘h5! 8 ♗g5 h6 9 ♗h4 ♘f4 10 ♗c4 g5 11 ♗g3 e5 12 c3 ♘b6 13 ♗b3 ♗g4 ∓ O'Kelly-Geller, Budapest 1952) 7 ... c6 8 0-0 ♕c7 9 ♗h2 e5 10 c3 ♘h5 11 a4 a6 12 ♘c4 b5 = Bogoljubow-Réti, Berlin 1919.

6 ... ♘c6!

Making every effort to prepare ... e5!. More passive is 6 ... ♘bd7 7 ♗c4 c6 8 0-0 ♘xe4 9 ♘xe4 d5 10 ♗d3 dxe4 11 ♗xe4 ♘f6 12 ♗c2 ♗g4 13 h3 ♗xf3 14 ♕xf3 ± Keres-Matulović, USSR v Yugoslavia 1961.

7 ♗b5 e5!

Despite doing his best, White is unable to prevent this liberating move. 7 ... ♘d7?! 8 0-0 e5 9 ♗g5 ♕e8 10 ♖c1 ± Keres-Polugayevsky, Illustrative Game No 76.

8 dxe5 dxe5
9 ♗e3

It turns out that the pawn is too hot to touch: 9 ♘xe5? ♘h5! 10 ♘xc6 bxc6 11 ♗xc6 ♘xf4 12 ♗xa8 ♘xg2+ 13 ♔f1 ♗h3 ∓.

9 ... ♕d6
10 b4 b6
11 0-0 ♗b7
12 ♕c2 a6

The chances are even. Keres-Boleslavsky, USSR 1965.

ILLUSTRATIVE GAMES

1 d4 ♘f6 2 ♘f3 g6 3 ♗f4

68) **S.Nikolić-Ermenkov**
Smederevska Palanka 1980

3 ... d6 4 e3?! ♘h5! 5 ♗g3 5 ♗g5 h6 6 ♗h4 g5 7 ♘fd2 ♘g7! 8 ♗g3 ♘f5 ∓. **5 ... ♘xg3 6 hxg3 ♗g7 7 ♗c4 e6! 8 ♘c3!? ♕e7 9 ♕d2 ♘d7 10 0-0-0?! a6 11 ♖h4?! b5 12 ♗d3 ♗b7 13 ♔b1 c5 14 ♖dh1 h6 15 ♘d1 c4 16 ♗e2 ♘f6 17 ♘e1 ♘e4 18 ♕c1 d5 19 c3 a5 20 ♘f3 ♕c7 21 ♘e5?** A miscalculated simplification in a lost position. **21 ... ♗xe5 22 dxe5 ♕xe5 23 ♖xh6 ♖xh6 24 ♖xh6**

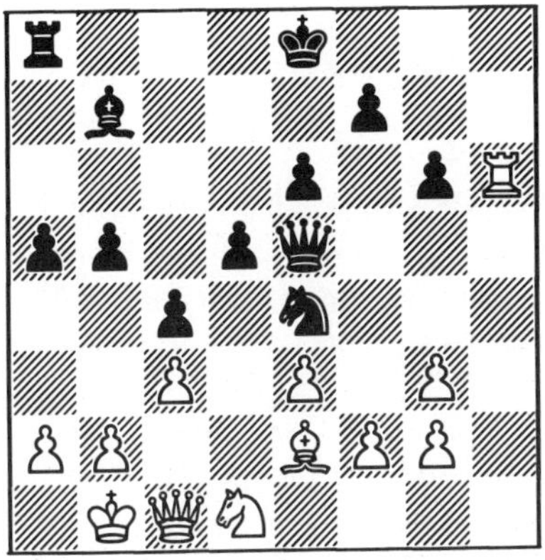

24 ... ♘xf2! 25 ♗xc4 dxc4! 26 ♘xf2 0-0-0! 27 g4 ♕g3 28 ♕e1 28 ♘h1 ♗e4+ 29 ♔a1 ♕xe3 −+; 28 ♘d1 ♕e1 −+. **28 ... ♗e4+ 29 ♔c1 ♗xg2 30 a4 b4 31 cxb4 axb4 32 ♘d3 ♕xe1+ 33 ♘xe1 ♗c6! 34**

a5 ♗a4 35 ♘c2 c3 36 bxc3 36 ♖h2 ♖d1+! 37 ♔xd1 cxb2. **36 ... bxc3 37 ♘d4 e5 0-1** (Ermenkov)

69) **Keres-Bronstein**
USSR Championship 1959

3 ... ♗g7 4 ♘bd2 d5 5 e3 0-0 6 ♗e2 c5 7 0-0 7 dxc5 ♘fd7. **7 ... cxd4 8 exd4 ♘c6 9 c3 ♘h5** The position now reaches a well-known variation of the Caro-Kann, but with the d3 bishop on e2. **10 ♗e3 ♕c7?!** 10 ... f5 11 ♘b3 ♘f6. **11 ♖e1 ♗g4 12 ♘b3 ♘f4 13 ♗b5! ♘h5 14 h3 ♗d7?! 15 ♕c1 ♖fe8** 15 ... ♘xd4?! 16 ♘bxd4 c5 17 ♗xd7 exd4 18 ♗xd4 ±. **16 ♗h6 ♗h8 17 ♗f1** 17 ♘c5? ♘xd4! 18 ♗xd7 ♘xf3+ 19 gxf3 ♕xc5 20 ♗xe8 ♖xe8 ∓. **17 ... ♖ad8 18 ♘c5 ♘f6 19 b4! ♗f5 20 ♘h4** 20 g4!? ♗e4 21 ♗f4 ♕c8 22 ♘e5. **20 ... ♗d7 21 ♗f4 ♕c8 22 g4!? h5 23 f3 hxg4 24 hxg4 ♘h7** It is not easy to tell where Black made a mistake, but he has been gradually forced back. **25 ♘d3 ♗f6** 25 ... ♗xg4?! 26 fxg4 g5 27 ♘f5! gxf4 28 ♕xf4 ±. **26 ♘g2 ♘b8 27 a4 ♘a6 28 ♘e3 ♘c7 29 ♗g2 ♗h4 30 ♖e2 b5 31 a5 ♘e6 32 ♗h2 ♗c6 33 ♕c2 ♗f6 34 ♘e5 ♗b7 35 ♖f1!** After lengthy preparations White begins the offensive. The threat is f4-f5. **35 ... ♘ef8** 35 ... ♘hg5 36 ♘xg6! fxg6 37 ♕xg6+ ♔h8 38 ♘f5 ±. **36 ♕d3 ♘g5 37 f4 ♘e4 38 ♘xd5! ♘d6** 38 ... ♗xd5 39 ♗xe4 ♗xe5 40 ♗xd5 ♗xd4+ 41 ♕xd4 e6 42 f5! ♖xd5 43 fxe6!!. **39 ♘e3 ♗xg2 40 ♖xg2 ♗g7 41 g5 ♕b7** 41 ... ♘f5!? 42 ♘5g4 ±.

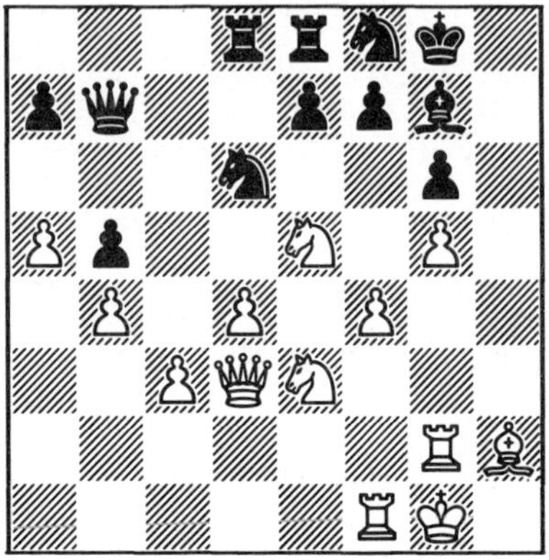

42 f5! ♕e4 43 ♕xe4 ♘xe4 44 ♖g4! The game suddenly hots up and White finishes with a brilliant attack. **44 ... ♘xc3 45 f6! ♗h8** 45 ... exf6 46 gxf6 ♗h6 47 ♘f5!. The bishop is not only passive, but it also restricts the mobility of its own king. **46 ♖h4! exf6 47 gxf6 ♖xd4 48 ♘3g4 g5** A futile effort to give the king space. 48 ... ♘d7 49 ♘h6+ ♔h7 50 ♖h3! ♘xf6 51 ♘g4+ ♔g8 52 ♖xf6 ±±. **49 ♖h5 ♖xe5**

(see diagram)

50 ♘h6+ ♔h7 51 ♘f5+! ♔g8 52 ♘e7+ ♖xe7 53 ♖xh8+! 1-0

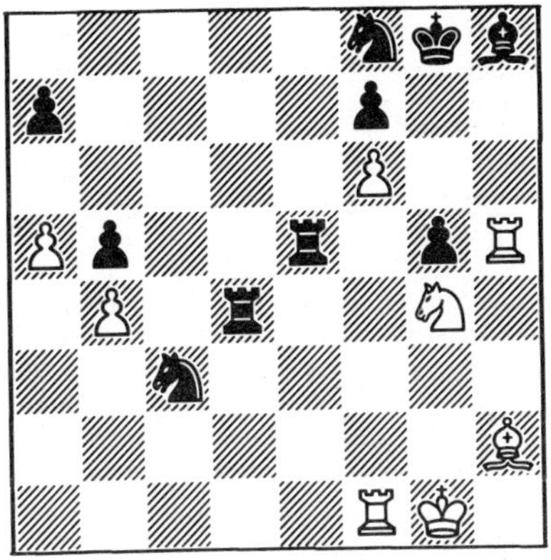

70) **Alekhine-Euwe**
London 1922

3 ... ♗g7 4 ♘bd2 c5 5 e3 d6 6 c3 ♘c6 7 h3 0-0 8 ♗c4 ♖e8? 8 ... a6. **9 0-0 e5 10 dxe5 ♘xe5?** 10 ... dxe5! 11 ♗h2 ♗e6 12 ♗xe6 ♖xe6 13 ♘c4 gives Black less trouble. **11 ♗xe5! dxe5 12 ♘g5!** Securing the domination on the d-file. **12 ... ♗e6?!** 12 ... ♖f8 13 ♘de4! ♕xd1 14 ♖fxd1 ♘xe4 15 ♘xe4 b6 ±. **13 ♗xe6 fxe6 14 ♘de4 ♘xe4 15 ♕xd8! ♖exd8 16 ♘xe4** Doubled pawns and a hemmed in bishop on one side, a stong knight and a strong-hold (e4) on the other – everything points to White's victory. Still, there is lengthy, intricate footwork to be accomplished before White can register the full point. The technique of the later world champion is highly instructive. **16 ... b6 17 ♖fd1 ♔f8 18 ♔f1!** 18 ♘g5?! ♔e7 19 ♘xh7 ♗h6 ±. **18 ... ♔e7 19 c4!** Preventing the 20 ... c4 and ... ♖d5 threats, and at the same time vacating the 3rd rank for the important manoeuvring of the rook. **19 ... h6 20 ♔e2 ♖xd1 21 ♖xd1 ♖b8** For 21 ... ♖d8 22 ♖xd8 ♔xd8, Alekhine gives the following winning process: (1) 23 h4 then g2-g4-g5, forcing ... h6-h5; (2) b2-b3, then ♔d3, ♘c3, ♔e4; (3) ♘d3, tying Black's king to d6; (4) f2-f4, winning a pawn after the forced exchange on f4. **22 ♖d3 ♗h8**

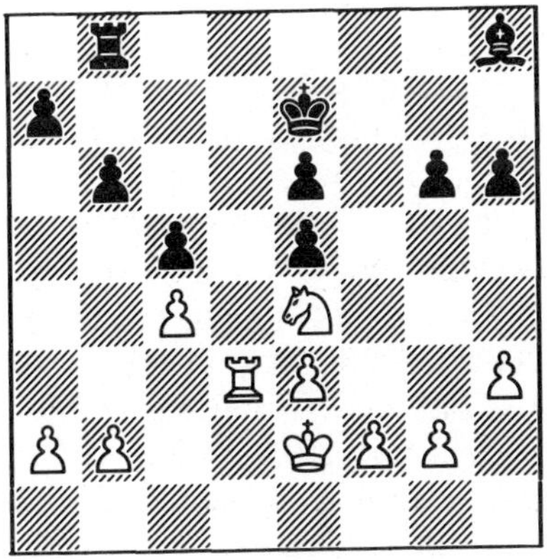

23 a4! The only way to force the decisive penetration of the white rook. 23 ... a5 24 ♖b3! costs a pawn. **23 ... ♖c8 24 ♖b3 ♔d7 25 a5! ♔c6 26 axb6 axb6 27 ♖a3 ♗g7 28 ♖a7 ♖c7 29 ♖a8 ♖e7 30 ♖c8+ ♔d7 31 ♖g8! ♔c6 32 h4** Locking up the bishop before the decisive manoeuvre of the knight! **32 ... ♔c7 33 g4 ♔c6 34 ♔d3**

♖d7+ 35 ♔c3 ♖f7 36 b3 ♔c7 37 ♔d3 ♖d7+ 38 ♔e2 ♖f7 39 ♘c3! The knight makes for b5, the king for e4. **39 ... ♖e7 40 g5 hxg5 41 hxg5 ♔c6 42 ♔d3 ♖d7+ 43 ♔e4 ♖c7 44 ♘b5 ♖e7** 44 ... ♖f7 45 ♖c8+!. **45 f3 ♔d7** 45 ... ♔b7 46 ♘d6+ and 47 ♘e8 +-. **46 ♖b8 ♔c6 47 ♖c8+ ♔d7** 47 ... ♔b7 48 ♘d6+ ♔a7 49 ♖g8 +-. **48 ♖c7+ ♔d8 49 ♖c6! ♖b7 50 ♖xe6 1-0**

A textbook example of 'good knight' versus 'bad bishop'.

71) **Keres-Fischer**
Candidates', Yugoslavia 1959

3 ... ♗g7 4 ♘bd2 c5 5 c3 cxd4 6 cxd4 d5! The position is similar to the Slav, but with easy equality for Black. **7 ♗xb8?!** This pawn-snatching is double-edged because Black is going to gain a considerable advantage in development. **7 ... ♖xb8 8 ♕a4+ ♗d7 9 ♕xa7 ♘e4 10 e3 ♘xd2 11 ♘xd2**

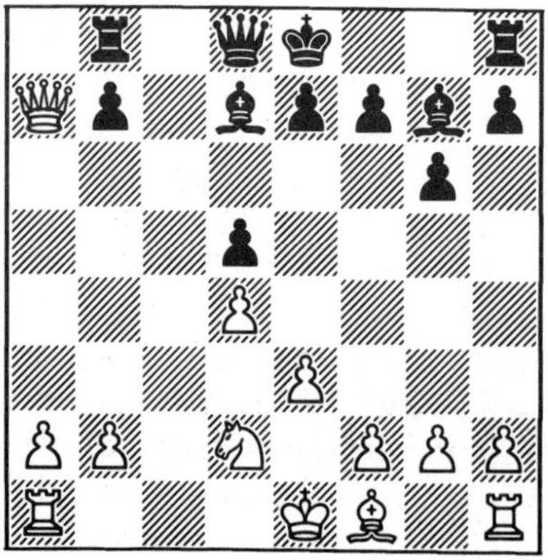

11 ... e5! The better development and the two bishops demand an open position. Black has ample compensation for the pawn; White has problems in maintaining the balance. **12 ♘b3** 12 ♘f3!?. **12 ... 0-0 13 ♕c5** 13 ♗e2 ♕g5!?. **13 ... ♖c8 14 ♕b4 ♖e8 15 ♗e2 exd4** 15 ... ♖c2!?; 15 ... ♕g5!?. **16 ♘xd4 ♕h4 17 ♕xb7!** 17 0-0?? ♗xd4 -+; 17 ♖d1 ♖xe3! 18 g3 ♖xe2+ 19 ♔e2 ♕e4+ +-. **17 ... ♗xd4 18 ♕xd7 ♗xb2 19 ♖d1 ♗c3+ 20 ♔f1 d4** 20 ... ♖cd8 21 ♕g4 ♕xg4 22 ♗xg4 d4 23 exd4 ♖xd4! 24 ♖c1 ♗b2 25 ♖b1 ♖d2 26 ♖e1 ♖xe1+ 27 ♔xe1 ♗c3 28 ♔f1 ♖xa2 =. **21 exd4 ♕e4 22 ♕g4 ♕c2** The threat is 23 ... ♕xd1+!. **23 g3 ♕xa2 24 ♗b5?** Going astray. 24 ♗f3! =. **24 ... ♕d5! 25 ♗xe8 ♕xh1+ 26 ♔e2 ♖xe8+ 27 ♔d3 ♗e1! 0-1** (Gligorić and Trifunović)

72) **Bondarevsky-Aronin**
USSR Championship 1952

3 ... ♗g7 4 e3 0-0 5 ♘bd2 c5 6 c3 The Lasker Variation of the Réti Opening, with colours reversed. **6 ... b6 7 ♗d3 ♗a6** The exchange of the light-squared bishops favours Black, even if he has to lose a tempo with the knight. **8 ♗xa6 ♘xa6 9 0-0 ♕c8 10 ♕e2 d5! 11 h3 ♕b7 12 ♘e5 ♖ac8 13 a4 ♖fd8 14 ♖fb1! ♘b8 15 a5 b5?** This leads to the opening of the position in White's favour. 15 ... ♘fd7 =.

16 dxc5! ♖xc5 17 ♘b3 ♖cc8

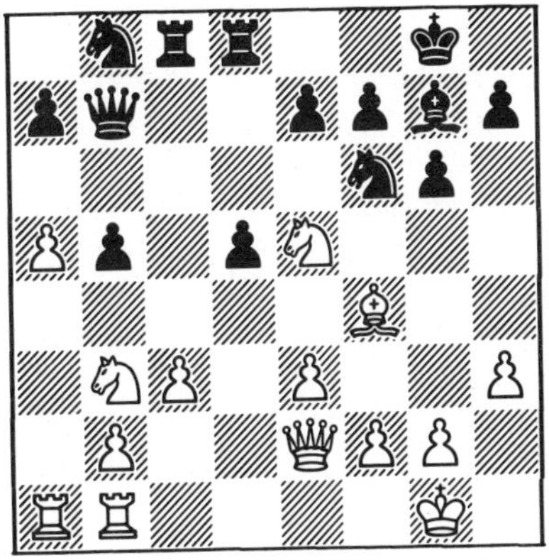

18 a6! ♘xa6 19 ♘d4 ♘c5 19 ... ♘c7 20 ♘dc6 ±. **20 ♕xb5 ♕xb5 21 ♘xb5 a6 22 ♘a7! ♖a8 23 ♘ac6** White has recaptured the pawn with interest; he has the upper hand. **23 ... ♖e8 24 ♖a5 ♘b7 25 ♖a3 ♘e4 26 ♖ba1 ♗xe5 27 ♗xe5 f6 28 ♗h2 ♘bc5 29 ♘b4 ♖ed8 30 ♘xa6 ♘d3 31 f3 ♘d6 32 ♘b4 ♖xa3 33 bxa3 ♘c5? 34 ♘c6! ♖d7 35 ♘xe7+ ♔f7 36 ♘xd5 ♘c4 37 e4**, etc. Black resigned only on the 65th move! **1-0**

73) **Ilivitzky-Geller**
USSR Championship 1952

3 ... ♗g7 4 e3 0-0 5 ♘bd2 c5 6 c3 cxd4 7 cxd4 ♘c6 8 ♗e2 d5 9 0-0 ♕b6 10 ♕b3 ♕xb3 11 ♘xb3 ♗f5 White has not played too sharply so far, and on top of that he now gives away his two bishops voluntarily. **12 ♖fc1?!** 12 h3! =. **12 ... ♘h5! 13 ♗c7 ♖fc8 14 ♗a5 ♘xa5!** Black thinks that keeping the two bishops is a greater asset than White's temporary pressure on the queenside. **15 ♘xa5 ♖xc1+ 16 ♖xc1 ♖c8 17 ♖xc8+ ♗xc8 18 ♘e1 ♘f6 19 ♔f1 ♔f8 20 ♗b5 e6 21 ♔e2 ♔e7 22 f4?! ♘e8 23 ♗d3 ♘d6 24 ♘f3 f6 25 h4?!** White has weakened his position 'systematically' on moves 22 and 25. **25 ... ♗d7 26 ♘b3?** The blunder, at last!

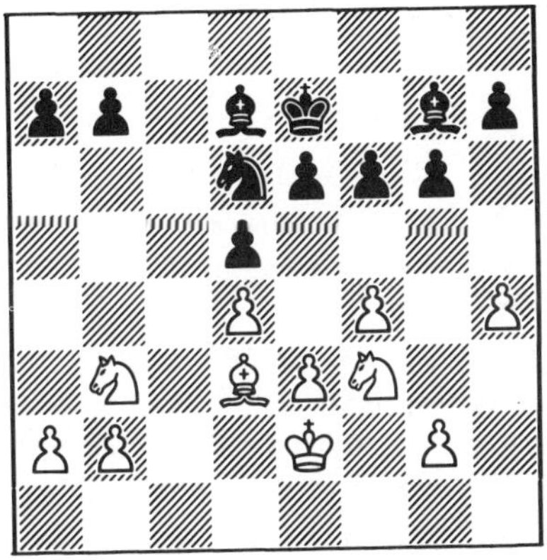

26 ... ♘c4! 27 ♘c5 The exchange is forced. Otherwise after 27 ♗xc4 dxc4 the two bishops and the queenside pawn majority leave White with a hopeless game. **27 ... ♘xb2 28 ♘xb7 ♘xd3 29 ♔xd3 ♗b5+ 30 ♔c3 ♗e2 31 ♘e1 e5! 32 ♘c5 ♔d6 33 a4 ♗f8 34 ♘ed3 ♗xd3 35 ♔xd3 h5 36 fxe5+ fxe5 37 e4?!** Accelerating the end, though because of his fixed pawns on the dark squares, White definitely has an inferior game. ... e4+

was threatened, followed by the king's march to g4 or a5. **37 ... ♗e7 38 g3 exd4 39 ♘b3** 39 ♔xd4?? ♗f6+!. **39 ... ♔e5 40 exd5 ♔xd5 41 ♘xd4 ♗c5 42 ♘e2 ♔e5 43 ♘f4 ♔f5 44 ♔e2 ♗d6 0-1** 45 ♔f3 ♗xf4! 46 gxf4 a5 ∓∓.

74) **Vidmar-Flohr**
Bled 1931

3 ... ♗g7 4 ♘bd2 0-0 5 e3 d6 6 h3 ♘bd7 7 ♗c4 e6 A typical manoeuvre: Black prepares ... ♕e7 and ... e5. **8 c3 ♕e7 9 e4 e5 10 dxe5 dxe5 11 ♗e3 b6 12 ♕e2 a6 13 g4?!** Too sharp. 13 0-0 =. **13 ... ♘c5 14 ♗g5 ♗b7 15 ♕e3 ♕e8!** Owing to the pressure on e4, White has to surrender the asset of the two bishops to his opponent. **16 ♗xf6 ♗xf6 17 0-0-0** Rather risky, but there is no better. **17 ... ♕e7 18 h4 b5 19 ♗d5 c6 20 ♗b3 a5 21 ♘g5!** Threatening to attack, White provokes a weakening of Black's camp. **21 ... a4 22 ♗c2 h6 23 ♘f3 ♗g7 24 h5?** Forcing the weakening of f5, but this is too small a concession. Better is 24 g5! h5 25 ♘f1! ♗c8 26 ♘g3 ♗e6 27 ♘f5!?. **24 ... g5 25 ♘f1 ♗c8! 26 ♘3h2** 26 ♘g3 ♗xg4 27 ♘f5 ∓. **26 ... ♗e6 27 ♘g3** 27 ♔b1 ♖fb8 ∓. **27 ... ♗xa2! 28 ♘f5 ♕a7 29 ♖d6 ♗e6 30 ♖xc6**

(diagram)

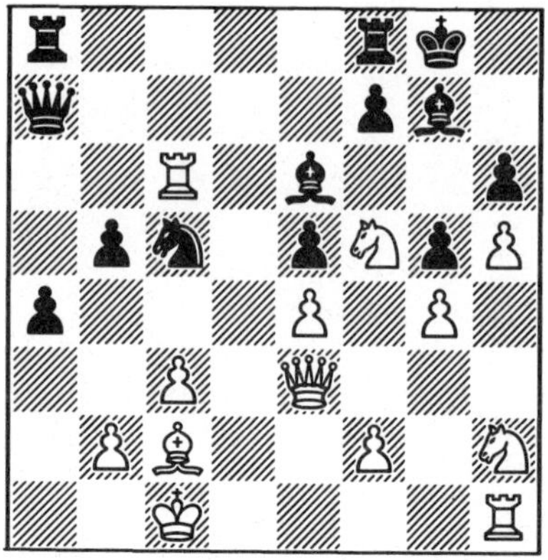

30 ... a3! The point of the counterattack! **31 ♕xc5** 31 bxa3 ♕xa3+ 32 ♔d2 ♘b3+!. **31 ... a2 32 ♔d2 ♖fd8+ 33 ♔e2 ♗c4+ 34 ♔f3 ♕xc5 35 ♖xc5 a1=♕ 36 ♖xa1 ♖xa1 37 b3 ♗e6 38 ♘e7+** 38 ♖xb5 ♖c1 39 ♘e3 ♖d2. **38 ... ♔h8 39 ♘d5 ♖c1 40 ♗d3 ♗f8 41 ♖xb5 ♖xc3!** Pretty! **42 ♔e2 ♖c5! 43 ♖xc5 ♗xc5 44 b4** 44 ♗c4 ♖a8. **44 ... ♗d6! 45 ♘e3** 45 ♗c4 ♗xb4!. **45 ... ♗xb4 46 ♘f3 f6 47 ♗c4 ♗d7** After the exchange of the light-squared bishops, f5 would remain annoyingly weak. **48 ♘h2 ♗c5 49 ♘hf1 ♖b8 50 ♔f3 ♖b2 51 ♗d5 ♗a4 52 ♗e6 ♗b4 53 ♘c4 ♗d1+ 54 ♔g2 ♖b1 55 ♘ce3 ♗c5 56 ♗c4 ♗a4 57 ♔f3 ♗d7 58 ♗f7 ♔g7 59 ♗g6 ♖b2 60 ♗f5 ♗b5 61 ♘g3 ♔f8 62 ♗e6 ♗xe3** With the immobile pawn structure, it is advisable to get rid of the opposing knight. **63 ♔xe3 ♔e7 64 ♗c8**

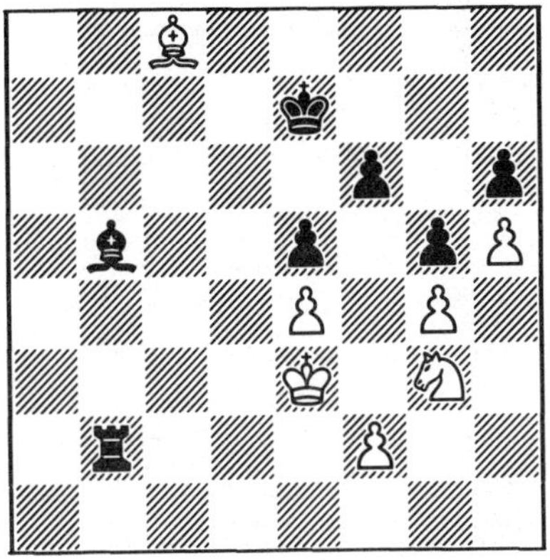

The pawns all being on one flank, it requires a precise endgame technique to make good the advantage of the exchange. **64 ... ♗c4 65 ♗f5 ♔d6 66 ♗g6 ♖b3+ 67 ♔d2 ♗e6 68 ♗f5 ♖xg3!** An elegant simplification! **69 fxg3 ♗xf5 70 exf5 ♔c5 71 ♔e3 ♔d5 72 ♔d3 ♔c6 73 ♔e4 ♔d6 74 ♔e3 ♔d7 75 ♔d3 ♔c6 76 ♔e4 ♔c5 77 ♔e3 ♔d5 78 ♔d3 e4+ 79 ♔e3 ♔e5 80 ♔e2 ♔d4 81 ♔d2 e3+ 82 ♔e1 ♔d5 83 ♔f1 ♔e5 84 ♔e1 ♔d4 85 ♔d1 ♔d3 0-1**

A remarkably instructive game! It seems that our forefathers knew how to play the game.

75) **Capablanca-Réti**
London 1922

3 ... ♗g7 4 ♘bd2 0-0 5 e3 d6 6 h3 ♘bd7 7 c3 c5 8 ♗c4 b6 9 0-0 ♗b7 10 ♕e2 ♕c7 11 ♗h2 ♖ae8? 12 e4! cxd4 13 cxd4 e5 14 ♖ac1 ♕b8 15 d5 ♖c8 16 ♗b5! White has gained hold of c6 with his last two moves. **16 ... ♖xc1 17 ♖xc1 ♖c8 18 ♗c6 ♗h6 19 b4! ♗xd2** The exchange does not seem so urgently required. **20 ♘xd2 ♗xc6 21 dxc6 b5 22 ♘b3 ♘f8 23 ♕d3 ♘e6 24 ♔f1!** As the game gets closer to the ending, the king should make for the centre. In addition, the bishop can be activated via g1. **24 ... ♕b6 25 ♘a5 ♕d4 26 ♕xd4 ♘xd4 27 f3 ♖c7?** 27 ... ♘h5 28 g4! ±.

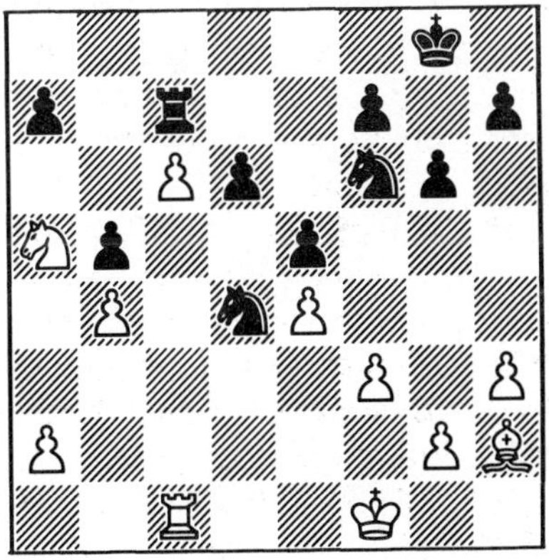

28 ♗g1 ♔f8 29 ♗xd4 exd4 30 ♖d1 ♔e7 31 ♖xd4 ♔e6 32 ♔e2 ♘g8 33 ♘b7! The clockwork precision of Capablanca! **33 ... ♘f6 34 ♖xd6+ ♔e7 35 ♔e3 ♘e8 36 e5! ♘g7 37 f4 h5 38 g4! hxg4 39 hxg4 1-0**

76) **Keres-Polugayevsky**
USSR Championship 1959

3 ... ♗g7 4 ♘bd2 0-0 5 e4 d6 6 c3 ♘c6 7 ♗b5 ♘d7?! 8 0-0 e5 9 ♗g5 ♕e8 10 ♖c1! Maintains the tension in the centre, since the rook helps defend d4 indirectly. **10 ... a6 11 ♗a4 ♘b6** 11 ... h6!?. **12 ♗b3 ♗g4 13 h3!** White frees himself from the pin by a temporary pawn sacrifice. **13 ... ♗xf3 14 ♘xf3 exd4 15 cxd4 ♕xe4!? 16 d5 ♘a5** 16 ... ♘e5 17 ♖xc7 ♘xf3+ 18 ♕xf3 ♕xf3 19 gxf3 ±. **17 ♖xc7 ♖ac8**

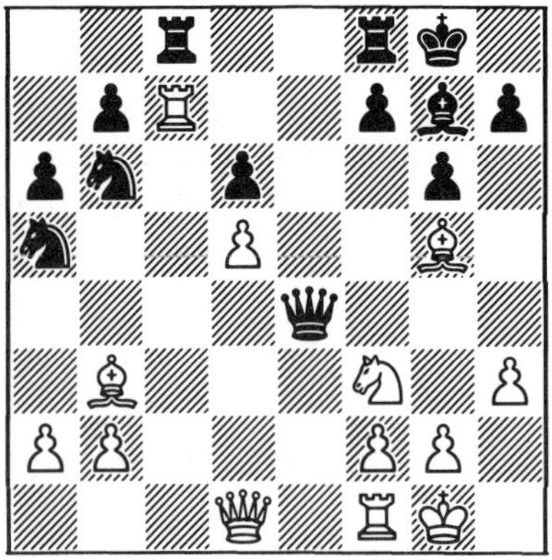

18 ♖e7! An attack from the rear! Black has to undertake an unfavourable simplification. 18 ... ♕f5? 19 g4. **18 ... ♕b4 19 ♗d2 ♕b5 20 ♗xa5 ♕xa5 21 ♖xb7 ♗xb2 22 ♘g5! ♘a8!** A delicate defensive move to neutralise the 7th rank pressure. **23 ♕e2?!** 23 ♕g4! ♖c7 24 ♖xc7 ♘xc7 (24 ... ♕xc7 25 ♕e2 ±) 25 ♕h4 h5 26 ♘e4 ±. **23 ... ♗e5 24 h4!? ♖c7 25 ♖xc7 ♘xc7 26 h5 ♕b4 27 g3 ♘b5 28 ♔g2 ♗f6 29 ♘e4 ♗g7 30 hxg6 hxg6 31 ♕g4** 31 ♕f3!?. **31 ... a5! 32 ♕h4 f5?** Too weakening. 32 ... ♖e8! 33 ♘f6+? (33 f3 ♔f8) 33 ... ♗xf6 34 ♕xf6 ♕e4+ 35 f3 ♕e5 = **33 ♘g5 ♕xh4 34 gxh4 ♘d4 35 ♗a4 ♖b8 36 ♖c1 ♗e5** 36 ... ♖b2? 37 ♖c8+. **37 ♖c7?!** First White should have played 37 ♗d7! since after the text he cannot make the ♗d7-e6 manoeuvre. **37 ... ♘b5! 38 ♖e7 ♗f6 39 ♖d7 ♗e5? 40 ♘f7?! ♘c3 41 ♘h6+ ♔h8 42 ♘f7+ ♔g8 43 ♘xe5 dxe5 44 ♗b3!** 44 ♗c6 ♘xa2 45 d6 ♘b4 46 ♗b7 a4 47 ♖c7 ♔f8! 48 d7 ♖d8. **44 ... a4 45 ♗c4 ♘e4 46 d6+ ♔h8 47 f3!** White lets Black's attack unroll: 47 ... ♖b2+ 48 ♔g1 ♖b1+ 49 ♗f1 ♘d2 50 ♖d8+ ♔g7 51 d7 ♖xf1+ 52 ♔g2 ♖xf3 53 ♖g8+!. **47 ... ♘d2 48 ♗d5 ♖b2 49 ♖b7! ♖c2 50 ♖c7 ♖b2 51 d7 ♘e4+ 52 ♔f1 ♖b1+ 53 ♔e2 ♖b2+ 54 ♔e3 1-0**

13 Countering the King's Indian and the Grünfeld: 'Wait and See' Variation, improved

1	d4	♘f6
2	♘f3	g6
3	♗f4	♗g7
4	e3	

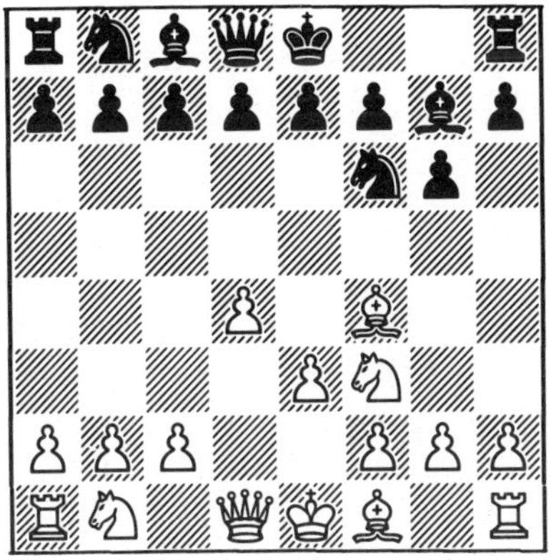

Unlike the case with 4 ♘bd2, Chapter 12, White has the alternative to develop his knight either to d2 or, after c2-c4, to c3. This is undoubtedly a more flexible line than those discussed in the previous chapters, and if the 'Wait and See' Variation occurs at all in contemporary master play, it is almost always in its improved, modernised form seen below. Still, despite White's apparent pressure Black will have the opportunity to play ... e7-e5, and quite often he even has other freeing moves at his disposal, too.

4 ... 0-0

(a) 4 ... d6 (4 ... ♘h5? 5 ♗e5 f6 6 g4 ±) 5 ♗e2?! (In most cases the exchange of the queen's bishop ought to be prevented. 5 h3! 0-0 6 a4 c5 7 ♗e2 ♕b6 8 ♖a3!? ♗f5 9 ♖b3 ♕a5+ 10 ♘c3 ♘d5 11 0-0 ♘xf4 12 exf4 ♘c6 13 ♖b5 ♕d8 14 dxc5 dxc5 15 ♖xc5 ♕xd1 16 ♖xd1 ∞ Ye Rongguang–Grószpéter, Lucerne 1989) 5 ... ♘h5! 6 ♗g5 h6 7 ♗h4 g5 8 ♘fd2 gxh4 9 ♗xh5 e5 10 dxe5 ♘c6 11 ♘c3 ♘xe5 = Klaman-Gufeld, USSR 1971.

(b) 4 ... c5 5 c3 b6 6 ♗e2 ♗b7 7 0-0 0-0 8 a4 d6 9 a5 ♗a6 10 ♗xa6 ♘xa6 11 ♕e2 ♕c8 12 e4 ♕b7 13 ♖e1 ♖fc8 = Dreyev-Fishbein, Moscow 1989 or 6 ♘bd2 0-0 7 h3

♗b7 8 ♗h2 d5? (8 ... d6 9 ♗c4!?) 9 ♗e2 ♘bd7 10 a4 a6 11 0-0 ♖c8 12 ♕b3! ± Ribli-Lautier, Clermont-Ferrand 1989.

5 ♗e2

5 h3 c5 6 c3 ♕b6 7 ♕b3 ♘c6! (7 ... d6 8 ♘bd2 ♗e6 9 ♗c4 ♗xc4 10 ♘xc4 ♕xb3 11 axb3 ♘bd7 12 ♔e2 b5 13 ♘a5 ⩲ Anastasian-Khenkin, Minsk 1990) 8 ♘bd2 ♕xb3 9 axb3 d6 10 dxc5 dxc5 11 e4 b6 12 ♗a6 ♗xa6 13 ♖xa6 ♘a5 14 ♘e5 ♘h5 = Portisch-Uhlmann, Leipzig 1960; 5 ... b6?! 6 ♗e2 ♗b7 7 0-0 d6 8 ♗h2 ♘bd7 9 c4 e6?! (9 ... c5!) 10 ♘c3 ♘e4 11 ♘xe4 ♗xe4 12 ♘d2! ♗b7 13 ♗f3! ⩲ Speelman-Haik, Illustrative Game No 77.

5 ... d6

Black can delay this move with 5 ... c5, and now:

(a) 6 0-0 b6 7 a4 d6 8 ♘a3 ♘c6 9 h3 ♗b7 10 c3 ♖c8 11 ♖e1 ♕d7 12 ♗f1 ♕f5 13 ♗h2 ♖fd8 14 ♘c4 ⩲ Taimanov-Doroshkevich, USSR 1967.

(b) 6 ♘bd2 ♘c6 7 c3 cxd4 (7 ... d6 see c.) 8 exd4 d6 9 h3 e5!? 10 dxe5 dxe5 11 ♘xe5 ♘d5 12 ♘xc6 bxc6 13 ♗g3 ♖e8 14 0-0 ♗xc3! = Cvitan-Sideif Zade 1983.

(c) 6 c3 b6 7 h3 (7 0-0 ♗b7 8 a4 see 4 ... d6) 7 ... ♗b7 8 ♘bd2 d6 9 0-0 ♘c6 (9 ... ♘bd7 10 a4!) 10 ♗h2 cxd4 (10 ... ♖e8?! 11 a4 ♕d7?! 12 ♘c4 ♖ac8 13 ♕b3 ⩲ Sapis-Kupreichik, Leningrad 1989; 10 ... ♕d7 11 a4 ♖fc8 ∞) 11 exd4 ♗h6 12 a4 ♘d5 13 ♖e1 ♗f4 14 ♘e4 ♗xh2+ 15 ♔xh2 e6 16 ♕d2 ⩲ Kamsky-Ftačnik, Manila 1990.

6 h3

13.1

6 ... c5

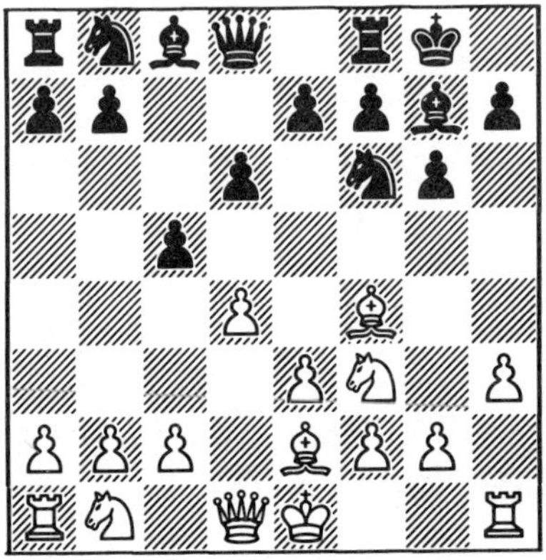

An acceptable move, but after e7-e5 Black has better chances to equalise. Another offbeat attempt: 6 ... ♘fd7 7 ♘c3 (7 c4!) 7 ... e5 8 dxe5 dxe5 9 ♗g5 f6 10 ♗c4+ ♔h8 11 ♗h4 ♕e7 12 0-0 ♘b6 13 ♗b3 ♘c6 = Portisch-Uhlmann, Madrid 1960.

7 c3

(a) 7 ♘bd2 cxd4! (7 ... ♘c6 8 ♗h2 a6 – 8 ... b6!? – 9 a4 cxd4 10 exd4 ♖b8 11 0-0 ♘d7 12 c3 ♘f6 13 ♖e1 b5 14 axb5 axb5 15 ♘f1 ⩲ Ye Rongguang-El Taher, Manila 1990) 8 exd4 ♘c6 9 0-0 ♗f5 (9 ... ♗e6 10 c3 a6 11 a4 ♖c8 12 ♖e1

♘a5 13 ♗d3 ♕d7 14 ♕e2 ♗f5 15 ♗g5 ♖fe8 16 ♘h2 Kovacevic-Gufeld, Vinkovci 1982; 16 ... ♗xd3! 17 ♕xd3 ♕f5 =) 10 c3 ♖c8 11 ♗h2 a6 12 a4 ♖e8 13 ♘c4 d5 14 ♘ce5 ♕b6 ∞ Polugayevsky-Gufeld, Illustrative Game No 78.

(b) 7 0-0 b6 8 c4!? ♗b7 9 ♘c3 ♘e4! 10 ♘xe4 ♗xe4 11 ♕d2 (11 ♘d2) 11 ... cxd4 12 exd4 ♘c6 13 d5 ♗xf3 14 ♗xf3 ♘d4 15 ♗e4 ♖c8 16 b3 e5 17 dxe6 ♘xe6 18 ♖ae1 ± Hort-Ftačnik, Prague 1990.

7 ... b6

7 ... ♗e6!? 8 dxc5!? dxc5 9 ♕xd8 ♖xd8 10 ♘bd2 h6 11 ♗c4 ♗xc4 12 ♘xc4 ½-½ Seirawan-Nunn, Zürich 1984.

8 0-0

8 a4 ♗a6 9 ♗xa6?! ♘xa6 10 0-0 ♘c7 11 ♘bd2 ♘e6 12 ♗h2 ♕d7 13 ♕b3 ♕b7 14 ♖fe1 cxd4! = Hulak-Krnić, Yugoslavia 1981.

8 ... ♗a6
9 ♘bd2 ♗xe2
10 ♕xe2 ♕c8
11 e4 ♕a6
12 ♕e3! ±

Sturua-Pavlov, Trnava 1980.

13.2

6 ... ♘bd7

Black's goal is to make the ... e5 move, preceded by ... e6 and ... ♕e7, or by ... ♕e8. This plan is probably his best chance.

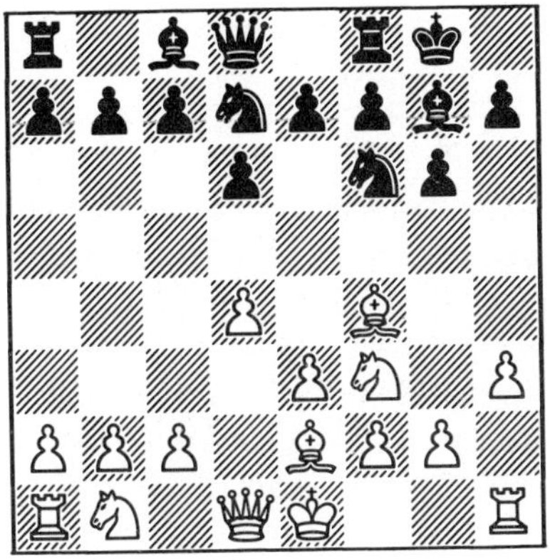

7 0-0

7 c4 ♘e4 8 ♕c2 e5 9 ♕xe4 ♘f6 10 ♕c2 exf4 11 exf4 ♗f5 12 ♗d3 ♖e8+ 13 ♔f1 ♗xd3+ 14 ♕xd3 c5 15 ♘c3 cxd4 16 ♘xd4 d5! 17 c5! ♘e4 18 ♘b3 ∞ (±) Nikolić-Douven, Wijk aan Zee 1989.

7 ... ♕e8

(a) 7 ... e6 8 ♗h2 ♕e7 9 c4 ♘e4! 10 ♘bd2?! (10 ♗d3 ♘g5! ∞) 10 ... ♘xd2 11 ♕xd2 b6 12 ♘e1 ♗b7 13 ♗f3 ♗xf3 14 ♘xf3 = Speelman-Ree, Wijk aan Zee 1983.

(b) 7 ... c5?! (This is a bit passive after ... ♘bd7; among other things, Black has lost the opportunity to play ... ♗c8-a6) 8 c3 b6 9 a4 ♗b7 10 ♗h2 ♘e4?! (10 ... a6!) 11 a5! ♖b8 12 ♘a3 cxd4 13 exd4 bxa5 14 ♘c4 ♗a8 ± Seirawan-Biyiasas, Lone Pine 1981.

(c) 7 ... h6 8 a4 a5 9 ♘bd2 ♗b7

10 c3 ♖e8 11 ♗h2 e5 12 ♕b3 ♘e4 13 ♘xe4 ♗xe4 14 ♖fd1 ♕e7 15 ♖ac1 ± Piket-Hamdouchi, Lucerne 1989.

8 c4!

The only way to take the initiative. It would be unwise to cling to the Anti-Indian here, e.g. 8 c3 e5 9 ♗h2 ♕e7 10 a4 a5 11 ♖e1 b6 12 ♘a3 ♗b7 13 ♘b5 Hort-Pribyl, Havirov 1971; 13 ... ♘e8! =.

8	**...**	**e5**
9	**♗h2**	**♘e4!**

9 ... ♕e7 10 ♘c3 e4? (10 ... ♘e8 11 b4 f5 12 c5 e4 13 ♘d2 ♘df6 14 cxd6 cxd6 15 ♕b3+ ♔h8 16 ♖ac1 g5 ± Andrianov-Poldauf, Budapest 1989) 11 ♘d2 ♖e8 12 ♘b5 ♕d8 13 c5! (The basic idea of the variation!) 13 ... a6 14 cxd6! ± Spassky-Bukic, Illustrative Game No 79.

10 ♘bd2

10 ♘c3!? ♘xc3 11 bxc3 b6 12 a4 a5 13 ♘d2 f5 14 ♘b3 ♗b7 15 c5!? bxc5 16 dxc5 ♕e6 ∞ Anastasian-Gligorić, Erevan 1989.

10	**...**	**♘xd2**
11	**♕xd2**	**e4**
12	**♘e1**	**♕e7**

12 ... ♘f6?! 13 ♖ac1 h5 Yusupov-Fuller, Esbjerg 1980; 14 c5! ±.

13	**b4**	**f5**
14	**♘c2**	**g5**
15	**c5**	**♘f6**
16	**♘a3**	**f4!**
17	**exf4**	**g4**
18	**hxg4**	**♘xg4**

A sharp position with mutual chances – Yusupov-Tukmakov, USSR Championship 1978.

ILLUSTRATIVE GAMES

1 d4 ♘f6 2 ♘f3 g6 3 ♗f4 ♗g7 4 e3

77) **Speelman-Haik**
Lucerne 1982

4 ... 0-0 5 h3 b6 6 ♗e2 ♗b7 7 0-0 d6 8 ♗h2 ♘bd7 9 c4! e6 9 ... c5!. **10 ♘c3 ♘e4?!** The following exchanges will weaken Black's queenside. **11 ♘xe4 ♗xe4 12 ♘d2! ♗b7 13 ♗f3! ♗xf3 14 ♘xf3** 14 ♕xf3?! e5!. **14 ... ♕e7** After 14 ... ♘f6 15 ♕a4 ♕d7 16 ♕xd7 ♘xd7, the b4-c5 breakthrough looms large in the endgame, with the assistance of the key bishop on h2. This remains a permanent threat throughout the game. **15 ♕a4! a5?! 16 ♖ac1 e5 17 ♕c6 ♖a7 18 ♖fd1 a4 19 b4 axb3 20 axb3 exd4** 20 ... ♖fa8 21 b4 again with the basic threat of c4-c5. **21 ♘xd4!? ♘b8!** 21 ... ♘c5 22 ♘b5 ♖a2 23 ♘xc7 ±. **22 ♕f3 ♖a3?** 22 ... ♗xd4? 23 exd4 ±; 22 ... ♖a2 ±.

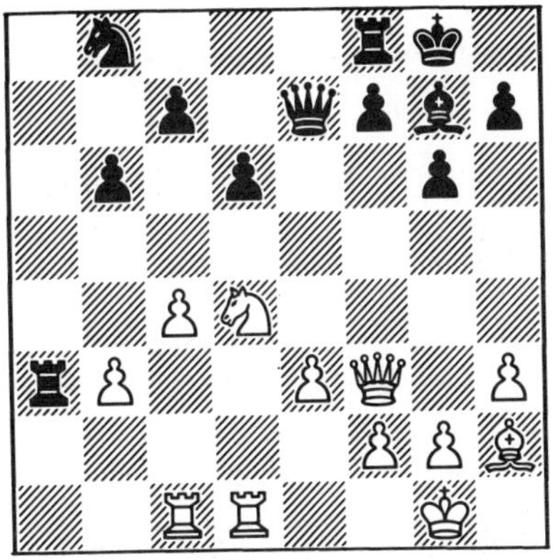

23 ♘b5! 23 b4 ♗xd4!. **23 ... ♖xb3 24 ♕b7 ♗b2?** 24 ... ♗e5! 25 ♕xc7! ♕xc7 26 ♘xc7 ±. **25 ♗xd6 ♕e8 26 ♗xf8 ♗xc1 27 ♗h6 ♖b1 28 ♘xc7 1-0**

(Notes based on Speelman's)

78) **Polugayevsky-Gufeld**
USSR 1979

4 ... d6 5 h3 0-0 6 ♗e2 c5 7 ♘bd2 cxd4! 8 exd4 ♘c6 9 0-0 ♗f5 10 c3 ♖c8 Black has a comfortable game. **11 ♗h2 a6 12 a4 ♖e8** 12 ... ♘a5!?. **13 ♘c4 d5 14 ♘ce5 ♕b6 15 ♖a2 ♘e4 16 ♘xc6?!** 16 g4!?. **16 ... bxc6** 16 ... ♖xc6? 17 a5 ±. **17 a5 ♕b7 18 g4 ♗d7 19 ♘e5**

(diagram)

19 ... ♗xe5! Unprejudiced!

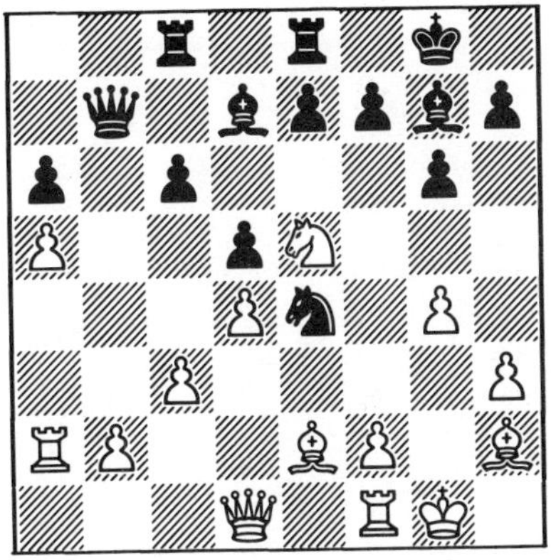

20 ♗xe5?! 20 dxe5!?. **20 ... f6 21 ♗h2 c5** Black's game is already a bit better. **22 f3 ♘g5 23 h4 ♘f7 24 ♖e1 ♗b5 25 b3** 25 ♕b3 c4! 26 ♕c2 e5 27 dxe5 ♘xe5 ∓. **25 ... cxd4 26 cxd4 ♖c3 27 ♔g2 e5! 28 ♗xb5 ♕xb5 29 ♖ae2 ♖d3 30 ♖d2 ♖xd2 31 ♕xd2 ♕xb3 32 ♖e3 ♕b5 33 g5 ♘d6! 34 ♖e1 ♘c4 35 ♕f2 exd4 36 ♖xe8+ ♕xe8 37 gxf6 ♘e3+ 38 ♔g1 ♕b5! 39 ♗e5 ♕b1+ 40 ♔h2 ♕f5 41 ♗g3 ♕c2 42 ♕xc2 ♘xc2 43 ♗e5 ♔f7 44 ♔g2 d3! 45 ♔f2 d2 46 ♔e2 ♘e3 0-1** (Gufeld)

79) **Spassky-Bukić**
Bugojno 1978

4 ... 0-0 5 ♗e2 d6 6 0-0 ♘bd7 7 h3 ♕e8 8 c4 e5 9 ♗h2 ♕e7? Allowing White to activate his knights. 9 ... ♘e4!. **10 ♘c3 e4? 11 ♘d2 ♖e8 12 ♘b5! ♕d8** 12 ... ♘f8 13 c5!. **13 c5! a6**

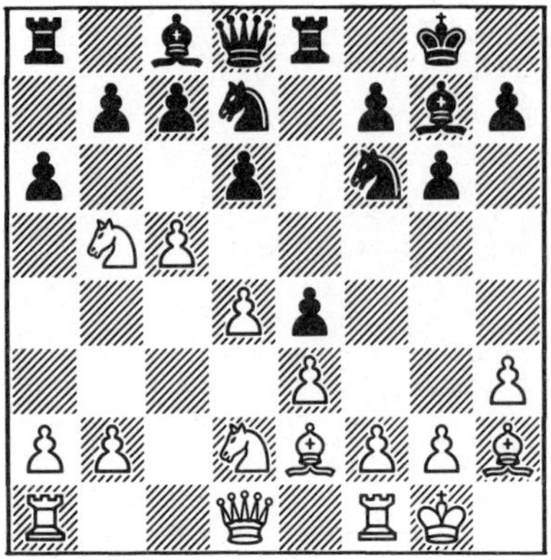

14 cxd6! The triumphant culmination of the system: White's dark-squared bishop is in full cry. **14 ... axb5 15 dxc7 ♕c7 16 ♗xb5** White's compensation is three pawns plus a considerable positional advantage for the piece. The well protected c7 pawn paralyses the opponent's forces. **16 ... ♗f8 17 ♘c4 ♕e6 18 ♕c2** 18 ♕b3!. **18 ... ♕d5** 18 ... ♘d5. **19 a4 ♖e6 20 ♖fc1 ♘e8 21 ♕c3 ♘ef6** 21 ... ♘d6? 22 ♗xd7! +−. **22 ♘e5 ♘b6 23 ♘c4 ♘fd7 24 ♕b3 ♖f6 25 ♗xd7! ♘xd7 26 ♕b5!** After some manoeuvring, White accelerates the tempo. 26 ... ♕xb5? would lose straightaway owing to the opening of the a-file after 27 axb5. **26 ... ♕f5 27 ♗g3 ♖fa6?** 27 ... h5. **28 d5! ♕f6 29 a5 h5 30 b4 h4 31 ♗h2 ♕f5 32 ♖f1!** To open a file on the kingside. **32 ... g5 33 f3 ♖g6 34 ♖ad1 exf3 35 ♖xf3 ♕c2 36 ♖d2 ♕c3 37 d6 ♖a6 38 e4 ♕c1+ 39 ♖f1 ♕c3 40 ♕d5 ♘f6 41 ♖xf6! 1-0**

(Notes based on Bukić's)

14 Countering the King's Indian and the Grünfeld: KB Line, Black playing a Benoni- or Grünfeld-like set-up

1	d4	♘f6
2	♘f3	g6
3	g3	♗g7
4	♗g2	0-0
5	0-0	

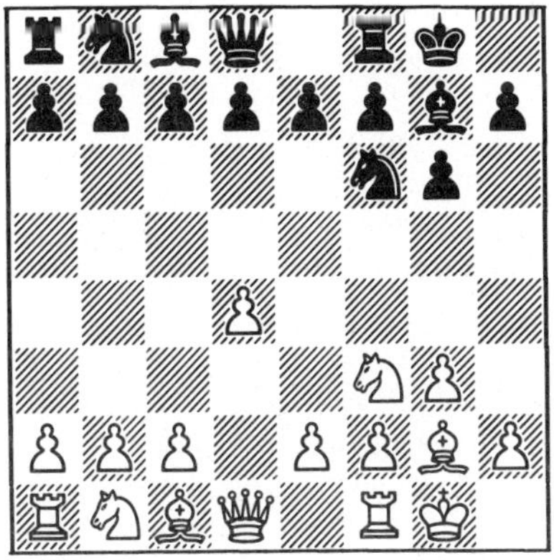

Unlike the previous, rather venturesome variations given in this book, the King's bishop line is a positionally well-established system. White does not attempt to overrun his opponent on the very first moves – on the other hand, equalising is a fairly demanding task for Black. The efficiency and richness of the line is increased by the fact that Black has always to be on the alert to meet the main variations of the King's Indian as well.

White's play suits the subject of this book inasmuch as he plays 2 ♘f3 and makes no haste to play c2-c4. The emerging positions often resemble those of the King's Indian with the c-pawn still being on the 2nd rank. There are several advantages of this: the d4 square and the long diagonal are not weakened and White can execute an extra move with a piece.

On the other hand, the lack of c2-c4 makes the control of the centre more difficult since Black can get a strong-hold by ... d7-d5 too, as will be shown in this chapter.

Just a few brief notes concerning the introductory moves:

(a) 3 ... d5 4 ♗g2 c5?! 5 dxc5! ♕a5+ 6 ♘fd2 ♗g7 7 ♘c3 ♕xc5 8

♘b3 ♕c7 9 ♘xd5 ♘xd5 10 ♕xd5! ♕xc2 11 ♘d4 ♕a4 12 ♕b5+ ♕xb5 13 ♘xb5 ♘a6 14 ♗e3! ± Korchnoi-Djindjihashvili, Tilburg 1985.

(b) 4 ... c5 and 4 ... d5 have no individual significance, except for Azmaiparashvili-Romanishin, Illustrative Game No 80.

(c) 5 b3 d6 6 ♗b2 e5 (6 ... ♘fd7 and 6 ... ♘bd7 are dealt with in Chapter 15 and Illustrative Game No 81.) 7 dxe5 ♘g4 (For 7 ... ♘h5 see Illustrative Game No 83) 8 h3! ♘xe5 9 ♘xe5 dxe5 (9 ... ♗xe5 10 ♗xe5 dxe5 11 ♕xd8 ♖xd8 12 ♘d2 ♘a6 13 0-0-0! – the point of the change in the sequence! – 13 ... c6 14 ♘c4 ♖e8 15 ♖d2 ± Barcza-Yudovich, corr. 1955; 12 ... ♘d7 13 0-0-0! ♖e8 14 ♘e4 ♔g7 15 g4 ± Polugayevsky-Tal, Illustrative Game No 82) 10 ♕xd8 ♖xd8 11 ♘d2 ♘d7 (11 ... ♘c6 12 0-0-0 ♗e6 13 g4! f6 14 ♘e4 ± Timman-Bachman, Stockholm 1972/73) 12 0-0-0 ♖e8 (12 ... ♖b8 13 a4 ♖e8 14 ♘c4 h5 15 ♖d2 ± Barcza-Kuijpers, Amsterdam 1967) 13 ♘c4 ♘b6 14 ♘a5! ♖b8 15 ♖d2 ± Smyslov-Polugayevsky, Palma de Mallorca 1970. However, Black has a comfortable game after 5 ... c5!, e.g. 6 ♗b2 (6 e3 ♕a5+) 6 ... cxd4 7 ♘xd4 d5!, and this a variation from Chapter 15 with an extra tempo for Black.

5 ... d5

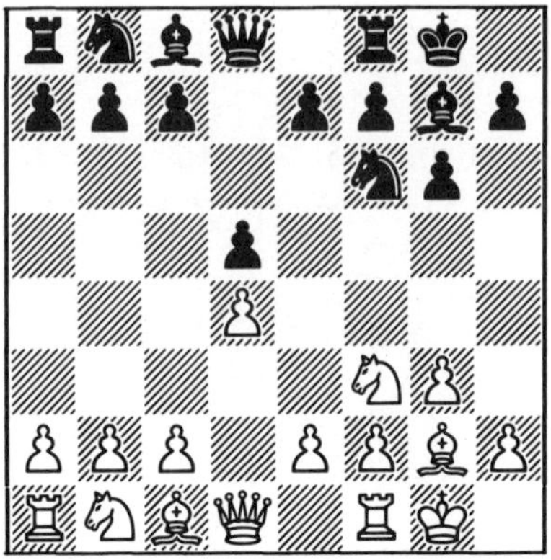

In this symmetrical position, usually called Grünfeld or Neo-Grünfeld by the textbooks, Black has not got too many opportunities to play an active game, but his set-up is solid. Sharper is 5 ... c5!?, after which White can transpose into the King's Indian by 6 c4, or into the English Opening. Others:

(a) 6 d5 b5!? 7 c4 d6 8 ♘fd2 (8 ♖e1!?; 8 cxb5!?) 8 ... ♘bd7 9 ♘c3 a6 (This is rather like the Benko Gambit!) 10 a4 b4! 11 ♘ce4 ♖b8 12 ♘xf6+ ♘xf6 13 ♖a2 e5 14 b3 ♘e8 Bönsch-Vaganian, Lvov 1984; 15 e4 f5 16 exf5 gxf5 17 ♗b2 then f2-f4 ∞.

(b) 6 c3 (Black should not be frightened of this move) 6 ... ♘a6 (6 ... b6 7 ♘e5 d5 8 a4 ♘fd7 = Filip-Tal, Curaçao 1962; 6 ... cxd4 7 cxd4 d5 = the Neo-Grünfeld; 6 ... ♕c7 7 b3 d6 8 ♗b2 ♘c6 9 c4 e5 10 d5 ♘a5 11 ♘e1 ♖b8 12

♘c2 ♗d7 13 ♘d2 ♘h5 = Filip-Petrosian, Erevan 1965; 7 ♖e1 d6 8 e4 ♘c6 9 ♘bd2 e5 10 dxe5 dxe5 11 a4?! ♗e6 12 ♕e2 ∞ Todorčević-Velimirović, Szirák 1987) 7 ♘bd2 d5! 8 dxc5 ♘xc5 9 ♘b3 ♘ce4 10 ♘g5 ♘d6 11 ♘f3 a5 12 a4 ♘c4 ∓ Kozma-Doda, Poland 1971.

(c) 6 dxc5! ♘a6 7 ♗e3! ♕c7 (7 ... ♘g4? 8 ♗d4 e5 9 ♗c3 ♘xc5 10 h3 +−; 7 ... ♘e4!? 8 ♗d4 ♗h6 – 8 ... ♘exc5!? – 9 ♘e5 ♘exc5 10 ♘g4 ♗g7 11 ♗xg7 ♔xg7 12 ♕d4+ f6 13 ♘c3 d6 14 ♕f4 ♗xg4 15 ♕xg4 ± Geller-Cuellar, Stockholm 1962) 8 ♘c3!? (8 c4 ♘xc5 9 ♘c3 b6 10 ♖c1 ♗b7 11 ♗d4 ♖ac8 12 ♘d5!? ♘xd5 13 cxd5 ♕d6 14 ♗xg7 ♔xg7 15 ♘d4 – 15 ♕d4+ – 15 ... ♕e5 16 ♖c3 ± Romanishin-Gelfand, Palma de Mallorca 1989) 8 ... ♘xc5 9 ♘b5 ♕b6 10 a4 ♘g4 11 ♗d4 (11 b4!? ♘xe3 12 bxc5 ♕xc5! – 12 ... ♘xd1? 13 cxb6 ♗xa1 14 ♖xd1 ♗f6 15 ♘c7 +− – 13 fxe3 ♕xe3+ 14 ♖f2! ♗xa1 15 ♕xa1 d6 16 ♘c7 ♖b8 17 ♘d5 ± Varnusz-Hevér, Budapest 1989) 11 ... d6 12 b4 (12 ♗xg7 ♔xg7 13 b4 ♘e6 14 h3 ♘f6 15 ♘d2 d5 16 c4 a6 17 a5 ♕d8 18 ♘c3 ♘c7 19 cxd5 ♘cxd5 20 ♘xd5 ♘xd5 21 ♕b3 ♗e6 22 ♕b2+ ± Grószpéter-Szalánczi, Hungarian Championship 1989) 12 ... ♗xd4 13 ♘fxd4 ♘a6 14 a5 ± Varnusz-Meleghegyi, Budapest 1984. Thus after 5 ... c5 the immediate capture seems good for White.

In the position shown in the diagram above, both sides ought permanently to consider the possibility of c2-c4, transposing into the Neo-Grünfeld. This in fact, happens quite often and that is why there are so few Illustrative Games in the present chapter. In the spirit of this book, we are not going to treat 6 c4 since 6 ... dxc4 7 ♘a3 c3! provides Black with good prospects of equalising. Still, some lines of the Neo-Grünfeld are going to occur in the book occasionally.

The main variations of this chapter are 6 ♗f4 and 6 ♘bd2. Others:

(a) 6 c3 b6 (6 ... c6 7 ♘bd2 ♗f5 8 ♘h4 ♗e6 9 ♘df3 ♕c8 10 ♕b3 = Pfleger-Romanishin, Lone Pine 1981, or 6 ... ♘c6 7 ♗f4 ♘h5 8 ♗e3 ♘f6 9 ♘bd2 ♘g4 10 ♗f4 e5 11 dxe5 ♘cxe5 12 h3 ♘xf3+ 13 ♘xf3 ♘f6 14 ♗e5 = Balashov-Oll, USSR Championship 1989) 7 ♘e5 (7 ♗f4!?) 7 ... ♗b7 8 ♕a4?! ♘fd7! 9 ♘xd7 ♘xd7 10 ♖d1 ♕c8 11 ♗g5 c5 12 ♘d2 e5! ∞ Barcza-Pachman, Helsinki 1952.

(b) 6 ♘c3 c6 7 b3 ♗f5 8 ♗b2 ♘e4 9 ♘h4 ♘xc3 10 ♗xc3 ♗e6 11 ♕d2 ♘d7 12 ♖ad1 ♘f6 13 f3 ♖c8 14 e4 dxe4 15 fxe4 ♗g4 16 ♖de1 e5! ∓ Kholmov-Vasyukov, USSR 1971.

(c) 6 b3 c6 (6 ... c5!?) 7 ♗b2 (7 a4 ♘e4 8 ♗b2 c5?! 9 e3 ♘c6 10 ♘bd2 ♗f5 11 ♘e5! ♘xe5 12 dxe5

♕a5 13 ♘xe4 dxe4 14 ♕d5! ± Spassky-Shianovsky, USSR 1961; 7 ... ♘bd7!, 8 ... ♘d7!) 7 ... ♗f5 8 h3?! (Better is 8 ♘bd2) 8 ... ♘e4 9 ♘fd2 ♕b6 10 ♘xe4 ♗xe4 11 ♗xe4 dxe4 12 ♘d2 ♖d8! 13 e3 f5 14 ♕e2 ♕c7 15 ♔h2 ♘d7 16 f3 exf3 ∞ Mariotti-Hartston, Praia da Rocha 1969.

(d) 6 ♗e3 c6 (6 ... ♘c6!?; 6 ... ♗f5!?) 7 ♕c1 ♖e8 (7 ... ♗f5!?) 8 ♗h6 ♗h8 (8 ... ♘bd7 9 ♗xg7 ♔xg7 10 c4 ±) 9 c4 ♗f5 10 ♘bd2 ∞/± ♘bd7 11 ♘h4!? (11 h3 e5 ∞) 11 ... ♗g4 12 f3 ♗e6 13 ♔h1! (13 e4? dxe4 14 fxe4 ♘g4 15 ♘df3 ♗xc4! ∓) 13 ... dxc4 14 e4 b5?! 15 f4! ± Goldin-Cvitan, Warsaw 1990; 14 ... ♘b6!? 15 ♗e3 ♘h5 16 e5! ♘d5! 17 ♘e4 ∞ Goldin. Clearly transposition into the 6 ♗f4 variation is possible.

14.1

6 ♗f4

A simple, natural developing move in a symmetrical position. (Fianchettoing is dealt with in 14.2.)

6 ... c6

(diagram)

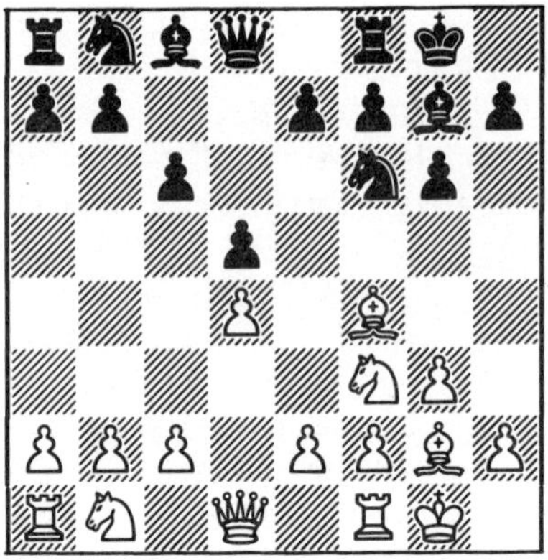

After 6 ... c5 7 c3 cxd4 8 cxd4 the game is a Neo-Grünfeld, playable for both sides. 7 dxc5!? ♕a5 (7 ... ♘a6 8 ♘c3 ♘xc5 9 ♗e5 b6 10 a4 ♗b7 ∞, maybe =, Schvidler-Rechlis, Tel Aviv 1989) 8 ♘c3 ♕xc5 9 ♘d4, threatening 10 ♘b3 and 10 ♘db5 followed by e2-e4, needs testing in tournaments. 6 ... ♘bd7 7 c3?! c6 8 ♘bd2 ♖e8 9 ♖e1 ♘h5 10 ♗e3 = Andersson-Unzicker, Hastings 1971/72.

7 ♘bd2

(a) 7 ♕c1 ♖e8 (7 ... ♗f5 8 c4 ♖e8 9 ♘bd2 ♘bd7 10 ♘b3?! ♕b6 11 h3 a5 12 ♖d1 a4 13 ♘bd2 a3 ∓ Romanishin-Smirin, Lvov 1990; 10 ♖d1 =) 8 ♘bd2 ♘bd7 9 c4 ♘f8 10 ♖d1 ♗g4 11 h3 ♗xf3 12 ♘xf3 ♘e6 13 ♗e5 dxc4 14 ♕xc4 ♘d7 15 ♗xg7 ♘b6 16 ♕b3 ♘xg7 17 ♘g5 ± Smyslov-Wittmann, Graz 1984.

(b) 7 ♘a3!? e6 8 c4 (In the actual game the sequence went 6 c4 c6 7 ♘a3 e6 8 ♗f4) 8 ... b6 9 ♕c1 ♗b7 10 ♗h6 ♘bd7 11 ♗xg7 ♔xg7 12 b3 ♖c8 13 ♕b2 ♕e7 14 ♖ac1 ♔g8 15 b4! ± Smyslov-Averbakh, USSR Championship

1955.

7 ... ♕b6

7 ... ♘h5?! 8 ♗e5! f6 9 ♗xb8 ♖xb8 10 c4! ± Romanishin-Kasparov, Illustrated Game No 83.

8 ♕c1 c5

8 ... ♗e6 9 ♖e1 ♖e8 10 c4 ± Varnusz-Haág, Budapest 1986; 8 ... ♗g4 9 c4 ♘bd7 10 c5 ♕d8 11 ♖e1 ♘h5 12 ♗e3 ♖e8 13 b4 e5 14 ♘b3 ♗xf3 15 ♗xf3 ♘hf6 16 ♖b1 h5 ∞ Romanishin-Khalifman, Simferopol 1988.

9	**dxc5**	**♕xc5**
10	**♘b3**	**♕b4**
11	**c3**	**♕a4!**
12	**♗h6**	**♗g4**
13	**♗xg7**	**♔xg7**

The most White has got is a tiny plus. A Smyslov-Korchnoi, Montpellier 1985, game went 14 ♕e3! ♗xf3 15 ♗xf3 ♘c6 16 ♖fd1 ♖ad8 17 ♘d4 ♖fe8 18 b3 ♕a6 19 ♖d2 ♘xd4 20 cxd4 ♖c8 21 g4 with White having a slight initiative.

14.2

6 ♘bd2

White prepares c2-c4 or e2-e4 after (or even before) fianchettoing his queen's bishop, to dampen Black's counterplay starting with ... c7-c5. The line often transposes into the Neo-Grünfeld (6 c4 c6 7 ♘bd2), but White, postponing c2-c4, does not ease Black's task in choosing a defence and he also avoids the 6 ... dxc4 7 ♘a3 c3 variation.

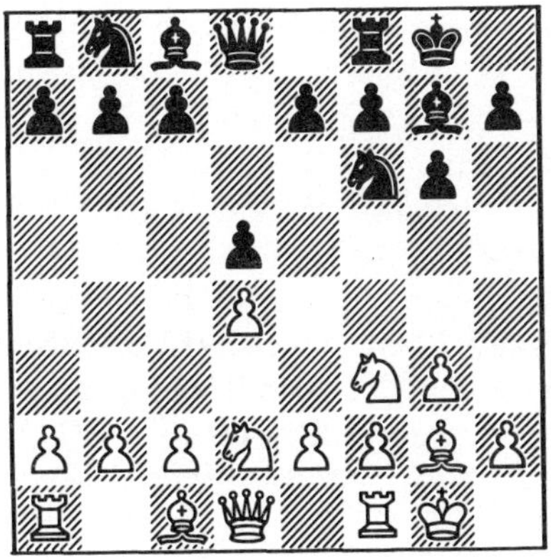

6 ... c6

(a) 6 ... c5? 7 dxc5 ♘bd7 8 ♘b3 ♕c7 9 c3?! (9 ♕d4!?) 9 ... ♘xc5 10 ♗f4 ♕c6 11 ♘fd4 ♕b6 12 ♘xc5 ♕xc5 13 ♗e5! ± Kasparian-Belavenets, USSR 1937.

(b) 6 ... ♘c6!? 7 b3?! e5! 8 dxe5 ♘g4 9 ♗b2 ♘gxe5 10 ♕c1 ♗f5 11 ♘xe5 ♘xe5 12 c4 c6 = Csom-London, New York 1987.

(c) 6 ... ♘a6!? 7 ♘b3! c6 (7 ... ♗f5 8 ♘a5 c6 9 ♘xb7 ♕b6 10 ♘c5 ♘xc5 11 dxc5 ♕xc5 ∞; 7 ... b6!? 8 ♘e5 ♗b7 9 ♗e3?! ♘e4! = Ye Rongguang-Stohl, Manila 1990; 9 c4 e6 10 ♗f4 ♕e7 ∞) 8 ♗f4 (8 ♘e5 ♘d7 9 ♘d3 e5 = Granda Zúñiga-Ftačnik, New York 1987) ♖e8 (8 ... ♘e4 9 ♘fd2 ♘d6 10 e4 ± Polugayevsky-Ftačnik, Haninge

1990; 8 ... ♗f5!?) 9 ♖c1 ♗f5 10 ♘e5! ♘d7 11 ♖e1 ♘xe5 12 dxe5 f6 13 exf6 ♗xf6 (13 ... exf6 14 ♘d4 ±) 14 e4! dxe4 15 c3 ♕xd1 16 ♖cxd1 ± Andersson-Ftačnik, Haninge 1990.

14.21

7 b3

7 c4 ♗f5 8 b3 is the Neo-Grünfeld, the main line being here 8 ... ♘e4 9 ♗b2, and then 9 ... ♕a5, 9 ... ♘xd2 or 9 ... ♘d7.

7 ... ♗f5

7 ... a5 8 a4 ♗f5 9 ♘h4 ♗e6 10 ♗b2 ♘a6 11 ♖e1 ±. 7 ... c5?! 8 c4 cxd4 9 ♗b2 d3 10 exd3 ♘c6 11 d4 ♗f5 12 ♘e5 dxc4 13 ♘dxc4 ♖c8 14 ♘xc6 bxc6 15 ♘e5 ± Polugayevsky-A.Sokolov, Haninge 1989.

8 ♗b2 a5

8 ... ♘e4 9 c4 is again the Neo-Grünfeld, but also possible is 9 ♘e5 ♘xd2 10 ♕xd2 ♘d7 or 9 ♘h4!? ♘xd2 10 ♕xd2 ♗e6 11 ♖c1 ±.

9 a3

For 9 a4! ♘a6 10 ♘h4 see 7 ... a5.

9 ... ♘e4

Interesting is 9 ... a4!?.

10 ♘h4

10 c4 ♘d7 11 ♘xe4?! (11 ♖c1!) 11 ... ♗xe4 12 ♘d2 ♗xg2 13 ♔xg2 dxc4! 14 ♘xc4 ♘b6 15 ♔g1 a4! ∓ Blau-Stahlberg, Moscow 1956.

10 ... ♘xd2

10 ... ♕b6?! 11 ♘xf5 gxf5 12 ♘f3, threatening 13 ♘h4 ±.

11 ♕xd2 ♗e6
12 f4!? f5

Chances are equal.

14.22

7 c3

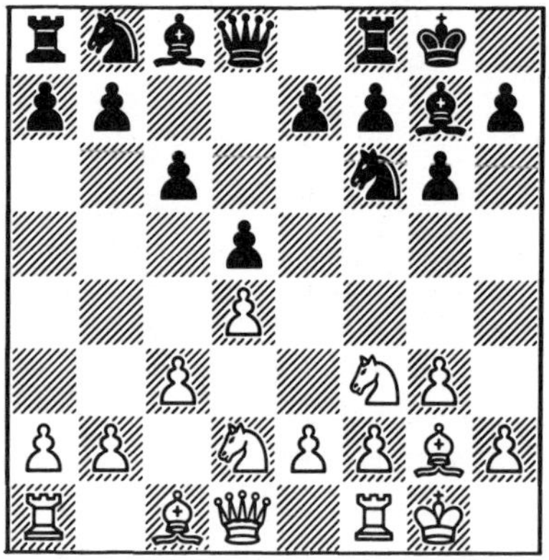

An utterly different strategy compared with 7 b3.

7 ... ♗f5

(a) 7 ... ♕c7 8 ♖e1 c5 9 dxc5 ♖d8 (9 ... ♕xc5 10 ♘b3 ♕c7 11 ♗f4 ♕d8 ±; 9 ... ♘a6 10 ♘b3 ♘xc5 11 ♗f4 ♕c6 12 ♘fd4 ♕b6 13 ♘xc5 ♕xc5 14 ♗e5 ±) 10 ♕a4 ♕xc5 11 ♘b3 ♕c6 12 ♕h4 ± Kovačevic-Nikolić, Yugoslavia

1989.

(b) 7 ... ♘bd7 8 ♖e1 ♖e8 9 e4 ♘xe4 10 ♘xe4 dxe4 11 ♖xe4 ♘f6 ± Pfleger-Hartston, Hastings 1971/72.

8 a4!?

With the idea 9 a5! Others:

(a) 8 ♖e1 ♘bd7 9 ♘h4 ♗e6 10 e4 dxe4 11 ♘xe4 ♘xe4 12 ♗xe4 ♕b6 13 ♕c2 ♖fe8 14 ♗e3 ♗d5 15 ♗d3 ♕a5 ∞ Andersson-Hellers, Haninge 1990.

(b) 8 ♘h4 ♗e6 9 ♖e1 ♖e8 (9 ... ♘bd7 10 e4 see (a)) 10 e4 dxe4 11 ♘xe4 ♗d5 12 ♘c5 b6 13 ♘d3 ♘bd7 14 ♘f3 c5 15 ♗e3 ♕c7 16 ♘de5 ♖ad8 17 ♗f4 ± Motwani-W.Watson, London 1990.

(c) 8 h3 ♘e4 9 g4 ♘xd2 10 ♘xd2 ♗e6 11 f4 f5 12 g5 ♘d7 13 b3 c5 14 ♘f3 ♖c8 15 ♗e3 ♕a5 16 ♕d2 ♗f7 17 ♖fc1 = Pfleger-Andersson, Hastings 1971/72.

(d) 8 ♘e5 ♘bd7 9 ♘df3 ♘e4 10 ♗f4 f6 11 ♘d3 ♕b6 12 ♕b3 ♗e6 13 ♘d2 ♘xd2 14 ♗xd2 ♗f7 = Hartoch-Hort, Wijk aan Zee 1972.

8 ... a5
9 ♘h4 ♕c8?!

9 ... ♘a6!?; 9 ... ♗e6!?.

10 ♘xf5 ♕xf5
11 e4! dxe4
12 ♖e1

With somewhat better play for White (Averbakh-Polugayevsky, Alma Ata 1969).

ILLUSTRATIVE GAMES

1 d4 ♘f6 2 ♘f3 g6 3 g3 ♗g7 4 ♗g2 0-0

80) **Azmaiparashvili-Romanishin**
USSR 1983

4 ... d5 5 0-0 c6 6 ♘bd2 ♗e6 7 ♘e5 ♘bd7 8 ♘d3! ♗f5 9 c4 ♗xd3?! 9 ... 0-0 10 ♕b3 ♕b6 11 c5!? ♕xb3 12 ♘xb3 a5 13 a4 b6 14 ♗d2 ±; 10 ♘f4 ±. **10 exd3 0-0 11 ♖e1 e6 12 ♘f3 ♕b6?!** 12 ... b5!? 13 c5 ±. **13 c5! ♕a6 14 ♗f4 ♖e8 15 a4** 15 b4? ♕a3!. **15 ... b6 16 b4 bxc5 17 dxc5! ♘h5 18 ♗e5 ♘xe5 19 ♘xe5 ♖ab8 20 ♖b1 ♗xe5 21 ♖xe5 ♘f6 22 d4 ♘e4!** In an unfavourable position, Black's best chance is the endgame with major pieces. **23 ♗xe4 dxe4 24 ♕c2?!** 24 ♖xe4 ♕c4 25 ♕b3 ♕xb3 26 ♖xb3 ♖e7 27 ♖e2 ±. **24 ... ♖e7?** 24 ... ♕d3! 25 ♕xd3 exd3 26 ♖e3 d2 27 ♖d3 ♖b7 28 ♖xd2 ♖eb8 29 ♖b2 ♖d7 30 b5 ±.

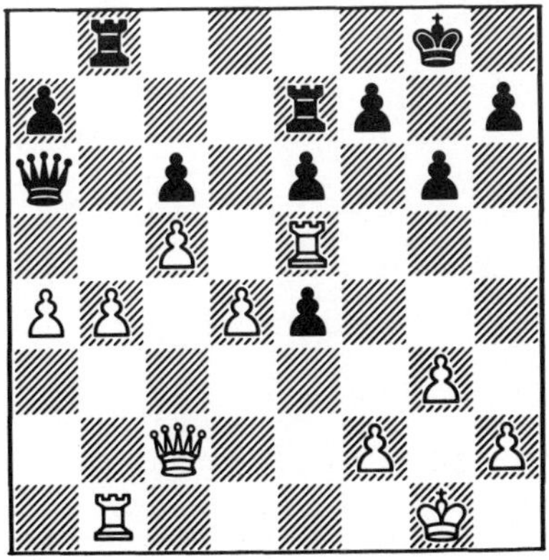

25 b5! After this witty pawn sacrifice, White's steamroller can get under way. **25 ... cxb5 26 d5 b4 27 ♖xe4! ♕a5 28 dxe6 fxe6 29 ♕c4 ♕xa4 30 ♖xe6 ♖f7 31 ♖e7 ♖f8 32 c6 ♕a5 33 c7 ♕f5 34 ♖xf7 1-0**
(Azmaiparashvili's notes included)

81) **Lehmann-Polugayevsky**
Solingen 1974

5 b3 d6 6 ♗b2 ♘bd7 7 c4 This actually started life as a King's Indian, but the ideas are so similar to this section's that it is worth our while to demonstrate what a comfortable game Black has (the order of moves has been changed). **7 ... e5! 8 dxe5 dxe5 9 0-0** 9 ♘xe5? ♘g4! 10 ♘d3 ♗xb2 11 ♘xb2 ♕f6 ∓∓. **9 ... e4 10 ♘g5 ♖e8** The e-pawn permanently annoys White. **11 ♕c2 e3 12 f4 ♘c5 13 ♖d1 ♕e7 14 ♘c3 c6 15 b4?** White's plan seems logical, hoping to grab the initiative on the long diagonal, but it is Black who is to deliver the first blow – on the kingside. 15 ♗a3!. **15 ... ♗f5 16 ♕c1 ♘e6 17 b5** 17 ♘xe6 ♗xe6 ∓. **17 ... ♘xg5 18 fxg5**

(diagram)

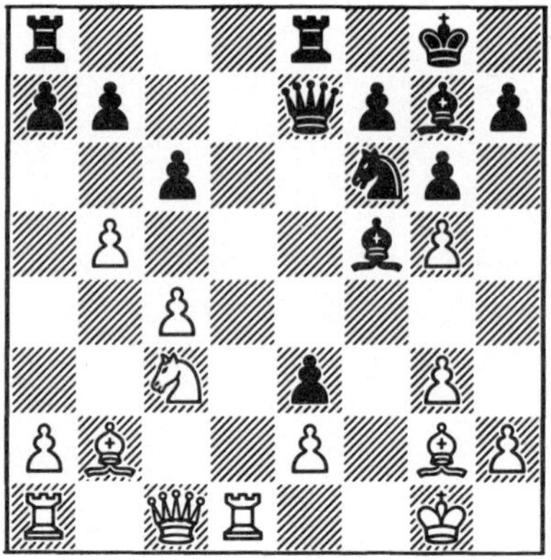

18 ... ♘h5! Introducing a sacrifice of the exchange, and then a piece! The idea is that after the disappearance of the g2 bishop, White's king remains unprotected. White probably considered only 18 ... ♘e4. **19 bxc6 bxc6 20 ♘a4** 20 ♗xc6 ♕xg5 21 ♗xa8 ♘xg3! 22 ♗g2 ♗h3! 23 ♗xh3 ♘xe2+ 24 ♔h1 ♘xc1 25 ♖axc1 ♕h4! ∓∓. **20 ... ♗xb2 21 ♕xb2 ♕xg5!** Intending the lethal 22 ... ♘xg3! threat. **22 ♕c3?!** Tougher is 22 ♕b7 ♘xg3 23 hxg3 ♕xg3 24 ♖f1 ♖ab8 25 ♕xa7 ♖a8 26 ♕b7 ♖xa4 27 ♕xc6 ♖aa8 etc. **22 ... ♗e4 23 ♖d4 ♘xg3! 24 hxg3 ♕xg3 25 ♖xe4 ♖xe4 26 ♕e1 ♕g5 27 ♔f1 ♖g4 0-1**

82) **Polugayevsky-Tal**
Leningrad 1971

5 b3 d6 6 ♗b2 e5?! 7 dxe5 ♘g4 8 h3! ♘xe5 9 ♘xe5 ♗xe5 Having learnt from his loss to Smyslov (Palma de Mallorca 1970), Polugayevsky plays this system with colours reversed here. The game in Spain went 9 ... dxe5 10

♕xd8 ♖xd8 11 ♘d2 ♘d7 12 0-0-0 ♖e8 13 ♘c4 ♘b6 14 ♘a5! ♖b8 15 ♖d2 c6 16 ♖hd1 f6 17 ♖d8 ♔f7 18 ♖xe8 ♔xe8 19 ♗a3! ♘d5 20 ♗d6 ♖a8 21 c4 ±±. **10 ♗xe5 dxe5 11 ♕xd8 ♖xd8 12 ♘d2 ♘d7** 12 ... ♘a6 13 0-0-0 c6 14 ♘c4 ±. **13 0-0-0 ♖e8 14 ♘e4 ♔g7** 15 ♖xd7! was threatened. **15 g4! h6** 15 ... f5?! 16 gxf5 gxf5 17 ♘c3 ♘f6 18 ♘b5! ±; 17 ... c6 18 ♖d6 ±. **16 ♖d3 ♘f6 17 ♘xf6 ♔xf6 18 ♖hd1 c6 19 ♖f3+ ♔g7** 19 ... ♔e7? 20 ♖e3 ♔f6 21 f4!. **20 ♖e3! g5! 21 a4 ♔f6?!** 21 ... a5! would have hindered White gaining the dark squares.

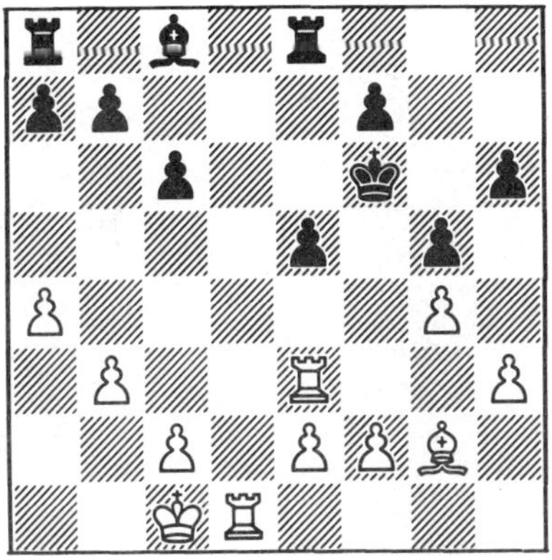

22 a5! a6 23 ♔b2 ♗e6 24 ♔c3! ♖ac8 24 ... h5!?. **25 ♔b4!** The king threatens to penetrate via the dark squares. Should Black parry this by 25 ... c5+ then White would hem him in after 26 ♔c3 ♖c7 27 ♖d6 and ♖b6. **25 ... h5 26 ♗f3 hxg4 27 hxg4 ♖cd8 28 ♖xd8 ♖xd8 29 ♔c5 ♖d4?!** Tougher is 29 ... ♖d7 although 30 ♔b6 and then c4-b4-b5 would be difficult to parry. **30 c4! ♗xg4 31 ♗xg4 ♖xg4 32 ♔b6 ♖f4 33 f3?!** 33 ♔xb7 ±±. **33 ... e4! 34 ♔xb7 ♔e5 35 ♔xa6 ♔d4 36 ♖xe4+ ♖xe4 37 fxe4 g4 38 ♔b7 g3 39 a6 g2 40 a7 g1=♕ 41 a8=♕ c5 42 ♔b6 ♔c3 43 ♕d5 ♕g8 44 ♔xc5 ♔xb3 45 ♕d3+ ♔b2 46 ♕d6 ♔b3 47 ♕b6+ ♔c2 48 ♔b5 ♕g4 49 ♕d4 ♕xe2 50 ♔b6 ♕h2 51 e5 ♔b3 52 c5 f6 53 c6 fxe5 54 ♕d5+ ♔a4 55 ♕b5+ ♔a3 56 c7 1-0**

83) **Romanishin-Kasparov**
USSR 1982

5 0-0 d5 6 ♗f4 c6 7 ♘bd2 ♘h5?! 8 ♗e5! f6 9 ♗xb8 ♖xb8 10 c4 f5 10 ... e5?! 11 cxd5 cxd5 12 ♕b3 ±. **11 cxd5 cxd5 12 ♕b3 ♘f6 13 ♘e5 ♗e6**

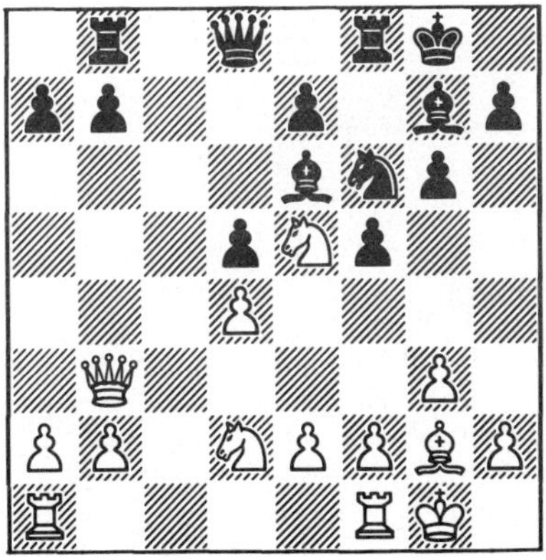

14 ♖ac1?! 14 e4! fxe4 15 ♘xe4

♘xe4 16 ♗xe4 ♕b6 17 ♗xd5 ♕xb3 18 ♗xb3 ♗xb3 19 axb3 ±. **14 ... ♕d6 15 ♘b1?!** 15 ♖c2. **15 ... g5! 16 ♘c3 a6 17 ♘a4 ♘e4 18 ♗xe4 fxe4?** 18 ... dxe4! 19 ♕e3 h6 20 ♘c5 ♗xe5 21 dxe5 ♕xe5 22 b3 ∓. **19 ♘c5 ♗xe5 20 dxe5 ♕xe5 21 ♖fd1 ♖bd8 22 ♘xe6 ♕xe6 23 ♕xb7 ♕f5?** 23 ... ♕f6 =. **24 ♖f1 ♖f7 25 ♕xa6 d4 26 ♕b6 ♖d5 27 b4 ♔g7 28 a4 ♖d6 29 ♕c5 ♖d5 30 ♕c8 ♕e5 31 ♖c5 e6 32 a5 e3 33 f4! gxf4 34 ♖xf4 ♖xf4 35 gxf4 ♕f5** 35 ... ♕xf4 36 ♖c7+ ♔f6 37 ♕h8+. **36 ♖xd5 ♕xd5 37 ♕c7+ ♔g6 38 ♕c2+ ♔f6 39 a6 ♕a8 40 ♕c4 ♕e4 41 ♕c5 ♕b1+** 41 ... ♔f7 42 a7 d3 43 ♕h5+ ♔g7 44 exd3 e2 45 dxe4. **42 ♔g2 ♕d1 43 ♕g5+ ♔f7 44 ♕h5+ ♔g7 45 a7 1-0**

15 Countering the King's Indian and the Grünfeld: KB Line, Black's King's Indian is answered by 6 b3

1	d4	♘f6
2	♘f3	g6
3	g3	♗g7
4	♗g2	0-0
5	0-0	d6
6	b3	

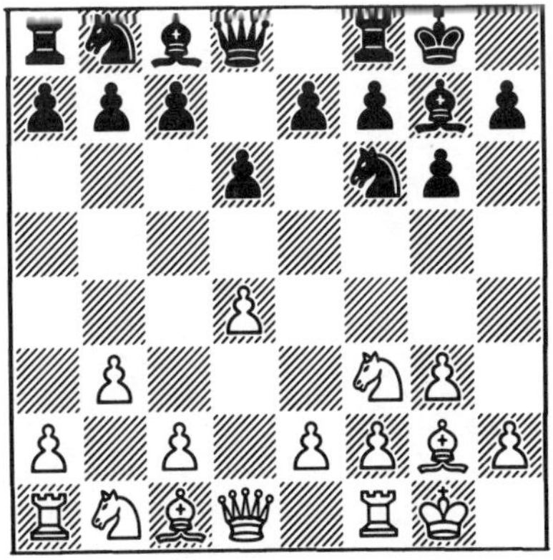

Once labelled as 'neo-romantic', or 'hypermodern', this variation is characterised by White's intention to exert pressure along both long diagonals. His dream would come true if he hindered ... e7-e5 successfully. This however, is impracticable.

The position in the diagram shows that the two camps have not yet come into contact, so it takes time to reach the stage of actual threats and hand-to-hand battles. That is why Black has so many alternatives on move 6. Here 6 ... ♘bd7, 6 ... e5 and 6 ... c5 are regarded as the mainstream variations, but, of course, there are also several lesser continuations:

(a) 6 ... c6 7 ♗b2 ♗g4 (7 ... ♕a5 8 ♘bd2 ♕h5 9 e4 ♗g4 10 ♖e1 ♘fd7 11 ♕e2 c5 12 c3 cxd4 13 cxd4 ♘c6 14 ♕f1! ± Pomar-E.Torre, Malaga 1973; 10 e5 dxe5 11 dxe5 ♘fd7 12 ♖e1 ♘a6 13 ♘c4 ♖ad8 14 ♕e2 ♘b4 15 ♘e3! ± Djindjihashvili-Kavalek, Buenos Aires 1978. 8 ♖e1 is also possible, with a likely transposition, e.g. 8 ... ♕h5 9 e4 ♗g4 10 ♘bd2 ♘bd7 11 ♘f1!? d5 12 exd5 ♘xd5 13 c4 ♘b4 14 a3 ♘a6 15 ♖xe7 ♖ad8 ± Kristiansen-Hebden, Hastings 1989-90) 8 h3 ♗xf3 9 ♗xf3 ♘bd7 10 ♗g2 e5 (10 ... a5!?) 11 dxe5 dxe5 12 ♘d2 ♕c7 13 ♘c4 ± Korchnoi-Nunn, Illustrative Game No 84.

(b) 6 ... a6 7 ♗b2 (7 a4!?) 7 ... b5 8 ♘bd2 (8 ♘e5 ♖a7 9 ♘d3 ♗b7 ∞) 8 ... ♗b7 9 ♖e1 ♘bd7 10 e4 e5 11 dxe5 ♘g4 12 ♘f1 (12 ♘d4!? dxe5? 13 ♘e6!, Flohr; 12 ... ♘gxe5 13 f4?! c5! =; 13 ♕c1 ∞) 12 ... ♘c5 13 ♘e3 ♘xe5 14 ♘xe5 ♗xe5 15 ♕c1 ± Taimanov-Spassky, USSR 1956.

(c) 6 ... ♘c6 7 ♗b2 a5 (7 ... ♗f5 8 d5 ♘b4 9 ♘d4! ♗e4 10 c4 ♗xg2 11 ♔xg2 ♕d7 12 ♘c3 e5 13 ♘c2 ♘xc2 14 ♕xc2 h5 15 e4 h4 ± Kogan-Christiansen, USA 1984; 7 ... ♗g4 8 d5 ♘b8 9 c4 ♕c8 10 ♖e1 ± Barcza-Gereben, Reggio Emilia 1963/64) 8 ♘c3 ♗f5 9 d5 ♘b4 10 ♘d4 ♗d7 11 a3 ♘a6 12 ♕d2 ± Trifunović-Korchnoi, Yugoslavia-USSR match 1956.

(d) 6 ... ♗d7 7 ♗b2 ♕c8 8 ♖e1 e5 (8 ... ♗h3 9 e4 ♗xg2 10 ♔xg2 e5 11 dxe5 ♘fd7 12 ♘c3 ♘xe5 13 ♘d5 ♘bc6 14 ♘xe5 ♗xe5 15 ♕c1 ♕d8 16 f4 ± Reshevsky-Kagan, Netanya 1971) 9 dxe5 ♘g4 10 ♘c3 ♘xe5 11 ♘xe5 dxe5 12 ♘d5 ♖e8 13 ♕d2 c6 14 ♘e3 ♗e6 15 ♖ed1 ± Savon-Taimanov, USSR 1971.

(e) 6 ... ♗f5 7 ♗b2 (7 ♘h4!) 7 ... c6 8 ♘bd2 ♖e8 9 ♖e1 e5 10 dxe5 dxe5 11 e4 ♗g4 12 h3 ♗xf3 13 ♘xf3 ± Polugayevsky-Zaitsev, Sochi 1976.

(f) 6 ... ♘fd7 7 ♗b2 e5 (7 ... ♘c6 8 e4 e5 9 ♖e1 exd4 10 ♘xd4 ♕f6 11 c3 ♘c5 Pirc-Matulović, Yugoslavia 1954; 12 ♘a3 ♘xd4 13 cxd4 ♘e6 14 ♘c2 c5 15 e5! ±) 8 d5! e4 9 ♘d4 ± (Pirc).

(g) 6 ... a5 7 a4 (7 c4 a4 8 b4 c5 9 bxc5 dxc5 10 ♘a3 cxd4 11 ♘xd4 ♘a6 ∞ Szabó-Spassky, Amsterdam 1956; 7 ♘c3 c6 8 e4 a4 9 ♗g5 axb3 10 axb3 ♖xa1 11 ♕xa1 h6 12 ♗d2 ∞ Mariotti-Nemet, Lugano 1987) 7 ... e5 (7 ... ♘c6 8 ♗b2 ♗f5 9 ♘h4 ♗d7 10 ♘a3 ± Smyslov-Borisenko, Illustrative Game No 85; 7 ... c6 8 ♗b2 ♘a6 9 ♘bd2 ♗f5 10 ♘h4 ♗d7 11 e4 ♖b8 12 ♖e1 b5 13 e5! ± Gheorghiu-Peev, Varna 1971; 7 ... d5 8 ♗b2 ♘c6 9 ♘bd2 ♘e4 10 e3 e6 11 c4 f5 12 ♘e1 b6 13 ♘d3 ± Kholmov-Simagin, USSR 1956; 7 ... ♗g4 8 ♗b2 – 8 h3! – 8 ... ♕c8 9 ♖e1 ♘c6 10 ♘bd2 ♗h3 11 ♗h1 h6 12 ♘c4 ♖e8 13 e4 ♘g4 14 d5 ♗xb2 15 ♘xb2 ♘ce5 = Tarasov-Taimanov, USSR 1957) 8 dxe5 ♘g4 9 ♗b2 ♘c6 10 ♘a3 ♘gxe5 11 ♘xe5 ♘xe5 12 ♕c1 (12 ♖b1!?) 12 ... c6 13 ♘c4?! (13 e4!) 13 ... ♘xc4 14 ♗xg7 ♔xg7 15 bxc4 ♕b6 ∓ Krogius-Gurgenidze, USSR 1960.

15.1

6	**...**	**♘bd7**
7	**♗b2**	**e5**

7 ... c6 8 ♘bd2 (8 c4!?) 8 ... ♕c7 9 e4 e5 (9 ... a5 10 ♖e1 a4 11 a3 axb3 12 cxb3 e5 13 dxe5 ♘xe5 14 ♘xe5 dxe5 15 ♘c4 ♘d7 16 ♕c2

♘c5 17 ♗c3! ♖d8 18 ♗a5 ± Lechtinsky-Flis, Polanica Zdrój 1983) 10 ♖e1 exd4 (10 ... ♖e8 11 ♘c4 ♗f8 12 a4 ♘b6 13 ♘xb6 axb6 14 ♕d2 ♗g4 15 h3 ♗xf3 16 ♗xf3 ± Pirc-Gojak, Yugoslavia 1963) 11 ♘xd4 ♘c5 12 a4 a5 13 ♕f3 ♘fd7 14 ♖ad1 ♖e8 15 ♕c3! ♘e5? Pomar-Hort, Gothenburg 1971; 16 f4! ♕b6 17 fxe5 dxe5 18 ♘c4 ±; 15 ... ♗f6! ±.

8 dxe5 ♘g4

8 ... ♘h5 9 ♘a3! dxe5 10 e4 ♖e8 11 ♕e2 ♘b6 (11 ... b6 12 ♖fd1 ♕e7 13 ♘b5 ♗a6 14 c4 ±) 12 ♖fd1 ♗d7 13 c4 ♕e7 14 ♘c2 ♗c6 15 ♗a3 ♕e6 16 ♘e3 ♖ad8 17 ♘d5 ♗xd5 18 cxd5 ± Smyslov-Unzicker, Hastings 1954/55.

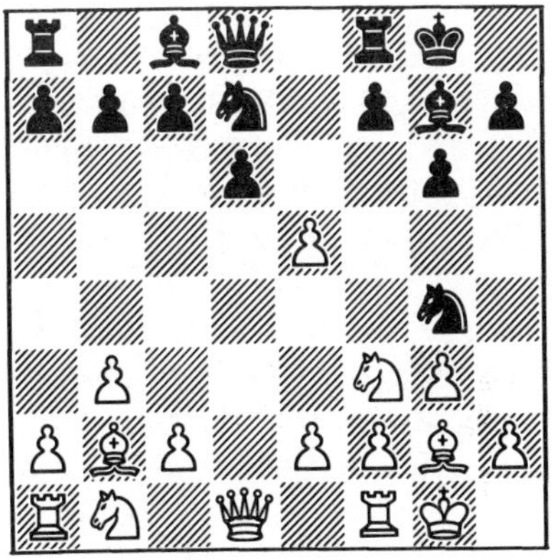

9 ♕d2!

Should Black recapture on e5 with a piece, White has 10 c4!; should he do it with a pawn, then White has 10 e4!. Others:

(a) 9 ♘bd2?! ♘gxe5 (9 ... dxe5?! 10 h3 ♘h6 11 e4 f6 12 ♘c4 ♘b6 13 ♕xd8 ♖xd8 14 ♘a5 ♗f8 15 a3 ♘f7 16 ♖fd1 ± F.Olafsson-Najdorf, Wijk aan Zee 1971) 10 ♘xe5 ♘xe5 11 ♕c1 (11 ♖b1 d5 12 h3 ♕e7 13 e4 dxe4 14 ♘xe4 ♗f5 15 ♖e1 ♕b4 = Eliskases-Najdorf, Mar del Plata 1948; 11 ♔h1 d5 12 ♘f3 ♘xf3 13 ♗xg7 ♔xg7 14 ♗xf3 ♗e6 = Filip-Fischer, Portoroz 1958) 11 ... d5 12 ♖d1 ♗g4 13 h3 ♗e6 = Rukavina-Bukić, Yugoslav Championship 1972.

(b) 9 ♘c3 dxe5? (9 ... ♘gxe5!) 10 ♘d2 ♖e8 11 ♘c4 ♘b6 12 ♘xb6 cxb6 13 ♕xd8 ♖xd8 14 ♖ad1 ± Yusupov-Zapata, Innsbruck 1977.

(c) 9 ♘d4 dxe5 (9 ... ♘gxe5!) 10 ♘b5 a6 11 ♘5a3 ♖e8 12 ♘c4 ♘h6 13 ♘c3 ♘f5 14 ♕d2 ♖b8 15 ♖ad1 ± Rukavina-Bogdanović, Sarajevo 1971.

(d) 9 h3?! ♘gxe5 10 ♘c3 ♘xf3+ 11 ♗xf3 ♘c5 12 ♗g2 ♗f5 13 g4 ♗d7 14 b4 ♘e6 15 f4 ♕h4 16 e3 a5 ∞ Plaskett-Hjartarson, Vestmanna Islands 1985.

(e) 9 c4!? ♖e8 (9 ... ♘gxe5?! 10 ♘xe5 ♘xe5 11 ♘c3 ♘g4 12 h3 ♘f6 13 ♕d2 ♖e8 14 e4 ± Mariotti-Valenti, Illustrative Game No 86; 9 ... dxe5?! 10 h3 ± Polugayevsky-Honfi, Illustrative Game No 87) 10 h3 (10 ♘c3 ♘gxe5 11 ♕c2 a5 12 ♖ad1 ± Sanguinetti-Idigoras, Argentina 1955) 10 ... ♘h6 11

♘c3 (11 ♕c2?! dxe5 12 ♖d1 f5 13 ♘bd2 e4 14 ♗xg7 ♔xg7 = Hartston-Najdorf, Illustrative Game No 88) 11 ... dxe5 12 e4 c6 13 ♕c2 ± Kholmov-Gufeld, Moscow 1969.

9 ... ♘gxe5

9 ... dxe5 10 e4 ♖e8 11 a4 f6 12 ♖d1 ♕e7 13 ♘c3 ♘f8 14 a5 ± Andersson-Spraggett, Clermont-Ferrand 1989.

10 ♘xe5 dxe5
11 ♖d1

11 ♘c3 c6 (11 ... ♘f6 12 ♕xd8 ♖xd8 13 ♖fd1 ♖xd1+ 14 ♖xd1 ♗f5 15 ♗xb7 ± Korchnoi-Spassky, USSR 1956) 12 ♖ad1 (12 ♗a3 ♖e8 13 ♘e4 ±) 12 ... ♕a5 13 ♘d5 ♕c5 14 ♘e3 ♘b6 15 ♕c1 ± Robatsch-Ojanen, Moscow 1956.

11 ... c6
12 ♘a3 ♕c7
13 ♘c4 ♘b6
14 ♕a5! ±

Möhring-Babrikowski, East Germany 1981.

15.2

6 ... e5!?

The simplest way to verify that not even 6 b3 is able to hinder this freeing move is by playing it! All Black's problems, however, are not solved by this move. The following exchange is forced, for 7 c4 e4! would be a comfortable King's Indian for Black.

7 dxe5

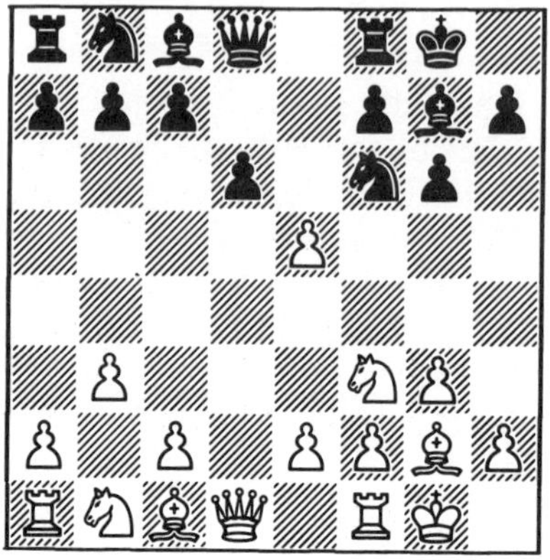

15.21

7 ... ♘fd7

Apart from 7 ... dxe5 (15.22), 7 ... ♘g4 is worth considering: 8 ♗b2 ♘c6 (8 ... ♘d7 – see 15.1. Bad is 8 ... ♘xe5? 9 ♘xe5! dxe5 10 ♕xd8 ♖xd8 11 ♘a3 ±) 9 ♕c1 (9 c4 dxe5! 10 h3 ♘h6 11 e3 ♗f5 12 ♘c3 ♗d3 13 ♖e1 e4 ∞ Lukács-Balogh, Budapest 1972; 11 ♕c1 e4 12 ♗xg7 ♔xg7 13 ♘e1 = Portisch; 11 e4!? ♕xd1 12 ♖xd1 f5 13 ♘c3 ± may be best, Varnusz-Pirisi, Budapest 1989. 9 ♘bd2 dxe5? – 9 ... ♘gxe5! = – 10 h3 ♘h6 11 e4 f5 12 ♘c4 ♕xd1 13 ♖axd1 ♘f7 14 exf5 gxf5 15 ♘h4 ± Polugayevsky-Krogius, Sochi 1963) 9 ... dxe5 (9 ... ♘gxe5!?) 10 h3 ♘h6 11 ♖d1 ♕e8 12 e4 f5 13 ♘c3 ∞.

8 ♗b2

8 ♗g5!? ♕e8 9 ♘c3 h6 ∞ – Ristić-Marjanović, Illustrative Game No 89.

8 ... ♘c6

8 ... dxe5 9 ♘fd2 (9 e4 ♘c6 10 ♘bd2! b6 11 ♕e2 ♕e7 12 ♖fd1 ♘c5 13 ♘f1 Polugayevsky-Medina, Palma de Mallorca 1972; 13 ... ♗e6! 14 ♘e3 ♘xe4 15 ♘c4 ±) 9 ... f5 10 ♘c4 ♕e8 11 e4 ♘b6 12 exf5 gxf5 13 ♕e2 ♘8d7 14 ♘bd2 ♕e6 ± Steinberg-Rashkovsky, USSR 1967.

9 ♕d2!

This fine move maintains the possibility of both 10 c4 and 10 e4. Others:

(a) 9 c4 dxe5! (9 ... ♘dxe5?! 10 ♘c3 Capablanca-Yates, Illustrative Game No 90) 10 ♘e1 ♘d4 11 ♘c3 c6 12 ♘d3 f5 13 e3 ♘e6 14 ♘a4 ♕e7 15 ♕c1 ♖e8 = Barcza-Fischer, Zürich 1959.

(b) 9 ♕c1?! dxe5! 10 ♘c3 ♖e8 11 ♖d1 ♘d4 12 ♘e1 h6 13 e3 ♘e6 14 ♔h1 f5 = Prins-Damjanović, Leipzig 1960.

(c) 9 e4 dxe5 10 ♘c3 (10 ♘a3 ♘c5 11 ♘c4 ♕e7 12 ♕e2 ♖d8 13 h3 b6 14 ♖fd1 ♗a6 = Antoshin-Bronstein, USSR 1953) 10 ... b6 (10 ... ♘d4!?) 11 ♘d5 ♖e8 12 ♕d2 ♘c5 13 ♖fe1 ♗g4 = Polugayevsky-Stein, USSR 1969.

9 ... ♘dxe5?!

9 ... dxe5 10 e4 ♘c5 etc. should be tested in practice. An idea for White is 10 ♖d1! ♖e8 11 e4 ♘c5 12 ♕xd8 ♘xd8 13 ♗xe5! ♘xe4 14 ♖e1! ♗xe5 15 ♖xe4, Miles-N. Ristić, Belgrade 1988, 15 ... f6 ±. 9 ... ♖e8 10 ♖d1 ♘dxe5 11 ♘xe5 (11 c4!?) 11 ... ♘xe5 12 c4 ± Miles-Marjanović, Manila 1974.

10 c4 ±

Or 10 ♘xe5, as in 15.21.

15.22

7 ... dxe5!?

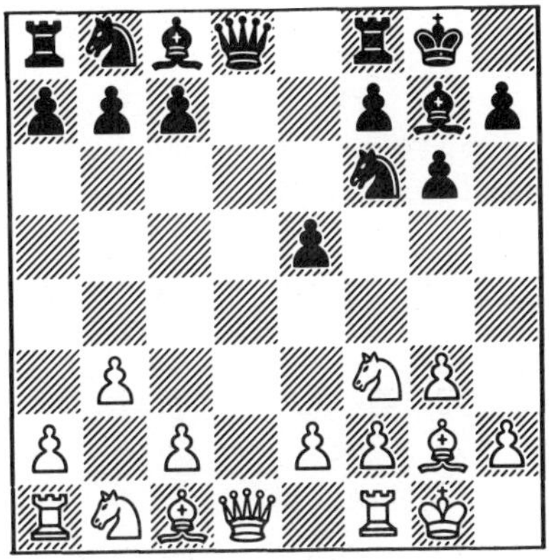

8 ♗a3

8 ♗b2?! (Do all 'natural' moves lose?) 8 ... e4 9 ♕xd8? (9 ♘d4 =) 9 ... ♖xd8 10 ♘g5 ♗f5 11 ♘a3 (11 g4 ♗xg4 12 ♘xe4 ♘xe4 13 ♗xg7 ♔xg7 14 ♗xe4 ♘c6 ∓ Filip-Geller, Amsterdam 1956) 11 ... h6 12 ♖ad1 ♘bd7 13 ♘h3 c6 14 ♘c4 ♘d5 ∓ Espig-Casper, East Germany 1984.

8 ... ♕xd1

8 ... ♖e8 9 ♘c3 e4 10 ♘g5 ♗f5 11 ♕xd8 ♖xd8 12 ♖ad1 ±.

9 ♖xd1 ♖e8
10 ♘c3 e4

10 ... ♗d7? 11 ♘xe5! ♖xe5 12 ♗xb7 ♗c6 13 ♗xa8 ♗xa8 14 ♖d8+ ♖e8 15 ♖ad1 ± Kholmov-Khasin, USSR 1957.

11 ♘d4

11 ♘e1?! c6 12 ♖ab1 ♘bd7 13 ♗h3 ♘b6 14 ♗xc8 ♖axc8 15 e3 ♘fd5 ∓ Barcza-Szabó, Budapest 1961.

11 ... a6
12 ♘a4 b6
13 c4 =

15.3

6 ... c5

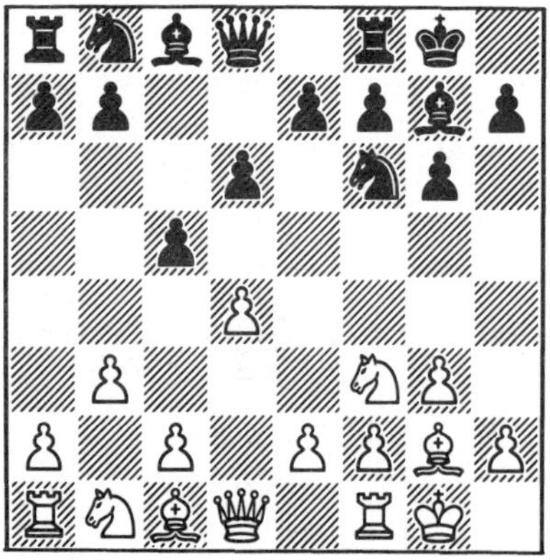

To control the centre and the long diagonal simultaneously.

7 ♗b2

To avoid the following space-winning manoeuvre, White can transpose into the King's Indian by 7 c4 ♘e4 8 ♗b2 ♘c6 9 e3 ♗g4 10 ♕c2! (10 ♕c1 ♗xf3! 11 ♗xf3 ♘g5 12 ♗xc6 bxc6 13 dxc5 dxc5 14 ♗xg7 ♔xg7 = Korchnoi-Gligorić, USSR-Yugoslavia match, 1956) 10 ... f5!? (10 ... ♗f5 11 ♕e2 cxd4? 12 ♘xd4 ♘xd4 13 exd4 d5 14 cxd5 ♘d6 15 ♘a3 ± Varnusz-Nagy, Budapest 1987; 11 ... ♗g4! ⩲) 11 d5 ♘b4! 12 ♕e2 ♗xb2 13 ♕xb2 ♘d3 14 ♕c2 ♘b4 15 ♕d1 e6! 16 dxe6 ♕f6 17 ♘a3 d5 18 ♘b5 ♖ad8 19 ♕c1 a6 ∞ Korchnoi-Jadoul, Brussels 1985.

In master play 7 e3 (to meet 7 ... cxd4 by 8 exd4) has not yet been encountered. Bizarre is 7 dxc5!?, e.g. 7 ... ♘e4! (7 ... dxc5 8 ♗b2 ♕xd1 9 ♖xd1 ♘c6 10 ♘e5! ♘g4 11 ♘d3 ♗xb2 12 ♘xb2 ♘d4 13 ♖d2 ♗f5 14 ♘a3 ♖ad8 15 ♗xb7 ± Barcza-Siaperas, Moscow 1956; 8 ... ♘c6 9 ♘e5! ♘xe5 10 ♗xe5 ♕b6 11 c4 ♗e6 12 ♘c3 ±) 8 c3 ♘xc5 (8 ... ♘xc3? 9 ♘xc3 ♗xc3 10 ♗h6! ±; 8 ... dxc5!?) 9 ♗e3 ♘c6 10 ♕c1 ♗d7 11 ♖d1 ♕c7 12 ♗h6 ♖ad8 13 ♗xg7 ♔xg7 14 c4 then ♘b1-c3-d5 ∞ (Analysis).

7 ... cxd4

7 ... ♘e4 (7 ... ♘fd7 8 c4! ±; 7 ... ♘c6 8 ♘bd2 ♗d7 ∞) 8 ♘bd2 (8 c4 is the previously mentioned

English-King's Indian hybrid) 8 ... f5 (8 ... ♘xd2 9 ♕xd2 ±) 9 c3!? (9 e3 ±) 9 ... ♕a5 10 b4 cxb4 11 ♕b3+ e6 12 cxb4 ♕b5 13 e3 ♘c6 ∞ Barcza-Flórián, Gyula 1965.

8 ♘xd4 d5!
9 c4!? dxc4

9 ... e5!? 10 ♘c2?! (10 ♘f3! e4 11 ♘d4 ±) 10 ... dxc4 11 bxc4 ♘c6 12 ♘c3 ♗e6 13 ♘d5 ♖c8 14 ♘ce3 ♘g4! 15 ♘xg4 ♗xg4 16 h3 ♗e6 17 ♕a4 ♖e8 18 ♖fd1 ♕a5 = Zysk-Sznapik, Poland 1984.

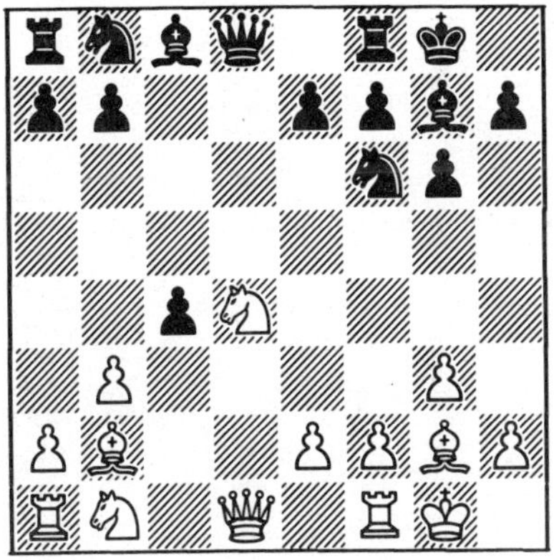

10 bxc4

10 ♘a3!? recalls the romanticism of the gambits: 10 ... cxb3 11 ♕xb3 ♕b6 12 ♘c4 (12 ♕xb6 axb6 13 ♘c4 ♘fd7 14 a4 ♘a6 ∞) 12 ... ♕xb3 13 axb3 ♘bd7 14 ♖fc1 a6 15 ♖c2 (15 b4 ♖b8 16 b5 axb5 17 ♘xb5 ♘e8 ∞) 15 ... ♖b8 16 ♖ac1 ♖e8 17 ♗a3 ♘d5 18 ♗xd5 ♗xd4 Bistrić-Vogt, Bugojno 1983; 19 e3 ♗f6 20 ♘a5 ♘b6 21 ♗f3 ♗e6 22 ♖c7 ∞.

10 ... ♘bd7

10 ... ♕c7!? 11 ♘d2 ♘c6 12 ♘xc6! bxc6 13 ♕a4 ♗d7 14 ♘b3 ♖fc8? 15 ♘c5 ♗e8 16 ♖ab1 ± Varnusz-Dobos, Eger 1984; 10 ... ♕b6 11 ♘b3 ♖d8 12 ♕c1 ♗e6 (12 ... ♘c6!?) 13 ♘1d2 ♘c6 14 ♗c3 ♗g4 ∞ (±) – Azmaiparashvili-Kochiev, Illustrative Game No 91.

11 ♘b3 a5
12 a4 ♘b6
13 ♘1d2 ♗e6
14 ♕c2 ♕c7
15 ♖fc1 ♗d7
16 ♘d4 ♖fc8
17 c5 ♘bd5
18 ♘b5 ♕b8 ±

Yap-Kengis, Jurmala 1986.

ILLUSTRATIVE GAMES

1 d4 ♘f6 2 ♘f3 g6 3 g3 ♗g7 4 ♗g2 0-0 5 0-0 d6 6 b3

84) **Korchnoi-Nunn**
Johannesburg 1981

6 ... c6 7 ♗b2 ♗g4?! 8 h3 ♗xf3 9 ♗xf3 ♘bd7 10 ♗g2 e5?! This move opens up the position in favour of the two bishops. Even worse, d6 is weakened. 10 ... a5!?. **11 dxe5! dxe5 12 ♘d2 ♕c7 13 ♘c4 ♖ad8 14 ♕d6! ♕c8 15 ♕a3 ♕b8 16 ♖ad1 ♖fe8 17 b4!** White begins to force Black back on the queenside. **17 ... ♘b6 18 ♘a5 h5?!** It is more advisable to regroup by 18 ... ♘fd5!, e.g. 19 c4 ♘c7 20 c5 ♘bd5 (20 ... ♘c8? 21 ♖xd8 ♖xd8 22 ♗xc6!!) 21 e4 ±. The text begins Black's kingside action but even that is going to favour White. **19 c4 h4 20 ♖xd8 ♖xd8 21 c5 ♘bd5 22 e4 ♘e7 23 ♘c4 ♘h5**

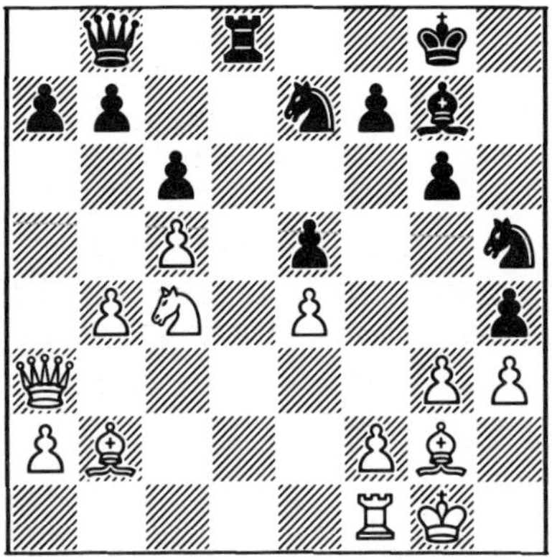

24 ♗f3! After the pawn sac the kingside will open up for White. **24 ... hxg3 25 ♗xh5 g2** 25 ... gxf2+ 26 ♖xf2 gxh5 27 ♘d6 ±. **26 ♔xg2 gxh5 27 ♖g1! ♘g6 28 ♔h2 b6 29 ♕f3 bxc5 30 bxc5 ♖d7 31 ♗c3 h4 32 ♕f5 ♖e7 33 ♘d6 ♕f8 34 ♗d2!** Another white piece appears on the kingside to force the issue. **34 ... ♖e6 35 ♗g5 ♘f4 36 ♗f6 ♘h5** 36 ... ♘g6 37 ♖xg6!. **37 ♕xh5 ♖xf6 38 ♘f5 1-0**

85) **Smyslov-Borisenko**
USSR Championship 1955

6 ... a5 7 a4 ♘c6 8 ♗b2 ♗f5 9 ♘h4! Hindering the opponent's counterplay. **9 ... ♗d7 10 ♘a3 ♕c8 11 ♘b5 ♘b4 12 ♖e1** White does not want to exchange his White-squared bishop! **12 ... c6 13 ♘a3 ♗h3 14 ♗h1 d5 15 ♘g2 ♘h5?** To prevent 16 ♘f4, but the knight will be out of play here. 15 ... c5!. **16 c3 ♘a6 17 e4! e6** After 17 ... dxe4 the knight would occupy c4. **18 e5! f6** The outpost must be eliminated because of the 19 ♗c1 and 20 g4 threats – but the backward e6 pawn will be a target of White's attack. **19 exf6 ♖xf6 20 ♗c1 ♕f8 21 ♖a2 ♖e8 22 ♘h4!**

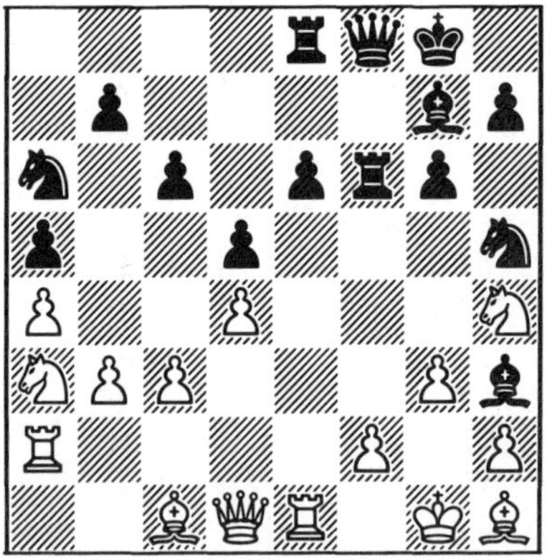

Smyslov has found the best set-up, his knight makes for f3 and his pawn for f4. **22 ... ♖f7 23 f4 c5 24 ♘b5 ♘c7 25 ♘f3 ♗g4 26**

♕d3 ♗f5 26 ... ♗xf3 is the lesser of two evils. **27 ♕e3 cxd4 28 ♘bxd4 ♗h6 29 ♗a3 ♕g7 30 ♘e5 ♖f6 31 ♗f3 ♗h3 32 ♖f2** White has gathered his forces on the kingside. Positionally losing, Black attempts to fish in troubled waters with an unsound sacrifice. **32 ... ♘xf4 33 gxf4 ♗xf4 34 ♕e2 h5 35 ♗g2 ♗xg2 36 ♖xg2 ♔h7 37 ♘df3 ♖g8 38 ♗c1 ♗xc1 39 ♖xc1 ♖f5 40 ♘g5+ ♔h8 41 ♖ce1 ♖gf8 1-0**

86) **Mariotti-Valenti**
Rome 1977

6 ... ♘bd7 7 ♗b2 e5 8 dxe5 ♘g4 9 c4 ♘gxe5 9 ... ♖e8!?. **10 ♘xe5 ♘xe5** 10 ... dxe5 11 ♕d2 ♘c5 12 ♗a3 e4 13 ♖d1 ♕e7 14 ♗b2 ±. **11 ♘c3 ♘g4?** Black cannot have counterplay without moving his pawns. 11 ... a6, then ... ♖b8 and ... b5 was required. Now White will have a small but long-lasting advantage. **12 h3 ♘f6 13 ♕d2 ♖e8 14 e4 ♗d7 15 ♖fe1 ♗c6 16 b4! a6 17 a4 ♖e7 18 a5 ♕e8 19 f3 ♖b8 20 ♗f1 b6?!** Slightly better is 20 ... b5!? 21 axb6! ♖xb6 22 c5 ♖xb4 23 cxd6 cxd6. **21 b5! axb5 22 cxb5 ♗a8 23 axb6 ♖xb6 24 ♗c4 ♖b8 25 ♔g2 ♖d8 26 ♗a3 ♘d7**

(diagram)

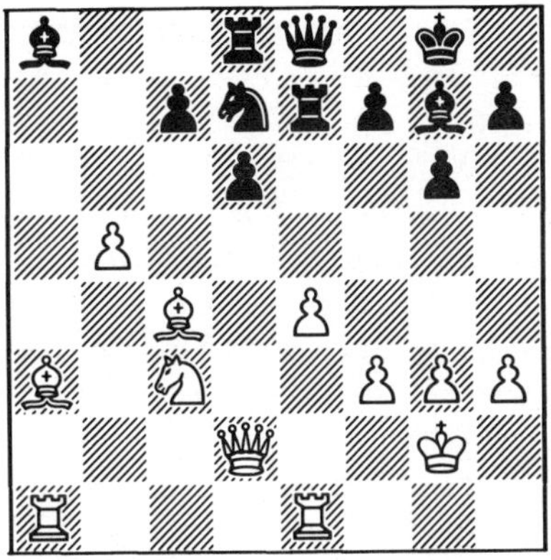

27 ♘d5! A decisive sacrifice of the exchange. **27 ... ♗xd5 28 ♗xd5 ♗xa1 29 ♖xa1 ♘f6** 29 ... ♔g7 30 ♕c3+ f6 31 ♕xc7 ♘c5 32 ♕b6 ±±. **30 ♗c6 ♕f8 31 ♗b2 ♘e8** 31 ... ♘d7 32 ♗d5! ♘b6 33 ♕d4 ♖e5 34 f4 ♘xd5 35 fxe5 ±±. **32 ♖a7 h6 33 ♕d4 ♔h7 34 b6! f6 35 b7 ♖e5 36 ♖a8 ♘g7 37 ♕a7 ♖c5 38 ♖xd8 ♕xd8 39 ♕a8 ♖c2+ 40 ♔g1 1-0**

87) **Polugayevsky-Honfi**
Solingen 1974

6 ... ♘bd7 7 ♗b2 e5 8 dxe5 ♘g4 9 c4 dxe5?! 10 h3 ♘h6 11 e4 f6 12 ♘c3 ♘f7 13 h4! White begins to loosen the black king's defences. **13 ... c6?!** 13 ... h5!?. **14 h5 ♗h6** 14 ... g5? would give up the f5 square. **15 ♘h4 ♔g7 16 ♕e2 ♕c7 17 ♖ad1** 17 ♘d1!?. **17 ... ♖d8** 17 ... ♖e8! **18 ♘a4!** Hindering 18 ... ♘c5. So far this defence has been impracticable owing to ♗a3!. **18 ... ♘f8 19 ♖xd8 ♕xd8 20 hxg6 hxg6 21 f4!** Initiating the kingside offensive!

21 ... b6 22 ♕f2?! Better is 23 ♕f3!, preventing ... ♗g4. **22 ... ♕e7 23 ♘c3!** Having fulfilled its duty on the queenside, the knight heads for the other flank. **23 ... ♗g4! 24 ♘d1 ♗xd1** The exchange is a small relief for Black. **25 ♖xd1 ♖d8 26 ♖f1!?** To collect the full point, White has to keep his rook for the offensive. **26 ... ♘e6?** Apparently the signal of the counter-attack, this move in fact accelerates White's attack. 26 ... ♖d3!.

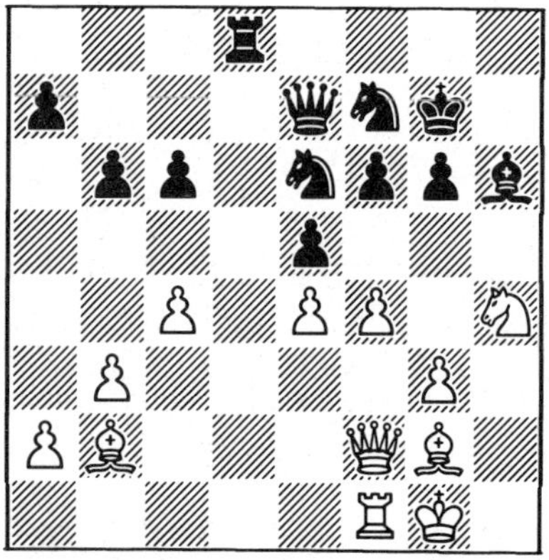

27 ♕e2! White's initiative on the light squares is decisive, whereas Black's attack on the h-file should not be taken too seriously. **27 ... ♕c5+ 28 ♔h1 ♖h8 29 ♕g4 ♘f8 30 ♗h3! ♖h7 31 ♔g2 ♕a5** 31 ... b5!?. **32 ♖f2 ♕e1 33 fxe5 ♘xe5 34 ♗xe5 fxe5 35 ♘f5+!** The final blow. **35 ... ♔g8 36 ♘xh6+ ♖xh6 37 ♕f3 ♘h7 38 ♕f7+ ♔h8 39 ♕e8+ 1-0**

88) **Hartston-Najdorf**
Hastings 1971/72

6 ... ♘bd7 7 ♗b2 e5 8 dxe5 ♘g4 9 c4 ♖e8 10 h3 10 ♘c3!?. **10 ... ♘h6 11 ♕c2?! dxe5 12 ♖d1 f5! 13 ♘bd2 e4 14 ♗xg7 ♔xg7 15 ♘d4 c6 16 ♘f1 ♕f6 17 b4 ♘e5 18 ♖ab1** 18 b5!?. **18 ... ♘hf7 19 ♘d2?!** Black's counterplay on the kingside should have been prevented. 19 f4!. **19 ... a5! 20 a3 axb4 21 axb4 h5! 22 f4?** Too late! **22 ... exf3 23 exf3** 23 ♘2xf3!?. **23 ... ♘g4! 24 ♘f1 ♘e3 25 ♘xe3 ♖xe3 26 ♕d2 f4! 27 gxf4 ♖8a3!** It was probably on this move that Najdorf decided to give up his two rooks for the white queen. **28 ♘c2 ♖ad3 29 ♘xe3** 29 ♕c1 ♖xd1+ 30 ♕xd1 ♖c3 ∓. **29 ... ♖xd2 30 ♖xd2 ♕xf4** The white pawns are very weak. **31 ♖b3 ♘g5 32 ♖bd3 ♗xh3 33 ♘f1 ♕xc4 34 ♖d4? ♘xf3+ 35 ♗xf3 ♕xf1+ 36 ♔h2 ♕xf3 0-1**

89) **Ristić-Marjanović**
Smederevska Palanka 1980

6 ... e5 7 dxe5 ♘fd7 8 ♗g5!? ♕e8 9 ♘c3 h6! 9 ... ♘xe5 10 ♘d5!. **10 ♘d5!?** 10 ♗f6!? ♘xf6 11 exf6 ♗xf6 12 ♘d5 ♗d8! 13 c4 ∞. **10 ... hxg5 11 ♘xc7 ♕d8 12 ♘xa8** 12 ♕xd6 g4 13 e6 fxe6 ∞. 12 exd6 ♘b6 ∞. **12 ... ♘xe5 13 ♘d4?** 13 ♘xg5! ♕xg5 14 ♘c7 ∞. **13 ... a6! 14 c3 ♘bc6 15 f4?** 15 ♕d2!. **15 ... gxf4 16 gxf4 ♘g4**

17 ♘xc6 bxc6 18 ♕d3 18 ♗xc6 ♕h4! 19 h3 ♕g3+ 20 ♗g2 ♕h2+ mate. **18 ... ♗b7 19 ♖ad1 ♗xa8 20 ♕xa6 ♕h4 21 ♖f3 ♕xh2+ 22 ♔f1 c5 23 ♕d3 ♖e8 0-1**

90) **Capablanca-Yates**
Barcelona 1929

6 ... e5 7 dxe5 ♘fd7 8 ♗b2 ♘c6 9 c4 ♘dxe5?! 10 ♘c3 ♖e8 11 ♘xe5! ♘xe5 11 ... dxe5! 12 ♕c1! ♗d7 13 ♖d1 ♕c8 ±. **12 ♕d2 a5?!** Better is 12 ... ♖b8 and ... a6-a5. **13 ♖ac1 ♖b8 14 h3 ♗d7 15 ♘d5 b6?!** 15 ... ♗c6 16 ♕xa5 ♖a8 17 ♕xc7 ♖xa2 18 ♕xd8 ♖xd8 19 ♗xe5 ♗xe5 20 e3 ♗xd5 ±. **16 f4 ♘c6 17 ♗xg7 ♔xg7 18 ♕b2+ f6 19 g4! ♘b4 20 g5 ♘xd5**

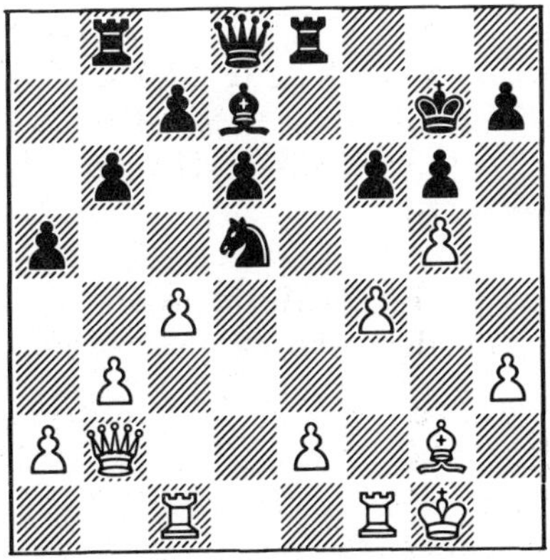

21 cxd5! The new weakness is c7. **21 ... ♖c8 22 e4! c6?** 22 ... ♔f7 23 gxf6 ♕xf6 24 e5!. **23 dxc6 ♖xc6 24 gxf6+ ♔f7 25 e5 ♖xc1 26 ♖xc1 dxe5 27 fxe5 ♕b8 28 ♕d4 ♗f5** 28 ... ♗e6 29 ♖c6 b5 30 ♖xe6!. **29 ♗d5+ ♔f8 30 ♕f4! ♖xe5 31 ♕h6+ ♔e8 32 f7+ 1-0**

91) **Azmaiparashvili-Kochiev**
USSR 1981

6 ... c5 7 ♗b2 cxd4 8 ♘xd4 d5 9 c4 bxc4 10 bxc4 ♕b6 11 ♘b3 11 ♕b3 ♘fd7 12 ♖d1 ♘c5!. **11 ... ♖d8 12 ♕c1 ♗e6** 12 ... ♘c6 13 ♘c3 ♗e6. **13 ♘1d2 ♘c6 14 ♗c3! ♗g4 15 ♖e1 e5 16 ♕b2** 16 ♗xc6?! ♕xc6 17 ♗xe5 ♖e8. **16 ... a5!** 16 ... ♘d7 17 ♘f1, then ♘e3-d5. **17 ♗xc6 ♕xc6 18 ♘xa5?!** 18 ♗xe5!. **18 ... ♕a4 19 ♘db3?!** 19 ♘ab3!. **19 ... ♘d7** 19 ... b6! 20 ♗xc5 ♘c8 21 ♗xg7 ♘xg7 22 ♘b7 ♖d7 23 ♘7c5 bxc5 24 ♘xc5 ♕xc4 25 ♘xd7 ♗xd7 =. **20 ♘xb7 ♖db8 21 ♘d6 ♕c6 22 ♖ad1 ♗h3** 22 ... ♗f8 23 c5! ♗h3! 24 f3 ♘xc5 25 ♗xe5 ♘xb3 26 axb3 ♕c5+ 27 ♕d4 ±. **23 f3 ♕b6+ 24 e3 ♘c5 25 ♗xe5 ♗xe5 26 ♕xe5 ♖xa2!**

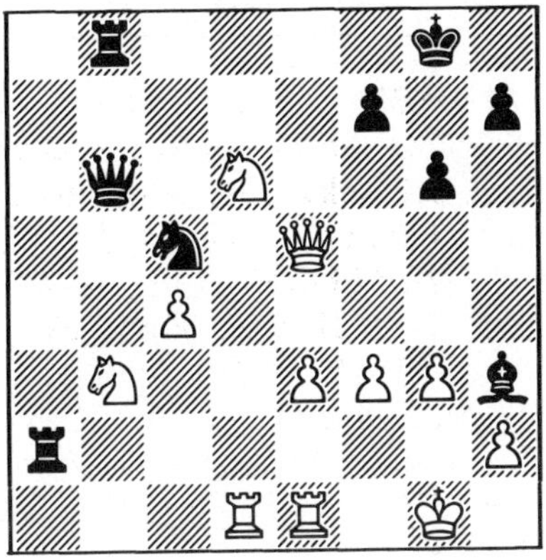

27 ♘xf7! 27 ♘xc5? ♕b2!. **27 ... ♔xf7 28 ♘xc5 ♖g2+?** 28 ... ♕b2! 29 ♕c7+ ♔g8 30 ♖d2! ♕xd2 31 ♕xb8+ ♔f7 =. **29 ♔h1 ♕b2 30 ♕c7+ ♔e8** 30 ... ♔g8 31 g4 ♖xg4 32 ♖d8+ ♖xd8 33 ♕xd8+ ♔f7 34 ♕d7+ ♔f6 35 ♕c6+ ♔g5 36 fxg4 +−. **31 g4 ♖xg4 32 ♕c6+ ♔f8 33 fxg4 1-0**

(Azmaiparashvili, Georgadze)

16 Countering the King's Indian and the Grünfeld: KB Line, rare replies on move 6

1	d4	♘f6
2	♘f3	g6
3	g3	♗g7
4	♗g2	0-0
5	0-0	d6

This chapter is a collection of rarely played quiet variations, usually dealt with quite briefly in textbooks. It will turn out, however, that Black cannot equalise automatically; no wonder that such grandmasters of positional play as Smyslov, Larsen, Andersson, Vaganian etc have a definite liking for these ideas. The main variations are 6 a4, 6 ♖e1, 6 ♘c3, 6 ♘bd2 and 6 miscellaneous.

16.1

6 a4

Rather odd at first glance, the aim of this move is to provoke ... a5 by threatening a5-a6. This sequence may weaken Black's queenside in certain lines. It should be noted that the a- (or h-) pawn quite often plays the role of the battering ram in modern chess; still the appearance of the pawn at such an early stage of the game is highly unusual.

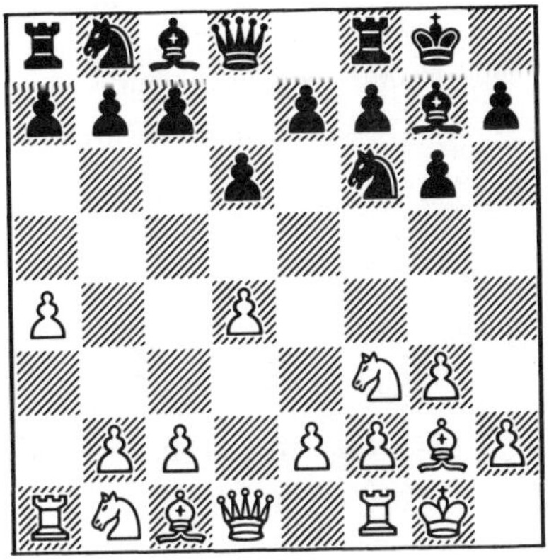

6 ... a5

A natural reply to prevent the further advance of the a-pawn. The following variations are also worth considering:

(a) 6 ... ♘c6 7 ♘c3?! (7 d5 ♘b4 8 ♘c3 c6 9 e4 cxd5 10 exd5 ♗f5 11 ♘d4 ♗g4 12 ♕d2 ♕d7 13 ♖e1 ♖fe8 ∞ – Simagin-Boleslavsky,

USSR 1966) 7 ... e5! 8 dxe5 dxe5 9 ♗g5 h6 10 ♗e3 ♕e7 11 ♕c1 ♔h7 12 ♖d1 ♗e6 13 a5 a6 14 ♘e1 ♖ab8 = Smyslov-Sax, Graz 1984. More consistent is 7 a5!? ♖b8?! (7 ... e5? 8 dxe5 dxe5 9 a6!) 8 b3 e5 9 dxe5 ♘g4 10 ♗b2 ♘gxe5 11 ♘xe5 ♘xe5 12 ♖a2 ♕e7 13 h3 a6 14 c4 ♗e6 ± Varnusz-Perhisco, Pula 1985.

(b) 6 ... ♘a6 7 ♘c3 c5 8 d5 e6 9 dxe6 ♗xe6 10 ♘g5! ♗c8 11 e4 h6 12 ♘f3 ♘b4 13 ♗f4! d5 14 exd5 ♘bxd5 15 ♘xd5 ♘xd5 16 ♗e5 ♖e8 17 ♗xg7 ♔xg7 18 ♕d2 ± Varnusz-Jadoul, Budapest 1985.

Maybe Black's best choice is 6 ... c5 7 d5 and either 7 ... ♘a6 or 7 ... ♗g4 with a similar position to that of the classic Benoni, the difference resting in the posting of White's King's bishop. Nevertheless, there is no example to be found of this in master play.

7 b3!

More vigorous than 7 ♘bd2 ♘c6 8 e4 ♘d7 9 ♘c4 e5 = or 7 ♘c3 c6 8 e4 ♗g4, etc.

7 ... ♘e4

Should Black follow the 7 ... c5 8 ♗b2 cxd4 9 ♘xd4 d5 variation (15.3), with a pawn move inserted, he would have difficulties owing to the b5 square. 7 ... ♘c6 8 ♗b2 ♗f5 9 ♘h4! gives a cramped game (as was seen in Illustrative Game No 85), or leads to 8 ... e5 9 dxe5 ♘g4 10 ♘a3 ♘gxe5 11 ♘xe5 ♘xe5 12 ♔h1! ♖e8 13 ♘b5 ♕e7 14 f4 ± Reshevsky-Feuerstein, Illustrative Game No 92.

7 ... c6 with a compressed yet solid game is to be considered, for example 8 ♗b2 ♘bd7 9 ♘bd2 ♕c7 10 e4 e5 11 dxe5 dxe5 12 ♖e1 ± ♖d8 13 ♘c4 ♘e8 14 ♕e2 b6 15 ♖ad1 ♗a6 16 ♗h3 ♘f8 17 ♖xd8 ♖xd8 18 ♗xe5! ± Galliamova-Akopian, Oakham 1990.

8	**♗b2**	**c5**
9	**♕c1**	**♘a6**
10	**♖d1**	**cxd4**
11	**♗xd4**	**♗xd4**
12	**♘xd4**	**♘ac5**
13	**♕e3**	**♘f6**

After 13 ... f5?! 14 ♘d2 White can get rid of the e4 knight, and has a slight advantage owing to the weakness of the e7 and e6 squares.

14	**♘c3**	**♗d7**
15	**♕d2!**	**♕b6**
16	**e4**	**♖fd8**
17	**♘d5**	

White has a significant advantage in space. Vaganian-Chiburdanidze, USSR 1982.

16.2

6 ♖e1

Threatening e2-e4 without letting the opponent know about the deployment of the queen's knight.

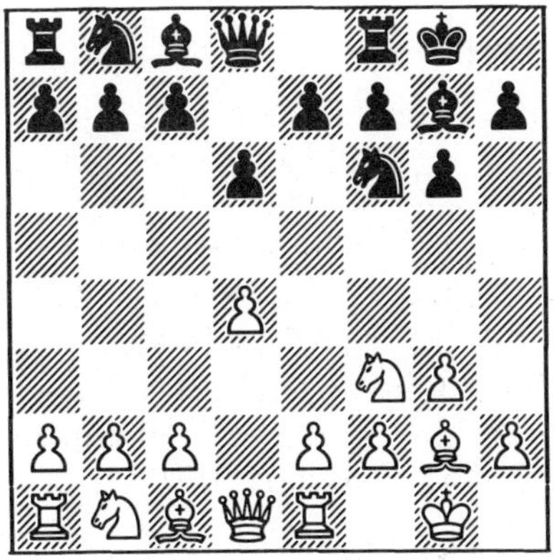

6 ... ♘bd7

(a) 6 ... d5 leads to the Neo-Grünfeld or the variations of Chapter 5 with an extra ♖e1 tempo for White – but that is not a great achievement.

(b) 6 ... ♘c6 7 d5 (7 e4 e5 8 c3 ♗g4 Panno-Quinteros, Manila 1976; 9 d5 ♘e7 10 h3 ±) 7 ... ♘b4 8 e4 e6 9 ♘c3 exd5 10 exd5 ♗g4 11 a3 ♘a6 12 h3 ♗xf3 13 ♕xf3 ♘c5 14 ♗d2 ♘cd7 15 ♕d3 ♘e5 16 ♕f1 ♘h5 17 g4 ♘f6 18 f4 ♘ed7 ± Makarov-Rishkin, USSR 1984.

(c) 6 ... c5 7 c3 (7 c4 ♘c6 8 ♘c3 cxd4 9 ♘xd4 ♘xd4 10 ♕xd4 ♗e6 = Andersson-Christiansen, Illustrative Game No 93. This is actually a variation of the English Opening with an unusually early ♖e1. 7 dxc5 dxc5 8 ♕xd8 ♖xd8 9 c3 – 9 ♘e5?! ♘a6 10 c3 ♘d5! 11 ♘c4 ♗e6 12 ♘ba3 ♖d7! 13 ♖b1 ♖ad8 14 e4? ♘bd4! ∓ Andersson-Quinteros, Mar del Plata 1981 – 9 ... ♗e6?! 10 ♘g5! ♗d5 11 e4 ♗c6 12 e5 ♗xg2 13 exf6 exf6 14 ♔xg2 fxg5 15 ♗xg5 f6 16 ♗e3 b6 17 ♘a3 ♘c6 18 ♘c4 ♗f8 19 a4 ± Andersson-Nijboer, Wijk aan Zee 1990. 7 e4!? is the 'Sicilian' move; White has a wide choice!) 7 ... ♗f5 (7 ... ♘c6!? 8 dxc5 dxc5 9 ♖xd8 ♕xd8 10 ♗e3 ♘d7 11 ♖d1 ♖e8 ± Varnusz-Széll, Budapest 1991) 8 dxc5 dxc5 9 ♕a4 ♗e4 (Preventing 10 ♕h4) 10 ♗g5 ♕b6 11 ♘bd2 (11 ♗xf6 ♗c6!) 11 ... ♗c6 12 ♕h4 ♕xb2 13 e4 ♘bd7 14 e5 ♘d5 15 ♗h6 ♘xc3 16 ♘g5 ♘e2+ ∞ Foigel-Ivanchuk, USSR 1984.

(d) 6 ... ♘e4!? 7 ♘bd2 (7 c4; 7 ♘fd2) 7 ... f5 8 c4 ♘c6 9 d5 ♘xd2 10 ♗xd2 ♘e5 11 ♕c2 (11 ♘xe5?!) 11 ... c5 12 dxc6 ♘xc6 13 ♗e3 e5 = Amura-Klimova, Azov 1990.

7 e4 e5
8 dxe5

8 ♘c3 is the Pirc Defence. Recent examples: 8 ... ♖e8 9 h3 exd4 10 ♘xd4 ♘c5 11 a4 ♗d7?! 12 a5 ± Barbero-Ernst, Lugano 1987, or 8 ... c6 9 a4 a5 (9 exd4!? 10 ♘xd4 a5 11 h3 ♘c5 12 ♗f4! ♖e8 13 ♕d2 ♕b6 Varnusz-I.Földi, Budapest 1991; 14 ♗xd6!?, possibly ±) 10 h3 ♖e8 11 ♗e3 exd4 12 ♗xd4! ♘f8 13 ♕d3 d5?! 14 ♗xf6 ± Varnusz-Balogh, Budapest 1987.

8 ... dxe5
9 b3

9 ♘c3 b6 10 ♕e2 ♗b7 = Grau-Czerniak, Buenos Aires 1939.

9 ... ♖e8

Very exciting is 9 ... ♘xe4!? 10 ♖xe4 ♘c5 11 ♕xd8? ♖xd8 12 ♘fd2 ♘xe4 13 ♗xe4 f5 14 ♗g2 e4 ∓ Przepiorka–Wojciechowski, Poland 1937; 11 ♘fd2! ♘xe4 12 ♗xe4 f5 ∞ (±).

10	**♗b2**	**♕e7**
11	**♘a3**	**♘b6**
12	**♕d2**	**c6**
13	**♕a5!?**	**♘fd7**
14	**♘d2**	**♗f8**
15	**♖ad1**	**♕e6**

White's advantage in space is tiny. Kärner-Gavrikov, Tallinn 1985.

16.3

6 ♘c3

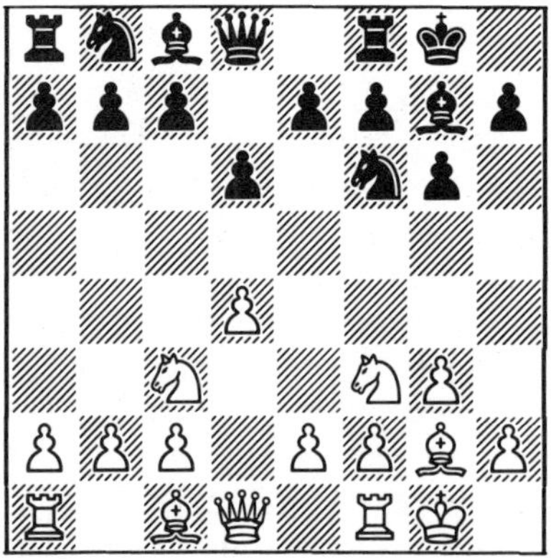

This line often transposes into the Pirc.

6 ... ♘bd7

(a) 6 ... d5 7 ♗g5 (7 ♘e5 c6 8 e4 dxe4 9 ♘xe4 ♘xe4 10 ♗xe4 ♗h3 = Ivkov) 7 ... c6 8 ♖e1 ♘e4 (8 ... ♕b6 9 ♖b1 ♗f5 10 ♘h4 ♗e6 11 ♘a4 ± Kluger-Haág, Budapest 1968) 9 ♘xe4 dxe4 10 ♘d2! e3 11 ♗xe3 ♗xd4 12 ♗xd4 ♕xd4 13 c3 ♕c5 14 ♘e4 ♕b6 15 ♕d2 ♗f5 16 ♘g5 ± Spassky-Bronstein, Illustrative Game No 94.

(b) 6 ... ♘c6 7 d5 ♘b8 leads to the Pirc Defence, or 7 ... ♘a5! 8 e4 c6 9 ♖e1 ♗g4 10 h3 ♗xf3 11 ♕xf3 ♖c8 12 ♕e2 a6 13 dxc6 ♘xc6 14 ♗e3 ♘d7 = Smyslov-Speelman, Subotica 1987.

(c) 6 ... c6 7 a4 ♗f5 8 ♘h4 ♗d7 9 e4 e5 10 ♘f3 ♖e8 11 a5 ♘a6 12 h3 b5 13 axb6 axb6 14 dxe5 dxe5 15 ♗g5 ♕c7 = Langeweg-Westerinen, Dortmund 1975; 11 h3!.

7 b3

7 e4 is already the Pirc. (1 e4 d6 2 d4 ♘f6 3 ♘c3 g6 4 g3 ♗g7 5 ♗g2 0-0 6 ♘f3 ♘bd7 7 0-0)

7 ... ♖e8

7 ... e5 8 dxe5 dxe5 9 e4 ♖e8 10 ♗a3?! = Kholmov-Fischer, Illustrative Game No 95.

8	**a4**	**e5**
9	**dxe5**	**dxe5**
10	**e4**	**♘c5**
11	**♕e2**	**c6**

Chances are equal.

16.4

6 ♘bd2

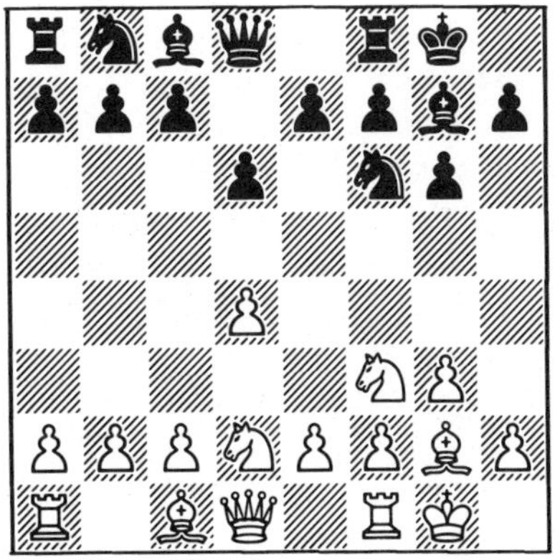

The threat is once again e2-e4 but the possibility of b3 and ♗b2 is also maintained. What is more, on the natural 6 ... c5 Black will be forced into a special variation.

16.41

6 ... c5

(a) 6 ... d5 is definitely bad since it is a Neo-Grünfeld with a tempo lost for Black.

(b) 6 ... ♖e8 7 e4 e5 8 ♖e1 ♘c6 9 ♘b3 (9 c3!?) 9 ... exd4 10 ♘fxd4 ♗d7 11 c4 a5 12 a4 ♘xd4 13 ♘xd4 ♘g4 14 ♘c2 ♘e5 15 ♘e3 ± Pirc-Stahlberg, England 1951.

(c) 6 ... ♘bd7 7 b3 c5 8 e3 ♕c7 9 ♗b2 ♖b8 10 c4 cxd4 11 exd4 b5 = Nimzowitsch-Bogoljubow, Baden-Baden 1925; or 7 e4 ♘e8?! 8 ♕e2 c5 9 d5 e6 10 dxe6 fxe6 11 ♖d1! b6 12 ♘f1 ♗b7 13 ♘g5 ♕e7 14 f4! h6 15 ♘f3 ♕f7 16 c3 ♔h7 17 g4! d5 18 e5 ♖c8 19 ♘g3 ± Varnusz-Apatóczky, Budapest 1987. A better defence to 7 e4 is 7 ... e5 8 dxe5 dxe5 9 b3 ♕e7 10 a4 a5 11 ♗a3 ♘c5 12 ♖e1 ♖d8 13 ♕e2 b6 14 ♘c4 ♗a6 = (±) Todorčević-Mäki, Haifa 1989.

7	**dxc5**	**dxc5**
8	**e4**	

8 c3 ♕c7 (8 ... ♘c6! 9 ♕a4!?) 9 ♘c4 ♗e6 10 ♗f4 ♕c8 11 ♘ce5 ± Bronstein-Gipslis, USSR 1963.

8	**...**	**♘c6**
9	**c3**	**h6**

9 ... ♗g4 (9 ... ♕d3!?) 10 h3 ♗xf3 11 ♕xf3 ♘e5 12 ♕e3 ♘fd7 13 f4 ± Cuderman-Suvalić, Yugoslavia 1961; 9 ... b6 10 ♕e2 ♘e8 11 ♖d1 ♘c7 12 ♘c4 ♕e8 13 ♘e3 ± Knezević-Bertok, Yugoslavia 1977.

10	**♕e2**	**♗e6**
11	**♘e1**	**♕b6**
12	**h3**	**♖ad8**

White's chances are slightly better. Petrosian-Reshevsky, Illustrative Game No 96.

16.42

6	**...**	**♘c6**
7	**♘c4**	

(a) 7 c3 e5 8 dxe5 dxe5 9 ♘b3 (9 ♘c4 ♕e7 10 a4 a5 11 ♘fd2 e4 12 ♕c2 ♖e8 13 b3 ♗g4 14 ♗a3 ♕e6 15 ♖fe1 ♗h3 16 ♗h1 h5 ∞ Todorčević-Marin, Szirák 1987) 9

... ♕e7 10 ♗e3 ♖d8 11 ♕c1 e4! 12 ♘fd4 ♘e5 13 ♗g5 ♘c4 = Stahlberg-Geller, Zürich 1953.

(b) 7 e4 e5 (7 ... ♗g4 8 d5 ♘e5 9 h3 ♘xf3+ 10 ♘xf3 ♗xf3 11 ♕xf3 ♘d7 12 a4!? c6 13 a5 ♕c7 14 ♕e2 cxd5 15 exd5 ♘e5 16 ♖a2! ± Larsen-Züger, New York 1986) 8 c3 ♗g4 9 ♕c2 exd4! 10 ♘xd4 ♖e8 11 h3 ♗d7 12 ♖e1 ♕c8 13 ♔h2 ♖e5!? ∞ Ledger-Gallagher, Hastings 1989/90.

7 ... ♗e6

7 ... ♗f5 8 c3 ♕c8 9 ♖e1 ♗h3 10 ♗h1 ±.

8 ♘e3

8 b3?! ♕c8 9 ♖e1 ♗xc4 10 bxc4 ♘a5 11 ♕d3 c5 ∓.

8 ... ♗d7
9 c4

9 d5 ♘b4 (9 ... ♘a5?! 10 b4 ♘e4 11 ♗a3) 10 c4 c6 ∞.

9 ... e5
10 d5 ♘e7
11 c5 ♘e8
12 ♘c4 f5

12 ... ♗b5!?.

13 ♕b3 e4
14 ♘g5 h6

The game is approximately level – Shabalov-W.Watson, Belgrade 1988.

16.5

Miscellaneous on move 6:

(a) 6 ♘e1 ♘c6 7 d5 ♘e5 8 ♘d3 ♘xd3 9 cxd3 ♗g4 10 ♘c3 ♕d7 = Barcza-Bronstein, Amsterdam 1954.

(b) 6 c3 ♘c6?! 7 ♘a3 a6 8 ♗f4 ♘d5 9 ♗d2 ♘b6 10 ♕c1 e5 11 dxe5 dxe5 12 ♗h6 ♕e7 Barcza-Petrosian, Bucharest 1953. Better is 7 ♘bd2 e5 8 dxe5 dxe5 9 ♕c2 ♕e7 10 e4 a5 11 a4 b6 12 b3 ♖d8 13 ♗a3 ♕e8 14 ♖fe1 ♗f8 15 ♗xf8 ♕xf8 16 ♘c4 ± Todorčević-De la Villa, Szirák 1987.

ILLUSTRATIVE GAMES

1 d4 ♘f6 2 ♘f3 g6 3 g3 ♗g7 4 ♗g2 0-0 5 0-0 d6

92) **Reshevsky-Feuerstein**
New York 1957/58

6 a4 a5 7 b3 ♘c6 8 ♗b2 e5 9 dxe5 ♘g4 10 ♘a3 ♘gxe5 11 ♘xe5 ♘xe5 Such positions do not allow of recapturing with the pawn because of 12 ♘b5!. **12 ♔h1 ♖e8 13 ♘b5 ♕e7 14 f4** White has to get rid of this knight to seize the initiative. **14 ... ♘c6** 14 ... ♘g4 15 ♗xg7 ♔xg7 16 e4!. **15 ♗xg7 ♔xg7 16 e4 f5! 17 ♖e1 ♕f7 18 ♕d2 fxe4 19 ♗xe4 ♗e6** 19 ... ♗f5 20 ♗d5 ♕d7 21 ♕c3+ ♔h6!?. The threat after the text move is 20 ... d5. **20 c4 ♖ab8!** Releasing the knight! **21 ♖e3! ♘b4 22 ♘c3 ♗f5?** 22 ... b6 23 ♖ae1 ♗d7 ±. **23 ♖ae1 ♗d7 24**

♘d5! ♘xd5 25 ♗xd5 ♗c6? 25 ... ♕f6 26 ♕xa5 ±.

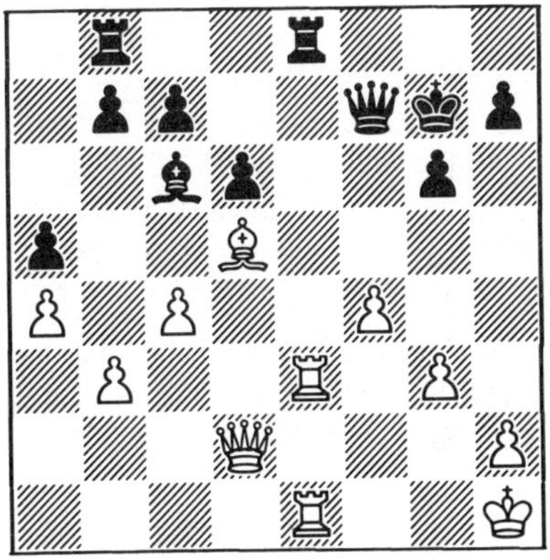

26 ♕d4+! 1-0

26 ... ♔f8 27 ♕h8+ ♕g8 28 ♕xg8+ mate, 26 ... ♕f6 27 ♖e7+! and 26 ... ♔h6 27 g4! are all lethal.

93) Andersson-Christiansen
Mar del Plata 1981

6 ♖e1 d5?! 7 c4 c6 8 cxd5 cxd5 A well-known position from the Neo-Grünfeld, with an extra tempo (♖e1) for White. But how much is it worth in an actual game? **9 ♘e5 ♘g4?!** 9 ... b6!?, 9 ... e6!?. **10 ♘xg4 ♗xg4 11 ♘c3 ♘c6** 11 ... ♗e6!?. **12 ♘xd5 ♘xd4 13 ♗e3** As it turns out, the e1 rook has an important function in defending the e2 pawn. **13 ... ♘c6?** 13 ... e5!?. **14 ♕b3 ♖b8 15 ♕a3! ♖e8** (15 ... e6 16 ♘c3! and ♖ad1 ±) **16 ♖ad1 ♕c8 17 ♖c1 ♗h3**

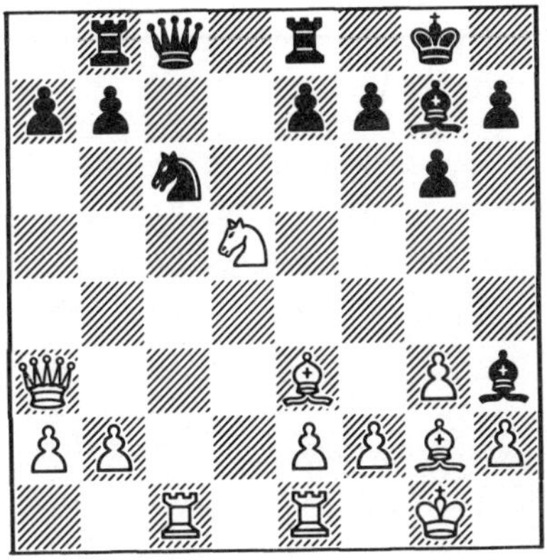

18 ♖xc6! Simplifying into a probably winning position. **18 ... bxc6 19 ♘xe7+ ♖xe7 20 ♕xe7 ♗xg2 21 ♔xg2 ♖b7** 21 ... ♖xb2 22 ♖d1 ±/+−. **22 ♕d6 ♖xb2 23 ♖d1 h5** 23 ... ♗f8 24 ♕f6 +−; 23 ... ♖xa2 24 ♕d8+ +−. **24 ♕e7 ♕e6** 24 ... ♕f5 25 ♖d8+ ♔h7 26 h4 ♖xe2 27 ♕e8 g5 28 ♕g8+ ♔g6 29 ♖d6+ f6 30 ♕e8+ etc. **25 ♖d8+ ♔h7 26 ♕xe6 fxe6 27 ♖d7 e5** The only move. **28 ♖xa7 ♖xe2 29 a4 ♔g8 30 a5 ♗f8 31 a6 c5 32 ♖c7 ♖a2 33 a7 e4 34 ♔h3 1-0**

(Larsen's and Minev's notes included)

94) Spassky-Bronstein
Moscow 1961

6 ♘c3 d5?! 7 ♗g5! c6 8 ♖e1! ♘e4 9 ♘xe4 dxe4 10 ♘d2! e3 11 ♗xe3 ♗xd4 12 ♗xd4 ♕xd4 13 c3 ♕c5 14 ♘e4 ♕b6 15 ♕d2 ♗f5 16

♘g5! ♖d8? Black overlooks the coming combination. 16 ... ♘a6 17 e4 ♖ad8 18 ♕f4 ♗c8 19 ♖e2, or 19 ♕h4 h5, are both playable here. **17 ♕f4 e5!?** The point of Black's strategy. Incidentally, 18 e4 and 18 ♘xf7 were threatened. **18 ♕xe5 h6 19 e4! ♗c8** 19 ... ♘d7 20 ♕e7.

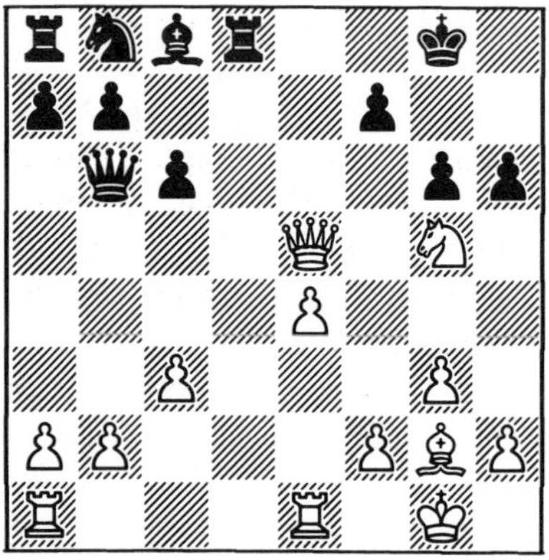

20 ♘xf7!! The ever so elegant destroying sacrifice. **20 ... ♔xf7 21 ♖e3 ♔g8** Parries the dual threats: 22 ♕f3+ and 22 ♗f1. **22 ♗f1 ♖d7 23 ♕e8+ ♔g7 14 ♖f3 ♕c5 25 ♖d1! h5 26 ♖xd7+ ♘xd7 27 ♖f7+ ♔h6 28 ♕h8+ ♔g5 29 h4+ 1-0**

95) **Kholmov-Fischer**
Skopje 1967

6 ♘c3 ♘bd7 7 b3 e5 8 dxe5 dxe5 9 e4 ♖e8 10 ♗a3 10 a4 or 10 ♗b2 are worth considering here. **10 ...c6 11 ♗d6?** The seemingly active bishop is going to get into trouble here. **11 ... ♕a5! 12 ♕d3** 12 a3!?

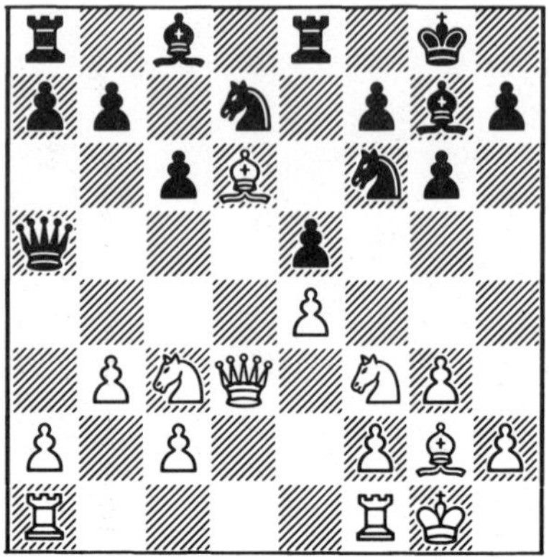

12 ... ♖e6! 13 b4 13 ♘g5? ♖xd6 14 ♕xd6 h6!. **13 ... ♕a3! 14 ♗c7 ♕xb4 15 ♖ab1 ♕e7!** 15 ... ♕f8? 16 ♘g5! and 17 ♗d6 ±. **16 ♖fd1 ♘e8 17 ♗a5 ♖d6 18 ♕e2 ♖xd1+ 19 ♕xd1 ♗f8 20 ♘d2 ♕a3! 21 ♘c4 ♕c5 22 ♗f1 b5 23 ♘d2** 23 ♗b4 ♕d4!. **23 ... ♕a3!** What an indefatigable queen! **24 ♘b3 ♘c5 25 ♗xb5** 25 ♗d8 ♘e6 26 ♗a5 ♘d6 -+. **25 ... cxb5 26 ♘xb5 ♕a4 27 ♘xc5** 27 ♕d5 ♕xe4!. **27 ... ♕xa5 28 ♕d5 ♖b8 29 a4 ♗h3 30 ♕xe5 ♖c8 31 ♘d3 ♕xa4 32 ♘e1 a6 0-1**

96) **Petrosian-Reshevsky**
Zürich 1953

6 ♘bd2 c5 7 dxc5 dxc5 8 e4 ♘c6 The actual order of moves was 1 ♘f3 ♘f6 2 g3 g6 3 ♗g2 ♗g7 4 0-0 0-0 5 d3 d5 6 ♘bd2 c5 7 e4 dxe4 8 dxe4 ♘c6. **9 c3 h6 10 ♕e2 ♗e6**

11 ♘e1! ♕b6 12 h3 ♖ad8 13 ♔h2

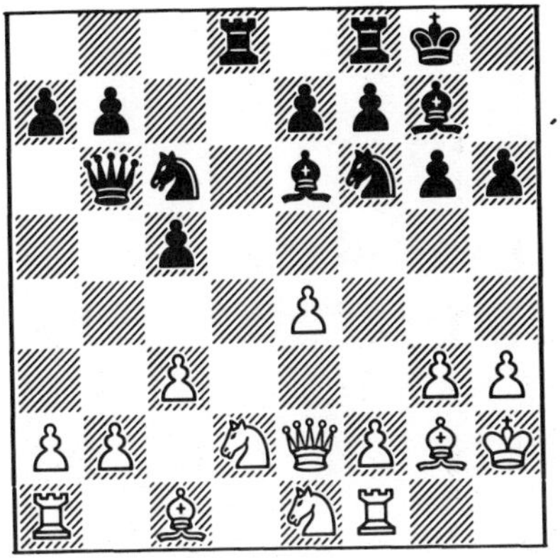

A weird position: Black has developed his pieces harmoniously while those of White are packed together on the first and second ranks. It is, however, White whose chances are more promising! Black has no suitable plan at hand whereas White gets an active game after playing f4. **13 ... ♘h7 14 f4 ♘a5 15 ♘ef3 ♗d7!** Introducing a correct re-grouping. **16 ♖e1 ♕c7 17 ♘f1 b6 18 ♘e3 ♗c6 19 ♘g4 ♘f6 20 ♘f2** Petrosian was the grandmaster of manoeuvring. **20 ... ♗b7 21 e5 ♘h7 22 h4 h5 23 f5! ♕d7 24 e6** 24 fxg6! fxg6 25 ♗f4 ±. **24 ... ♕d5 25 exf7+ ♕xf7 26 fxg6 ♕xg6 27 ♘g5** 27 ♗f4!?. **27 ... ♗xg2 28 ♔xg2 e5 29 ♕e4 ♖f5! 30 ♘xh7 ♔xh7 ½-½**

Part III: Countering the Benoni and the Benko Gambit 1 d4 ♘f6 2 ♘f3 c5 3 d5

Introduction to Chapters 17-20

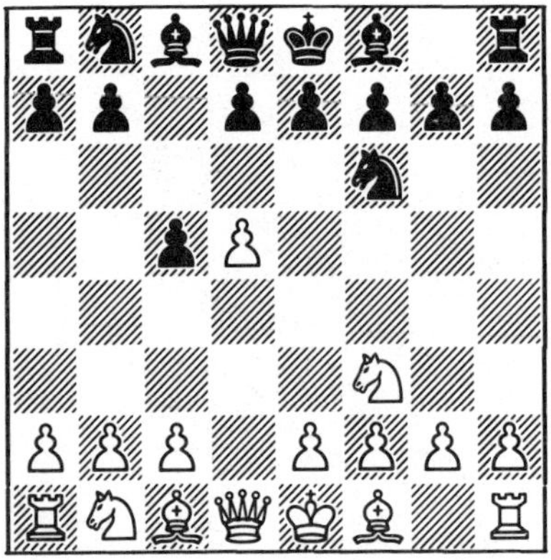

This section is also of great practical importance, as both the Benoni and the Benko Gambit appear frequently in tournament play.

Our move order permits White to avoid the heavily analysed lines of both defences. The connecting principle is again White's holding back of his c-pawn, although in other respects we are dealing with three by and large distinct systems: 3 ... e6 4 ♘c3, 3 ... g6 4 ♘c3 and 3 ... b5 4 ♗g5.

Of these the second is the most commonly encountered in practice, since it can arise via transposition from several openings.

17 Countering the Benoni and the Benko Gambit: Fighting the Modern Benoni

1	d4	♘f6
2	♘f3	c5
3	d5	e6
4	♘c3	

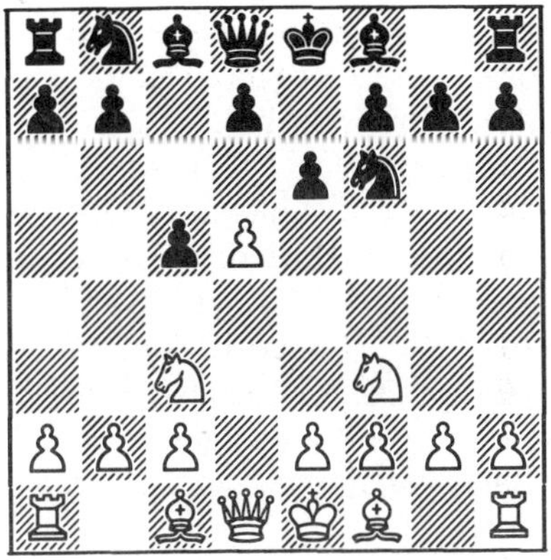

It is no exaggeration to say that after this particular sequence the Benoni gives a rather hazardous, or at least uncomfortable, game to Black. He will lack the quick, tactical counterplay he is used to in the main variations.

White's idea is to occupy d5 with a piece and to develop his forces as quickly as possible. 4 ... b5 and 4 ... exd5 are the main lines here. 4 ... a6 is a bit slow; 5 e4 b5 6 e5 b4 7 dxe6 dxe6 8 ♕xd8+ ♔xd8 9 ♘b1 ♘d5 10 ♘bd2 ♘d7 11 g3 h6 12 ♗g2 ♖b8 13 0-0 g5 14 ♘c4 ♗g7 15 ♖e1 ± Vaganian-Suba, Tallinn 1983.

17.1

4 ... b5

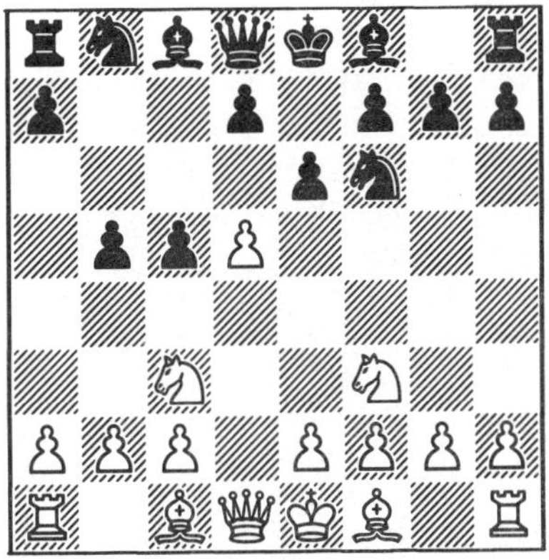

The idea resembles that of the Blumenfeld Counter-Gambit; Black offers a pawn to take hold of the centre. White's play, however, is superior to that of the Blumenfeld because he has a better development.

5 dxe6

5 ♗g5?! b4 6 ♘e4 ♗b7 7 c4 bxc3 8 ♗xf6 (8 ♘xc3? ♗xd5! ∓ – Figler-Sideif Zade, Illustrative Game No 98) 8 ... gxf6 9 ♘xc3 f5! (9 ... ♕a5? 10 e4 ♖g8 11 ♘d2 ± Varnusz-Perényi, Budapest 1982) 10 e3 ♗g7 11 ♗c4 0-0 12 0-0 ♘a6 ∓ Varnusz-Plachetka, Eger 1984.

5 ... fxe6
6 ♘xb5 d5
7 e4!?

7 e3 ♘c6 8 c4 (8 ♗e2 a6 9 ♘c3 d4 ∞) 8 ... ♖b8?! 9 ♗e2 a6 10 cxd5 exd5 11 ♘c3 d4 12 ♘a4 ♗f5 13 exd4 cxd4 14 ♗c4 ♗b4+ 15 ♗d2 ♕e7+ 16 ♕e2 ♗e4! 17 0-0 Plachetka-Podzielny, Trnava 1984; 17 ... ♗xf3! 18 ♕xf3 ♘e5 19 ♕b3! ♘xc4 20 ♖fe1 ♘e5 21 ♗xb4 ♖xb4 22 ♖xe5! ♖xb3 23 ♖xe7+ ♔xe7 24 axb3 ± (Plachetka).

7 ... ♘xe4

7 ... a6 (7 ... d4 8 ♗f4 ♕a5+ 9 ♕d2 ±) 8 e5 ♘e4 9 ♘c3 ±.

8 ♗f4 ♘a6?!

8 ... ♗d6 9 ♘xd6+ ♘xd6 10 ♗d3 0-0 11 ♗g3 ±.

9 ♗d3 ♕a5+!?
10 ♘d2! ♘f6
11 0-0! ♗e7

Accepting the offer is lethal: 11 ... c4? 12 ♘xc4 dxc4 13 ♗xc4 and the threats are ♕f3 and ♖e1+.

12 c4! 0-0
13 ♕e2 ±

Varnusz-S.Faragó, Illustrative Game No 99.

17.2

4 ... exd5

Black treats the opening in a Benoni-like way.

5 ♘xd5

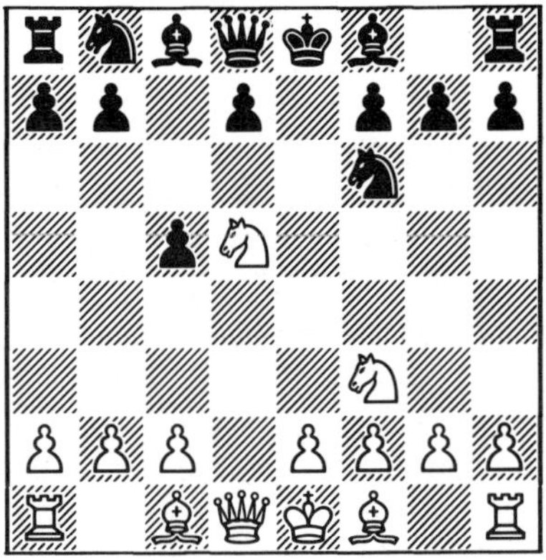

White's goal is the occupation of d5 with a piece.

5 ... ♘xd5

5 ... ♘c6 6 e4 d6 7 ♗c4 ♗e7 8 0-0 0-0 9 ♗f4 ♘xd5 10 ♗xd5 ♕b6 11 ♖b1 ♘b4 12 ♗b3 ♕a6 13 a3 ♘c6 14 ♗d5 ♗g4 15 c3 ± Lerner-Yap, Moscow 1986.

6 ♕xd5 ♘c6

6 ... d6 7 ♘g5!? (7 e4!? ♘c6 8 ♘g5 ♕c7 9 ♗c4 ♘e5 10 ♗b5+

♗d7 11 ♗xd7+ ♕xd7 12 ♗f4 ♘c6 13 0-0-0 h6 14 ♘f3 0-0-0 ± Hodgson-Armas, Wijk aan Zee 1989) 7 ... ♕f6 (7 ... ♕e7 8 ♗f4 ♗e6 9 ♘xe6 fxe6 10 ♕d2 d5 11 e4! ± Morovic-Alburt, Illustrative Game No 100) 8 ♕e4+ ♗e7 9 ♘xh7 ♕f5 10 ♘g5 ♕xe4 11 ♘xe4 ♗f5 ∞. Better is 7 ♗f4 ♘c6 8 ♘g5 ♕f6 9 ♕e4+ (9 ♗xd6? ♗e6! ∓) 9 ... ♗e7 10 0-0-0 ♗f5?! (10 ... h6 11 ♘f3 0-0 ∞) Khomiakov-Bangiev, USSR 1987; 11 ♕a4! ±.

6 ... ♗e7 7 ♗g5 (7 e4 ♘c6 8 c3 d6 9 ♗c4 ♗e6 10 ♕d3 ± Michel-Speelman, Semmering 1926; or 7 ... d6 8 ♗c4 0-0 9 ♕h5 ♕e8 10 ♗g5 ♗xg5 11 ♘xg5 h6 12 h4 ♘d7 13 0-0-0 ♘f6 14 ♗xf7+ ♖xf7 15 ♕xf7+ ♕xf7 16 ♘xf7 ♔xf7 17 ♖xd6 ♘xe4?! – 17 ... ♗e6 ∞ ± – 18 ♖d8 b6 19 f3 ± Dautov-Löffler, Dresden 1989) 7 ... 0-0 8 0-0-0 ♘c6 9 a3 h6 (9 ... b5? 10 e3 ♖b8 11 11 ♗d3 c4 12 ♗xh7+! 1-0 – Shereshevsky-Gusev, USSR 1977 – or 10 ♗xe7 ♕xe7 11 e3 ♖b8 12 ♗d3 b4? 13 ♗xh7+ 1-0 – Varnusz-Bodnár, Budapest 1989) 10 ♗e3 ± or 10 ♗f4 ±.

7 e4

7 ♗g5!? ♕b6 8 ♘e5! ♘xe5 9 ♕xe5+ ♕e6 10 ♕c7 f6 11 ♗f4 ♗e7 12 e3 d5 (12 ... 0-0!?) 13 ♗b5+ ♔f7 14 0-0-0 a6 15 ♗e2 Gheorghiu-Sindik, Zürich 1984; 15 ... ♖d8 16 c4 ±. Instead 7 ... ♗e7 8 0-0-0 (8 a3 ±) 8 ... ♘b4!? (8 ... 0-0 9 a3 h6 10 ♗f4 ±) 9 ♕e5!? ♘xa2+?! (9 ... f6 10 ♗xf6 gxf6 11 ♕h5+ ♔f8 12 ♘h4, given by the *Chess Informant* No 33, is incredibly complicated but probably playable for Black) 10 ♔b1 ♘c3+ 11 ♕xc3 ♗xg5 12 ♕e5+ ♗e7 13 ♕xg7 ♗f6 14 ♕g3 ♕b6 15 ♘e5 ♕e6 16 ♘g4 ± Dizdar-Rajković, Yugoslavia 1982.

7 ... d6

One of the critical positions in this line. Interesting is 7 ... ♘b4!? 8 ♕b3 (8 ♕d1 d5!?) 8 ... d5 9 exd5 (9 c3!?) 9 ... ♕xd5 10 ♗c4 ♕e4+ etc., ∞ Another line is 7 ... ♗e7 8 ♗c4! 0-0 9 c3 d6 10 ♕h5 ♗e6 11 ♗xe6 fxe6 12 h4!? (12 ♗e3 ±) 12 ... ♕e8 13 ♕xe8 (13 ♕g4!?) 13 ... ♖fxe8 (Schandorff-Rogers, Denmark 1989) 14 ♗e3 b5 15 0-0-0 ±.

8 ♘g5!

8 ♗c4 ♗e6 9 ♕d3 ♗e7 10 c3 0-0 11 0-0 ♔h8 12 ♗f4 ♕b6 13 ♖ab1 ♖ad8 14 ♖fd1 ♗g4 = Stean-Sax, Smederevska Palanka 1982.

8 ... ♕d7!

8 ... ♕c7?! 9 ♗c4 ♘e5 10 ♗b5+ ♗d7 (10 ... ♘c6? 11 ♘xf7! ♕a5+ 12 ♗d2 ♕xb5 13 ♘xh8 +− Sideif Zade-Tseshkovsky, USSR 1985) 11 ♗xd7+ ♕xd7 12 f4 ♘c6 13 c3 h6 14 ♘f3 ±.

9 c3

9 ♗b5 a6 10 ♘xf7 axb5 11 ♘xh8 ∞.

9 ... h6
10 ♘f3 ♗e7
11 ♗c4 0-0
12 0-0 ±

(Stoica)

17.3

4 ... d6

5 e4

5 dxe6 ♗xe6 6 e4 ♘c6 7 ♗b5 ♗e7 8 e5 dxe5 9 ♕xd8+ ♔xd8 10 ♗xc6 bxc6 11 ♘xe5 ♔c7 ± Levitina-Maksimović, Thessaloniki 1988.

5 ... exd5

5 ... a6 6 dxe6 ♗xe6 (6 ... fxe6? 7 e5!) 7 ♘g5 b5 8 ♘xe6 fxe6 9 g3! ♘c6 (9 ... b4 10 ♘e2 ♘xe4 11 ♗g2 d5 12 ♘f4 ♕f6 13 0-0 ±) 10 ♗g2 ♕c7 11 0-0 ♗e7 12 ♘e2 ♔f7 13 ♘f4 ♖he8 14 a4 b4 15 g4 ± Speelman-Suba, Illustrative Game No 97.

6 exd5 ♗e7
7 ♗b5+

7 ♗e2 0-0 8 0-0 b6?! (8 ... ♗g4 ±) 9 ♖e1 ♘a6 10 ♗b5! ♘b8 11 ♕e2! a6 12 ♕xe7 ♕xe7 13 ♖xe7 axb5 14 ♗g5 ♘bd7 15 ♘xb5 ♘xd5 16 ♘xd6! ± Chandler-Tseitlin, Palma de Mallorca 1989.

7 ... ♗d7

7 ... ♘bd7 8 a4!.

8 a4 0-0
9 0-0 ♘a6
10 ♗xa6! bxa6
11 b3 ♗f5
12 ♘d2 ♘d7
13 ♘c4 ♗f6
14 ♗b2

And White has the better chances: 14 ... ♘b6 15 ♘e3 ♗g6 16 ♕d2 ♖e8 17 a5 ± (Vaganian-Agzamov, USSR 1983).

ILLUSTRATIVE GAMES

1 d4 ♘f6 2 ♘f3 c5 3 d5 e6 4 ♘c3

97) **Speelman-Suba**
Dortmund 1981

4 ... d6 5 e4 a6?! Slow. **6 dxe6 ♗xe6** 6 ... fxe6 7 e5!. **7 ♘g5! b5 8 ♘xe6 fxe6** Not only are the two bishops gone, but

Black will have problems with the e6 square too. **9 g3!** Preparing the ideal development for the bishop. 9 ... b4? 10 ♘e2 ♘xe4 11 ♗g2 d5 12 ♘f4 ♕f6 13 0-0 threatening ♘xd5 would now be rather unpleasant for Black. **9 ... ♘c6 10 ♗g2 ♕c7 11 0-0 ♗e7 12 ♘e2!** The knight heads for e6. **12 ... ♔f7?!** 12 ... 0-0 13 ♘f4 ♕c8 14 ♗h3 ♘d8 15 ♘d5!; 13 ... ♕d7 14 ♗h3 ♘d8 15 ♘d5! ±. Black should have tried 12 ... e5!?. **13 ♘f4 ♖he8?** Deflecting a defending piece from the kingside. 13 ... ♖ae8 14 ♗h3 ♘d8 gives a cramped but still tolerable game. **14 a4 b4**

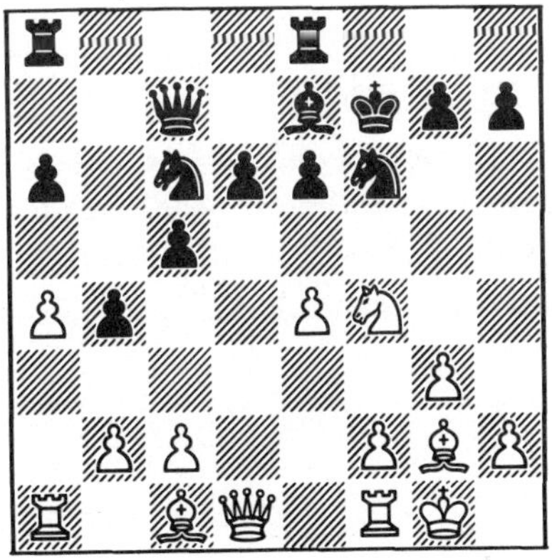

15 g4! h6 16 h4 g5 16 ... ♘h7? 17 ♘xe6!. **17 ♘h3 ♘h7 18 f4! ♔g7** 18 ... gxh4 19 g5!. **19 hxg5 hxg5 20 fxg5 ♘e5 21 g6!** Clearing the queen's route towards the opponent's king. **21 ... ♘xg6 22 ♕d2 ♘hf8 23 ♘f4 ♘xf4 24 ♕xf4 ♗d8 25 e5 d5 26 ♕h6+ ♔g8 27 ♖xf8+!** The simplest. White will soon win back the exchange, with two extra pawns. **27 ... ♖xf8 28 ♕xe6+ ♕f7** There is no better. **29 ♕xf7+ ♖xf7 30 ♗xd5 ♖c8 31 ♗e3 ♔g7 32 ♗xf7 ♔xf7 33 ♖f1+ ♔g7** 33 ... ♔e6 34 ♖f8. **34 ♔g2 ♗e7 35 e6 ♔g6 36 ♖f5** etc. Black prolonged his sufferings and did not resign until move 52! 1-0

(Minić and Sindik)

98) **Figler-Sideif Zade**
Correspondance Game 1983

4 ... b5 5 ♗g5 b4 6 ♘e4 ♗b7 7 c4 bxc3 8 ♘xc3? ♗xd5! 9 ♘xd5 exd5 10 ♗xf6 10 e3 ♕a5+!. **10 ... ♕xf6 11 ♕xd5 ♕xb2 12 ♖d1 c4! 13 ♕e4+** 13 ♕xa8? ♗b4+ 14 ♘d2 0-0. **13 ... ♔d8! 14 ♘d2 ♗b4 15 ♕xa8?** 15 e3 c3 16 ♕xa8 c2 17 ♕xb8+ ♔e7 18 ♕xb4+ ♕xb4 19 ♖c1 ♕b2 20 ♘b3 ♕c3+ 21 ♔e2 ♖b8 ∓. **15 ... ♗xd2+ 16 ♖xd2 ♕b1+ 17 ♖d1 ♕b4+ 18 ♖d2 c3 19 ♕xa7 c2! 20 ♕xb8+ ♕xb8 21 ♖xc2 h5 0-1**
(Sideif Zade)

99) **Varnusz-S.Faragó**
Budapest 1986

4 ... b5 5 dxe6 fxe6 6 ♘xb5 d5 7 e4!? ♘xe4 8 ♗f4 ♘a6?! 9 ♗d3 ♕a5+?! 10 ♘d2 ♘f6 11 0-0! ♗e7 12 c4! Fixing Black's centre; the text is better than 12 ♘d6+. **12 ... 0-0 13 ♕e2 ♕d8! 14 ♖ad1 ♘b4**

15 ♗b1 ♘c6 16 ♘b3 16 ♘f3 ♘h5!. **16 ... d4 17 ♗g3!** 17 ♘c7 e5!. **17 ... e5! 18 ♘c3! ♗g4!? 19 f3 ♗d7 20 ♘a4 ♕a5??** Time trouble! 20 ... d3 21 ♕xd3 ♘d4 (21 ... ♘b4 22 ♕e3 ±±) 22 ♘axc5 ±±; 20 ... ♘h5!? 21 f4! ♘xf4 22 ♗xf4 ♖xf4 23 ♖xf4 exf4 24 ♕e4 g6 25 ♕d5+ ♔h8 26 ♘axc5 ♗e8?! 27 ♘e6! ♕xd5 28 cxd5 ♘d8 29 ♘c7! ±±; 22 ... exf4 23 ♕e4 g6 (23 ... ♖f5 24 ♘axc5!) 24 ♘axc5 ±±; 21 ♕e4 ♘f6 22 ♕h4 ±; 22 ♕e1 ±. **21 ♘xa5 1-0**

100) **Morovic-Alburt**
Malta 1980

4 ... ♘xd5 5 ♘xd5 exd5 6 ♕xd5 d6 7 ♘g5! ♕e7 8 ♗f4 ♗e6 9 ♘xe6 fxe6 10 ♕d2 d5 11 e4! ♘c6 12 ♗g5 ♕c7 13 exd5 ♕e5+ 14 ♕e3 ♕xe3+ 15 ♗xe3 exd5 16 ♗b5 a6?! 16 ... ♖c8 17 0-0-0 d4 ±. **17 ♗xc6+ bxc6 18 0-0-0 ♗d6 19 c3 ♔d7**

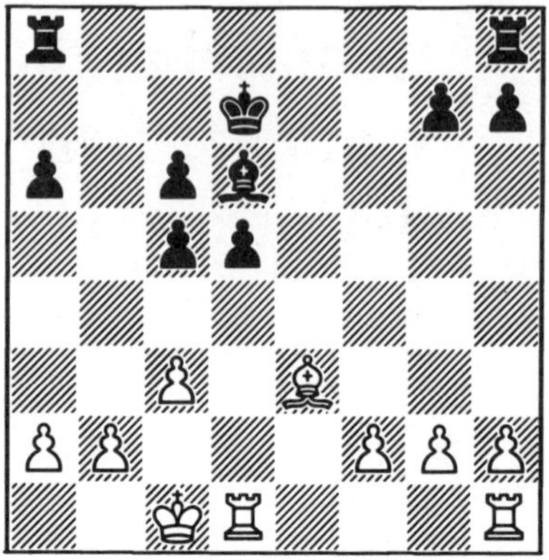

20 c4! A pretty combination, unleashing the minority attack. **20 ... d4 21 b4! cxb4 22 ♖xd4 ♔c7 23 ♖hd1 ♗c5** 23 ... ♖d8?? 24 ♖xd6!. **24 ♖d7+ ♔b6 25 ♗f4! ♗xf2 26 ♖f7 ♗h4 27 ♗c7+ ♔c5 28 ♖f5+ ♔xc4 29 ♗b6! 1-0**

18 Countering the Benoni and the Benko Gambit: Benoni, Schmid Variation, deviations on moves 5 and 6

1	d4	♘f6
2	♘f3	c5
3	d5	g6
4	♘c3	♗g7
5	e4	

This popular and flexible variation is looked at in depth when the Sicilian and the Pirc are considered in textbooks. Here we summarise briefly, emphasising novelties.

18.1

5 ... 0-0

Books tend to forget about this move which, on the one hand, avoids the 5 ... d6 6 ♗b5+ line, and, on the other, answers the natural ♗e2 with 6 ... b5!? 7 ♗xb5? ♘xe4! 8 ♘xe4 ♕a5+ 9 ♘c3 ♗xc3+ 10 bxc3 ♕xb5. The latter line can be prevented by 6 a4 but this move does not always suit White's intentions.

6 a4

(a) 6 ♗e2 b5!? 7 e5 ♘g4 8 ♗f4 (8 ♗xb5 ♘xe5 9 ♘xe5 ♗xe5 10 ♗h6 ∞) 8 ... b4 9 ♘e4 d6 10 exd6 exd6 11 0-0 (11 ♘xd6 ♗xb2 12 0-0 ♕f6! 13 ♘xc8! ♕xf4 ∞) 11 ... ♘f6?! 12 ♘xd6 ♗a6 (12 ... ♘h5 13 ♕d2 ♕c7 14 g3 ±) 13 ♗xa6 ♘xa6 14 ♘c4 ♕xd5 15 ♕xd5 ♘xd5 16 ♗e5 ± – Zilberman-Kaidanov, USSR 1984.

(b) 6 e5 ♘g4 7 ♗f4 d6 8 exd6 exd6 9 ♗e2 ♕b6 10 ♖b1 ♘d7 11 0-0 a6 12 ♕d2 ♘de5?! 13 ♘xe5 ♘xe5 14 ♗h6! ♗xh6? 15 ♕xh6 f5 16 f4 ♘d7 17 h4! ♘f6 18 h5 ♔f7

19 ♘d1 ♗d7 20 ♘f2 ± Van der Wiel-Jadoul, Brussels 1985.

(c) 6 ♗g5 d6 7 ♘d2 h6 8 ♗h4 e6 9 ♗e2 exd5 10 exd5 ♘a6 11 0-0 ♘c7 12 f4 b5? (12 ... ♕d7!) 13 ♗xb5 ♘xb5 14 ♘xb5 ♕d7 15 ♗xf6 ♗xf6 16 a4 ♗xb2 17 ♖b1 ♗g7 18 ♘c4 ± - Ivanchuk-Velimirović, Lucerne 1989.

The positions after 6 a4 often inter-transpose with those given in Chapter 19.

6 ... d6
7 ♗e2 ♘a6

The most coherent line. Others:

(a) 7 ... e5?! 8 ♗g5 h6 9 ♗h4 g5 10 ♗g3 ♘h5 11 h4! ♘xg3 12 fxg3 f5 13 hxg5 hxg5 14 ♘d2 ♘a6 15 exf5 ♗xf5 16 ♗g4 ± Sorokin-Minakhsian, Minsk 1990.

(b) 7 ... e6 8 ♘d2 exd5 9 exd5 ♘bd7 10 ♘c4 ♘b6 11 ♘e3 ♗d7 12 0-0 a6 13 ♖e1 ♖e8 14 ♗f3 ♕c7 15 ♗d2 ± Ftačnik-Gdanski, Stara Zagora 1990.

8 0-0

8 ♗xa6 bxa6 ∞.

8 ... ♘b4
9 ♗f4 b6
10 ♕d2 ♖e8
11 ♗b5 ♗d7
12 ♖fe1

White stands slightly better (King-Hebden, London 1988).

18.2

5 ... d6

The main variation here is 5 ... d6 6 ♗e2 0-0, analysed in Chapter 19; here we will analyse the 6 ♗b5+ and the 6 ♗e2 ♘a6 lines. Interesting is 6 ♗f4 0-0, but not now 7 ♗e2? b5! 8 ♗xb5 ♘xe4 ∓ Beliavsky-Razuvaev, USSR 1978. Better is 7 ♘d2 ♘a6 8 ♗e2 ♘c7 9 a4 a6 10 0-0 ♗d7 11 a5 ♘b5 12 ♘a4 ♘d4 13 ♘b6 ♘xe2+ 14 ♕xe2 ♖b8 15 ♖ab1 ♘h5 16 ♗g5 h6 17 ♗e3 f5 18 exf5 ♖xf5 19 b4 ± Ermolinsky-Yudasin, Simferopol 1988.

18.21

6 ♗b5+

Attempting to confuse Black's set-up.

18.211

6 ... ♘fd7

6 ... ♘bd7 7 a4 0-0 8 0-0 a6! (8 ... ♘e8 9 ♖e1 e5? 10 dxe6 fxe6 11 e5! d5 12 ♘xd5 ♘xe5 13 ♘e7+ ♕xe7 14 ♘xe5 ±; 9 ... ♘c7 10 ♗f4 a6 11 ♗f1 ±) 9 ♗e2 ♖b8 10 ♖e1?

(10 Nd2 and Nc4 should be played to meet ... b5 with Na5-c6. White has to avoid a couple of pitfalls here: 10 Nd2! Ne8 11 Nc4?! – 11 a5! ⩲ – 11 ... Nb6! 12 Ne3 Bd7 13 Bd2 Nc8 14 Rb1 b5 15 axb5 axb5 16 b4 Nc7 17 bxc5 dxc5 18 Na4 Na6 19 Bc3 f6! ∞ I.Sokolov-Veličković, Yugoslav Championpionship 1988) 10 ... Ne8 11 Bf4 Nc7 12 a5 b5 13 axb6 Rxb6 14 Qc1 e5! ∓ Adorján-T.Horváth, Illustrative Game No 101.

7 a4

7 0-0?! a6 8 Bd3 b5 9 a4 b4 10 Nb1 a5 11 Nbd2 Nb6 12 Nc4 N8d7 13 Nfd2 0-0 14 Qe2 Ba6 = Keres-Browne, San Antonio 1972.

7 ... Na6

7 ... 0-0 8 0-0 Na6 9 Bf4?! (9 Re1! leads back to the Lerner-Razuvaev game below) 9 ... Nc7 10 Be2 f5 11 exf5 Rxf5 12 Bg5! Bxc3 13 bxc3 Nxd5 14 Bd3! Nxc3 ∞ Larsen-Browne, Illustrative Game No 102.

8 0-0 Nc7
9 Re1!?

9 Bc4!? 0-0 10 Bf4 b6 11 Qd2 Bb7 12 Bh6 a6 13 Bxg7 Kxg7 ⩲ Bischoff-Hansen, Munich 1989.

9 ... 0-0
10 Bf1 Nf6
11 h3 e5!

11 ... b6?! 12 Bf4 Bb7 13 Qd2 a6 14 Rab1! Qd7 15 b4 ± Lerner-Razuvaev, USSR 1981.

12 dxe6 Nxe6

12 ... Bxe6 (12 ... fxe6?! 13 e5! ±) 13 Bf4 Ne8 14 Ng5 ⩲.

13 a5 Ne8
14 e5!

14 Nd5 Bd7 15 c3 Bc6 ∞.

14 ... dxe5
15 Qxd8 Nxd8
16 Nxe5

⩲ Kir.Georgiev-Barlov, Vršac 1987 (Kir.Georgiev).

18.212

6 ... Bd7
7 a4 0-0

7 ... Bxb5!? 8 axb5 0-0 9 0-0 Nbd7 10 h3 Ne8 11 Bg5 (Perhaps 10 Bg5, or 11 Bf4, would have been better) 11 ... Nc7 12 Qe2 Nb6 13 Ra5 Qd7 14 Rfa1 a6 15 bxa6 bxa6 = Browne-Alburt, Thessaloniki 1984.

8 0-0 Na6

8 ... a6 9 Be2 e5 10 dxe6! Bxe6 11 Bf4 Ne8 12 Qd2 Nc6 13 Bh6 Bg4 14 Bxg7 Kxg7 15 Rfe1 Nc7 16 Rad1 ± Taimanov-Matulović, USSR-Yugoslavia match 1964; 8 ... Bg4 9 Re1 Nbd7 10 h3 ⩲ Kasparov.

9 Re1!

9 Bxa6 bxa6 10 Nd2 Rb8 11

♕e2 e6! 12 ♕xa6 (12 dxe6 ♗xe6 13 ♕xa6 d5!) 12 ... exd5 13 ♕xd6 (13 exd5 ♗f5) 13 ... d4 14 ♘b5 ♖e8 15 ♕xc5 ♘xe4 16 ♘xe4 ♖xe4 17 ♗g5 ♕b6 = Dorfman-Tal, Illustrative Game No 103.

9 ... ♘c7

9 ... ♘b4? 10 h3 e6 11 ♗f4! e5 12 ♗g5 ♗c8 13 ♘d2 h6 14 ♗h4 g5 15 ♗g3 g4 16 hxg4 ♘xg4 17 f3 ♘f6 18 ♗h4! ± Kasparov-Beliavsky, Illustrative Game No 104.

10 ♗f1 a6

10 ... ♗g4 11 h3 ♗xf3 12 ♕xf3 b6 13 ♗d2 a6?! 14 ♖b1! e6 15 ♗g5 h6 16 ♗h4 exd5 17 exd5 ♖b8 18 b4 ± Varnusz-Halász, Budapest 1986; 10 ... e6 11 ♗f4! ±.

11 ♖b1 b5
12 axb5 axb5
13 b4 cxb4

The consequences of 13 ... c4 14 ♘d4 e5 or 14 e5 are unclear.

14 ♖xb4 ♘a6
15 ♖b1 b4
16 ♘b5 ♕b6

The critical position. White's prospects seem a bit better.

18.22

6 ♗e2 ♘a6

White wants to complete his development while Black does not even bother to castle before

carrying out his plan (... ♘c7, ... ♖b8, ... b5) as quickly as possible. Comparison should be made with 18.1, where Black castles early but White is not allowed the option of 6 ♗b5+.

7 0-0 ♘c7
8 a4 a6
9 ♘d2

The knight makes for c4 to assist the e4-e5 breakthrough. 9 a5?! ♗d7 10 ♘d2 ♘b5 and Black has got hold of b5. 9 ♗f4!?.

9 ... ♗d7
10 ♘c4

10 e5? ♘fxd5 11 ♘xd5 ♘xd5 12 ♘e4 ♘c6 13 exd6 0-0 ∓.

10 ... b5
11 e5!

11 ♘b6? b4! 12 ♘xa8 ♕xa8 13 ♘b1 ♘xe4 14 ♗f3 f5 ∓.

11 ... dxe5

11 ... bxc4? 12 exf6 ♗xf6 13 ♗h6 ±; 12 ... exf6 13 ♗f4 ±.

12 axb5 ♘xb5

12 ... axb5 13 ♖xa8 ♕xa8? (13 ... ♘xa8! 14 ♘xe5 b4 15 ♘xd7 ♘xd7 16 ♘e4 0-0 ±) 14 ♘xe5 b4 15 d6! ± Botvinnik-Schmid, Illustrative Game No 105. 12 ... ♗xb5?! 13 d6! exd6 (13 ... ♗xc4 14 dxc7! ♕xd1 15 ♖xd1 ♗xe2 16 ♘xe2 0-0 17 ♖a5 ±) 14 ♘xd6+ ♔e7 15 ♘dxb5 axb5 16 ♗e3 ±.

13 ♘a4!?

13 ♘xe5 ♘xc3 14 bxc3 ♘e4? (14 ... a5!?) 15 ♕d3! ♗xe5 (15 ... ♗f5 16 ♗f4 ♕d6 17 ♕b5+!) 16 ♕xe4 ♗xc3 17 ♖xa6 ♖xa6 18 ♗xa6 0-0 19 ♗e3 ± (Kondratiev and Stoliar).

13 ... ♕c7
14 c3!

The critical position. 15 ♗e3 ± is threatened. 6 ... ♘a6, however, is not popular these days.

ILLUSTRATIVE GAMES

1 d4 ♘f6 2 ♘f3 c5 3 d5 g6 4 ♘c3 ♗g7 5 e4 d6

101) **Adorján-T.Horváth**
Budapest 1984

6 ♗b5+ ♘bd7 7 a4 0-0 8 0-0 a6 This must not be delayed since after 9 ♖e1, the bishop can retreat comfortably to f1. **9 ♗e2 ♖b8 10 ♖c1?!** This move suits the system but White need not have hurried with it. 10 ♘d2! ♘e8 11 ♘c4 b6 12 ♗g5 ±. **10 ... ♘e8 11 ♗f4 ♘c7 12 a5** The only way to restrain ... b7-b5. But there is no good way to prevent the opening of the b-file. **12 ... b5 13 axb6 ♖xb6 14 ♕c1 e5! 15 ♗h6 ♗xh6!?** 15 ... f5 16 ♗xg7 ♔xg7 17 exf5 gxf5 18 ♘d2 ♘f6 19 ♘c4 ♖b4 ∞. **16 ♕xh6 ♕e7?!** 16 ... ♖xb2? 17 ♘g5 ♘f6 18 f4! exf4 19 ♖f1 ♘ce8 20 ♖xf4 ±; 16 ... f6!?. **17 ♘g5 f5?** 17 ... f6 18 ♘e6 ♘xe6 19 dxe6 ♕xe6 20 ♘d5 ♖xb2 would have been an exciting struggle with chances for both sides.

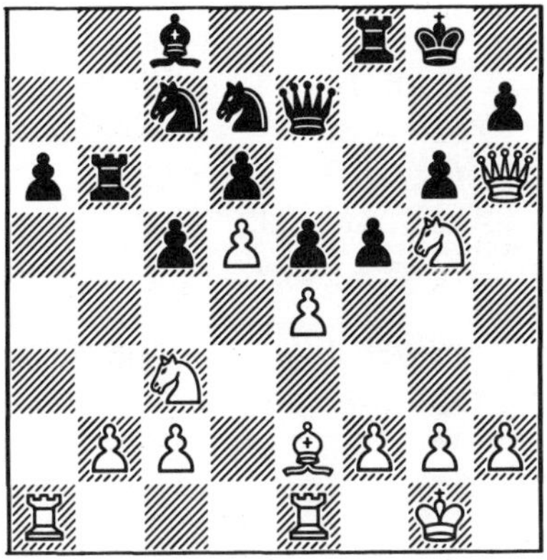

18 ♘e6! This witty pawn sacrifice opens up the position for White's pieces. The taking of the d5 square will be of special importance. **18 ... ♘xe6 19 dxe6 ♘f6** 19 ... ♕xe6 20 exf5 ♖xf5 21 ♗g4

♖xb2 22 ♖ad1 ♖xc2 23 ♘e4 ±±; 20 ... ♕xf5 21 ♘d5! ♕xf2+ 22 ♔h1 ±±. **20 ♘d5 ♘xd5 21 exd5** Thus the protected e6 pawn provides White with a decisive advantage in the middle game and the endgame. **21 ... ♖xb2 22 ♗xa6 ♖xc2 23 h4 ♗xa6 24 ♖xa6 ♖c4 25 ♕g5! ♕xg5 26 hxg5 ♖d8 27 ♖ea1 ♖b4 28 ♖xd6! 1-0**

28 ... ♖xd6 29 ♖a8+ ♔g7 30 e7 ♖xd5 31 e8=♕ ♖d1+ 32 ♔h2 ♖h4+ 33 ♔g3 ♖g4+ 34 ♔f3 ♖f4+ 35 ♔e2 etc. (Notes based on T. Horváth's)

102) **Larsen-Browne**
USA 1972

6 ♗b5+ ♘fd7 7 a4 0-0 8 0-0 ♘a6 9 ♗f4 ♘c7 10 ♗e2 f5!? 11 exf5 ♖xf5 12 ♗g5! ♗xc3?! 13 bxc3 ♘xd5 14 ♗d3 ♘xc3 15 ♕d2 15 ♕e1! ♖xf3 16 ♗c4+! ♖f7 17 ♗xf7+ ♔xf7 18 ♕xc3 ♘e5 ±. **15 ... ♖xf3! 16 gxf3?** 16 ♗c4+!. **16 ... ♘e5 17 ♗c4+**

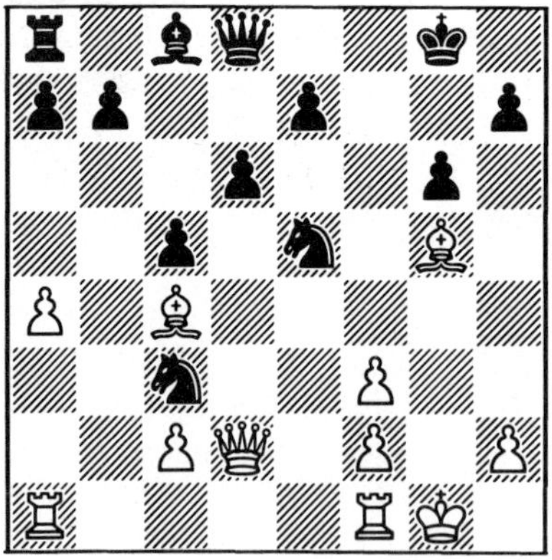

17 ... e6!! An unexpected winning move! **18 ♕xc3 ♕xg5+ 19 ♔h1 b6 20 ♖fd1 ♕f4! 21 ♖xd6 ♘xf3 22 ♖d8+ ♔f7 23 ♔g2 ♕g5+ 24 ♔h3** 24 ♔xf3 ♗b7+. **24 ... ♕h4+ 25 ♔g2 ♘d4! 26 ♖xd4 ♗b7+ 27 ♗d5 ♗xd5+ 28 ♖xd5 ♕e4+ 29 f3 ♕xd5 30 a5 b5 31 ♖e1 ♖d8 32 ♖e2 ♕g5+ 33 ♔f2 ♖d1 34 ♖e1 ♕h4+ 0-1**

103) **Dorfman-Tal**
USSR Championship 1977

6 ♗b5+ ♗d7 7 a4 0-0 8 0-0 ♘a6 9 ♗xa6?! bxa6 10 ♘d2 ♖b8! 10 ... e6 11 ♘c4 exd5 12 exd5 ±. **11 ♕e2** 11 ♘c4 ♖b4 12 b3 e6. **11 ... e6! 12 ♕xa6! exd5 13 ♕xd6 d4 14 ♘b5! ♖e8** 14 ... ♖c8!?. **15 ♕xc5 ♘xe4 16 ♘xe4 ♖xe4 17 ♗g5! ♕b6! 18 ♕xb6 ♖xb6 19 ♖ad1** 19 c3? ♗xb5 20 axb5 ♖xb5 ∓. **19 ... a6** 19 ... ♗xb5 20 axb5 ♖xb5 21 ♗c1 ♖e2 22 c3! =. **20 f3 ♖e8 21 ♘xd4 ♖xb2 22 a5 ♗a4 23 ♗h4! ♗xc2 24 ♘xc2** 24 ♖d2 ♖b4!. **24 ... ♖xc2 25 ♖fe1 ♖ec8 26 ♗d8 ♗c3 27 ♖e4 ♗g7 ½-½**

104) **Kasparov-Beliavsky**
Candidates' match 1983

6 ♗b5+ ♗d7 7 a4 0-0 8 0-0 ♘a6 9 ♖e1 ♘b4? The knight gets out of play here. **10 h3 e6** After 10 ... ♗xb5 11 ♘xb5, the threat is 12 c3. **11 ♗f4! e5 12 ♗g5 ♗c8** 12 ... h6 13 ♗xf6 ♗xf6 14 ♗xd7

♕xd7 15 ♘d2 ±. **13 ♘d2 h6 14 ♗h4 g5** 14 ... ♕c7 15 ♗e2! ♘e8 16 ♘b5 ♕d7 17 ♘c4 f5 18 exf5! gxf5 19 ♗h5 ±. **15 ♗g3 g4?!** 15 ... h5!? 16 ♗e2! g4 17 ♗h4!? gxh3 18 g3! ±. **16 hxg4 ♘xg4 17 f3 ♘f6**

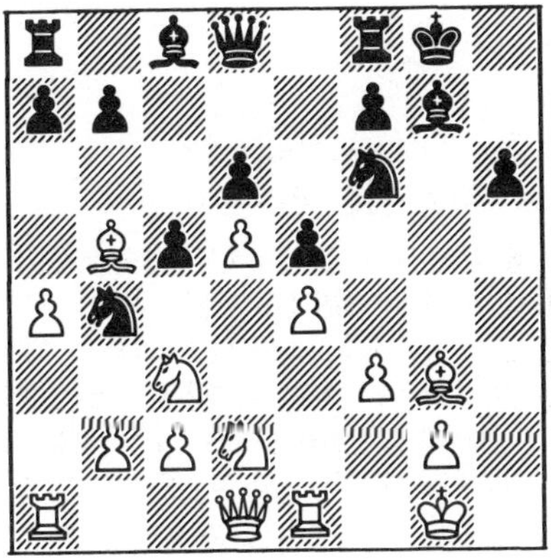

18 ♗h4! ♔h8 19 ♘e2! ♖g8 20 c3 ♘a6 21 ♘g3 ♕f8? Tougher is ... ♗f8-e7. **22 ♘df1 ♘h7 23 ♘e3 ♗f6 24 ♗xf6+ ♘xf6 25 ♘gf5 ♘h5 26 ♔f2 ♗xf5 27 ♘xf5 ♘f4 28 g3 ♘h3+ 29 ♔e2 ♖xg3!?** 29 ... ♘g5 30 ♖h1 ♖g6 31 ♖h5 ±±. **30 ♘xg3 ♕g7 31 ♖g1! ♖g8** 31 ... ♘xg1+ 32 ♕xg1 ♖g8 is followed by 33 ♕h2!. **32 ♕d2 1-0**

(Notes based on Kasparov's)

105) **Botvinnik-Schmid**
Leipzig 1960

6 ♗e2 ♘a6 7 0-0 ♘c7 8 a4 a6 9 ♘d2 ♗d7 10 ♘c4 b5 11 e5! dxe5 12 axb5 axb5 13 ♖xa8 ♕xa8? 14 ♘xe5 b4

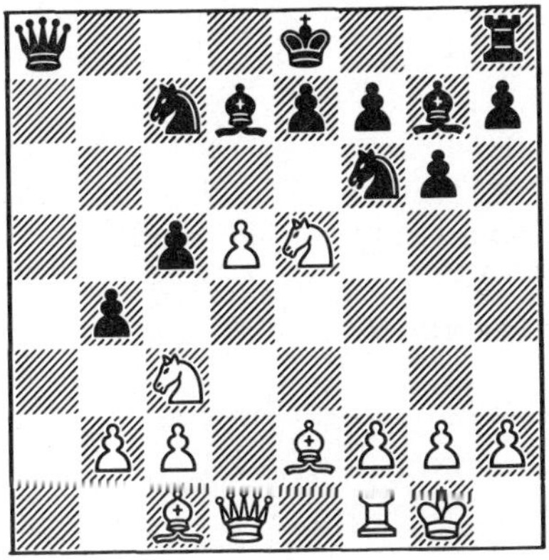

15 d6! bxc3 15 ... exd6 16 ♕xd6 bxc3 17 ♗f3! ♕c8 18 ♘xd7 ♘xd7 19 ♗g5 ±±. **16 dxc7 ♕c8 17 ♗f4 cxb2 18 ♘xd7 ♘xd7** 18 ... ♕xd7 19 ♗b5!. **19 ♗b5 ♗d4** Otherwise 20 ♕xd7+ ♕xd7 21 c8=♕+ mate! **20 c3! e5 21 cxd4 exf4 22 ♗xd7+ ♕xd7 23 ♕e2+** 23 ♕a4!. **23 ... ♔f8 24 ♕e5 ♔g8 25 ♖b1 f6 26 ♕xc5 ♔g7 27 ♖xb2 ♖e8 28 ♖b1 f3 29 gxf3 ♕h3 30 ♕c6 1-0**

19 Countering the Benoni and the Benko Gambit: Benoni, Schmid Variation, main line

1	**d4**	**♘f6**
2	**♘f3**	**c5**
3	**d5**	**g6**
4	**♘c3**	**♗g7**
5	**e4**	**d6**
6	**♗e2**	**0-0**
7	**0-0**	

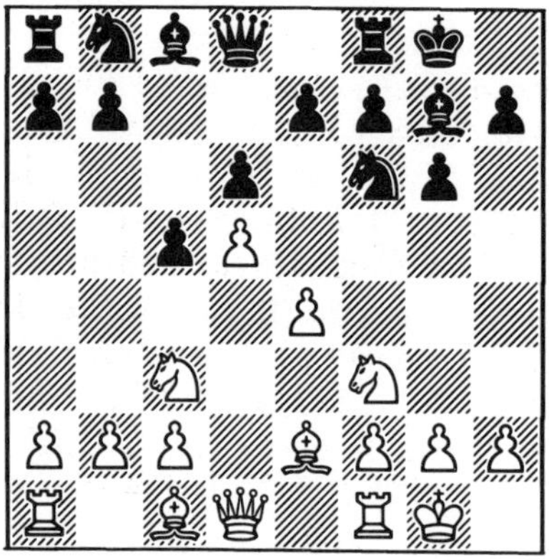

This position can emerge from a number of openings, e.g. the Pirc: 1 e4 d6 2 d4 ♘f6 3 ♘c3 g6 4 ♘f3 ♗g7 5 ♗e2 c5 6 d5 0-0 7 0-0, or the Sicilian: 1 e4 c5 2 ♘f3 g6 3 d4 ♗g7 4 d5 d6 5 ♗e2 ♘f6 6 ♘c3 0-0 7 0-0, etc.

Because of his pawn formation, Black strives for ... b7-b5, or tries to break up the centre with ... e7-e6,or sometimes attempts to get rid of his bishop playing ... ♗c8-g4xf3. White has to watch out for these plans, with the e4-e5 break-through as his trump card. Unlike in the King's Indian variations, White has the opportunity to post a piece on the strategically important c4 square.

A deviation from the main line:

6 ... ♗g4 7 a4 (7 0-0 a6?! 8 a4 0-0 9 ♘d2 ♗xe2 10 ♕xe2 ♘bd7 11 ♘c4 ♘b6 12 ♘e3 e5 13 dxe6 fxe6 14 a5 ♘bd7 15 ♘c4! ± Varnusz-I.Horváth, Budapest 1983; 12 ... ♖e8! 13 ♖d1 ♕c7 14 f3 ♖ad8 15 a5 ♘c8 16 ♘c4 ♘d7 17 ♗f4 ♘a7 18 ♘a4 ± Andersson-Zapata, Wijk aan Zee 1987) 7 ... ♗xf3 8 ♗xf3 0-0 9 0-0 ♘e8?! 10 h4! e6 11 dxe6 fxe6 12 e5! d5 13 ♗g5 ♕b6 14 ♘xd5 ± Smyslov-Bilek, Sochi 1963.

White may also deviate: 6 ... 0-0 7 h3!? b5! 8 ♘xb5 ♘xe4 9 0-0 ♘d7 10 ♗d3 a6 11 ♘a3 ♘ef6 = Norwood-Hodgson, London 1988.

7 ... ♘a6

(a) 7 ... ♗g4 8 ♘d2! (8 ♗g5 ♘bd7?! 9 ♘d2 ♗xe2 10 ♕xe2 ♖e8 11 f4 h6 12 ♗h4 ♕b6 13 ♘c4 ♕a6 14 e5 dxe5 15 fxe5 ± Larsen-Stein, Sousse 1967; 8 ... ♗xf3!) 8 ... ♗xe2 9 ♕xe2 ♘bd7 (9 ... ♘a6 10 ♘c4 ♘c7 11 a4 a6 12 a5 ♘d7 13 ♘a4 ♘b5 14 c3 ± Tukmakov-Georgadze, Decin 1977) 10 ♘c4 ♘b6 11 ♘e3 ♖e8 12 a4 e6 13 dxe6 ♖xe6 14 a5 ♘bd7 15 f3 ± Stein-Bilek, Illustrative Game No 106.

(b) 7 ... e6 8 dxe6! (8 ♗c4 e5! 9 ♗e2! ♘a6 10 ♘d2 ♘c7 11 a4 b6 12 ♘c4 ♗a6 = Speelman-Velimirović, Banja Luka 1983; 8 ♘d2 exd5 9 exd5 ♘bd7 10 a4 – 10 ♘c4!? ♘b6 11 ♘e3 ♗d7 12 a4 ± – 10 ... ♘b6 11 ♗f3 ♗d7 12 a5 ♘c8 13 ♖a3! ♖b8 14 ♘c4 b5 15 axb6 axb6 16 ♗f4 ♕c7 17 ♖a6 ± Zaid-Cr.Ionescu, Sofia 1988) 8 ... ♗xe6 9 ♗e3 ♘c6 (9 ... b6!?) 10 ♕d2 ♕e7? (10 ... ♘g4! is the only chance!) 11 ♗g5! ♖fe8 12 ♖ad1 ♖ad8 13 ♕f4! a6 14 ♕h4 ♘e5 15 ♘xe5 dxe5 16 f4 +– Timman-Jadoul, Illustrative Game No 107.

19.1

8 h3!?

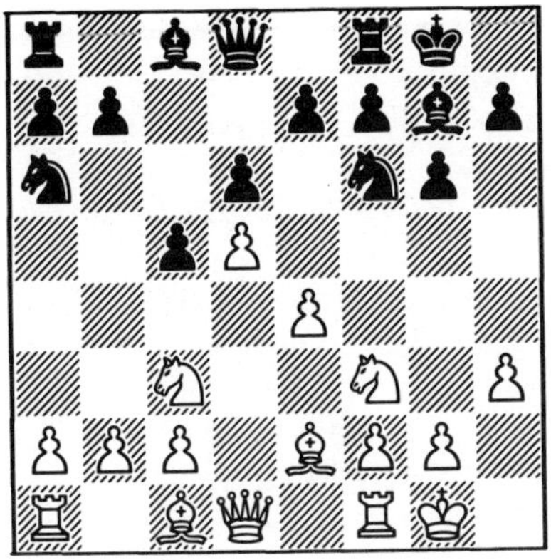

Apart from the other main line (19.2: 8 ♗f4) the following are worth considering:

(a) 8 ♘d2 ♘c7 9 a4 a6! (9 ... b6 10 ♘c4 ♗a6 11 ♗f4 ♖b8 12 b3 ♘d7 13 ♕d2 ± Smyslov-Schmid, Illustrative Game No 108; 11 ... ♗xc4 12 ♗xc4 a6 13 ♖e1 ♘d7 14 ♕d2 ♖b8 15 ♗h6 b5 16 ♗xg7 ♔xg7 17 ♗f1 ± Bukić-Janošević, Kralevo 1967) 10 f3 (10 a5? ♗d7 11 ♘c4 ♘b5 ∓; 10 ♘c4 b5! 11 axb5 axb5 12 ♖xa8 ♘xa8 13 ♘xb5 ♘xe4 =; 10 ♖e1!? ♗d7 11 f4!? – 11 ♘c4 – 11 ... b5 12 ♗f3 ♖b8 13 e5 ♘fe8 14 ♘b3 bxa4?! – 14 ... b4!? – 15 ♘xa4 ♖b4 16 ♘c3 ♘b5 17 ♘xb5 ♗xb5 18 ♗d2 ± Torre-Inkiov, Zagreb 1987) 10 ... ♗d7 11 ♘c4 b5 12 ♘b6 ♖b8 13 a5 ♗e8 = Reshevsky-Larsen, Palma de Mallorca 1971, or 10 ♖e1 ♗d7 11 ♘c4 b5 12 ♘b6 ♖b8 13 ♘xd7 ♕xd7 = Nikitin-Tal, USSR 1969.

(b) 8 ♖e1 ♘c7 9 a4 (9 ♗f4? b5!

10 ♘xb5 ♘xe4 11 ♘xc7 ♕xc7 12 ♗c4 ♘f6 = Tal-Speelman, Reykjavik 1988) 9 ... a6?! (9 ... e6!; 9 ... e5!) 10 a5 (10 ♗g5 h6 11 ♗f4 ♗d7 12 ♕d2 b5? 13 e5 dxe5 14 ♗xe5 b4 15 ♗xf6 ♗xf6 16 ♘e4 ♗g7 17 ♘xc5 ♗xb2 18 ♖ad1 ± Spassky-Schmid, Varna 1962; 12 ... g5!? 13 e5 gxf4 14 exf6 ♗xf6 15 ♕xf4 ♗g7 ∞) 10 ... ♘b5 (10 ... ♖b8!?) 11 ♘b1! ♗g4 12 ♘bd2 e6 13 h3 ♗xf3 14 ♗xf3 ♖e8 15 c3 exd5 16 exd5 ♖xe1+ 17 ♕xe1 ♗h6 18 ♘c4 ± Vaganian-Velimirović, Nikšić 1978.

Obviously, the text move is intended to hinder ... ♗g4.

8 ... ♘c7
9 a4

9 ♖e1 ♖b8 10 a4 b6 11 ♗f4 ♘d7 12 ♕d2 a6 13 ♗h6 ♗xh6 14 ♕xh6 f6 ∞ Gligorić-Adorján, Hastings 1973/74.

After 9 a4, Black has natural replies of 9 ... a6 and 9 ... b6, both of which transpose into lines considered in 19.2 below after White's 10 ♗f4 (thus 8 ♗f4 ♘c7 9 a4 b6 10 h3, or 9 ... a6 10 h3). The one line of independent significance is 9 ... e6 10 dxe6 fxe6 (10 ... ♘xe6 11 ♗c4 ±; 10 ... ♗xe6 11 ♗f4 ♘fe8 12 ♘g5 ±) 11 e5 dxe5 12 ♕xd8 ♖xd8 13 ♗g5 ± Ftačnik-Hodgson, Lugano 1988.

19.2

8 ♗f4

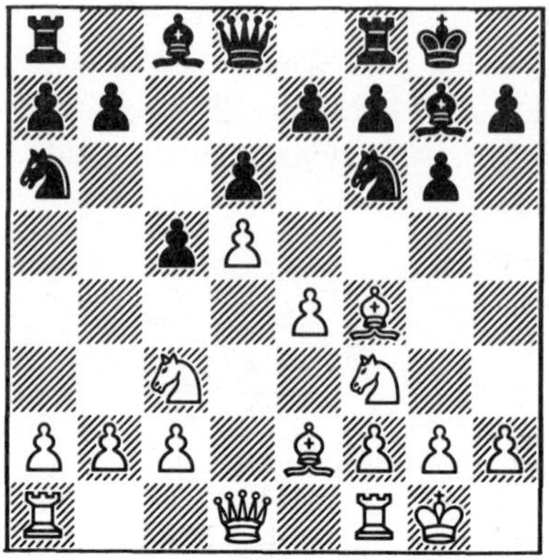

Before moving his knight to c4, White prevents ... e7-e6/e5.

8 ... ♘c7
9 a4

9 ♘d2 b5 10 ♘xb5 ♘xb5 11 ♗xb5 ♖b8 12 a4 ♘h5 13 ♗g5 ♗xb2 14 ♖b1 ♗g7 15 ♘c4 ♘f6 ∞ Najdorf-Tal, Moscow 1967.

9 ... b6

(a) 9 ... ♗g4 10 ♖e1! (10 h3 ♗xf3 11 ♗xf3 ♘d7 12 ♕d2 a6 – 12 ... ♖e8!? – 13 ♗e2 ♖b8 14 ♗h6 b5 15 ♗xg7 ♔xg7 16 ♘d1 ♘f6 17 ♗f3 e6 18 axb5 axb5 19 ♘e3 exd5 20 exd5 Karpov-Browne, Madrid 1973; 20 ... b4! =) 10 ... a6 11 ♘d2 ♗xe2 12 ♕xe2 ♖e8 13 a5 e6 14 ♕d3 (14 ♘c4? ♘fxd5!) 14 ... exd5 15 exd5 ± Stein-Ljubojević, Vrnjačka Banja 1971.

(b) 9 ... ♗d7 10 ♕d2 (10 ♖e1!?; 10 ♘d2!?) 10 ... a6 11 e5 dxe5 12 ♘xe5 ♗f5 13 ♗f3 ♘ce8 14 ♖fe1 (14 ♘c4!?) 14 ... ♘d6 15 g4 ±

Smyslov-Seret, Lucerne 1985.

(c) 9 ... a6 10 ♖e1 (10 ♘d2 ♖b8 11 ♘c4 b5 12 axb5 axb5 13 ♘a5 ♗d7 14 e5 ♘e8 ∞; 10 h3!? ♖b8?! 11 e5 dxe5! – 11 ... ♘fe8 12 ♖b1! b5 13 axb5 axb5 14 b4 ± Savchenko-Khmelnitsky, USSR 1988 – 12 ♘xe5 ♘fxd5 13 ♘xf7 ♖xf7 14 ♘xd5 e5 15 ♘xc7 ♕xc7 16 ♗g3 ♗e6 ± Savchenko; or alternatively for White 13 ♘xd5 ♕xd5 14 ♘xg6 hxg6 15 ♗xc7 – 15 ♕xd5 ♘xd5 16 ♗xb8 ♗xb2 ∞ – 15 ... ♕xd1 16 ♖fxd1 ♖a8 17 c3 ± Ivanchuk) 10 ... ♖b8 11 a5 (11 e5 ♘h5 12 ♗e3 b5) 11 ... b5 12 axb6 ♖xb6 13 b3 (13 ♖a2!) 13 ... ♘h5 14 ♗d2 ♖b8 15 ♖a2 ♘b5 16 ♘xb5 axb5 – Tal-Velimirović, Belgrade 1979. For 10 ... b6, see note to 9 ... b6 10 ♖e1 a6.

(d) 9 ... ♘h5?! 10 ♗g5 h6 11 ♗e3 ♘f6 12 ♘d2 b6 13 ♗c4 ±; 13 ♘c4 ♗a6 14 h3 ♔h7 15 ♕d2 ♖b8 = Polugayevsky-Haág, Havana 1962.

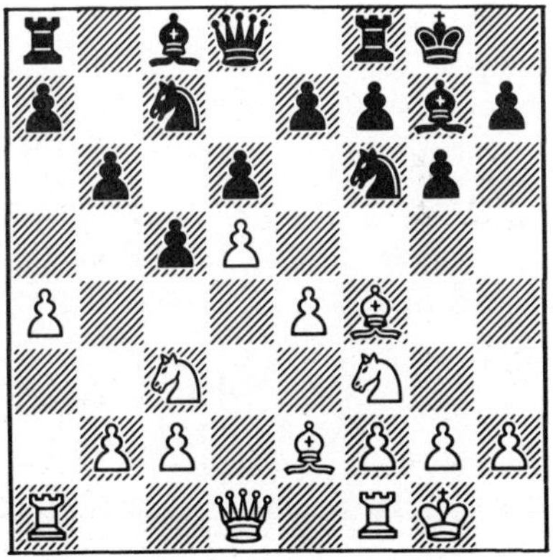

10 ♖e1

(a) 10 h3 (The threat is 11 e5!) 10 ... a6!? (10 ... ♗b7 11 ♗c4! ± Petursson-W.Watson, Illustrative Game No 109; also 11 ♖e1 ♕d7 12 ♕d2 ♖fe8 13 ♗c4 ♖ad8 14 ♗h6 e6 15 ♗xg7 ♔xg7 16 dxe6 fxe6 17 ♗b5 ± Alburt-Tal, USSR Championship 1974; 10 ... ♘d7?! 11 ♗c4 ♘e5 12 ♘xe5 dxe5 13 ♗e3 ♘e8 14 a5 ♘d6 15 ♕e2 ±; 10 ... ♗b7 11 ♖e1 ♖e8 12 ♗c4 ♘d7 13 e5 dxe5 14 ♘xe5 ♘xe5 15 ♗xe5 ♕d7 Zilberstein-Furman, USSR 1973; 16 ♕d3! ±; 11 ... ♕d7 12 ♗c4 ♖fe8 13 ♕d2 ♖ad8 14 ♗h6 – 14 e5?! ♘fxd5! – 14 ... e6! 15 ♗xg7 ♔xg7 16 dxe6 fxe6 ± – Kondratiev and Stoliar; 11 ... a6 12 ♖b1 ♕d7 13 b4? cxb4 14 ♖xb4 ♘xe4! 15 ♘xe4 ♘xd5 ∓ Rajković-Velimirović, Yugoslavia 1988) 11 e5 dxe5 12 ♘xe5 ♘cxd5 13 ♘xd5 (13 ♘c6 ♘xc3!) 13 ... ♕xd5 14 ♗f3 ♕xd1 15 ♖fxd1 ♖a7 16 ♘c6 ♖b7 ∞. Probably better is 11 ♗c4 or 11 ♖e1 (Kondratiev and Stoliar).

(b) 10 ♘d2 a6 11 ♘c4 (11 ♖e1 ♖b8? 12 ♘c4 b5 13 axb5 ♘xb5 14 ♘xb5 axb5 15 ♘a5 ♗d7 16 e5 dxe5?! 17 ♗xe5 ♖a8 18 ♘c6 ± Varnusz-Morvay, Tapolca 1986; 11 ... ♗d7 12 ♗f3 b5 13 e5 ♘fe8 ±) 11 ... b5 12 axb5 axb5 13 ♖xa8 ♘xa8 14 ♘xb5 ♘xe4 15 ♗f3 ♗a6 16 ♘ba3 ♘f6 17 ♖e1 ± Barcza-Pribyl, Brno 1975. 10 ... e6!? 11 dxe6 ♘xe6 12 ♗e3 ♘d4 ∞ (Kondratiev and Stoliar).

(c) 10 ♕d2 ♖e8 11 ♖fe1 ♗g4! 12 h3 ♗xf3 13 ♗xf3 ♘d7 14 ♗h6 ♗h8 15 ♗e2 a6 16 h4! e6! 17 ♗g5 (17 dxe6 ♘xe6 18 ♕xd6 ♕xh4) 17 ... ♗f6 18 g3 ♗xg5 19 hxg5 e5! = Durić-Gheorghiu, Kastel Stari 1988.

10 ... ♗b7

10 ... a6 11 h3 ♘d7 12 ♕d2 ♖b8 13 ♗h6 ± Beliavsky-Stoica, Illustrative Game 110. 11 ... ♗b7 12 ♖b1 ♖b8 (12 ... ♕d7 13 b4 ♘h5 – 12 ... ♘xe4? 14 ♘xe4 ♘xd5 15 ♕d2 ♘xb4 16 ♗c4 ± Greenfeld-Hodgson, Tel Aviv 1988 – 14 ♗d2 ♖ab8 15 ♘h2! ♘f6 16 ♘f1 ± Greenfeld) 13 ♕d2 b5 14 axb5 axb5 15 b4 c4 16 ♗h6 ♕d7 17 ♗xg7 ♔xg7 18 ♖a1 ♖a8 19 ♕d4 e5 20 ♕b6 ♗a6 (Gavrikov-Torre, Lugano 1988) 21 ♖a5! ±.

White can also vary on move 11: 11 ♕d2 (delaying h3) 11 ... ♗b7 12 ♖ab1 ♖c8! 13 h3 ♖e8 14 ♗h2 ♘d7 15 ♗f1 ± Dzandzanzaga-Rechlis, Oakham 1988. White's piece play always seems a little freer than Black's.

10 ... ♖e8 11 h3 ♗b7 12 ♗c4 a6 13 ♕d2 (13 ♕d3!?) 13 ... ♘d7 14 ♖ad1 (14 e5 ±) 14 ... ♘e5?! (14 ... ♖b8 15 e5 dxe5 16 ♘xe5 ♘xe5 17 ♗xe5 ♗xe5 18 ♖xe5 ♕d6 19 f4 ± Zysk) 15 ♗xe5! dxe5 16 d6! ± Zysk-Short, West Germany 1987/88.

11 ♗c4 ♘h5?!

11 ... a6, 11 ... ♕d7 and 11 ... ♖e8 are worth considering here (see notes to Illustrative Game No 111).

12 ♗g5 ♘f6
13 ♕d3! a6
14 ♖ad1 ♖b8
15 h3

For 15 e5! see the analysis of the Illustrative Game No 111.

15 ... ♘d7
16 ♕e3

16 ♗f4 is also sufficient, e.g. 16 ... ♘e5 17 ♘xe5 dxe5 18 ♗e3 a5 19 ♘b5 then c3 and b4.

16 ... ♗a8
17 ♗h6 b5
18 ♗xg7 ♔xg7
19 ♗f1

White's prospects on the king-side are slightly better than Black's on the other flank – Karpov-Korchnoi, Illustrative Game No 111.

ILLUSTRATIVE GAMES

1 d4 ♘f6 2 ♘f3 c5 3 d5 g6 4 ♘c3 ♗g7 5 e4 0-0 6 ♗e2 d6 7 0-0

106) **Stein-Bilek**
Moscow 1967

7 ... ♗g4 8 ♘d2! ♗xe2 9 ♕xe2

♘bd7 10 ♘c4 ♘b6 11 ♘e3 ♖e8 12 a4 e6 13 dxe6 ♖xe6 14 a5 ♘bd7 15 f3 Having fixed the centre, White has slightly the better game due to the d5 and d6 weaknesses. Nevertheless, Black has a fairly comfortable position, making the advantage difficult to exploit. **15 ... ♖b8 16 ♖d1 ♘e5 17 ♘c4 ♘xc4 18 ♕xc4 ♘d7! 19 ♘d5 ♘e5 20 ♕a4** 20 ♕e2 ♘c6 21 c3 f5! **20 ... g5!?** A bold decision. Black has thwarted f3-f4 and in certain situations he himself threatens ... g5-g4.

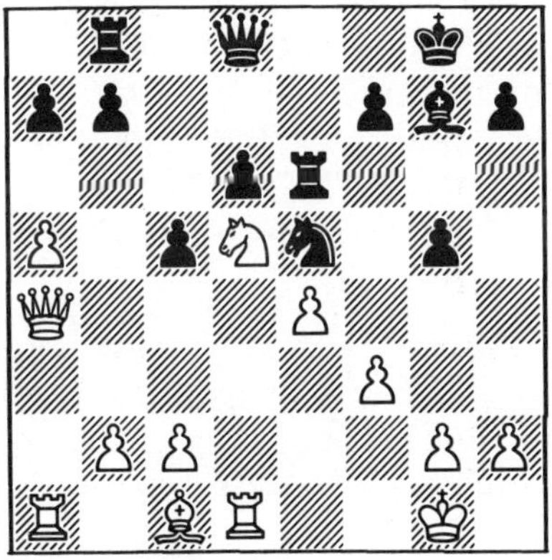

21 ♖a3! ♘c6 21 ... g4!?. **22 ♘e3 ♗d4** 23 ♘f5 must be prevented. **23 ♔h1 ♗xe3 24 ♗xe3 ♕f6 25 ♖d5!?** 25 ♖b3. **25 ... h6** 25 ... ♕xb2 26 ♖xg5+ ♖g6 27 h4. **26 ♖b3 a6** 26 ... g4? 27 ♖f5 ♕g6 28 a6!. **27 h3 ♘e5 28 ♕a1! ♕g6 29 ♕d1 ♘c4 30 ♗d2 b5?!** 30 ... ♕f6!. **31 axb6 ♖xb6 32 ♖xb6 ♘xb6 33 ♖d3 f5?** Opening up the position is a fatal blunder. 33 ... ♘c4!. **34 ♖b3! ♘d7 35 ♖b7 ♖e7** 35 ... ♘e5 36 exf5 ♕xf5 37 ♗c3. **36 exf5 ♕xf5 37 ♗c3 d5 38 b4 d4 39 bxc5! ♕d5 40 ♖c7 ♕e5 41 ♖c8+ ♔f7 42 ♕xd4 ♕xd4 43 ♗xd4 ♘f8 44 c6 ♘e6 45 ♗b6 ♖e8 46 ♗d8!** Elegant! **46 ... a5 47 ♖b8! a4 1-0**

107) **Timman-Jadoul**
Brussels 1986

7 ... e6 8 dxe6! ♗xe6 9 ♗e3 ♘c6?! 10 ♕d2 ♕e7? This can be seen as the losing move. **11 ♗g5! ♖fe8 12 ♖ad1 ♖ad8 13 ♕f4! a6 14 ♕h4 ♘e5 15 ♘xe5 dxe5**

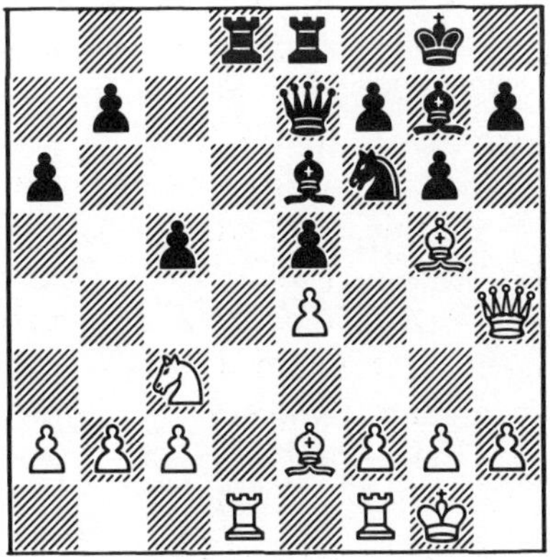

16 f4! ♖xd1 17 ♖xd1 h6 There is no better to be seen. **18 ♗xh6 ♗xh6 19 ♕xh6 c4?** 19 ... exf4 puts up a much tougher defence. **20 f5! gxf5 21 ♕g5+ ♔h8 22 exf5 ♗d7 23 ♕h4+ ♔g7 24 ♕g5+ ♔h8 25 ♕h6+ ♔g8 26 ♗xc4 1-0**

108) **Smyslov-Schmid**
Helsinki 1952

7 ... ♘a6 8 ♘d2 ♘c7 9 a4 b6?! 9 ... a6!. **10 ♘c4 ♗a6 11 ♗f4 ♖b8 12 b3! ♘d7 13 ♕d2 f5** Weakens his pawn structure, but Black would suffocate without counterplay. **14 ♖ad1!** A fine pawn sacrifice! **14 ... fxe4** 14 ... ♗xc3 15 ♕xc3 fxe4 16 ♗h6 ♖f7 17 ♗g4 ♗xc4 18 bxc4 ♘e5 19 ♗h3 then ♖de1 and ♖xe4 ±. **15 ♘xe4 ♖f5?!** Better is 15 ... ♗b7 16 ♗g5! ♕e8 17 ♗g4 ♗xd5 18 ♘exd6! exd6 19 ♘xd6 ♕e5 20 ♘b5 although White regains the piece and has a superior game.

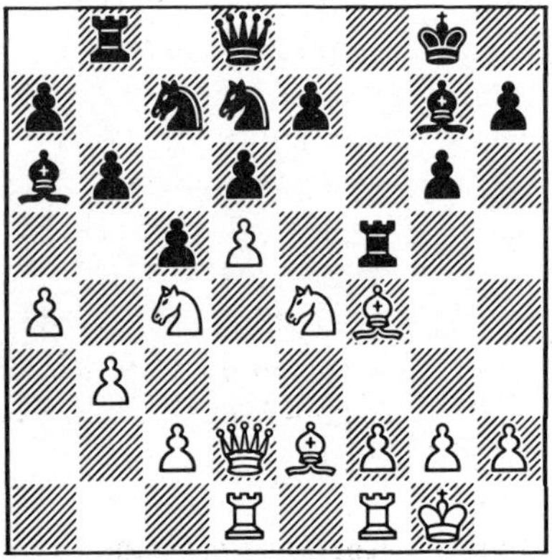

16 ♗g4! ♖xd5 17 ♗e6+ ♘xe6 18 ♕xd5 ♘df8 19 ♘g5 ♗b7 19 ... ♕c8!? 20 ♘xe6 ♕xe6 21 ♖fe1 ♕xd5 22 ♖xd5 ♗b7 23 ♖d3 ♗f6 24 ♗d2 ♔f7 25 ♗c3 ±. **20 ♘xe6 ♕c8** 20 ... ♗xd5 21 ♘xd8 ♗xc4 22 ♘c6 ♗xf1 23 ♘xb8 ♗e2 24 ♖e1 e5 25 ♖xe2 exf4 26 ♖e7 +−. **21 ♘xd6! exd6 22 ♕xd6 ♕xe6 23 ♕xe6+ 1-0**
(Smyslov)

109) **Petursson-W.Watson**
Reykjavik 1989

7 ... ♘a6 8 ♗f4 ♘c7 9 a4 b6 10 h3 ♗b7 11 ♗c4! a6 12 ♖e1 ♕d7 13 ♕d3! A strange looking square for the queen, but an effective one. Black's b5 is prevented, while White's break with e5 still threatens. With the e5 square out of range of either Black knight, both queen and c4 bishop are very hard to dislodge. **13 ... ♖ad8 14 ♖ab1** In Ivanchuk-Torre, Biel 1989, White tried 14 ♖ad1, play continuing 14 ... ♕c8 15 ♕e3 ♖fe8 16 ♗h6 ♗h8? 17 ♘g5 ♘d7 18 f4 ±. Ivanchuk suggests two possible improvements for Black: 14 ... ♘h5!? 15 ♗h2 ♗xc3 16 ♕xc3 ♕xa4 ∞, or 16 ... e6. Maybe after 14 ♖ab1 instead, Black should still try the ... ♘h5 plan. **14 ... e6?! 15 b4!** A standard plan to stop Black's queenside pawns rolling, and indeed even to show them to be weak. **15 ... exd5?** Now White has a stable positional edge. Black had to steer into the complications with 15 ... ♘xe4!; Petursson gives 16 ♖xe4 ♗xc3 17 ♕xc3 exd5 18 ♗h6 d4 19 ♘xd4 ♗xe4 20 ♘f5 ♘e6 21 ♗xe6 fxe6 22 ♘xd6 ♗d5 23 bxc5 bxc5 24 ♗xf8 ♖xf8 25 ♕xc5 ♕xa4; White is only slightly better. **16 exd5**

cxb4 17 ♖xb4 b5 18 axb5 axb5 19 ♗b3 ♘a6 20 ♖xb5 ♘c5 21 ♕c4 ♗a6

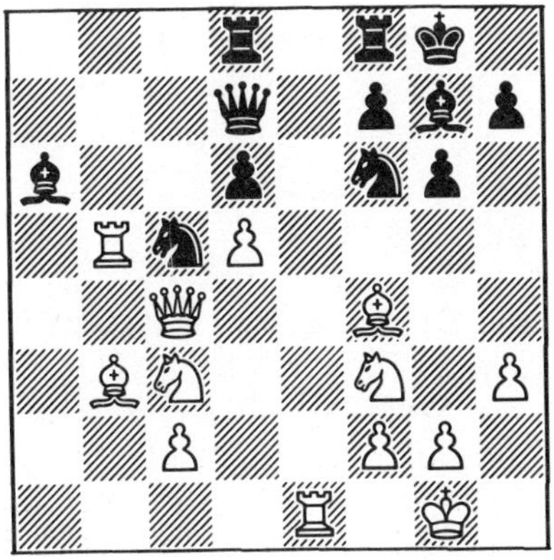

22 ♗xd6! ♘xb3 White's connected passed pawns outweigh the sacrificed exchange after 22 ... ♕xd6 23 ♕xc5 ♗xb5 24 ♕xd6 ♖xd6 25 ♘xb5 ±. **23 ♗xf8 ♘a5** 23 ... ♗xf8 24 ♕xb3 ±. **24 ♕a4 ♗xb5 25 ♕xa5 ♗xf8 26 ♘xb5 ♕xd5 27 c4 ♕d7 28 ♕b6 ♔g7 29 ♖a1 ♖c8?** Missing White's combination; 29 ... ♕c8 ±. **30 ♖a7! ♕d1+ 31 ♔h2 ♗c5 32 ♖xf7+ ♔xf7 33 ♕b7+ ♘d7 34 ♕xc8 ♗xf2 35 ♕d8!** The point; 36 ♘e5+ is threatened. **35 ... ♔g7 36 ♕e7+ ♔h6 37 ♘d6 ♕c1 38 ♘f7+ ♔g7 39 ♘7g5+ ♔g8 40 ♕f7+ 1-0**

(Notes based on Petursson's)

110) **Beliavsky-Stoica**
Lucerne 1985

7 ... ♘a6 8 ♗f4 ♘c7 9 a4 b6 10 ♖e1 a6 11 h3 ♘d7 12 e5! was threatened. **12 ♕d2 ♖b8** 12 ... ♖e8!? 13 ♗h6 ♗h8. **13 ♗h6 b5 14 ♗xg7 ♔xg7 15 axb5 axb5 16 b4! cxb4 17 ♘a2! ♗b7 18 ♘xb4 ♘f6 19 ♕e3 e6!** The only way to start counterplay. **20 ♘d4! ♖a8 21 ♖xa8 ♕xa8 22 ♕c3! ♕c8!** 22 ... ♖c8? 23 ♖a1 ♕b8 24 ♘dc6 ± **23 ♘dc6! exd5** 23 ... ♖e8 24 g4! h6 25 f4! ±. **24 ♗g4 ♕a8 25 exd5 ♗xc6** 25 ... ♖e8? 26 ♖a1 +−. **26 dxc6 ♖e8 27 ♖a1 ♕d8 28 ♖a7 ♖e5! 29 ♖xc7??** A gross blunder in a better position! **29 ... ♕xc7 30 ♘a6 ♘d5! 31 ♕xe5+** 31 ♘xc7! ♘xc3 32 ♗d7 b4 33 ♘e8+ ♖xe8 34 ♗xe8 ♘b5 ∓. **31 ... dxe5 32 ♘xc7 ♘xc7** The knight is much more powerful than the bishop, and the c6 pawn needs permanent protection. **33 ♗d7 ♔f8 34 ♔f1 ♔e7 35 ♔e2 ♔d6 36 ♔d3 ♘d5! 37 ♗e8 f5 38 c4 ♘f4+ 39 ♔c3 bxc4 40 ♔xc4 ♘xg2 41 ♔b5 ♔c7 42 ♔c5 ♘f4 43 h4 ♘d3+ 44 ♔d5 e4 45 h5 ♘xf2! 0-1**

46 ♔d4 g5 47 ♗g6 e3! 48 ♔xe3 hxg6 (Stoica).

111) **Karpov-Korchnoi**
match (32) 1978

7 ... ♘a6 8 ♗f4 ♘c7 9 a4 b6 10 ♖e1 ♗b7 11 ♗c4 11 h3 ♕d7! 12 ♗c4 ♖ad8 13 ♕d3 e5!. **11 ... ♘h5?!** 11 ... ♕d7 12 e5 dxe5 13 ♘xe5 ♕f5 14 ♘xg6 fxg6 15 ♗xc7 ♘g4 ∞; 12 ♕d3 ±. **12 ♗g5 ♘f6 13 ♕d3! a6 14 ♖ad1 ♖b8 15 h3**

Karpov does not want to take any risks in the last game of the World Championship match: 15 e5! is more convincing. E.g. 15 ... dxe5 16 ♘xe5 b5?! 17 axb5 axb5 18 ♗xb5 ♘cxd5 19 ♘xd5 ♗xd5 (19 ... ♕xd5 20 ♕g3 ♕a2 21 ♗c4 ♕xb2 22 ♘xf7) 20 c4 ♗a8 (20 ... ♗e6 21 ♘c6!) 21 ♘d7 ±±. **15 ... ♘d7 16 ♕e3 ♗a8 17 ♗h6 b5 18 ♗xg7 ♔xg7 19 ♗f1 ♘f6 20 axb5 axb5 21 ♘e2!** The g7 bishop has disappeared from the board and Black's kingside has become weaker, so White concentrates his forces there. **21 ... ♗b7** 21 ... e5 22 dxe6 ♘xe6 23 ♘g3. **22 ♘g3 ♖a8 23 c3 ♖a4 24 ♗d3 ♕a8** Black has occupied the open file and seems to have prevented the typical breakthrough.

(diagram)

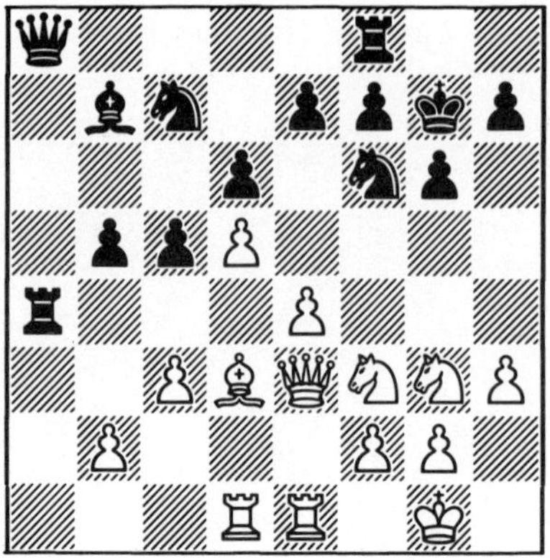

25 e5! Yet White breaks through all the same! The tactical justification of the idea is 25 ... ♘fxd5 26 ♘h5+! gxh5 27 ♕g5+ ♔h8 28 ♕f5. After Black's forced reply his c5 pawn will be weakened as well. **25 ... dxe5 26 ♕xe5 ♘cxd5 27 ♗xb5 ♖a7 28 ♘h4! ♗c8** The threat was 29 c4. 28 ... ♗c6 would be met by 29 ♗xc6 ♕xc6 30 c4 ♘b4 31 ♖d6!! exd6 32 ♘h5+ gxh5 33 ♕g5+ ♔h8 34 ♕xf6+ ♔g8 35 ♘f5, and White wins. If 28 ... ♕b8 29 c4 ±±. **29 ♗e2! ♗e6 20 c4 ♘b4 31 ♕xc5 ♕b8 32 ♗f1 ♖c8 33 ♕g5 ♔h8 34 ♖d2** The c4 pawn is taboo. **34 ... ♘c6 35 ♕h6!** The main battlefield alternates from the queenside to the kingside and vice versa. **35 ... ♖g8 36 ♘f3 ♕f8 37 ♕e3 ♔g7?** Overlooks White's blow in a lost position. Fixing the b2 pawn would have set a more difficult task. **38 ♘g5 ♗d7 39 b4! ♕a8 40 b5 ♘a5 41 b6 1-0**

20 Countering the Benoni and the Benko Gambit: Keres Variation

1	d4	♘f6
2	♘f3	c5
3	d5	b5

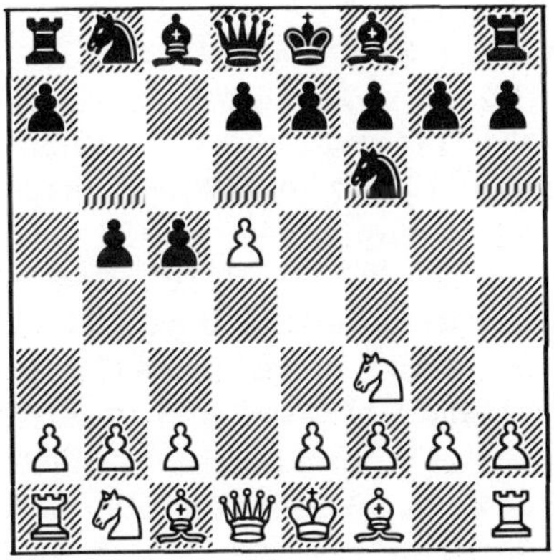

White's e-pawn has not been moved yet and, exploiting this, Black gains space on the queenside, hindering the protection of the d5 outpost. A shortcoming of the concept is that later White can get hold of c4 after having played a2-a4. We are not going to analyse 4 c4 which leads to the popular Benko Gambit or the exciting Blumenfeld Counter-Gambit. Less popular is 4 a4, e.g. 4 ... ♗b7 (4 ... b4!?) 5 e4 ♘xe4 6 ♗xb5 e6 7 dxe6 fxe6 8 ♘bd2 ♘f6 9 ♘g5 ♘c6 10 ♘de4 ♘d4 11 ♗d3 ♘xe4 12 ♘xe4 ♗e7 13 c3 ♘f5 ∞ Lutikov-Furman, USSR 1969.

4 ♗g5

Hinders Black's smooth development and occasionally threatens ♗xf6. The main variations here are 4 ... ♕b6, 4 ... ♗b7, and 4 ... ♘e4. Others:

(a) 4 ... ♕a5+?! 5 c3 ♘e4 6 ♘bd2 ♘xg5 7 ♘xg5 h6?! 8 ♘gf3 d6 9 e4 ♘d7 10 a4 ± Stahlberg-Petrosian, Illustrative Game No 112.

(b) 4 ... d6 5 ♗xf6! (5 e3 a6 6 a4 b4 7 ♗c4 ♘bd7 8 ♘bd2 g6 9 e4 ♗g7 10 h3 0-0 11 0-0 ♘b6 12 ♖e1 a5 ∞ Larsen-Browne, Hastings 1972/73) 5 ... exf6 6 e4 a6 7 a4 b4 8 ♗d3 (8 ♘bd2 f5!? 9 e4 ±; 8 ... ♗e7 9 ♗c4 0-0 10 0-0 ♘d7 11 a5 ♖e8 12 c3 bxc3 13 bxc3 ♘e5 14 ♘xe5 fxe5 15 ♗d3 ± – Tisdall-Ernst, Gausdal 1987) 8 ... ♘d7 (8 ... g6!? 9 ♘bd2 ♗g7 10 ♘c4 a5 11 0-0 ♕c7 12 ♘fd2 0-0 13 f4 ♘d7 14

♔h1 ♖e8 15 ♕f3 ♗a6 16 ♖ae1 ♖e7 17 g4 ♖ae8 18 ♖g1! ± Yusupov-Vaganian, USSR 1979) 9 0-0 ♘e5?! (9 ... a5! ± 9 ... g6?! 10 ♘bd2 ♘e5?! 11 ♘xe5 fxe5 12 a5! ♗h6 13 ♘c4 0-0 14 c3! ± Bonin-Alburt, New York 1986) 10 ♘bd2 (10 ♘xe5 fxe5 11 a5 ±) 10 ... g6 11 ♘xe5 fxe5 12 a5 ± Yusupov-Miles, Bugojno 1986.

(c) 4 ... e6?! 5 e4 ♕a5+ 6 ♕d2! ♕b6 (6 ... ♕xd2+ 7 ♘bxd2 a6 8 a4 ±) 7 ♗xf6 gxf6 8 a4 bxa4 9 c3 ±.

(d) 4 ... g6 5 ♘bd2 (5 d6 ♗g7 6 e3 ♘c6 7 ♘c3 ♕a5 8 ♘d2 0-0 9 ♗xb5 exd6 10 ♘c4 ♕c7 11 ♗xf6 ♗xf6 12 ♘d5 ♕d8 13 ♘xf6+ ♕xf6 14 ♕xd6 +− Weingold-Adriane, Budapest 1989) 5 ... ♗g7 (5 ... ♘xd5?? 6 ♘e4! +−) 6 e4 0-0 7 a4 b4 ± Ingbrandt-Tisdall, Oslo 1986.

20.1

4 ... ♕b6

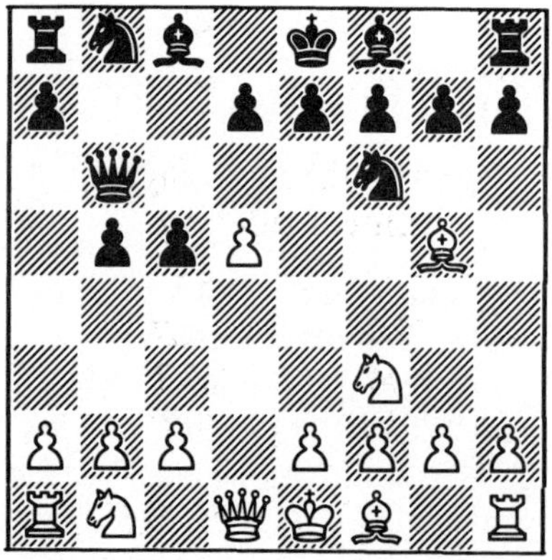

Defends the b5 pawn and prepares recapturing with the queen after 5 ♗xf6.

20.11

5 ♗xf6

An original idea; giving up the advantage of the two bishops, White entices the black queen away from the queenside.

(a) 5 a4 bxa4 6 ♗xf6 gxf6 7 ♕c1? ♗g7 8 ♖xa4 f5 9 b3 ♗b7 10 ♕d2 0-0 11 e3 e6 ∓ Jacobsen-Bobotsov, Kapfenberg 1970. Better is 6 ♘c3! ♕xb2 7 ♗d2 ♕b6 8 e4 d6 9 e5! dxe5 10 ♘xe5 g6 11 ♖b1 ♕c7 12 ♗b5+ ♗d7 13 ♗f4 ♕c8 14 d6 +− Vizhmanavin-Arbakov, USSR 1986.

(b) 5 e3 ♗b7 6 c4 bxc4 7 ♗xc4 ♕xb2 8 ♘bd2 ∞ (Dezso).

(c) 5 c3 d6?! (5 ... ♘e4 6 ♗h4 e6 7 e3 c4 8 a4 ♗b7 9 dxe6 fxe6 10 axb5 ♕xb5 11 ♘bd2 ♕xb2 12 ♖b1 ♕xc3 13 ♖xb7 ♗b4 14 ♖xb4 ♕xb4 15 ♗xc4 ± - De Boer-Weemaes, Amsterdam 1986) 6 ♗xf6 exf6 7 a4 bxa4 8 ♕xa4+ ♗d7 9 ♕c2 ± Barlov-Forintos, Bela Crkva 1986.

5 ... ♕xf6

5 ... exf6 6 e4 g6 7 c3 ♗g7 8 ♗d3 0-0 9 0-0 d6 10 ♘bd2 ♘a6 (10 ... c4 11 ♗e2! a6 12 a4 ±) 11 a4 b4 M. Gurevich-Bareyev, Saltsjöbaden 1987/88; 12 ♗b5! ±.

6 c3 g6

6 ... ♗b7?! 7 e4 ♕g6 8 ♘bd2 e6 9 ♗xb5! exd5 10 exd5 ♗xd5 11

0-0 ♗e7 12 ♖e1 ♗e6 13 ♘e5 ± Varnusz-Pasman, Budapest 1983.

Interesting is 6 ... d6 7 e4 a6 8 ♘bd2 g5 (8 ... ♘d7 9 g3 g5 10 a4! b4 11 cxb4 cxb4 ± Grünfeld-Keres, Illustrative Game No 113) 9 g3 g4 10 ♘h4 h5 11 ♗g2 ♗h6 12 0-0 ♗g5 (Black spends too much time on winning a pawn) 13 a4 ♗d7 14 axb5 ♗xb5 15 e5! ± Panchenko-Forintos, Tallinn 1987.

7	**e4**	**♕b6**
8	**♘bd2**	**♗g7!**

8 ... d6? 9 a4! bxa4 10 ♘c4 ♕c7 11 ♕xa4+ ♘d7 12 ♕c6! ♕b7 13 e5! ♗g7 14 exd6 e6 15 ♕xb7 ± Razuvaev-Vaganian, USSR 1982.

9	**a4**	**b4**
10	**♘c4**	**♕d8**
11	**♕c2 ∞**	

11 cxb4? cxb4 ∓ – Lukács-Arkhipov, Budapest 1984.

20.12

5 ♘c3

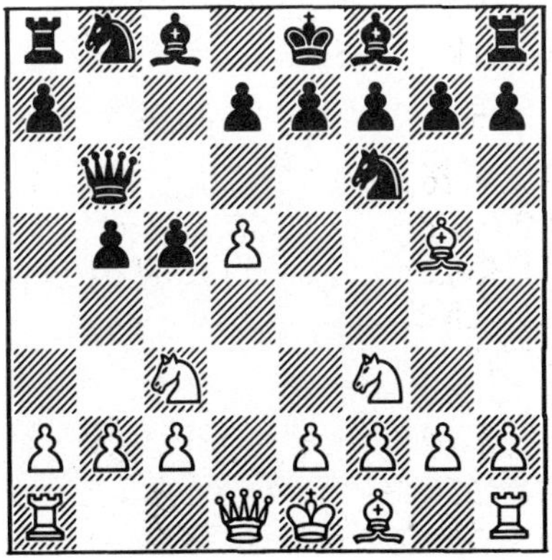

This developing move meets general principles, more than the previous ones.

5	**...**	**♗b7**

5 ... b4 (5 ... h6? 6 ♗xf6 exf6 7 e4 a6 8 a4 bxa4 ± – Tierpugov-Petrosian, USSR 1951) 6 ♘a4 ♕a5 (6 ... ♕c7 7 ♗xf6 gxf6 8 b3 d6 9 e4 ♗g7 10 ♗d3 f5 11 exf5! ± Smyslov-Szmetan, Buenos Aires 1978) 7 ♗xf6 gxf6 (7 ... ♕xa4 8 b3 ♕a5 9 ♗b2 ±) 8 b3 (8 c4!?) 8 ... f5 (8 ... ♗g7 9 e4!? d6 10 ♗d3 ♗a6 11 ♗xa6 ♕xa6 12 ♘h4 f5 13 ♘xf5 ∞ Varnusz-Morvay, Illustrative Game No 116) 9 e3 d6 10 ♗d3 ♗g7 11 ♖b1 ♘a6 12 ♘h4! e6 13 dxe6 fxe6 14 ♕h5+ ♔e7 15 0-0 Browne-Evans, Illustrative Game No 114; 15 ... d5! 16 ♖bd1 c4 17 ♗xf5 ∞ (Browne).

6	**e4**	**b4**
7	**♘a4**	**♕a5**
8	**♗xf6**	**exf6**
9	**b3**	**d6**
10	**♗d3**	**g6**
11	**h4!?**	

Here and on the following moves a3 ± is worth considering.

11	**...**	**h5**
12	**♘b2**	**♗g7**
13	**♘c4**	**♕c7**
14	**0-0**	**0-0**
15	**a3 ±**	

15 ... a5 16 axb4 cxb4 17 ♕d2 ± Dreyev-Glek, Illustrative Game No 115.

20.2

4 ... ♗b7

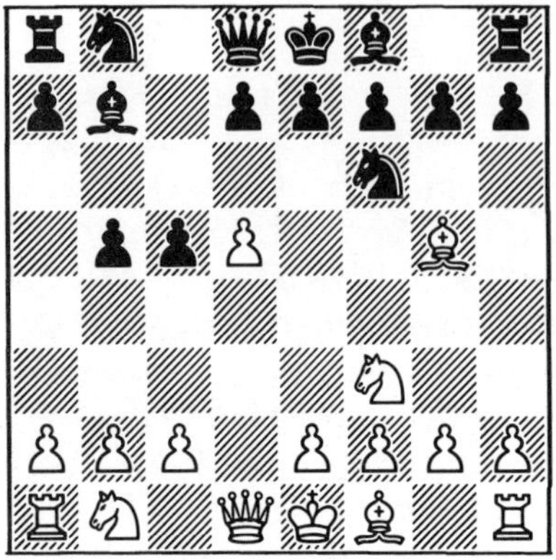

By exerting pressure on the d5 outpost, Black forces the coming exchange but somewhat weakens his pawn structure.

5 ♗xf6 exf6

5 ... gxf6 6 e4 ♕b6 (6 ... a6 7 a4 b4 8 c4 ♗g7 9 ♗d3 d6 10 ♖a2! ♘d7 11 ♘h4 ± Varasdy-S.Faragó, Kecskemét 1987) 7 c4 b4 8 ♘h4 ♕d6 9 ♘d2 ♕e5 10 ♕c2 ± Prokeš-Hromadka, Prague 1928.

6 e4

6 a4 a6 7 e4 c4 8 ♗e2 ♗c5 9 b3 f5?! 10 exf5 cxb3 11 c3 ♕b6 12 0-0 bxa4 13 ♖xa4 0-0 14 ♗c4 b2 15 ♘bd2 ± Savchenko-Nesterov, USSR 1986. For 9 0-0 see note (b) below; for 7 ... ♕e7 see note (c).

6 ... ♕e7

This gives a sharp game. More modest moves offer a slight advantage for White:

(a) 6 ... g6 7 a4 (7 ♘c3!?) 7 ... bxa4 8 ♘c3 ♗h6 9 ♗e2 0-0 10 ♘xa4 ♕a5+ 11 ♘c3 ♕b6 12 0-0 d6 13 ♘d2 ± Vizhmanavin-Kiseliov, USSR 1986.

(b) 6 ... c4 7 a4! a6 8 ♗e2 ♗c5 9 0-0 0-0 10 axb5 axb5 11 ♖xa8 ♗xa8 12 ♘c3 ♕b6 (12 ... ♕a5? 13 ♕a1! +−) 13 b3! cxb3 14 cxb3 Browne-Quinteros, Buenos Aires 1978; 14 ... ♖e8! ±.

(c) 6 ... a6 7 ♗e2 (7 a4 ♕e7 8 ♘bd2 ♗xd5 ∞; 8 ... c4? 9 axb5 axb5 10 ♖xa8 ♗xa8 11 ♕a1 ♗xd5 12 ♕a7 ♘c6 13 ♕a8+ +−) 7 ... ♗d6 8 a4 ♕b6 9 axb5 axb5 10 ♖xa8 ♗xa8 11 ♘c3 b4 12 ♘b5 0-0 13 0-0 ♗b7 14 ♘xd6 ♕xd6 15 ♗c4 ± Browne-Korchnoi, Wijk aan Zee 1980.

(d) 6 ... ♕b6?! 7 a4 a6 8 ♘c3 c4 9 ♗e2 ♗c5 10 0-0 0-0 11 axb5 axb5 12 ♖xa8 ♗xa8 13 b3! cxb3 14 cxb3 ♖e8 15 ♕d3 ± Piket-Brenninkmeyer, Groningen 1987.

7 ♕e2

7 ♗e2 a6 8 0-0 g6 9 c4 b4 10 a3 ∞ Petursson-Alburt, Reykjavik 1984. 7 ♘bd2 b4 (7 ... ♗xd5? 8 ♗xb5 ♗xe4? 9 0-0 +−) 8 ♗c4 g6 9 0-0 ♗g7 10 a3 0-0 11 axb4 cxb4 12 ♘b3?! (12 ♖e1 ±) 12 ... ♕xe4 13 ♘a5 ♗a6 14 ♖e1 ♕f4 15 ♕d3 ± Huzman-Rashkovsky, Irkutsk 1986.

7 ... g6

8	**♘bd2**	**♗h6**
9	**♕xb5**	**♗xd5**
10	**♗c4!**	**♗xc4**
11	**♕xc4**	**0-0**
12	**0-0**	**♘c6**
13	**♘b3**	**d6**
14	**♖ad1**	**♖fd8** ±

Martin-Alburt, Hastings 1983/84.

20.3

4 ... ♘e4!?

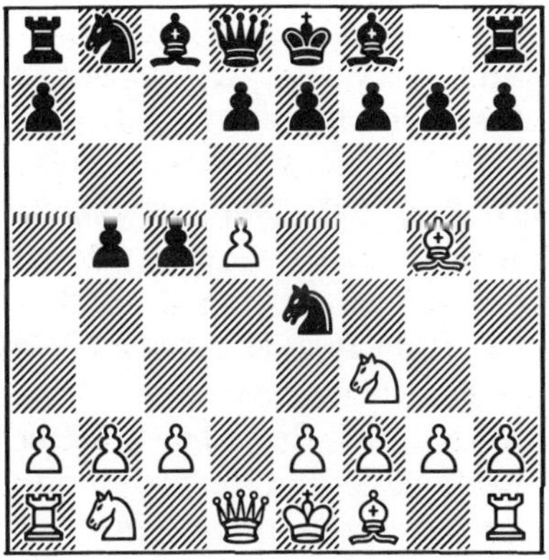

Trying to interrupt White's plans. At the time of going to press this seems the best chance for Black.

5 ♗h4

(a) 5 ♕d3!? ♘xg5 6 ♘xg5 h6?! 7 ♘h7! ♕a5+ 8 c3 d6 9 ♘xf8 ♔xf8 10 e4 a6 11 ♘d2 ♘d7 12 ♕g3 ± Wells-Buckmire, Oakham 1986.

(b) 5 ♗f4!? ♕a5+ 6 ♘bd2 g6 7 a4 ♘xd2 8 ♘xd2 ♗g7 9 axb5 ♕xb5 10 e4 ♕b7 11 ♘c4 d6 12 c3 0-0 13 ♗d3 ± Zsuzsa Polgar-Fedorowicz, Wijk aan Zee 1990.

5 ... ♕a5+

5 ... ♗b7 6 ♕d3 ♘d6 7 e4 ±.

6 ♘bd2

6 c3!? b4 7 ♕c2 f5 8 ♘fd2 bxc3 9 bxc3 (9 ♘xc3!?) 9 ... ♗b7 10 ♘xe4 fxe4 11 ♕xe4 e6 12 ♕c2 ♗xd5 13 e4 ♗c6 14 a4 ♗d6 15 ♗g3 ♕c7 16 ♘d2 0-0 17 ♗d3 ♗f4 18 0-0 = Kogan-Alburt, USA 198?.

6	**...**	**♗b7**
7	**a4**	**♗xd5**
8	**axb5**	**♕c7!**

8 ... ♕b4?! 9 c4 ♗b7 10 ♕c2 a6 11 ♖a4! axb5 12 ♖xb4 ♖a1+ 13 ♘b1 ±.

9 ♖a4! ♕b7

After 9 ... ♘xd2 10 ♘xd2 the threats are 11 e4 and 11 ♕a1 (±).

10 c4 ♘xd2

The critical position. Kasparov-Miles, Basle (match) 1986, continued with 11 cxd5? ♘xf1 12 ♕d3 d6 13 e4!, and Black could have equalised by playing 13 ... ♘xh2! 14 ♖xh2 ♘d7 15 ♘d2! ♖b8 16 ♘c4 ♕xb5. Therefore Kasparov suggests the pawn sacrifice 11 ♕xd2! ♗e4 12 e3 d6 13 ♗d3!, since 13 ... ♗xf3? 14 gxf3 ♕xf3 15 ♖g1 is too risky. 12 ... a6 or 12 ...

h6 13 ♗d3 g5 are worth considering.

ILLUSTRATIVE GAMES

1 d4 ♘f6 2 ♘f3 c5 3 d5 b5 4 ♗g5

112) **Stahlberg-Petrosian**
Budapest 1952

4 ... ♕a5+? 5 c3 ♘e4 6 ♘bd2! ♘xg5 7 ♘xg5 h6?! 7 ... e6, 8 ... ♗e7. **8 ♘gf3 d6 9 e4 ♘d7 10 a4! bxa4 11 ♖xa4 ♕c7 12 ♕a1!** The threat is 13 ♗b5, 14 ♗c6. **12 ... ♘b6 13 ♗b5+ ♗d7 14 ♗xd7+ ♕xd7 15 ♖a6 ♘c8 16 0-0 e5** 16 ... g6 17 e5! **17 dxe6 fxe6 18 ♘h4! ♔f7 19 f4 ♕d8** 19 ... ♗e7 20 f5! ♗xh4 21 fxe6+ ♔xe6 22 ♕a2+ ±±. **20 ♘hf3 ♕e8 21 f5! exf5 22 ♕a2+ ♕e6**

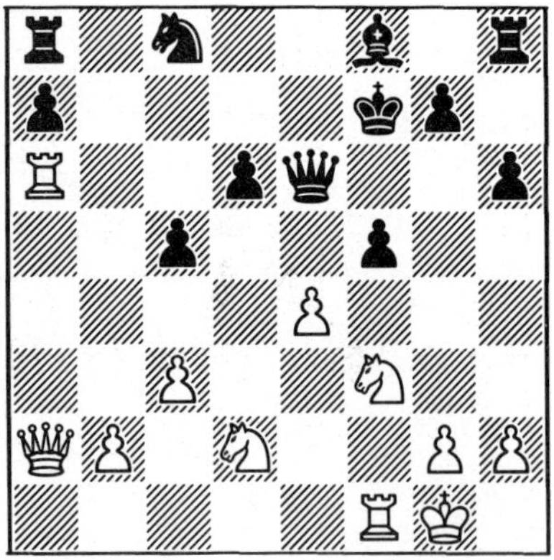

23 ♘e5+! Exploiting the double pin, White puts an end to the game with a beautiful mating attack. **23 ... ♔e7 24 ♘c6+ ♔d7 25 ♕a4 ♔e8 26 exf5 ♕e3+ 27 ♔h1! 1-0**

113) **Grünfeld-Keres**
Szczawno Zdrój 1950

4 ... ♕b6 5 ♗xf6 ♕xf6 6 c3 d6?! 7 e4 a6 8 ♘bd2 ♘d7 9 g3 9 ♗e2!?. **9 ... g5!? 10 a4! b4** 10 ... g4 11 ♘h4 b4 12 ♖c1!. **11 cxb4 cxb4 12 ♖c1?** A naive trap! 12 ♘c4 ±. **12 ... g4! 13 ♕c2 ♘c5 14 ♘h4 ♗h6! 15 f4?!** A sly pawn sacrifice but somewhat dubious: the king will wind up in the centre. 15 ♖d1 would parry the loss of the pawn (... ♗xd2+). **15 ... ♗xf4 16 gxf4 ♕xh4+ 17 ♔e2 g3 18 ♔e3** The position White had in mind. He hopes to launch an attack on the kingside and to secure his king in the centre. **18 ... ♗g4 19 ♗g2 gxh2 20 ♘f3 ♕g3 21 ♖xh2 e5!** Opening the position around White's king and blocking the b1-h7 diagonal simultaneously. 21 ... 0-0? 22 e5!. **22 fxe5 0-0! 23 ♖ch1** 23 exd6 ♘xe4! 24 ♔xe4 ♖fe8+ 25 ♔d4 ♕f4+. **23 ... f5! 24 exd6?** Missing the chance for a stunningly original brilliancy in which White sacrifices his queen in order to use his king as an attacking piece! Instead White should play 24 ♖xh7! f4+ 25 ♔d4 dxe5+.

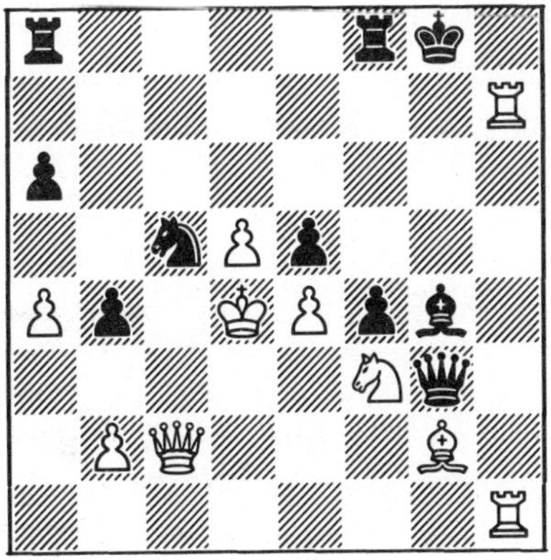

analysis diagram

Now 26 ♔xe5? ♖ae8+ 27 ♔d6 ♘xe4+ wins for Black and 26 ♔c4 ♘d7! ∓ is uncomfortable, but 26 ♔xc5!! ♖ac8+ 27 ♔d6! and 27 ... ♖xc2? is amazingly a forced win for White: 28 ♖h8+ ♔f7 29 ♖1h7+ ♔f6 (29 ... ♔e8 30 ♖e7+ ♔d8 31 ♖xf8+ mate!; 29 ... ♔g6 30 ♘xe5+ ♔g5 31 ♖g7+ ♔f6 32 ♖g6+ mate) 30 ♖xf8+ ♔g6 31 ♖ff7!! and the threat of a knight mate leaves Black nothing better than sacrificing into a lost endgame with 31 ... ♗xf3. Black must not be greedy; better to take a draw with 27 ... ♖fd8+! 28 ♔xe5 ♗xf3!? (28 ... ♖e8+ =) 29 ♖h8+ ♔g7 30 ♖8h7+ ♔g6 31 ♖7h6+ ♔g7 =; 31 ... ♔g5? 32 ♗xf3! ±. **24 ... fxe4 25 ♔d4 ♗xf3 26 ♗xf3**

(diagram)

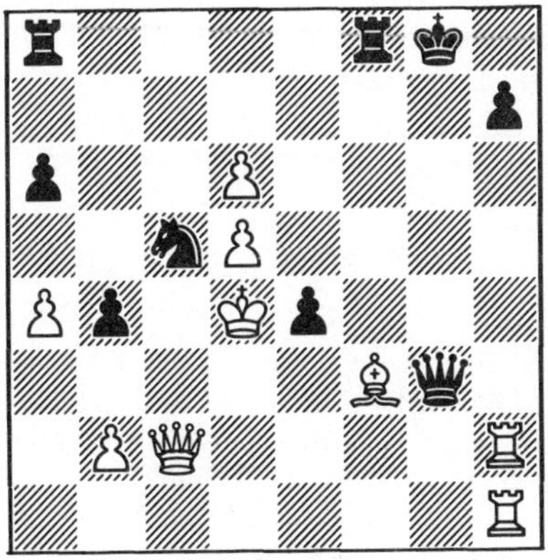

26 ... ♘b3+! A decisive blow! **27 ♕xb3 ♕g7+! 28 ♔c5 ♕a7+ 29 ♔xb4 ♖ab8+ 0-1**

(Note to move 24 by Crouch)

114) **Browne-Evans**
Philadelphia 1979

4 ... ♕b6 5 ♘c3 b4 6 ♘a4 ♕a5 7 ♗xf6 gxf6 8 b3 f5 9 e3 d6 10 ♗d3 ♗g7 11 ♖b1 ♘a6 12 ♘h4! e6 13 dxe6 fxe6 14 ♕h5+ ♔e7 15 0-0 ♗d7? The touchstone of White's play was the 15 ... d5 16 ♖bd1 c4!? 17 ♗xf5!? sacrifice.

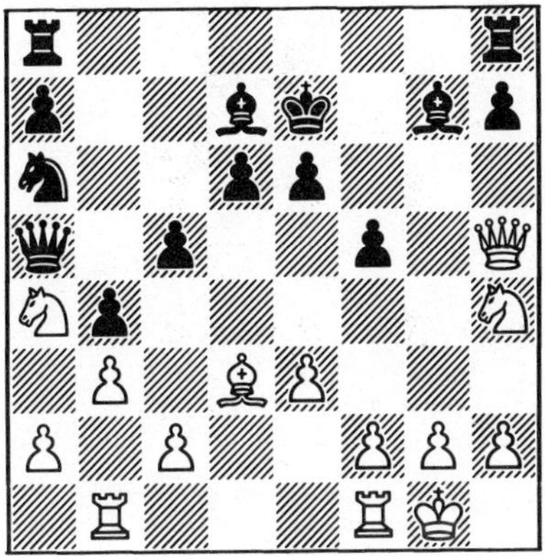

16 e4! f4 16 ... fxe4 17 ♗xe4 d5? 18 ♗xd5! exd5 19 ♕g5+ ♔f7 20 ♖be1 ♕d8 21 ♕xd5+ ♔f8 22 ♕d6+ ♔f7 23 ♕xa6 ♕xh4 24 ♕b7 ♖ad8 25 ♘xc5 ♕d4 26 ♘e6 etc. **17 ♖be1 ♖af8 18 ♘f3 ♗xa4?!** 18 ... e5 19 ♗c4 ±. **19 bxa4 ♔d7?** 19 ... ♕xa4 20 e5! d5 21 ♕g5+ ±±. **20 ♗b5+ ♔c7 21 ♘g5 1-0**
(Browne)

115) **Dreyev-Glek**
USSR 1986

4 ... ♕b6 5 ♘c3 ♗b7 6 e4 b4 7 ♘a4 ♕a5 8 ♗xf6 exf6 9 b3 d6 10 ♗d3 g6 11 h4!? 11 a3!. **11 ... h5 12 ♘b2 ♗g7 13 ♘c4 ♕c7 14 0-0 0-0 15 a3 a5 16 axb4 cxb4** 16 ... axb4? 17 ♖xa8 ♗xa8 18 ♕a1 ♘d7 19 ♕a6 ±±. **17 ♕d2 ♘d7 18 ♕f4! ♖a6** 18 ... ♘e5 19 ♘fxe5 fxe5 20 ♕e3 ±. **19 ♘e3 ♖aa8 20 g4! hxg4 21 ♘xg4 ♕d8** For 21 ... ♘e5 the reply is not 22 ♘xf6+ ♗xf6 23 ♕xf6 ♕d8!, but 22 h5! instead. **22 h5 ♘e5 23 h6 ♗h8**

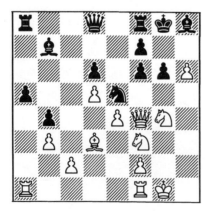

24 h7+! White must open the h-file at any cost. The outcome of the struggle however is still unclear. **24 ... ♔xh7 25 ♔g2 ♘xg4 26 ♖h1+ ♔g8 27 ♕xg4 ♖e8 28 ♖ag1** 28 ♖h2? f5!. **28 ... ♗g7 29 ♖h2 ♕c8?!** Black could have fished in troubled waters after 29 ... ♗c8! 30 ♕f4 ♕d7! 31 ♔g3 g5! 32 ♘xg5 fxg5 33 ♕xg5 ∞. **30 ♕f4 ♗a6? 31 ♖gh1 ♗xd3 32 cxd3 ♖e5** Sacrificing the exchange in despair. 32 ... ♔f8 33 ♖h7!. **33 ♖h7! g5 34 ♕h2** White proves that the Black king's position is even worse than that of his own. **34 ... ♕g4+ 35 ♔f1 ♔f8** 35 ... ♕xf3 36 ♖h8+!. **36 ♖xg7 ♔e7** 36 ... ♕xf3 37 ♖xf7+! leads to mate! **37 ♘xe5 dxe5 38 ♕h5 ♕xh5 39 ♖xh5 a4** The last chance is the attempt to promote the b-pawn. **40 bxa4 b3 41 ♔e2 b2 42 ♖h1 ♖h8! 43 d6+!** After 43 ♖b1 ♔f8! White still has problems, whereas now 43 ... ♔xd6 44 ♖b1 ♔e7 45 ♖xb2 ♔f8 46 ♖b8+ ♔xg7 47 ♖xh8 ♔xh8 48 a5 forces the issue. **1-0**
(Dreyev's notes included)

116) **Varnusz-Morvay**
Budapest 1987

4 ... ♕b6 5 ♘c3 b4 6 ♘a4 ♕a5 7 ♗xf6 gxf6 8 b3 ♗g7 9 e4!? White has a sacrifice of the exchange in mind to get hold of the a1-h8 diagonal. Though 8 e3 is safer, the text is more exciting. **9 ... d6 10 ♗d3 ♗a6!** 11 ... c4! is threatened. **11 ♗xa6 ♕xa6 12 ♘h4! f5!** The best chances for both sides. **13 ♘xf5 ♗xa1 14 ♕xa1 ♖g8** 14 ... ♖f8 15 ♕g7 ±. **15 ♘h6 ♖f8** 15 ... ♖xg2? 16 ♕h8+ ♔d7 17 ♘xf7 ±±. **16 ♕g7 ♘d7 17 ♕xh7** Otherwise Black plays 17 ... ♘f6. **17 ... 0-0-0?** The losing move. Black offers another pawn to complete his development and get lines for his rooks. He ignores, however, the weakness of e6. 17 ... ♘b6! 18 ♘xb6 axb6 19 ♘f5 is the touchstone of the sac: 19 ... ♕xa2?! 20 0-0 ♕xc2? 21 e5! ±; 19 ... ♕b5! 20 ♕h4! and chances are equal despite White's positional pressure and passed pawn. **18 ♘xf7 ♖de8 19 ♘g5 ♖h8 20 ♕f5 ♖h4 21 g3 ♖f8 22 ♕e6 ♖h5 23 ♘xc5! ♕b5 24 ♘xd7 ♕xd7 25 h4 ♕xe6 26 dxe6 ♔b7 27 f4 ♖c8 28 ♖h2 ♖c3 29 g4 ♖h6 30 f5 ♖g3 31 ♘f7 ♖h7 32 f6!** The point of the plan commenced on move 28. **32 ... ♖xg4 33 fxe7 ♖xe4+ 34 ♖e2 1-0**

Complete List of Variations

Page numbers in italic

Part I: Torre-Petrosian Attack